KJE10 CON

CONVERGENCE AND DIVERGENCE IN
EUROPEAN PUBLIC LAW

Convergence and Divergence in European Public Law

Edited by

PAUL BEAUMONT
CAROLE LYONS
and
NEIL WALKER

·HART·
PUBLISHING

OXFORD – PORTLAND OREGON
2002

Hart Publishing
Oxford and Portland, Oregon

Published in North America (US and Canada) by
Hart Publishing c/o
International Specialized Book Services
5804 NE Hassalo Street
Portland, Oregon
97213-3644
USA

Distributed in the Netherlands, Belgium and Luxembourg by
Intersentia, Churchillaan 108
B2900 Schoten
Antwerpen
Belgium

Hart Publishing is a specialist legal publisher based in Oxford, England.
To order further copies of this book or to request a list of other
publications please write to:

Hart Publishing, Salter's Boatyard, Folly Bridge,
Abingdon Road, Oxford OX1 4LB
Telephone: +44 (0)1865 245533 or Fax: +44 (0)1865 794882
e-mail: mail@hartpub.co.uk
WEBSITE: http//www.hartpub.co.uk

British Library Cataloguing in Publication Data
Data Available
ISBN 1–84113–211–X (hardback)

Typeset by Hope Services (Abingdon) Ltd.
Printed and bound in Great Britain on acid-free paper by
Biddles Ltd, www.biddles.co.uk

Preface

The title of this volume suggests a theme at least as old as the European Union (and its predecessor supranational Communities) itself, but one still central to the major debates and controversies about its current and future design and direction. The more that the European Union extends its powers, its jurisdiction and its influence within the changing political configuration of a post-Westphalian world, and the more that it engages the fears and aspirations of Europe's politicians and publics, the more pressing the fundamental question about the relationship between its legal order and the continuing legal orders of its member states becomes. Not surprisingly, for all the recent discussion about providing some fixed and final framework and ultimate vision for the European Union, contestation over the proper legal shape and scope of the European polity appears to be increasing in direct proportion to its growing political and economic significance.

Just as the old question has proved resilient, so too has the rhetorical opposition in terms of which it has often been framed. It may no longer be considered serious or respectable to view European Union law in general and European public law in particular as a one-way train towards integration. Equally, it may no longer be considered serious or respectable to view the European Union Treaty framework as a limited or reversible political experiment—one that does not and should not challenge the longstanding hegemony of the European nation state. Yet in making this obvious point, we must also concede two others. In the first place, we must continue to acknowledge as relevant to the convergence/divergence debate the sentiments that underpin the rhetorical opposition between statism and super-statism, if not the bald terms in which that opposition is still sometimes expressed. There are real normative issues at stake, genuine choices to be made, over the ways in which and the extent to which the European Union legal order should develop a framework of public law tending towards the retention or otherwise of the form, content and authority of the constituent national orders. As soon as we approach questions of democracy and its relationship to other political values such as fundamental rights and economic prosperity, as soon as we consider the proper meaning and articulation of ideas such as community, autonomy and solidarity in the insistent contemporary European politics of identity and difference, we are bound to revisit the question of the place of states relative to other polities in the new European framework.

The second point, however, is something of a corrective to the first. The future of European public law is about the re-articulation—and, hopefully, reconciliation—of strong normative positions about the continuing currency of the state as a steering mechanism and as a community of attachment, but it is also about much more than that. The evolving legal and political paradigm represented by European supranationalism continues to throw up new puzzles and offer new prospects. Wearing their technician hats, lawyers must acknowledge that convergence of law generally and public law in particular is still an emergent phenomenon and remains a poorly understood and refined area of legal technique, one whose complexity defies reduction to simple one-dimensional, more-or-less, terms. They must be prepared to address questions about the various different ways in which convergence might proceed, or divergence be sustained, and to examine the co-ordination problems raised and solutions available through this or that method in this or that particular area of public law. Equally, wearing their political hats, lawyers must be alive to the ways in which the evolution of European law allows normative questions to be framed other than in zero-sum terms—as more than a contest between the authoritative claims of the states on the one hand and the new European Union polity on the other. They must, for example, acknowledge the way in which Europeanisation stimulates the search for more consensual forms of accommodation between legal systems and their principal actors, or facilitates the mobilisation of a third-level of territorial claims at the sub-state level, or encourages the articulation and regulatory involvement of new voices within the spheres of civil society and the economy.

The purpose of this volume is to bring these various questions and issues together. It seeks to keep the resilient foundational tension between state-centred and EU-centred perspective directly in focus, while also analysing the legal intricacies of convergence in different areas and investigating the ways in which the working out of the foundational tension has given rise to new patterns of authority and influence and new normative possibilities. The essays differ in the emphasis that they place on each of these themes, as well as in the dimension of European public law on which they concentrate, but each in its own way enhances our appreciation of the relationship between all three themes. In order to contextualise the debate about public law convergence as widely as possible, we have also included essays from writers with a different disciplinary background. Michael Keating, from a political science background, and Pierre Legrand, whose main work is in the field of comparative private law, offer valuable alternative perspectives which considerably enrich our understanding both of the distinctiveness of the public law debate and its significant continuities with other questions at the heart of the new European legal and political order.

The volume is divided into five sections. In part one, Michael Keating and Joanne Scott apply the perspectives of political science and public law respectively to the question of how the European institutional framework nurtures both unity and territorial diversity within the European legal and political space. The emphasis in both chapters is on the opportunities and constraints contained in the range of mechanisms and influences through which the European centre recognises and channels sub-state political voices and interests, and on how we should make sense of and evaluate the new multi-level constitutional mosaic which is emerging as a result.

The following three sections are more specialist, tracking the dynamics of European convergence and divergence along three classical dimensions of public law, namely constitutional law, administrative law and fundamental rights. In part two, the emerging constitutional order of the European Union and its implications for convergence are examined both from a process-based perspective and from a structural perspective. From a process-based perspective, Bruno de Witte engages in a highly topical examination of the evolving IGC framework and of the ways in which it is metamorphosing into a more inclusive constitutional conversation—a development that is gathering new pace and generating new interest in the post-Nice period. From a structural perspective, Deirdre Curtin and Ige Dekker undertake a theoretically ambitious and normatively sensitive examination of the overall constitutional configuration of the European Union as a complex institutional unity—a unity which embraces not only the horizontal relationship between the three Union pillars but also the vertical relationship between the three pillar structure and the constitutional orders of the member states. Carole Lyons concludes this section by examining contrasting perspectives on convergence, drawing on recent jurisprudence to expose the different ways in which shared or converged national laws are treated within the EU legal order.

In part three, the dilemmas exposed by the interaction between national administrative law systems and the supranational legal framework are considered. Chris Himsworth provides an overview of the technical and political problems attendant in balancing respect for the integrity of national systems in an area where domestic styles and cultures are particularly strong and resilient against a commitment to effectiveness and reasonable uniformity at the European level. Ton Heukels and Jamilia Tib offer a more detailed and historical overview of the problems attendant upon achieving this balance in the particularly sensitive and crucial area of legal remedies.

In part four, the contributors examine the extent and evaluate the significance of the trend towards a common European jurisprudence of human rights. Common to all these chapters is a sensitivity to the complex articulation between national traditions, the European Convention system, the case-law of the Court of Justice, and other legislative and policy initiatives in the human rights field at the EU level—including its freshly minted Charter of Fundamental Rights. Gráinne de Búrca offers a framework for disaggregating the fundamental normative debate in this area into a number of discrete if inter-related questions, and offers a qualified argument for an active EU human rights profile. Paul Beaumont puts forward a robust defence of a more state-centred approach, arguing through a detailed examination of recent case-law that a unduly *dirigiste* and fundamentalist approach to rights encounters problems of legitimacy and tends to distort understanding of the substantive policy issues involved in rights-coded disputes. Niamh Nic Shuibhne provides a careful analysis of the problems involved in drawing firm boundaries between state and supranational jurisdiction in this area, and thus of the difficulties of framing precise normative questions about the proper allocation of competence

Finally, in part five, two long overview essays by Carol Harlow and Pierre Legrand set out reasons to be sceptical about a strong convergence project in the area of European public law. Drawing on her background as both a national and European public lawyer, Carol Harlow argues the democratic case for proceeding cautiously with convergence. Pierre Legrand is known for his view that the cultural specificity of national legal systems provides both technical and normative arguments against convergence in the private law domain and in this book he posits that the case for divergence is at least as strong in relation to public law. In response to these two essays, Neil Walker, while sympathetic to much of Harlow and Legrand's theses, cautions against overstating the sceptical perspective and argues for a more nuanced and agnostic approach to questions of convergence and divergence.

The collection grew out of a symposium held at the School of Law of the University of Aberdeen in May 2000. The keynote address, reproduced in this volume in an amended version, was provided by Carol Harlow in the form of the School's annual Ledingham Chalmers European Law lecture. The lecture, which maintained the standard of excellence set by previous contributors to the series,[1] provided a central point of reference for the symposium as a whole, and we are immensely grateful to Carol Harlow for the expertise, intellectual range, style and commitment which she brought to this occasion. We are also very grateful to the other speakers, the fruits of whose labours are to be found in the pages below. Important contributions were made by other participants in the symposium, notably Zenon Bankowski, Nick Bernard, Robin Evans-Jones, Giorgio Monti, Jo Shaw, Victor Tadros and Steve Weatherill, and we thank them too for their efforts. In the background, invaluable support was offered by Amanda Walton as conference secretary, and we are immensely indebted to her. Many thanks are also due to several postgraduate students at the University of Aberdeen who assisted in the conference organisation.

Finally, a word for our sponsors and publisher. Thanks again to David Laing—managing partner of Ledingham Chalmers, Solicitors,—for his continuing support, financial and otherwise, for the annual lecture series. On this occasion, too, thanks are due to Duncan Rice, Principal of Aberdeen University, to Peter Sloane, Dean of the Faculty of Social Sciences and Law, and to Chris Gane, then Head of the School of Law, for using their good offices to provide a generous measure of funding without which we would have been unable to

---

[1] Previous lecturers were David Edward (1997), Joseph Weiler (1998) and Robert Reed (1999). The fifth lecture was given in May 2001 by Neil MacCormick. On the occasion of the second annual lecture by Joseph Weiler in 1998 a broader conference was also organised, with financial support from the European Commission, leading to an earlier collection published by Richard Hart: P Beaumont and N Walker (eds.), *Legal Framework of the Single European Currency* (Oxford: Hart, 1999).

organise the conference on such an ambitious scale. Thanks, too, to Richard Hart, for his characteristic encouragement and solid but unobtrusive support in bringing the present volume to publication.

The Editors
1st August 2001

Contents

List of Contributors

Paul Beaumont, Professor of European Union and Private International Law, School of Law, University of Aberdeen

Deirdre Curtin, Professor of Law of International Organisations at the Europa Instituut, University of Utrecht

Gráinne de Búrca, Professor of European Union Law, European University Institute, Florence

Bruno de Witte, Professor of European Law, University of Maastricht and European University Institute, Florence

Ige Dekker, Senior Lecturer in the Law of International Organisations at the Europa Instituut, University of Utrecht

Carol Harlow, Professor of Public Law, London School of Economics and Political Science

Ton Heukels, sometime Professor of the Law of International Organisations and Jean Monnet Professor "Judicial Protection", Europa Institute, Leiden University; currently Co-ordinating Legal Adviser at the Ministry of Justice, The Netherlands

Chris Himsworth, Professor of Law, Faculty of Law, Edinburgh University

Michael Keating, Professor of Political Science, European University Institute, Florence and Professor of Scottish Politics, University of Aberdeen

Pierre Legrand, Professor of Law, Université Panthéon-Sorbonne

Carole Lyons, Lecturer in European Union Law, School of Law, University of Aberdeen

Niamh Nic Shuibhne, Lecturer in Law, Faculty of Law, Edinburgh University

Joanne Scott, Reader in European Law, Cambridge University and Fellow of Clare College, Cambridge

Jamila Tib, former Lecturer in European Law, Europa Institute, Leiden University

Neil Walker, Professor of European Union Law, European University Institute, Florence and Professor of Legal and Constitutional Theory, University of Aberdeen

Part One
The Territorial Dimension

1

Europe's Changing Political Landscape: Territorial Restructuring and New Forms of Government

MICHAEL KEATING

THE STRANGE PERSISTENCE OF SPACE AND TIME

I T IS A staple of much modern social science to argue that the old constraints of time and space have been conquered by new forms and technologies of communication, dissolving old solidarities and hierarchies. So within a short interval, Fukayama[1] could declare the end of history, and Badie,[2] among others, could announce the end of territory. Yet everywhere we look territory seems to be of increasing importance while history has emerged as one of the key weapons of modern political debate. The argument I want to develop here is that understanding of time and space have been hampered by the obsession with the state whose rise coincided with the development of modern social science and which has come to be seen as the very incarnation of modernity itself. European political space is currently restructuring in complex ways as the nation state is increasingly called into question as the sole or principal basis for political authority and legitimacy. This has presented a challenge to state-focused social science, whether in politics, economics, sociology, history or law. Some interesting work is being done within these disciplines to understand the nature of the changes under way, but the most fruitful avenue for understanding comes from the emerging interdisciplinary approaches. There are many dimensions to state restructuring, but the one on which I focus here is to do with territory.

Territory is such a fundamental element in political order that it is often unconsciously filtered out of the analysis. One reason is that the state constantly gets in the way. For many international relations specialists, the state is the only form of territorial polity imaginable and thus the only unit of analysis; international relations are inter-state relations. For country specialists, the state is

---

[1] F Fukayama, *The End of History and the Last Man* (New York: Free Press, 1992).

[2] B Badie, *La fin des territoires. Essais sur le désordre international et sur l'utilité social du respect* (Paris: Fayard, 1995).

taken for granted, providing the frame of analysis and the very data sets on which social science relies. There may be territorially based political and social movements but these are contained within state boundaries. Often, the significance of territory itself is denied, or reduced to a mere coincidence in space of other factors. At best, the territorial effect features as a mere residual to explain things that do not respond to the main functional variables. Lawyers have had difficulty in enunciating principles of legal authority that are not rooted in the sovereign state. Nationalising historians have presented state history as a teleological progress to national unity. Social science has also contained a strong normative bias to the nation state, as scholars have presented the consolidated nation state as not merely the contingent accompaniment, but the necessary condition for liberal democracy (most recently Dahrendorf)[3] and the embodiment of universal values. Indeed, one book entitled "The end of the nation state"[4] had earlier appeared in French as "The end of democracy".[5] In recent years, as the state has been demystified and challenged, scholars are becoming more aware of its historically contingent and contested nature and the way it continually changes in form and function.[6] While it is still the most important social aggregate and the key level of collective action and legitimate authority, it is not the only one.

The state is being transformed from above, by globalisation, transnational integration and, specifically, by European integration; from below, by declining functional capacity in the management of territory and by the emergence of new forms of territorial politics; and laterally, by the rise of the market and of civil society. It has ceased to be the only actor in international politics, if it ever was,[7] and is no longer able to aggregate social demands and broker social compromises as in the past. It is true that few states have actually disappeared and that many new ones have been created but the very ease of state creation reflects the lightening of the burdens which statehood entails. Yet the weakening of the nation state has not meant the end of territorial politics. On the contrary, territory remains a vital principle of social, political and economic organisation. More concretely, territory comes back repeatedly for three reasons, functional, political and normative. Territory is intimately connected to social and economic functions, even in a supposedly borderless world. It provides the most widespread basis for political mobilisation; and it is the basis for most systems of representation, control and accountability. So we are witnessing not the end of territory but its reinvention as the relationship among space, function, identity and representation changes. New spaces are emerging, at the local and

---

[3] R Dahrendorf, "Preserving Prosperity", *New Statesmen and Society*, 13/29 December 1995; R Dahrendorf, "La sconfitta della vecchia democrazia", *La Repubblica*, 26 January 2000.

[4] J-M Guehenno, *The end of the nation state* (Minneapolis: University of Minnesota Press, 1995).

[5] J M Guehenno, *Fin de la démocratie* (Paris: Flammarion, 1993).

[6] An idea that comes much more easily to people in stateless nations like Scotland than to German or French scholars.

[7] Y H Ferguson and R W Mansbach, "Global Politics and the Turn of the Millennium: Changing Bases of 'Us' and 'Them' " (1999) 1 *International Studies Review* 78–107.

regional level, at the European level, and at the interstices of the evolving state system.

It was a staple of social theory from Durkheim on that, as society modernised, functional specialisation would replace territory as a principle of organisation.[8] This has always been questionable and probably arose from a failure adequately to conceptualise the relationship between territory and function. Moreover, the modernisation paradigm was not truly universal but implicitly bounded by the nation state. The same was true of the national integration scholars of the post-war era and their contemporaries in the behavioural school of social science. Deutsch[9] is typical, arguing that integration proceeds until it has produced homogeneous nation states; if this cannot be achieved, unassimilated territories secede to produce the same effect. Again, there is no mention that the nation state is itself a territorial form which may be historically contingent. Nor is it recognised that sustaining its integrity and managing territorial relations within it have been a constant feature of European statecraft.[10] In the nineteenth century, while the nation state was consolidating and extending its reach, tariff protection, Church-state relations and even class politics were shaped by territorial factors. Territorial intermediaries performed a vital role in sustaining support both for the regime and the government in office even in the most centralised systems like France and Italy. In the postwar era, regional and urban policies were important across European states. Often seen as a mere adjunct to centralised macro-economic strategies, these were gradually institutionalised and took on a political life of their own, shaping the policy agenda, interest group activity and citizen expectations on a territorial basis. In recent years, new links between territory and function have become apparent as scholars have identified new functional systems emerging above, below and across the nation state.[11]

The most important have been in economic development and change, where the global and European levels are recognised as being embedded in their own logic and undermining the role of the state. Capital mobility, increased trade and the rise of the transnational corporation are reshaping global economic

---

[8] "We can almost say that a people is as much advanced as territorial divisions are more superficial"; E Durkheim, *The Division of Labour in Society* (New York: Macmillan, 1964) p. 187.

[9] K Deutsch, *Nationalism and Social Communication: An Inquiry into the Foundations of Nationality* (Cambridge: MIT Press, 1966).

[10] M Keating, *State and Regional Nationalism: Territorial Politics and the European State* (London: Harvester-Wheatsheaf, 1988); M Keating, *The New Regionalism in Western Europe. Territorial Restructuring and Political Change* (Aldershot: Edward Elgar, 1998).

[11] J Agnew, *Place and Politics: The Geographical Mediation of State and Society* (London: Allen and Unwin, 1987); J Agnew and S Corbridge, *Mastering Space: Hegemony, Territory and International Political Economy* (London: Routledge, 1995).

space and curtailing the options of state governments in economic management. The European single market further undermines national control, while the Europeanisation of a series of policy sectors, culminating in the single currency, reduces the functional scope of national administrations.

Yet while Europeanisation and globalisation are eroding the territorial frame of the nation state they are not, *pace* some observers[12] eroding territory as a frame for economic restructuring. On the contrary, there is a resurgence of interest in local and regional economies, seen as the motors of change within the global system.[13] Space, which was previously seen merely as a matter of location, which could be neutralised through transport and communications, is now seen as a factor in economic competitiveness in its own right. Conventional market linkages, which have explained the tendency of firms to cluster, are supplemented by the idea of "untraded interdependencies", in which spatially bounded communities produce public goods and positive externalities for enterprises. Space is no longer a matter of mere topography but takes on a social and cultural meaning, which sustains different types of market economy and different degrees of competitiveness. Regions and localities have thus emerged as new spaces of production which, in a globalising economy, must compete against each other to gain advantage. Extreme versions of this theory present regions as engaged in a neo-mercantilist competition for absolute advantage in a Darwinian struggle for survival. Others recognise the old principle of comparative advantage, in which there is a niche for everyone, if only they can discover it. Economically determinist versions of the theory claim that politics must follow suit, with the pursuit of economic advantage as the only goal. Ohmae[14] goes so far as to equate the rise of regional economies with the end of the nation state itself. This is much too simplistic since the nation state is about a great deal more than economic development. Like other prophets of globalisation, Ohmae also hides a strong ideological message in his account of a purportedly irresistible force to which governments must bend. A more sophisticated analysis must recognise that these economic forces are mediated by institutions and political actors at supranational, national and substate levels, to produce different outcomes in different places. Even the market economy takes different forms and obeys distinct logics in different cultural and institutional environments.

Culture provides another, perhaps unexpected, example of reterritorialisation. Despite the internet, satellites and the whole paraphernalia of modern communication, linguistic and cultural communities seem more than ever in need of their own physical space. This probably reflects the fact that cultural production, development and progress, as opposed to mere diffusion, require

[12] Badie, n. 2 above.

[13] A J Scott, *Regions and the World Economy: The Coming Shape of Global Production, Competition, and Political Order* (Oxford: Oxford University Press, 1998); M Storper, *The Regional World: Territorial Development in a Global Economy* (New York and London: Guildford, 1997).

[14] K Ohmae, *The End of the Nation State: The Rise of Regional Economies* (New York: The Free Press, 1995).

interaction in space. They also require an institutional framework and control of other policy instruments, which are also spatially based. So we find more, not less, emphasis on territorialised language policies in places like Quebec, Catalonia, Flanders or Wales.

There is also some evidence that social solidarity may be becoming detached from the nation state framework and embedded in smaller local and regional units, especially when these have a cultural identity. This poses a challenge for national welfare states and for systems of territorial equalisation.

Since the postwar settlement but particularly in the 1990s, human rights have been increasingly detached from the nation state. Not only does the state no longer define and frame rights, but national judiciaries are no longer the sole interpreter and enforcer of them. So human rights are no longer the same as citizen rights and the promotion of rights has been freed of the ideological baggage of nationalism—something the French revolutionaries never quite succeeded in doing. This new transnational jurisprudence, both through the EU and the European Convention on Human Rights, has now also been able to penetrate the state to connect directly with sub-state governments. The implications of this, especially for stateless nations, are far reaching.

So functional systems are re-orienting themselves, migrating to new levels above, below and beyond the nation state. Yet none of these functional factors—one could cite more—are determinant and, indeed, they do not point consistently to one level of territory among the many possible ones between the global system and the parish. Their effects are mediated and shaped by politics, but this too is changing its territorial focus.

POLITICAL CHANGE

The reterritorialisation of politics has been an uneven process, taking different forms in different places and impelled by different forces. Again there is a dual process of sub-state mobilisation and supra-state integration. One factor is the reaction to functional change and the search for new levels of political action, at the supra-state or sub-state level, at which these forces can be contained and controlled. Another may be the weakening of class, religious and other cleavages that previously marked European political space, and the emergence of new (or re-emergence of old) forms of identity. Popular identification with sub-state territories varies widely, being greatest where there is a cultural or historical basis, as in the "stateless nations" like Scotland or the Basque Country. In these cases, political leaders have sought to link the issue of territorial assertion to that of European integration, attacking the state from above and below. They gain a certain amount of popular support for this. Evidence for a more general shift of loyalties upwards from the state to Europe is more elusive. Observers like Anthony Smith[15] deny the possibility of a European identity, since Europe

---

[15] A Smith, *Nations and Nationalism in a Global Era* (Cambridge: Polity, 1995).

lacks a unified demos (which Smith, but not all observers, tends to identify with an ethnic core). This, I believe is missing the point since what is required is a functional capacity rather than an all-embracing identity. Once again, we risk falling for a false analogy with the nation state as the only imaginable form of political order. I suspect, rather, that there is a process akin to that described by Anderson[16] for nations, in which certain strata of the population in their "pilgrimages" acquire a transnational identity. This would also be true of people working in specific geographic or functional locations like the European Commission, the Council of Europe, CSCE, certain firms and, indeed, the European University Institute. Such a European identity might be combined with varying types of state and sub-state identity.[17] Identity thus ceases to be fixed or determined by social status and becomes more open and malleable.[18] Identities are also multiple, with different ones, or combinations, invoked according to need and circumstance.

An important role in demystifying the state and encouraging notions of plural identity has been played by historians. Scholars like Tilly,[19] Spruyt[20] and Osiander[21] have shown that the nation state is a historically contingent form, which has taken different shapes in various parts of Europe and whose triumph was not inevitable or complete. In response to current political debates, a new historiography has emerged, questioning the centrality of the state and rehabilitating older principles of political authority.[22] The experience in Scotland, where devolution has given history a new currency, is paralleled in Catalonia, the Basque Country and Quebec where dominant state-centred historiographies are being challenged. This historical revisionism, closely linked to a revalorisation of sub-state cultures, provides an important element in the reinvention of identity and the construction of new or rediscovered imagined communities at various spatial levels.

INSTITUTIONAL CHANGE

There have also been institutional changes, at European level, with the consolidation of continental institutions, and at local and regional level. European

---

[16] B Anderson, *Imagined Communities: Reflections on the Origins and Spread of Nationalism* (London: Verso, 1983).

[17] Again, it is much easier to make this point in Aberdeen or Barcelona than in London or Paris.

[18] D McCrone, *The Sociology of Nationalism* (London: Routledge, 1998).

[19] C Tilly, *Coercion, Capital and European States, AD 990–1990* (Boulder: Westview, 1990); C Tilly, "Entanglements of European States and Cities", in C Tilly and W P Blockmans (eds.), *Cities and the Rise of States in Europe, AD 1000 to 1800* (Boulder: Westview, 1994).

[20] H Spruyt, *The Sovereign State and Its Competitors* (Princeton: Princeton University Press, 1994).

[21] A Osiander, *The State System of Europe, 1640–1990. Peacemaking and the Conditions of International Stability* (Oxford: Clarendon, 1994).

[22] M Keating, "How Historic are Historic Rights? Competing Historiographies and the Struggle for Political Legitimacy", in *Etnicidade e Nacionalismo*, (Santiago de Compostela: Consello da Cultura Gralega, 2001).

integration has progressed in stages, acquiring new dimensions as it goes. The most advanced element is that of market integration, with its own system of regulation. There is also an advanced process of institution building, although caught between the logic of intergovernmentalism, incarnated in the Council of the EU, and supranationalism, represented by the Commission, the Parliament and much of the consultative machinery. There is a European social space, less developed than the market and, since the Maastricht Treaty a European citizenship. This citizenship, like other aspects of the European project, is not monopolistic and is rather functionally specific. Again, the analogy with the nation state is misleading. European citizenship is there to be invoked and used in specific contexts, rather than itself determining the context for social and political identity. The latest stage of the European project, the single currency, while ostensibly part of the process of market integration, goes to the heart of state sovereignty, with huge practical and symbolic effects. It also introduces another actor in the form of the European Central Bank, independent of political control both at national and European levels.

The larger states of Europe have all established forms of intermediate, regional, or "meso" government. In some cases, this responds to a functional need for a new level of intervention and coordination (France, Italy). In others it is a response to bottom up pressures for recognition of cultural and historic entities (Spain, UK) or the management of linguistic and ethnic conflict (Belgium, Northern Ireland). The very heterogeneity of this meso level has led some observers to dismiss it but, in the context of the general restructuring of functions and powers discussed above, it is surely no coincidence that states have all tended to institutionalise an intermediate form of management. The powers and status of the meso level do, it is true, vary greatly, from the cooperative federalism of Germany, to the asymmetrical devolution of the UK, the strong, quasi-federal system of Spain, or the largely administrative regionalism found in France and Italy. European influences have also been important. States have been persuaded that a more coherent system of regional administration and management is needed to face the needs of the single market, although this conflicts with their reluctance to surrender power (hence the dilemma of the last and present British government over English regions). In some cases, the Commission itself has been the catalyst, insisting that regional institutions be set up in order to manage the Structural Funds since their reform in 1988. Commission pressure has been largely responsible for regionalisation in Greece, Sweden and the candidate countries of Central and Eastern Europe and the abortive regionalisation plans in Portugal.[23] Regions gained some institutional recognition in the Maastricht Treaty, which established a Committee of the Regions as a consultative body but ambitions to entrench them as a "third level"

---

[23] Regions were in fact mandated by the 1976 constitution of Portugal, but it took European pressure to bring the issue to the fore in 1998. Since the voters then turned down regionalisation in a referendum, we now have the interesting situation of an entire electorate being in breach of its own constitution.

of European government have not succeeded. Regions are too heterogeneous to be reduced to the same institutional logic and do not even exist in some parts of Europe. The Committee of the Regions itself has suffered from this heterogeneity and from the limitations on its own powers, but it has sustained the "Europe of the Regions" movement at a certain level.

Complicating matters is the fact that this territorial decentralisation is accompanied by functional decentralisation and a shifting of the boundaries between government, the market and civil society. Deregulation and privatisation have shifted back the boundaries of the state. The European project involves both the construction of a new level of regulation and an overall programme of deregulation. Private sector techniques and assumptions have been brought into government via the "new public management". In formerly state-dominated polities like France, Spain, or Italy, the autonomous institutions of civil society are being given more rein. Public-private partnerships, community-based partnerships and innovative forms of service delivery abound. This has not only made government more complex, it has created a great deal of conceptual confusion for social scientists used to working with old and familiar categories rooted in the hierarchical state. Worst of all, it has generated a slew of neologisms that tend to obscure more than they illuminate, especially in the areas of European integration and regionalism.

UNDERSTANDING CHANGE

Grasping the significance of these changes is a serious challenge, especially given that we are living in the midst of them. There are still those who insist that nothing has changed, that states remain the fundamental unit of analysis in both the international and domestic areas. Intergovernmentalist analysts of European integration note that states remain formally sovereign and can withdraw from the EU, despite the absence of treaty provision for this. They point to the concentration of power in the Council of the EU, representing the states. Their main thrust, however, is the assumption of old style *realpolitik*, that state leaders see their interest in maintaining the power of the state as an institution and are guided by this in everything they do. This becomes a mere tautology, when even steps to strengthen European institutions are then interpreted as necessarily in the interests of the states as institutions.[24] Neo-functionalists, on the other hand, are vulnerable to the criticism that functional integration has not led ineluctably to the creation of a new European polity and the end of the nation state. On the contrary, functional integration, institution-building and the creation of a common European identity have progressed at quite different rates, creating a discrepancy that poses both intellectual and political problems.

---

[24] One is reminded of the old Marxist idea that the state, even when acting against the expressed interests of capitalists, must somehow still be working in the interests of capital.

It does appear, then, that we are seeing in Europe the creation of a new form of political order and that the tendency to interpret it using existing categories, whether as a state, a federation, a confederation or an international organisation, represent another instance of the statist fixation in social science. As a single market, it represents a limitation of the old powers of the member states and can be seen as a specific but deeper instance of globalisation and deregulation. Left wing opponents, at least until the 1980s, insisted that this is the essence of the project. On the other hand, it can be seen as a response to globalisation, an attempt to recapture at the continental level functions lost at the national level. It is also a social space and a political space, albeit of a different nature to those found at national level. This is the basis for opposition from British Thatcherites, who otherwise approve of the internal market as a contribution to free trade and deregulation. There is a rumbling conflict between those who see Europe purely as a market, undermining the regulatory capacity of states, and advocates of a social Europe in which the old social compromises can be renewed.[25] Some observers claim that Europe can never become a political space because it lacks a national basis.[26] This not only ignores the experience of existing multinational states that have managed to sustain multiple identities (Spain, UK), but also fundamentally misconceives the nature of European political identity. European integration was launched precisely to overcome nationalism, not to foster a new type of nationalism. It does, nevertheless, rest on a basis of common values and their institutionalisation. The fact that these values are universal ones shared elsewhere in the world no more disqualifies Europe than it disqualifies the United States, which is also an ethnically heterogeneous society built on universal values. So we can see an emerging European order of a single market, a sense of shared history (in this case a history of conflict to be overcome as well as of co-operation), a common set of values, a set of institutions, and a system of law. This is not a state but it is a great deal more than a mere intergovernmental organisation.

Similar difficulties arise in conceptualising the emerging sub-state spaces. Territorial restructuring has taken economic, political, social, cultural and institutional forms. Economic spaces can be defined by the presence of a dominant sector, or of complementary sectors, making up a productive system. Increasingly, they are seen as a nexus of traded and untraded interdependencies forming the basis of competitive units in global and European markets. Regions are social spaces in so far as they contain the institutions and associations of civil society. Cultural spaces may be defined by language, shared values, or identity. Political spaces are those which sustain political debate and in which issues are debated and decided in relation to their impact on the territorial society. Institutional spaces are defined by government. In some places, these meanings

---

[25] L Hooghe, and G Marks, "The Making of a Polity: The Struggle over European Integration", in H Kitschelt, P Lange, G Marks and J Stephens (eds.), *Continuity and Change in European Capitalism* (Cambridge: Cambridge University Press, 1999).

[26] Smith, n. 15 above.

of region coincide, while in others they do not. Economic regions do not always coincide with social or cultural spaces, *pace* the economic determinists like Ohmae. Territories can be political spaces with a sense of identity but lack autonomous institutions of government, like Scotland before 1999. Most French regions, on the other hand, do not constitute political spaces even though they are institutionalised. So the meaning of territorial units is shaped by the strength and degree of coincidence of these distinct meanings. There can therefore be no new hierarchy, with three levels, Europe, state and region, replacing the dyadic relationship of the past.

Matters are further complicated by the rise of cities. In the 1960s and 1970s, states sought to rationalise and modernise local government to fulfil specific roles within the national welfare state. Like the attempt to institutionalise regions, this ran into conflict as the technocratic rationale of state elites collided with the interests of social and political forces at the local level. Since the 1980s, cities like regions have been positioning themselves in the new European and global division of labour, competing in most instances, co-operating in others. Like regions, their activities are not contained within national boundaries. In some cases, there are competing bases for political mobilisation and institution-building, at the regional and urban level, as in the rivalry between the city of Barcelona and the Generalitat of Catalonia.

One distinct feature of the new regionalism is that it is no longer contained by the nation state on any of its dimensions.[27] Rather than serving complementary functions in a national division of labour, regions compete in global and European markets. Cultural and historic regions cross state frontiers. Regional leaders seek political support, economic resources and cultural sustenance outside state boundaries through an emerging paradiplomacy and strategic alliances with other territorial actors. European policies penetrate national space, bringing regions into contact with each other and the Commission, so that state territories are simultaneously Europeanised and regionalised.

This is a complex political order, comparable, although not identical to, the pre-state European order of overlapping and underlapping sovereignties, different types of authority in the state, the economy and civil society, and competing forms of legitimacy. Despite loose talk of a neo-medievalism, or analogies with the Holy Roman Empire, however, it is distinctly modern in that it coexists with universal norms of liberal democracy. Political scientists, seeking to make sense of it, have come up with a plethora of new concepts and neologisms, none of which quite fits the bill. What is needed is a set of concepts that allows us to place the new order in its historical context, to analyse its dynamics, to assess the distribution of power and resources. They must enable us to compare different times and places to identify their distinguishing features. We also need normative concepts to enable us to judge the new dispensation and its relationship with shared ideas of democracy, accountability and justice.

---

[27] Keating, n. 10 above (1998).

Perhaps the most widespread notion in contemporary analysis is that of "governance". This is a broad term, for which at least six different meanings have been identified[28] but the basic idea is that government, identified with the traditional hierarchical state form, has given way to a world of diffused authority in which the boundaries between public and private are blurred. Governance seems to refer to the regulatory capacity of the whole gamut of organisations in the public sphere, including governments at all levels, private firms, and associations. Applied to local and regional restructuring, this takes the form of "multilevel governance" in which the state shares power with emerging bodies above and below it as well as with the institutions of market and civil society. There are a number of problems with this concept. In the first place, it relies heavily on a mythical view of a past in which authority was monopolised by a centralised state which, in turn, was the only actor in the international system. At best, this describes an aspiration of European states from the mid-nineteenth century until the late twentieth century, not the historical experience of European space. Even in the archetypal centralised, hierarchical state, France, researchers for over thirty years have emphasised the complex dispersal of power and the need for continuous negotiation. Students of federalism, especially in Germany, have long recognised the interdependence of tiers of government and the complex patterns of co-operation and competition that this produces. In the minority nations of Europe the legitimacy of the state has always been seen as somewhat conditional and resting on a range of explicit and implicit concessions. In other words, there is nothing new about territorial politics.

More seriously, the concept of multilevel governance (and governance generally) is impossible to operationalise. It is never clear, in fact, whether it is meant to be an operational theory or a general comment on the state of the world. It does not seem to be possible to contrast instances of multilevel governance with instances where it is absent, or to calibrate degrees of multilevel governance. If multilevel governance is everything, then perhaps it is nothing—or maybe no more than a descriptive metaphor. The concept is loosely pluralistic, in its emphasis on the dispersal of authority and, like so much pluralist theory, suffers from a severe level of analysis problem. At some level of analysis, every social phenomenon is plural, since we can go on disaggregating until we come down to the level of the individual. This is very easy since the state, the region, Europe, social class or gender are no more than abstract concepts. What is more difficult in the social sciences is to choose appropriate levels of reaggregation. This is the work of theory. Theories of governance, which have their origins in organisation theory, tend to take the organisation as the unit of analysis. This in turn has a number of effects. It fillets out of the analysis other social aggregates like class, gender, residential location, which undergird much of the struggle over power and resources in society. This in turn confirms the pluralist analysis, since

[28] R A W Rhodes, "The New Governance: Governing without Government" (1996) 44 *Political Studies*, 652–67.

organisations are easily disaggregated and pluralistic theory becomes self-confirming. Eventually, disaggregation takes us down to the individual actor, yet theories of social action built purely from an individual basis are notoriously unreliable. So pluralism, and multilevel governance with it, becomes no more than an artefact of methodology; if you look for it anywhere at all, you will find it.[29] It also introduces a rather insidious conservative bias, since we are deprived of those very social aggregates needed to form normative judgements. Perhaps more generously, it sustains a "third way" type of politics in which there are no left and right, no two sides of industry, no north and south, no country and city (to name a few of the critical social cleavages that Tony Blair has denied in the last couple of years). It is a form of social science designed for a post-ideological age.

Federal and confederal theory have also been deployed in an effort to understand the new territorial politics in Europe. Federalism has a normative basis, founded on the dispersal of power, the limitation on government and a respect for how politics is conducted as well as for its outcomes. In studies of European integration it is usually invoked as a normative principle by those seeking closer unity and a strengthening of accountable institutions. It has proved less useful as an analytical theory about Europe, whether the EU or the broader European order. Federations come in many shapes and forms and the principle has often been extended to cover a great deal and thereby explain ever less. In particular, it has been stretched to cover vertical and horizontal divisions of identity and authority in society at large, rather than just in the state, thereby losing its original meaning. Federalism is also based on the existence of clearly demarcated levels of government and fits less well a world of "variable geometry" with multiple loci of power. On the other hand, there is a growing interest in the idea of asymmetrical federalism, especially in multinational states.[30]

A principle which is allied to federalism and which received a great deal of prominence in the 1990s was that of subsidiarity. This is another elusive idea, which has been interpreted in multiple ways and often manipulated to suit specific interests. In essence, it is a normative principle about the distribution of power that tries to reconcile the dispersal and decentralisation of power in state and civil society with the recognition of the unity of society and the need for social integration and solidarity. It has been particularly associated with Catholic and some forms of Protestant social thought but was incorporated into the Maastricht Treaty as a way of squaring various circles. This allowed different interests to use it to their own purposes, with the British government taking it to mean the primacy of member states in the European Union while the German Länder saw it as a means of securing their autonomy against the state and securing a direct link with Europe. Thereby the vagueness of the concept and the difficulties of its operationalisation were exposed.

[29] This is exactly what happened to the debate between pluralists and elitists about community power in the 1960s.

[30] E Fossas, and F Requejo, (eds.) *Asimetría federal y estado plurinaciona* (Madrid: Trotta, 1999).

Public choice theory has gained great prominence in some fields of social science, including the study of local government. Its analytical claims are based on certain assumptions about human behaviour, notably that people are rational, utility maximising individuals. It can in certain cases provide powerful insight into the behaviour of individuals and organisations in complex settings, but its utility is drastically limited by the founding assumption. It also has a powerful normative dimension. Explicitly or implicitly, public choice analysts believe that people *should* be rational utility maximisers[31] and that political institutions should be designed with this in mind. They favour creating market-like conditions in government, with agencies competing against each other for the public's custom. They believe that local government systems should be flexible and allow groups of individuals to associate or incorporate freely to provide services in common. So they favour complexity and are against the hierarchical state but, unlike multilevel government theorists, do have a normative basis and set of criteria for this. Essentially, they favour market competition in public administration and oppose anything that might militate against this. What they lack is any broader principle of social organisation that might sustain social solidarity or the unity of society. They do insist that people in a public choice world would be free to form any type of overarching organisation they want, including a welfare state. They do not show how or why this would happen in a world in which individuals are assumed to act in their own individual interest. Nor does this type of analysis get us far in understanding the new forms of collective action emerging in Europe.

THE CONSEQUENCES

We are left, then, with a shifting political mosaic in Europe. This is a new context but it does not raise essentially new issues in politics. Coining new concepts is both premature, since we do not know where things are heading, and it is distracting, since we can still ask many of the old analytical and normative questions. The analytical questions involve tracing the changing relationship between territory, function, political mobilisation and institution building. This requires both an overview of developments at European level, and detailed examination of the different forms that region building can take in different places.[32] We need to realise that the state is not the only bearer of territorial identities or the only territorial framework for functional systems and that the emerging functional systems do not always neatly coincide in space as in the ideal-type nation-state. Functional, political, cultural and administrative regions may differ in their boundaries and scope, and increasingly cross the borders of European states.

[31] Although in some cases it remains unclear whether the argument being advanced is that they are or that they merely should be.
[32] Keating, n. 10 above (1998).

The normative questions concern accountability and representation, as well as matters of distribution and equity. Ralph Dahrendorf[33] has recently been arguing that the erosion of the dominant nation state is a loss for democracy and social solidarity since both developed within it and it provided the necessary reason for their realisation. Europe, it is argued, cannot be democratised since it lacks a demos, while local and regional government are divisive and, where they correspond to cultural identities, dangerously tribalistic. These claims can certainly be questioned. There is no reason why the nation state should be the only framework for democracy.[34] Indeed, local and regional devolution have been promoted precisely as a way of extending and deepening democracy. One might also argue that there are untapped possibilities for deepening democracy in the EU and not just by strengthening the role of the Parliament or converting the Union into a nation state. Perhaps a more serious argument hinges on the complexity of the emerging order. Complex systems relying on co-operation among multiple agents obscure accountability and shift power into the networks of co-operation themselves. Those with the time, skills and resources to operate these systems are at an advantage. In particular, representative assemblies tend to lose influence to executives and bureaucracies. Yet if the nation state, in so far as it ever existed, is gone, it seems forlorn to hanker for its return. Besides, if it does fade away, it will take with it a lot of evil as well as good. It is perhaps more important to think about how to extend democratic principles and accountability within the newly emerging social, economic and political spaces. It may be possible to do so much better than within the consolidated state which itself has suffered from many democratic deficits.

Equity, however, remains a real problem. The nation state has served as a powerful instrument for redistribution, although varying in its real progressivity. Supporters of the nation state often argue that only large consolidated states have the tax base and resources to engage in redistribution and that only nation states have the common values to sustain a politics of redistribution. Yet these are two separate questions. If only large states could redistribute, then there would be no justification for the persistence of small states in Europe. Yet we find that small states like the Netherlands or the Scandinavian countries have a much larger distributive effort than the United States. What really matters is the political will to sustain redistributive policies and this depends on a sense of shared identity and values, as well as a rational calculation that this is part of an overall bargain to sustain social stability and the conditions of development. If power is decentralised to levels where these principles are more strongly rooted, then social solidarity may be favoured.[35]

---

[33] Dahrendorf, n. 3 above (2000).

[34] M Keating, *Nations against the State: The New Nationalism in Catalonia, Quebec and Scotland* (2nd edn., London: Macmillan, 2001).

[35] A Noel, "Is Decentralization Conservative?", in R Young (ed.), *Stretching the Federation: The Art of the State in Canada* (Kingston: Institute of Intergovernmental Relations, Queen's University, 1999) pp. 195–218.

The state still remains the main instrument of inter-territorial transfers. This, however, has depended on a social bargain in the context of a shared national project and identity. In the heyday of the integrated nation state, there was also an element of self-interest as wealthy regions could transfer resources to poorer ones knowing that the money would come back in the form of orders for their products. Diversionary regional policies in the Keynesian era were promoted as a way of helping developing regions to grow, relieving pressures in advanced regions, and adding to national output by mobilising idle resources. The weakening of the state has shifted the parameters for these social and territorial compromises. In the single European market and the context of globalisation, regions are now pitted in competition for absolute advantage. It is no accident that pressures against fiscal equalisation are growing in the contributing regions of Germany, Belgium, Italy and the UK. The logical response to this would be an increased effort for territorial redistribution at the European level, based on the same principles of solidarity and enlightened self interest that underlay state policies for territorial equalisation. There has been some such effort through the Structural Funds, which were increased and reformed in the 1980s in response to market integration and now form the second largest item in the EU budget. Yet they remain tiny in relation to national-level transfers and the political will to expand them further in response to the single currency and enlargement is lacking.

CONCLUSION

So we are seeing a shift of functions, of identities and of institutions from the nation state to new territorial and non-territorial bases. In some cases, these coincide or are nested—Scotland might be an example of this. In others these competing principles pull territorial societies in different directions as the experiences of Wales and, more dramatically, Northern Ireland, show. The social sciences have been slow in grasping this since it deprives them of many of their most basic analytical tools. It also, for some, puts in question the very project of modernity and liberal democracy itself, tied as these have been historically to the nation state. State sovereignty itself is called into question. For some sovereignty is by definition, indivisible and remains the unique property of states. This claim can be sustained only in the most formal sense and, if sovereignty belongs to states by definition, then the claim is a rather empty one, if not positively tautological. Others claim that particular states remain sovereign, as with the repeated declarations of British governments, incorporated into legislation, that nothing is being done to affect the sovereignty of Parliament. Yet if sovereignty is given any substantive meaning, then it is surely clear that it is being transformed radically and that there are many ways of adapting to a post-sovereign political order. Exactly how it is being transformed and what is replacing it remain unclear and will continue to do so as long as we evade the issue, hiding behind purely formal conceptions of sovereignty, or retreating into forms of organisational analysis that avoid the question altogether. We cannot yet frame a new paradigm for the new political order. We can, however, ask questions about the relationships among these forms of restructuring and about the power distribution within the emerging order. We can also ask normative questions about participation, accountability and distribution. This is surely enough to keep social scientists busy for a while yet.

2

Member States and Regions in Community Law: Convergence and Divergence

JOANNE SCOTT*

INTRODUCTION

IN THE PREVIOUS chapter Michael Keating addressed the theme of territorial restructuring in Europe, and the relationship between territory, function, identity and democracy. The picture which he painted was unstable and fragmented. It is not one which easily lends itself to conceptualisation or interpretation on the basis of existing categories in law and political science, predicated as these so often are upon the centrality of the (nation) state. Michael Keating observes that "[t]he larger states of Europe have all established forms of intermediate, regional, or 'meso', government". While this "meso" level is acknowledged to be heterogeneous in social, cultural, economic and political terms, the fact remains that the last decades have witnessed a rise in the "third level" of government in Europe.[1] He goes on to note, as have others, that "European influences have been important" here. He points in particular to the impact of structural funding since the seminal 1988 reforms and, rather more tentatively, to the establishment of the Committee of the Regions. Thus, in these respects at least he argues, the European Union has constituted a catalyst promoting "regionalisation" in the member and applicant states.[2]

* Thanks to the workshop participants for their comments on the paper. Thanks too to the editors for their help along the way.
    [1] See C Jeffrey (ed.), *The Regional Dimension of the European Union: Towards a Third Level in Europe?* (London: Frank Cass, 1997).
    [2] It will already be clear that there is a wide range of terminology available to describe the phenomenon under discussion; meso level, third level, sub-state, sub-national, regional etc.. This is due in part to the sensitivity of the subject at hand and the heterogeneity to which Keating alludes. This paper will adopt the language of "regional" government. This serves to distinguish sub-state government located at the "meso" and local level. Use of the term "regional" is, however, liable to offend, especially in the context of one of the cases discussed in this chapter, namely devolution in Scotland. Hence use of this term comes with a health warning. Regions may be sub-national or national. Use of the term is used merely to connote sub-state, and does not disparage any people's claim to historic nationhood.

It is against the backdrop of this claim that this chapter will proceed. It is in no sense intended to challenge Michael Keating's claim, but rather to place it within a broader framework of Community law. This chapter will consider how territory—state and sub-state—is conceived in Community law, and how this conception (or these conceptions) may be anticipated to shape territorial relations within the member states. One central objective is to illustrate the wide variety of different stances which Community law adopts in this respect. From the proactively regionalist, to the cautiously agnostic, Community law remains, at times, wilfully "statist" in its predilections. The following list provides an overview of the European Union's fragmented personality in this respect, highlighting the principal elements which define its stance vis-à-vis the regions. It seeks to provide a more comprehensive sketch-map in this respect, whereas the analysis which follows focuses upon only a small number of the elements adduced therein.

State-Centric Aspects of Community Law

—Article 226 EC Commission actions against member states, regardless of the identity of the state actor with responsibility for the breach;
—Inter-governmental make-up of institutional actors, including Council of the European Union, European Council, and comitology committees;
—Article 230 EC and central government as privileged actor, but sub-state actors enjoying no special status with regard to standing before the European Court;
—Closer Co-operation under the Treaty defines "ins" and "outs" in terms of the member states as a whole, and does not permit regions to opt-in or out;
—Treaty revision and *national* veto.

Community Law Accommodating the Regions

—Doctrine of direct effect, including vertical direct effect of directives ensuring enforcement against body with responsibility for breach, including sub-state actors;
—Indirect effect (doctrine of consistent interpretation) ensuring enforcement against body with responsibility for breach, including sub-state actors;
—State liability in damages, leaving it open to member states to enforce liability against central government, or against sub-state authorities with responsibility for the breach;
—The open-ended concept of a "competent authority" with responsibilities pursuant to much Community legislation. This may be situated at whichever level of governance the member state concerned deems appropriate;
—Increasing "flexibility" which characterises much Community law, leaving much scope for differences in implementation decisions. This is closely associated with the concept of proportionality as defined in the Protocol on the application of the principles of subsidiarity and proportionality;

—Article 203 EC and the possibility of sub-state ministerial representatives in Council;

—Open Method of Coordination; Though "statist" in its form, there is sufficient flexibility inherent in it for sub-state actors to be involved and for European guidelines to be translated into regional as well as national policies, though this will vary from area to area according to the nature of the Community objective pursued.

Community Law Giving Voice to the Regions

—Committee of the Regions;

—Partnership in Community Structural Funding;

—Article 1 TEU which talks of decisions being taken as closely as possible to the citizen.

"STATISM" AND COMMUNITY LAW

If the Community's personality is fragmented vis-à-vis its regions, in respect of enforcement it exhibits some strongly statist tendencies. Of particular importance in this respect is the functioning of Article 226 TEC, and the concept of state responsibility which inheres in it. Regardless of which organ of the state is responsible for an alleged breach of Community law, Article 226 TEC posits the myth of the unitary state and pursues the member state, in its central government guise, before the European Court. That member state will be responsible for ensuring compliance with any judgment of the Court and for the payment of any fine which may be imposed as a result of a failure to do so.[3] This gives rise, potentially, to a disjunction between political authority and legal responsibility; a disjunction which may be anticipated to expand as the actual powers of sub-state actors increase.

---

[3] The European Court's authority to impose pecuniary sanctions on defaulting member states arises from the Maastricht Treaty. It is a power which, it recently deployed for the first time in Case C–387/97 *Commission* v. *Greece*, [2000] ECR I–5047. This stands in contrast to the observations of the European Court that reparation for damage does not necessarily need to be provided by the federal state in the context of state liability for damages. A member state cannot plead the distribution of powers and responsibilities between the bodies which exist in national law in order to free itself from liability, but subject to the effectiveness and non-discrimination principles, it would appear to be acceptable for state liability to be enforced against a devolved authority or sub-state entity. See Case C–302/97 *Klaus Konle and Republic of Austria* [1999] ECR I–3099. This was recently confirmed in Case C–424/97 *Haim and Kassenzahnartzliche Vereinigung Nordrhein,* [2000] ECR I–5123 in which the Court noted that in member states with a federal structure, reparation need not necessarily be provided by the federal state, in order for Community law obligations to be fulfilled, "and nor does Community law preclude a public-law body, in addition to the member state itself, from being made liable to make reparation for loss and damage caused to individuals as a result of measures which it took in breach of Community law". See paras. 27–34.

It may be thought that this "statist" bias in Community law would tend to "exercise a centralising effect in relations between central, regional and local government",[4] as member states seek to close down the disjunction by clawing back powers in so far as their exercise may impact upon member state compliance with Community law. And indeed in the context of Scottish devolution in the United Kingdom this does appear to be the case. The Scotland Act 1998 is resoundingly imbued with the logic of (UK) parliamentary sovereignty, and the concept of a voluntary—and perhaps temporary—delegation of powers. The Scottish Parliament enjoys broad legislative competence in respect of all matters which are not reserved.[5] Reserved matters include foreign policy, defence and national security, immigration and nationality, employment and social security, regulation of markets and monetary and fiscal policy. Nonetheless, even outside of these areas, the Secretary of State for Scotland (a member of the UK government) may, where he has reasonable grounds to believe that any action proposed by the Scottish Executive would be incompatible with international obligations, direct that the proposed action should not be taken. He may similarly direct that action be taken where this is required to give effect to such obligations.[6] More specifically, and even more forcefully, in relation to the European Union, it is provided that any function of a Minister of the Crown (UK executive) shall continue to be exercisable by him as regards Scotland, for the purposes specified in section 2(2) of the European Communities Act 1972.[7] This empowers the UK government to enact delegated legislation in a variety of forms for the purpose of implementing Community law obligations or enabling Community law rights to be exercised, or arising out of or related to any such rights or obligations.[8] Thus, perhaps the most striking legacy of EU membership to Scottish devolution is a broadly framed statutory "legislative override" whereby even in non-reserved areas the UK government may legislate for Scotland.

This phenomenon of legislative override is neither unique to Scotland and the UK, nor yet common to all member states incorporating strong regional government. Thus, in Belgium for example, while the Communities and Regions enjoy some international relations powers in their spheres of exclusive competence, the federal state is entitled to suspend a treaty making initiative where this appears to be inconsistent with Belgium's international interests or obligations.[9] Equally, the federal government may act within the exclusive competences of the Communities or Regions where the federal state has been

---

[4] V Bogdanor, *Devolution in the United Kingdom* (Oxford: Oxford University Press, 1999) p. 279.

[5] See s. 29 and Sched. 5.

[6] *Ibid.*, s. 58(2) and (3).

[7] *Ibid.*, s. 57 (1).

[8] This is subject to Schedule 2 of the Act which limits materially the areas in which such power to enact delegated legislation may be exercised.

[9] Art. 167(4) of the Belgian Constituton. See generally R Senelle, "The Role of the Communities and the Regions in the Making of Belgian Foreign Policy" (1999) 5 *European Public Law* 601.

found to be in breach of its obligations as a result of non-compliance on the part of a Community or Region. This override procedure is subject to certain conditions. Thus, the Community or Region concerned must have been declared in default at least three months prior by the federal government. In addition, the Community or Region must have been involved in the whole of the dispute settlement procedure, and the federal state must have adhered to the terms of the relevant "co-operation agreement" concerning the ways in which actions are brought before an international or supranational court in a mixed dispute.[10]

In Germany, as is well known, such federal override would be constitutionally unthinkable. Article 23 of the German Constitution guarantees the competences of the *Länder*, including their competence to implement directives which affect their legislative competences. The other side of this coin is that the federal government is not entitled to legislate in areas which fall exclusively or predominantly within the competence of the *Länder*. The lines separating the powers of central and regional government are constitutionally drawn and constitutionally guaranteed. These lines may not be breached in order to prevent, or reverse, a failure on the part of one or more of the *Länder* to respect their Community law obligations.[11]

It is clear on the basis of the above that the member states have responded to the statism inherent in Article 226 TEC in very different ways. The logic of the UK government which insists upon a correlation between responsibility and power has led, within a system predicated upon the idea of parliamentary sovereignty, to an emphatic rejection of the Scottish Parliament or Executive being endowed with exclusive competence, at least in so far as implementation of Community law is concerned. In Belgium the settlement is more nuanced, and the powers of central government more circumscribed, though the essential logic remains unchanged. In Germany, however, the statism which characterises Community law in this respect has done nothing to dent the confidence with which constitutionally guaranteed legislative boundaries are upheld. It is true that whatever the domestic political arrangements of a member state, whether it is federal or unitary, the European Union holds the state (and not its constituent parts) liable for obligations under European Community Law.[12] It is, however, by no means inevitable that this will lead to centralising effects within the member states. The implications of EU law in this respect may seem inevitable to one or other member state. But this apparent inevitability takes shape within a given constitutional constellation, the fundamental premises of which are not shared throughout the Union. It is a truism to assert that the impact of Community law on territorial

---

[10] Co-operation agreement of 11 July 1994 concerning the way in which actions are brought before an international or supranational jurisdiction in a mixed dispute. See Art. 169 thereof, and Senelle, n. 9 above, p. 604.

[11] See A Cygan (1999) 24 *ELRev.* 483 and C Jeffrey, "Farewell the Third Level? The German Lander and the European Policy Process" in C Jeffrey (ed.), *The Regional Dimension of the European Union: Towards a Third Level in Europe?* (London, Frank Cass: 1997).

[12] *Commission* v. *Belgium* cases 227–30/85 [1988] ECR 1.

relations within member states will be mediated through national constitutional filters.[13] Obvious, but nonetheless important.

It is, of course, similarly apparent that member state responses to the Article 226 phenomenon take shape within a broader framework for the management of the reality of concurrent competences across different levels of government within member states arising from membership of, and participation in, the European Union. Thus in Germany, for example, the continuing autonomy of the *Länder* in respect of the implementation of EU obligations within their spheres of competence coincides with the powerful legislative function which they exercise in respect of EU level decision-making. Thus, even where Germany is represented by federal government in Council, the *Länder* participate in the legislative process via the Upper Chamber of the German Parliament, or the Bundesrat. Not only does the German Constitution secure a channel of communication between the federal government and the Bundesrat, the latter being informed of Community proposals with relevance to the *Länder* (and enjoying an opportunity to debate and review these, where the legislative or administrative competences of the *Länder* are involved), the Bundesrat's position is binding upon the German government. On other occasions their views are to be taken into account. Add to this the fact that transfers of further sovereignty to the EU, through amendment of the Treaties, is subject to a two-thirds majority in the Bundesrat, and it is clear that the *Länder*, acting collectively through the Upper Chamber, enjoy a substantial and sometimes a decisive influence upon law-making in Europe.[14]

In neither Belgium nor the UK do such entrenched constitutional guarantees exist to secure the participation of the regions in the formulation of federal policy on European questions. Interestingly, however, both Belgium and the UK have adopted a similar course of action in securing certain rights of participation for the regions. In Belgium a Co-operation Agreement between federal government and the Communities and Regions set up a system of co-ordination between the different levels of government. The Federal Foreign Ministry Directorate for Foreign Affairs (P. 11) holds meetings on a weekly basis, at which issues arising in the Council of the European Union will be discussed. These meetings are attended by the ministers-president of the Communities and Regions, as well as representatives of the federal prime minister, and of the federal vice-prime ministers, and those ministers across the board with responsibility for the subject matter at hand. Also in attendance is the Belgian Permanent Representative to Brussels. It is within this framework that the Belgian policy position in Brussels is determined. Where no decision is reached, it is referred to

[13] As the UK Concordat on Co-ordination of European Union Policy Issues recognises: "It is implicit in the sovereignty of the UK Parliament that it will continue to have the ability to legislate to give effect to EU obligations in Scotland"; ch. 5, para. 5.8; see n. 16.

[14] See below for a discussion of the direct influence played by the *Länder* through their capacity to represent Germany as a whole in the Council of Ministers, and their participation in the advisory groups of the Commission and Council.

an Inter-Governmental Conference on Foreign Policy operating at ministerial rather than representative level. Where no agreement can be reached there will be no instruction given to the Belgian representative in Brussels, and Belgium will abstain during the relevant vote in Council. As Keeremans and Beyers note:

> "A crucial element of this system is the fact that it grants the Belgian federal and sub-national entities a right of veto in the determination of Belgium's policy in the Council. Theoretically, they have this veto in all cases, including exclusive federal or sub-national matters, since the representatives of the ministers-president are ex officio members of the co-ordination meetings. Practice shows however that these representatives keep a low profile whenever issues are discussed which do not fall within their jurisdiction. On all other matters however—and there are a lot since many competences are shared between the federal and sub-national authorities—they are anxious to protect their prerogatives".[15]

It is interesting to observe that though the German and Belgian positions are marked by important differences, both in terms of the origin of the powers of the regions, and in terms of their specific scope, in both member states these arrangements have been characterised as giving rise to a type of "co-operative federalism", based upon communication, co-ordination (sometimes consensus), deliberation and, fundamentally, interdependence in European policy making. In both member states these developments took shape around the time of the conclusion/entry into force of the Maastricht Treaty on European Union.

Looking to the UK, one might anticipate that such notions of co-operative federalism would be anathema in a system predicated upon the supremacy of Parliament and the devolution rather than federalisation of political power. And certainly the Scotland Act is silent as to the issue of the management of concurrent competences which fall within the Scottish Parliament's and Executive's devolved powers, but also within the competence of central government by virtue of its reserved powers over EU affairs. In Scotland, as in Belgium, the issue has fallen for resolution by way of an agreement between the Scottish Ministers and the UK Government. A "Concordat on Co-ordination of European Union Policy Issues" has been agreed. This agreement, like the plethora of others drawn up, is characterised as being "binding in honour only" and as not intended to constitute a legally enforceable contract or to create any rights or obligations which are legally enforceable.[16] It sets out the mechanisms between the UK Government and the Scottish Executive for the handling of EU business dealing, *inter alia*, with the provision of information and the formulation of UK policy on Europe. In terms of the former it provides a commitment to the provision to the devolved administrations of "full and comprehensive information,

---

[15] B Kerremans, and J Beyers, "The Belgian Sub-National Entities in the European Union: Second or Third Level Players" in C Jeffrey (ed.) n. 11 above, pp. 45–6.

[16] "Concordat on Co-ordination of European Union Policy Issues—Scotland", B1.2. See generally <http://www.scotland.gov.uk/concordats>. For an excellent discussion see A Scott, "The Role of Concordats in the New Governance of Britain: Taking Subsidiarity Seriously" Jean Monnet Paper 8/00 at: http://www.jeanmonnetprogram.org/

as early as possible, on all business within the framework of the European Union which appears likely to be of interest to the devolved administrations, including notifications of relevant meetings within the EU".[17] In terms of Scottish participation in the formulation of UK policy:

> "It is the Government's intention that Ministers and officials of the devolved administrations should be fully involved in discussions within the UK Government about the formulation of the UK's policy position on all issues which touch on matters which fall within the responsibility of the devolved administrations."[18]

It is provided that the nature of the consultative procedure pursued will vary according to the nature of the specific issue at hand, including the degree of urgency which characterises it. The implication is that while in certain circumstances inter-departmental consultation across the two tiers of government might be foregone, at the very least bilateral consultation between the lead Whitehall department and the devolved administration will take place. As well as co-ordination by way of contact between civil servants, the Concordat provides for a degree of central co-ordination by way of a Joint Ministerial Committee (JMC),[19] consisting of Ministers of the UK Government, Scottish Ministers, Members of the Cabinet of the National Assembly for Wales [and, one hopes, Ministers in the Northern Ireland Executive Committee]. In the context of European affairs such meetings are to be convened where resolution of the matter at hand cannot be achieved by way of bilateral contacts between administrations. The JMC is presented thus as a forum for seeking to resolve differences between government at different levels, and the procedure to be followed for EU affairs is laid down in the supplementary agreement on the JMC.[20] This presents the JMC as one of the principal mechanisms for consultation on UK positions in respect of EU issues affecting devolved matters. It anticipates that the majority of business in this respect will be carried out through correspondence, meeting only where necessary, and emphasises the consultative rather than executive nature of the body, which enjoys authority only to reach non-binding agreements, and not to adopt binding decisions.

Thus it is clear that while there are certain similarities of style—in terms of the post-constitutional nature of the agreement—between the Belgian and Scottish model, the position of Scotland vis-à-vis the UK government in the formulation of European policy positions is weak. Not only does Scotland not possess any veto power—regardless of the extent to which the issue under discussion falls within its competence—but the Scottish Executive incurs duties (relating to confidentiality of proceedings for example) as well as rights under the terms of the Concordat. Once again, the United Kingdom' s response to the

---

[17] "Concordat on Co-ordination of European Union Policy Issues—Scotland", Common Annex, B3.2.

[18] *Ibid.*, B3.4.

[19] See *Memorandum of Understanding*, n. 16 above.

[20] n. 16 above, Supplementary Agreements, Part II, A. Agreement on the Joint Ministerial Committee.

reality of the continuing statism of the EU, be it in relation to the capacity of Scotland to represent the UK as a whole in Council or in relation to procedures for co-operation in the formulation of a single UK negotiating position, is mediated through its own constitutional framework and offers the Scottish institutions of government certain participatory privileges, rather than concrete rights. Whether in relation to the implementation issue, or in respect of the role of the member state in Council, the UK has engineered a solution that should ensure that shifting and contested territorial politics at home remain a matter of domestic house-keeping—somewhat inconvenient but not too intrusive on the European stage—and that they do not serve to disrupt the unity of the UK's relationship with the European Union. Scotland may look on with some envy, and perhaps surprised bemusement, at the willingness of both Belgium and Germany to accommodate the regional position even at the expense of the effectiveness and unity of external representation in Europe.

Nevertheless, one fact remains to be observed. Who would have guessed that it is the very statism which inheres in Community law which has generated such momentum in favour of federal relations in the member states? The crudeness of the EU's position towards the member states—the inability of the votes of such states to be split in Council to reflect regional differences, and the disjunction between regionalisation and unity in member state representation—serves to institutionalise concurrent rather than co-ordinate forms of federalism within the member states,[21] and thus to necessitate mechanisms and institutions for inter-governmental co-operation within the member states. Ironically, perhaps, it is the very statism of the EU, especially in the context of representation in Council, which, generates momentum for a version of co-operative federalism within the member states and to the institution—in a variety of guises—of pathways for communication, consultation, deliberation and agreement between the constituent parts of multi-tiered governments. These mechanisms may find weakest expression in the UK, as indeed one would anticipate, but that does not alter the fact that they at any rate find expression.

COMMUNITY LAW ACCOMMODATING REGIONALISM

There is something apparently disconcerting about "regionalisation" and increasing regional autonomy within member states, at just such a time as political power is slipping away to supranational (notably the EU) and international (notably the WTO) entities. Nonetheless, such is the reality of regional government in Europe that it is beginning to shape the supranational,[22] which is finding ways of accommodating the authority claims and aspirations of this tier. This is most starkly apparent in Article 203 TEC (ex Article 146) which opens up

---

[21] See R Cornes, "Intergovernmental Relations in a Devolved United Kingdom: Making Devolution Work" in R Hazell, (ed.), *Constitutional Futures: A History of the Next Ten Years* (Oxford: Oxford University Press, 1999).

[22] On regions within the framework of the GATT/WTO see *infra*.

the possibility for regional ministerial representation in Council, so long as the regional representative in question is authorised to commit the government of that member state. It is, however, also clear that the responsiveness of the EU to the regional dimension will depend not only upon such specific regionally focussed initiatives, but also upon the more general constitutional framework within which European integration takes shape. However substantial a role regional governments come to play in policy formation at European level, such regions will face important policy constraints deriving from the European level— constraints which, inevitably, will not always respect the position of all of the regions all of the time. Whichever way you look at it, regions, like member states, sacrifice some "sovereignty" in the framework of the European Union. In this respect the current mood of "flexibility" in Europe is important from the point of view of the accommodation of regionalism. The entity within which the European regions are participating today is less authoritarian, prescriptive and homogenising than it was some years ago.[23] Without wishing to exaggerate and claim the existence of a "moment" of change, the emphasis today is less upon uniformity and harmonisation, and more upon self-restraint, proportionality and diversity. This is certainly, and perhaps above all, true in respect of the role of the European Community in regulating markets. The national and/or regional auton- omy which inheres in notions of mutual recognition, where market integration is predicated upon a live and let live ethos, is matched today by a more hands-off approach to constraining regulatory outcomes in the member states. This is captured, and perhaps furthered, by the concept of proportionality as expressed in the Protocol on subsidiarity and proportionality to the TEC. This provides that the Community should legislate only to the extent necessary and that, other things being equal, there should be a preference for framework directives as the instrument of Community intervention, and that these should leave as much scope for national (or presumably regional) decision as possible. Equally, care should be taken to respect well established national arrangements and the organisation and working of member states' legal systems. Where appropriate, Community measures should provide member states (and regions) with alterna- tive ways to achieve the objectives of the measure.

This emphasis upon proportionality alongside subsidiarity is of the utmost importance for the Community's regional governments. It creates a legal system based upon framework legislation which leaves considerable room for manoeu- vre in its implementation. In the same way as it is predicated upon the accept- ance of diverse outcomes in different member states, it is wholly equipped to accept diversity of approach within a single member state. Thus the flexibility

---

[23] See generally G de Búrca and J Scott (eds.), *Constitutional Change in the EU: From Uniformity to Flexibility?* (Oxford: Hart Publishing, 2000). Some of the contributions to this volume demon- strate the long history of flexibility in practice, and the way in which the language of uniformity sometimes operated to conceal tolerance of substantial differences between and within member states. See especially de Búrca's contribution on the single market in this respect; "Differentiation Within the 'Core'? The Case of the Single Market" pp. 133–72.

in implementation which proportionality implies in a legislative context, accrues not only to the member states but equally to the regions. Recourse to notions such as the idea of the "competent authority" with responsibilities for allocated implementation tasks, and the unwillingness of the European Court to prescribe that such bodies operate at any particular level of governance,[24] further enhances the potential role of regional governments, and the acceptability of differentiated implementation within member states.

Of course flexibility in implementation is only as good as the European Court is prepared to accept it as being. And the Court, conceived traditionally as motor of integration, pursuing a distinct teleology taking it in the direction of ever closer union, emphasising uniformity not least because that appears to be the very purpose of the all important preliminary ruling reference system, might be anticipated to undermine the new flexibility bargain struck by the Community's legislature. There are, however, signs that the Court is not entirely out of synch with this new mood. Notable in this respect is the recent case of *Standley & Metson*[25] with its potentially far-reaching comments upon the post-harmonisation, regulatory, nature of Community environmental law, in the wake of the Community's new specific policy competences, operating independently of the internal market project. In construing the nitrates directive the Court acknowledged that:

> "The Directive may thus be applied by the Member States in different ways. Nevertheless, such a consequence is not incompatible with the nature of the Directive, since it does not seek to harmonise the relevant national laws but to create the instruments needed in order to ensure that waters in the Community are protected against pollution caused by nitrates from agricultural sources. The Community legislature necessarily accepted that consequence when, in Annex 1 to the Directive, it granted the Member States a wide discretion in the identification of waters covered by Article 3(1)".[26]

It is perhaps surprising that in another important respect the European Court has been seminal in the accommodation of regionalism in Europe. It was at the hands of this Court that the so-called constitutionalisation of the Treaties occurred. This constitutionalisation, while multi-faceted and contested, rested upon the twin pillars of direct effect and supremacy of EU law. Direct effect was the first of a number of mechanisms developed by the European Court to facilitate the decentralised enforcement of Community law by individuals in their national courts. It was openly, and explicitly, intended by the Court to augment the Article 226 procedure in ensuring the effective application of Community law. The "vigilance" of individuals in policing respect for their own rights is presented by the Court as a crucial supplement to the Treaty defined procedures for enforcement.[27]

---

[24] This is very common in, for example, the environmental sphere.
[25] Case C–293/97 *R* v. *Secretary of State for the Environment, Minister of Agriculture, Fisheries and Food, ex parte Standley and Others and Metson and Others* [1999] ECR I–2603.
[26] *Ibid.*, para. 39.
[27] See Case 26/62 *Van Gend en Loos* [1963] ECR 1.

STRUCTURAL FUNDING AND PARTNERSHIP

It is in the context of structural funding that the Community is perceived as having offered its greatest service to Europe's regions. This is due in part to the emergence of the concept of "partnership" which posits a role for sub-state governments in the implementation and management of Community funding. Article 8 of Council Regulation 1260/1999 laying down general provisions on the Structural Funds[28] provides in this respect:

> Community actions shall complement or contribute to corresponding national operations. They shall be drawn up in close consultation, hereinafter referred to as the "partnership", between the Commission and the Member State, together with the authorities and bodies designated by the Member State within the framework of its national rules and current practices, namely:
>
> —the regional and local authorities and other competent public authorities;
> —the economic and social partners;
> —any other relevant competent bodies within this framework.
>
> The partnership shall be conducted in full compliance with the respective institutional, legal and financial powers of each of the partners as defined in the first subparagraph.
>
>   In designating the most representative partnership at national, regional, local or other level, the Member State shall create a wide and effective association of all relevant bodies, according to national rules and practice . . .

Expressed today in terms which are somewhat more emphatic than previously, member states nonetheless continue to exercise an important "gatekeeper" function, filtering access to the partnership and an effective voice within it. It is instructive in this respect that the final chapter to Lisbet Hooghe's collection of country-based partnership case studies is entitled "Exploring and Explaining Variation in EU Cohesion Policy".[29] In his chapter Gary Marks observes the existence of widespread variation in the role and impact of sub-national actors in cohesion policy making, notably as between the member states. Focussing upon four sets of actors (central government, regional governments, local governments, and the European Commission), at four different stages of the cohesion policy chain (from the strategic task of drawing up development plans, to the more micro task of implementing and monitoring operational programmes), Marks classifies influence on a scale from insignificant, through weak and moderate, to strong.[30] Whereas the influence of regional government is uniformly

---

[28] [1999] OJ L 161/1.
[29] The collection is called *Cohesion Policy and European Integration* (Oxford: Oxford University Press, 1996).
[30] *Ibid.*, p. 407.

strongest at the implementation and monitoring stage, it remains "insignificant" or "weak" in four out of the eight member states considered.[31]

Marks observes that "the causal path from structural programming to institutional relations among levels of government is complex and convoluted",[32] and is cautious in his assertions of a causal chain. Drawing upon the individual country case studies he observes, for example, that in Ireland cohesion policy has "disturbed" relations between central and local government actors, generating a "new impetus for a major overhaul of Irish local government".[33] In Greece, "structural programming has energised subnational government, raising expectations and demands, modernising bureaucracies, and creating new communication channels for local and regional authorities".[34] In France and the UK "there are signs that the experience of structural programming . . . has buttressed demands on the part of subnational actors for participation in regional planning and, at the very least, intensified contention between subnational and central government".[35] Thus while Marks does not accept that "the role of subnational governments in structural policy" is simply "a reflex of prior domestic arrangements", or deny that Community cohesion policy generates an impetus towards change, his conclusions are appropriately nuanced in this respect. The concept has undoubtedly served as a convenient peg upon which regional and local authorities could hang their authority claims and aspirations, and indeed as a means to stimulate such claims. It has served moreover to highlight exclusionary practices in the most centralised of the member states,[36] and to provide a focal point for transnational regional collaboration, often under the auspices of Commission sponsored alliances.[37]

THE EU AND WTO AND TERRITORIAL POLITICS IN THE MEMBER STATES

It is clear from the above that territorial relations within the member states take shape against the backdrop of developments, including legal developments, in

---

[31] The findings were as follows for the fourth stage of structural programming (implementation and monitoring) for the eight member states under investigation: Belgium: moderate to strong; France: weak; Germany: strong; Greece: weak; Ireland: weak; Italy: weak to moderate: Spain: strong; United Kingdom: insignificant. For Ireland, Greece and the UK, countries without a tradition of "regional" as opposed to local government, local government played a role at this stage classified as moderate, moderate and weak respectively.

[32] *Ibid.*, p. 414.

[33] *Ibid.*

[34] *Ibid.*

[35] *Ibid.*, pp. 416–417.

[36] For UK experiences in this respect, see I Bache, V George and M Rhodes , "The Politics of Regional Policy"in Hooghe (ed.), n. 29 above; J Scott, "Law, Legitimacy and EC Governance: Prospects for 'Partnership' " (1998) 36 *JCMS* 175.

[37] Examples of such alliances include Exchange (poverty programme); Green links, Horizon (opportunities for the handicapped), Leader (rural development) and RETI (Region de tradition industrielle).

the European Union. A broad range of legal and constitutional developments are relevant in this respect, and not only those specifically concerned with territorial restructuring. One of the potentially most important of recent developments in this respect is the Community's (and the member states') accession to the World Trade Organisation. The range and intensity of the obligations which the World Trade Organisation Agreement implies for the Community and its member states is dramatic and increasingly well known. From subsidies to procurement, to, for example, technical standards, accession to the WTO will impact upon decision making at all levels of government.

The GATT, which forms just one part of the broader WTO Agreement, is unusual in international law in that it contains what has come to be known as a "federal clause". Article XXIV:12 provides that each contracting party shall take such reasonable measures as may be available to it to ensure observance of the provisions of this Agreement by the regional and local governments and authorities within its territories. The implications of this—and of similar provisions in other WTO side agreements—are as potentially profound as they are uncertain. Not yet the subject of post-WTO dispute settlement, the federal clause has fallen for consideration in two earlier panel reports. The first—*Canadian Measures Affecting the Sale of Gold Coins*—was not adopted, but provided that the federal clause applies only to those measures adopted at regional or local level which the federal government cannot control because they fall outside its jurisdiction under the constitutional distribution of competence.[38] This was followed by the second (and adopted) panel report which emphasised the necessity of construing the clause narrowly in order to avoid undue imbalances in the rights and obligations of contracting parties according to their status as unitary or federal states.[39]

Two issues in particular arise in respect of this federal clause. The first relates to the concept of reasonable measures, and the question of the premises according to which this is to be assessed. The panel in the Canadian report cited above observed that the only elucidation of the concept of reasonable measures included in the GATT is to be found in a note to Article III.1. The basic principle embodied in this note is, according to the panel, such that in determining which measures to secure compliance with the GATT are reasonable within the meaning of the federal clause, it is necessary to weigh the consequences of non-

---

[38] It also provided that the federal clause could be invoked in cases where the exact distribution of competence still remains to be determined by the competent judicial or political bodies, and hence there are uncertainties as to the distribution of authority within the federal state in question. On this see, T Cottier and C Germann, "The WTO and EU Distributive Policy: The Case of Regional Promotion and Assistance" in G de Búrca and J Scott (eds.), *The EU and the WTO* (Oxford: Hart Publishing, 2001). It was Thomas Cottier's contribution to the Florence workshop leading to the above volume that drew my attention to this issue at the level of the WTO.

[39] *United States—Measures Affecting Alcoholic and Malt Beverages* at: <http://www.wto.org/english/tratop_e/dispu_e/distab_e.htm>.

observance by local (or regional) government for trade relations with other parties, against the domestic difficulties of securing observance. This begs a host of difficult and important questions, relating first to the willingness of the Appellate Body to scrutinise the member's own conception of this balance, and to the range of factors which may be accepted as informing it. While on the one hand it is clear that the degree of domestic difficulty implied will vary according to constitutional context, and constitutional relations, it is less clear to what extent political, as opposed to constitutional or legal, difficulties, may inform the member's assessment of the balance. The language of Article XXIV:12 refers to reasonable measures available to [the contracting party in question]. This implies that constitutional context is relevant in informing the concept of reasonable and hence the concept of reasonable is contingent rather than fixed.

There is of course no direct parallel in the EU context. There is no federal clause as such. On the contrary it is clearly established that member states "may not plead situations in its internal legal order, including those resulting from its federal organisation, in order to justify a failure to comply with the obligations and time-limits laid down in a directive".[40] Thus, member states may not rely on provisions, practices, or circumstances in their own legal orders to justify a failure to comply with Community law obligations, and this includes the division of powers between central government and devolved regions.[41] Nonetheless, recent developments before the European Court in the area of the free movement of goods may shed some light in this respect. In *Commission* v. *France*[42] the scope and nature of member states' obligations under Article 28–30 were assessed having regard to the alleged failure of the French government to take adequate measures to prevent widespread and persistent protests by French farmers from disrupting free movement of goods within its territory. The European Court, adopting a functional analysis, construed Article 28 as not merely prohibiting measures emanating from the states, but as applying also where a member state abstains from adopting measures required in order to deal with obstacles to freedom of movement which are not created by the state. While recognising that it was not for the Community institutions to prescribe to the member states which measures they should adopt, and subject to a margin of discretion on the part of the member states, the European Court exhibited a willingness to assess the adequacy of the measures taken by the state, and whether all necessary, appropriate and proportionate measures had been adopted to guarantee the full scope and effect of Community law. In this respect it implied the existence of an exception in the event that member states could show that action on its part would have consequences for public order with

---

[40] Case C–236/99 *Commission* v. *Belgium*, [2000] ECR I–5657.
[41] Case C–274/98 *Commission* v. *Spain*, [2000] ECR I–2823.
[42] Case C–265/95 [1997] ECR I–6959.

which it could not cope by using all means at its disposal.[43] In this case the
European Court adopts an approach to the assessment of the adequacy of the
measures adopted by the member state which while based upon an objective
assessment, does not entirely preclude the relevance of factors specific to the
state and situation at hand.

The second issue relates to the consequences of successful reliance on the federal clause. It remains an open and contested question as to whether this clause
might serve to justify departure from GATT norms, and hence to evade state
responsibility for compliance. The Canadian panel report cited above, though
by no means authoritative, would suggest that it might. By approaching the
clause in terms of its role in facilitating the accession of federal states (while at
the same time minimising the risk of imbalances in the rights and obligations of
contracting parties), and by viewing the concept of "reasonable" in terms of a
balance between the costs of non-compliance for other states, and the internal
difficulties of the federal state in question, the panel appears to acknowledge
that—within strictly circumscribed circumstances—respect for prevailing federal relations within a contracting party may take precedence over the obligation of that party to comply with the GATT. It is interesting in this, and other
respects, to have regard to the TBT Agreement, one of the most important and
far-ranging of the WTO agreements regulating technical regulations and standards, even where these are applied on a non-discriminatory basis.

The TBT Agreement rests upon a distinction between different levels of government, and to this end defines the concepts of central and local government.
The former is defined as "[c]entral government, its ministries and departments
or any body subject to the control of the central government in respect of the
activity in question". It provides in the case of the European Communities that
the provisions governing central government shall apply. A local government
body is in turn defined as "[g]overnment other than central government (e.g.
State, provinces, Lander, cantons, municipalities etc.), its ministries or departments or any body subject to the control of such a government in respect of the
activities in question". Both central and local government bodies are bound by
most of the obligations laid down by the TBT Agreement, subject to certain
exceptions in the case of notification obligations for local government bodies,
other than those "on the level directly below that of the central governments in
Members". The Agreement explicitly provides that members are fully responsible for the observance of all provisions of the Agreement, and that they shall formulate and implement positive measures and mechanisms in support of the

---

[43] This case has important implications in terms of territorial relations within the member states.
Policing is traditionally a competence which falls partly or principally within the competence of sub-
state authorities. Nonetheless, as the export of live animals case in the UK demonstrated, the activities of local police forces, and the operational decisions of senior police officers, may have
implications for compliance with Community rules on free movement. See *R v. Chief Constable of
Sussex ex Parte International Traders* [1998] 3 WLR 1260 HL.

observance of certain core provisions by other than central government bodies (i.e. local government bodies as defined above, and non-governmental bodies). In addition, as regards the core obligations laid down, members are to take such "reasonable measures as may be available to them to ensure compliance" by both local and non governmental bodies.

There are then clear and important differences between the terms of the TBT Agreement and the GATT 1994, the central text of which remains unchanged since its conclusion in 1947. In particular, where the former explicitly provides for the (central government) identity of the EC, the latter of course has nothing to say on the constitutional identity (federal state or otherwise) of the EC.[44] Equally and crucially the TBT Agreement, while mimicking the GATT through recourse to the concept of "reasonable measures" in central/local government relations, does not imply that exhaustion of all such reasonable measures will exempt states from responsibility under the agreement.

Thus, in the same way as a disjunction between responsibility and power may arise in respect of the enforcement of the Treaty, and Community legislation, so too such a disjunction might arise with respect to (at least parts of) the WTO Agreement. Such is the range of substantive areas touched by this Agreement that an assertion of Community and/or member state authority vis-à-vis the regions to ensure compliance with it, would be of enormous significance for the regions in terms of the autonomy which they enjoy.

CONCLUSION

This chapter has sought to exemplify the significance of Community law for territorial relations within the member states. It has revealed a picture which is fragmented, in that Community law exhibits a variety of approaches to regional government, ranging from the proactively regionalist, to the unashamedly statist. What is clear is that Community law will impact upon territorial relations by virtue of doctrines, principles and concepts which at first glance would appear unrelated to this issue. Thus, broad general shifts in the nature of Community governance, such as those associated with flexibility and proportionality, will bear significantly upon the way in which Community law will impact upon relations between different tiers of government within the member states. In this way, those interested in regions and regionalism in the European Union, need to look beyond those parts of Community law which are self-conscious in their attempt to shape territorial relations within the member states, recognising that the constitutional system of the Union as a whole will impinge upon governance in the member states, albeit that impacts will be mediated through the lens of national constitutions.

---

[44] Of course it was the individual states which later came to form the EEC which signed the GATT in 1947. It was only later—pursuant to Art. 234—on the basis of the case law of the European Court that the GATT was found to be binding on the Community institutions.

Part Two
The Constitutional Dimension

3

The Closest Thing to a Constitutional Conversation in Europe: The Semi-Permanent Treaty Revision Process

BRUNO DE WITTE

BRUNO DE WITTE

INTRODUCTION: JUDICIAL AND POLITICAL CONVERSATIONS ON THE EUROPEAN CONSTITUTION

IN THE LETTER of invitation to the Aberdeen symposium, from which this book proceeds, I was asked to present "a process-based perspective on the development of a European constitutional law, with reference to the constitutional conversations taking place within and between the various levels of the European polity". When read in the light of the general theme of this volume, the term "constitutional conversation" seems to refer to non-hierarchical ways of articulating *divergences* and of, possibly, achieving greater *convergence* in European public law.

It is beyond doubt that the development of a European constitutional law is indeed a *process*, and even a very long-drawn out process. Unlike what happened with most national constitutions, the "European constitution" (if there is such a thing, which I will assume here)[1] has not been solemnly enacted at one particular moment in time by an authoritative constitutional assembly, but has been developed in a piecemeal fashion over the past fifty years.

It is less clear, though, to what extent this constitution-making process can be said to be carried on by means of constitutional *conversations*. The term "constitutional conversation" itself is not a term of art of European law or European Union politics. It stems from the deliberative democracy strand of contemporary

---

[1] The use of the term "European constitution" presupposes a broad understanding of the term "constitution", cutting the umbilical cord connecting the constitution and the nation-state. See, for an example of such a broader understanding, N MacCormick, *Questioning Sovereignty: Law, State and Nation in the European Commonwealth* (Oxford: Oxford University Press, 1999) at 103–4. For a detailed justification of the use of the term "European constitutional law", see J Gerkrath, *L'émergence d'un droit constitutionnel pour l'Europe* (Bruxelles: Editions de l'Université de Bruxelles, 1997), especially at 27–143.

political philosophy.[2] When applied to the evolution of the EU constitutional system, a first distinction, usefully made by Neil Walker in a recent paper, is that between *judicial conversations* involving the European Court of Justice and national constitutional courts, and *political conversations* taking place in successive Intergovernmental Conferences (IGCs) and within the EU institutions.[3] The former type of constitutional conversation has been the object of considerable interest in the recent English-language literature of European law and European integration studies.[4] Alec Stone Sweet does not hesitate to describe the interaction between the ECJ and national courts, and the resulting constitutionalisation of the treaty system, as a set of *constitutional dialogues*.[5]

This stretches the metaphorical capacity of the term "dialogue" very far. The members of these courts hardly know each other, and certainly never sit together formally to examine a particular case or abstract question. One may call the preliminary rulings mechanism a system of "court-to-court dialogue"[6] (albeit one occurring at a distance), but one should not forget that preliminary references emanate from "ordinary" national courts and not, or very seldom, from constitutional courts.[7] Moreover, these preliminary references are hardly ever formulated as queries about constitutional matters, even though the ECJ has occasionally seized upon seemingly anodyne questions to send a "constitutional" message back. Furthermore, the European Court of Justice has never in its judgments (at least as far as I know) referred to a judgment, or a doctrine, of a national constitutional court, not even in matters where such a mention would have come naturally, as for example where the ECJ extracts general principles of EC law from the "common constitutional traditions of the Member States". It may well be that national courts' attitudes are occasionally at the back of the ECJ members' minds when they deliver judgment, but how are we to tell? In fact, the concern is occasionally voiced that the ECJ is insufficiently sensitive to

---

[2] See, in particular: S Chambers, "Contract or Conversation? Theoretical Lessons from the Canadian Constitutional Crisis" (1998) 26 *Politics & Society* 143; J. Elster (ed.), *Deliberative Democracy* (Cambridge: Cambridge University Press, 1998). One of the main inspirations is Jürgen Habermas, particularly in his work *Faktizität und Geltung: Beiträge zur Diskurstheorie dse Rechts und des demokratischen Rechtsstaats* (Frankfurt: Suhrkamp, 1992); English translation: *Between Facts and Norms* (Cambridge: Polity Press, 1998).

[3] N Walker, "Flexibility within a Metaconstitutional Frame: Reflections on the Future of Legal Authority in Europe", in G de Búrca and J Scott (eds.), *Constitutional Change in the EU: From Uniformity to Flexibility* (Oxford: Hart Publishing, 2000) 9, at 21.

[4] See, in particular, A-M Slaughter, A Stone Sweet and J H H Weiler (eds.), *The European Court and National Courts—Doctrine and Jurisprudence* (Oxford; Hart Publishing, 1998).

[5] A Stone Sweet, "Constitutional Dialogues in the European Community", in *The European Court and National Courts*, n. 4 above, p. 305. This assessment is most strongly stated at 325–6: "The constitutionalisation of the treaty system generated a structured and ongoing, intra-judicial dialogue, judges speaking to each other through the medium of legal discourse."

[6] R Dehousse, *The European Court of Justice* (Houndmills: Macmillan, 1998), at 28.

[7] An exception is the preliminary reference by the Belgian Court of Arbitration in Case C–93/97, *Fédération Belge des Chambres Syndicales de Médecins* v. *Flemish Government*, [1998] ECR I–4837 (but this reference related to a "normal" question of the interpretation of an EC directive and did not raise an issue of European constitutional law).

the integrity of national legal orders, and to national judicial doctrines.[8] The national courts, from their side, do refer extensively to judgments of the ECJ (as they are bound to do because of the Article 234 reference mechanism), but their options are essentially restricted either to accepting the positions defined by the ECJ, or else to replacing the "European *diktat*" by a "national counter-*diktat*".[9] A real dialogue, with mutual exchange of arguments, requires a series of subsequent references in different cases raising similar problems, which is rather cumbersome and rarely happens.[10] A true *judicial conversation* would be made possible in an entirely different, and yet-to-be-created, institutional setting, such as the "Constitutional Council for the Community" advocated by Joseph Weiler. This Council would be composed of the President of the ECJ and members of the various national constitutional courts and their equivalents, and would decide issues of division of competences between the EU and its member states through intra-judicial conversation.[11]

In view of my doubts about the appropriateness of using the term "judicial conversations" in the constitutional field,[12] and also in view of the fact that these questions have been extensively examined in the recent literature, I will move, in the rest of this paper, to the "political conversations" mentioned by Neil Walker, and more particularly to the political conversations taking place in the framework of successive intergovernmental conferences for the revision of the European treaties. It has been stated, in recent international relations theory, that Habermasian argumentative rationality is an important element even of "secret" diplomatic relations between states;[13] *a fortiori*, this would seem to be

---

[8] See, for instance, Carol Harlow's contribution to this volume.

[9] I refer here to expressions used (with specific reference to the German Constitutional Court) by J H H Weiler and U R Haltern, "Constitutional or International? The Foundations of the Community Legal Order and the Question of Judicial Kompetenz-Kompetenz", in *The European Court and National Courts*, n. 4 above, 331, at 364.

[10] See, for example, the series of German court references on various questions of EC labour law, as described by J Kokott, "Report on Germany", in *The European Court and National Courts*, n. 4 above, 77, at p. 112 *ff.*, and the series of references by British courts on sex equality analysed by C Kilpatrick, "Community or Communities of Courts in European Integration? Sex Equality Dialogues Between UK Courts and the ECJ" (1998) 4 *European Law Journal* 121.

[11] This proposal is made in a number of Joseph Weiler's writings; see for instance, J H H Weiler, "IGC 2000: The Constitutional Agenda", in E Best, M Gray and A Stubb (eds.), *Rethinking the European Union—IGC 2000 and Beyond* (Maastricht: European Institute of Public Administration, 2000) 219, at 235.

[12] The same scepticism may be expressed about the interaction between the European Court of Human Rights and national constitutional courts. The Court in Strasbourg is, indeed, more ruthless than its counterpart in Luxembourg, as it does not hesitate to find that constitutional court judgments constitute violations of the ECHR, or even that aspects of the constitutional process are structurally in breach of procedural rights guaranteed by the European Convention. See J-F Flauss, "Droit constitutionnel et Convention européenne des droits de l'homme—Le droit constitutionnel national devant la Cour européenne des droits de l'homme" (2000) *Revue française de droit constitutionnel* 843.

[13] T Risse, "Let's Argue!: Communicative Action in World Politics" (2000) 54 *International Organization* 1; see his conclusion at 33: "the preconditions for argumentative rationality, particularly a 'common lifeworld' and the mutual recognition of speakers as equals in a nonhierarchical relationship, are more common in international relations than is usually assumed."

the case for the dense and highly regulated interaction pattern of an IGC. In the framework of EU Treaty revision negotiations, there is, in my view, much more of a true conversation going on than there is between judges, and that conversation is much more focused on the development of a constitutional order for Europe. It may also have contributed more to constitutional convergence in Europe, despite the fact that the main participants in this conversation (the member state governments) have studiously avoided the use of the words "constitution" and "constitutional" during or after IGCs.

THE TREATY REVISION PROCESS AS THE MAIN CONSTITUTIONAL CONVERSATION IN THE EUROPEAN UNION

An Ongoing Conversation

In most states (though not in all), a revision of the Constitution is a solemn event which, due to the rigidity of the revision procedure, occurs only rarely. One of the most extreme examples is the Constitution of the United States which has hardly been modified in the course of the past century. Similarly, the UN Charter (which is called, by many authors, the "constitution" of the world community),[14] seems almost impossible to revise. Compare this with the European Communities and now the European Union, where Treaty revisions have been frequent, particularly if one considers the treaties of accession of new member states as a form of revision.[15] For more than a decade, there has been, in effect, a semi-permanent revision process. In December 1989, the European Council in Strasbourg decided to call an intergovernmental conference in order to bring about Economic and Monetary Union. Six months later, the Dublin European Council decided to convene a separate IGC on what was then called European Political Union. Both IGCs formally started their work in Rome in December 1990. By the time the Maastricht Treaty, the common end-product of these conferences, was finally approved by all member states and was ready to enter into force (on 1 November 1993), the negotiations for the accession of Austria, Finland, Norway and Sweden were in full swing. The Treaty of Corfu, laying down the conditions for their accession, was signed in June 1994. The same European Council meeting in Corfu defined the procedural framework for the upcoming post-Maastricht IGC and defined, in very broad terms, the political objectives of that new Conference. Most of the year 1995 was spent by a Reflection Group of personal representatives of the national governments in laying the political groundwork for the revision conference. The new IGC was

---

[14] See, with extensive references to the literature, B Fassbender, "The United Nations Charter as Constitution of the International Community" (1998) 36 *Columbia Journal of Transnational Law* 529.

[15] Indeed, Art. 49 EU Treaty specifies that accession treaties may imply "adjustments" to the EC and EU Treaties, and they invariably do.

formally launched at the Turin European Council of March 1996, and its end-product, the Treaty of Amsterdam, eventually came into force, after the last of the fifteen member states had ratified it, on 1 May 1999. Only one month later, the European Council of Cologne, meeting in June 1999, decided to convene a new IGC for the revision of the EU and EC Treaties in early 2000. This led to the Treaty of Nice, signed on 26 February 2001, which again contains a Declaration by which the member states commit themselves to having another IGC in 2004, with preparatory debates to be held in the intervening period.[16]

When taking a general view of this past decade, one can say that the revision of the European treaties has ceased to be an incidental occurrence devoted to technical adjustments and has, instead, become an ongoing concern of the member states and the EU institutions, which involves important policy choices about the institutional architecture of Europe and, indirectly, about the political future of each member state. All the signs are that this process will continue relentlessly in the coming decade, and that the Treaty of Nice will again be nothing but a milestone along the long road of European constitution-making.

One can consider this semi-permanent revision process as one continuous conversation about the future of Europe between the member states of the Union. During IGC negotiations, papers are continually being submitted, not only by the country holding the presidency of the Conference, but by practically all other states as well. The papers are taken seriously by all the other countries, which study them, and prepare their reactions for the following meetings of the negotiation group. The national parliaments, or at least the specialised committees of the parliaments, are constantly informed about the progress in the negotiations and thus allowed to participate in the conversation from a distance. Once a new treaty text is agreed upon, the constitutional conversation is decentralised from Brussels (or whichever place the European Councils have made their final deal) to the capitals of the member states, where it continues until the text is ready for ratification, by which time a new stage in the conversation is launched at the European level.

There is also, usually, a formal link between subsequent IGCs. Issues that cannot be resolved at one IGC, or can be resolved only in a provisional and, to some countries, unsatisfactory way, are carried over to the next IGC by means of a *rendez-vous* clause inserted in the revision Treaty or in an accompanying document. At Maastricht, the states that felt unhappy with the creation of the pillar structure of the European Union obtained the insertion in Article N (now Article 48) EU Treaty of a second paragraph calling for a new IGC to be held in 1996, at which this institutional structure was to be reconsidered. In fact, this 1996–97 IGC paid little attention to the pillar structure, but it was undoubtedly the *rendez-vous* clause of Article N paragraph 2 that had forced the states to reconvene in the negotiation room in 1996. The Amsterdam summit of June 1997, in turn, ended with some important institutional "left-overs" which were,

---

[16] Treaty of Nice, Declaration on the Future of the European Union [2001] OJ C 80/85.

once again, entrusted to a later IGC by means of a Protocol. This later IGC elaborated the Treaty of Nice in which the Amsterdam left-overs were dealt with after a fashion; however, the Declaration on the Future of the European Union, appended to it, contains again a commitment of the states to launch a new and broader Treaty reform debate which is guaranteed to occupy the political minds between now and 2004.

The Structuring Rules of the Conversation: Consensus First, Unanimity Thereafter

Revision treaties are adopted "by common accord" of the member state representatives at the conference (Article 48 EU Treaty). This is not exactly the same rule as the unanimity rule which applies for the adoption of certain categories of secondary EU acts. The term "common accord" conveys rather well what has been the practice in the last rounds of Treaty revision, namely that states are prepared to accept certain amendments which they do not approve of or even positively dislike, because of the importance they attach to an overall accord on the revision Treaty.[17] The "package deal" negotiation style is more vigorously pursued at the level of the IGC than in day-to-day Council decision-making, and is much more vital for the success of the negotiation. It dramatically culminates in the final night of the European Council meeting at which, after some hasty last-minute deal-cutting between heads of government, the revision agreement is reached. The need to find a common accord takes decisive precedence, in this last phase of the negotiations, over the wish for rational deliberation and the need for legal and logical consistency. The requirement of the "common accord" has, thus, an effect on the conversation which varies in time. In the early stages of the negotiation, it acts as an incentive for all delegations to listen carefully to each other's opinions, and, indeed, there may be occasional room for rational argument; but, as negotiations proceed, the wish for constructive and relatively open dialogue gives way to the pressing need to reach agreement "notwithstanding all".[18] Power games and legal traps make the conversation distinctly less "Habermasian" then, but, nevertheless, eyewitnesses

---

[17] Thus, one commentator noted that the Dutch Presidency conducting the "Amsterdam" negotiations in the first half of 1997 "put forward proposals that should appeal to a sufficient majority. If the rest were not angered enough to make use of their veto, the Presidency knew that they could probably be bought off with more favourable proposals in other issue areas or put under so much pressure that they would give in at a later stage." (A-C Svensson, *In the Service of the European Union. The Role of the Presidency in Negotiating the Amsterdam Treaty 1995–97* (Uppsala: University Library, 2000).

[18] See the remarks of Philippe de Schoutheete on this point: "It has always been tacitly understood that an intergovernmental conference cannot be allowed to fail, because its failure would reflect on the European Council and its members. Tough negotiations will take place in the last weeks of the conference, and those negotiations will produce a result. Whether that result will be adequate is another matter." (P de Schoutheete, "Guest Editorial: The Intergovernmental Conference", (2000) 37 *Common Market Law Review* 845, at 848).

claim that at all stages of the IGC process personal interaction and face-to-face persuasion play an important role.[19]

Once the intergovernmental bargaining has led to the adoption of a Treaty text, the conversation ends, and the "common accord" mode of negotiation gives way to the cruder rule of unanimity, whereby every single government must separately deliver an act of ratification, after having received the constitutional green light at the domestic level. Although there is occasionally some interaction between the national approval processes (think, for instance, of how the original Danish No to the Maastricht Treaty almost derailed the British and French ratification processes), there is no meaningful cross-national "conversation" going on at this stage. Each government must fight, in almost total isolation, to convince its own parliament and its own public opinion of the benefits which the revision treaty may bring to the country.[20] At this stage, small incidents can bring down the whole patiently constructed edifice. In Belgium, for instance, the Treaty of Amsterdam had to be approved by no less than eight parliamentary bodies, and in the smallest of these bodies, a shift of one single vote could have blocked Belgian ratification and, hence, the Treaty revision process as a whole.[21] Similarly, the "no vote" delivered in the Irish referendum of June 2001 now threatens to derail the Treaty of Nice. The self-contained nature of the national ratification processes is also denoted by their lack of synchronisation. Thus, Luxembourg ratified the Maastricht Treaty as early as 24 August 1992, whereas Germany, the last of the twelve member states to do so, ratified only on 13 October 1993.

The Participants in the Conversation: the Member State Governments, the Persuaders and the Ghosts at the Table

The main actors of the Treaty-revision conversation are, of course, the "representatives of the national governments". In this respect, the text of Article 48 EU Treaty truly reflects the political and legal reality. However, different groups

[19] Eyewitnesses tend to emphasise the importance of the personal factor throughout the negotiations. See the following statement made by Dyson and Featherstone in the preface of their detailed account of the EMU negotiations: "As we looked closely at the EMU negotiations, we began to see that they had a life of their own. They were composed of flesh-and-blood people, whose motives were very complex and preferences by no means fixed, whose likes, aversions, ambitions, and manners played an important role in the dynamics of the process." (K Dyson and K Featherstone, *The Road to Maastricht. Negotiating Economic and Monetary Union* (Oxford: OUP, 1999), at ix). Putting this insight in more noble terms, they claim that the EMU IGC "was an arena not only for intensive bargaining but also for a shared process of policy learning and reflection" (at xii).

[20] A rare example of cross-border participation in a national ratification process was chancellor Kohl's brief appearance on French television on 4 September 1992, during the Maastricht referendum campaign there. (C Mazzucelli, *France and Germany at Maastricht. Politics and Negotiations to Create the European Union* (New York and London: Garland Publishing, 1997) at 220).

[21] H Bribosia, "La participation des autorités exécutives aux travaux du Conseil de l'Union et des conférences intergouvernementales", in Y Lejeune (ed.), *La participation de la Belgique à l'élaboration et à la mise en oeuvre du droit européen* (Bruxelles: Bruylant, 1999) 85, at p. 131.

of persons act as "representatives" of the governments in the course of the nego-tiations. The first level is that of the *government representatives group* (also sometimes called the *preparatory group*) which is composed of the countries' permanent representatives with the EU, or their secretary of state for European affairs, or some other person chosen by his or her government. This group meets every week or so during the whole duration of the IGC, and deals with the nuts and bolts of the negotiations with the help, of course, of a whole team of other officials and experts. The second level of the negotiations is formed by the min-isters of foreign affairs, who take stock of the progress of the negotiations at approximately monthly intervals (but more often in the final stages), either in the margin of their ordinary meetings of the General Affairs Council or in spe-cially convened formal or informal meetings. Generally speaking, the ministers of foreign affairs do not actively negotiate themselves, and insiders tend to con-sider this second-level type of meeting to be the least effective.

The third level is, of course, that of the heads of state and government, who discuss ongoing IGC negotiations at their ordinary trimestrial meetings, who may meet for exceptional informal meetings wholly devoted to the revision negotiations,[22] and who, above all, are called to bring the negotiations to a suc-cessful end at the European Council meeting which is scheduled in advance as having to deliver the final consensus on the new Treaty text: Maastricht in December 1991, Amsterdam in June 1997, Nice in December 2000. At these cru-cial concluding meetings, all the IGC participants at the lower echelons are pre-sent in the corridors, trying to prevent their heads of government from losing ground that was painfully won at earlier stages, or (in a more positive mode) tirelessly drafting or analysing last minute compromise texts. To an important extent, however, major deals are cut by the heads of government and ministers of foreign affairs themselves, or even during dinners at which only the "top dogs" are present.[23] Often, such discussions lack direction, and suffer from the ignorance of some heads of government about the "technical details" of the negotiations.[24]

---

[22] For instance, an extraordinary one-day "summit" of heads of state and government took place on 23 May 1997 in Noordwijk, only a few weeks before the regular European Council meeting in Amsterdam. It was entirely devoted to the negotiations on revision of the Treaties.

[23] This means that the personal representatives and the ministers of foreign affairs may occa-sionally be left in the dark on what exactly has happened among the heads of government. The con-fidential character of these meetings among heads of governments is ritually acknowledged by the other governmental representatives. See, for example, the following statement by the French Secretary of State for European Affairs Moscovici in his speech to the European Parliament of 24 October 2000, when reporting on IGC progress at the European Council meeting of Biarritz: "*ce qui m'a été rapporté de la discussion la plus cruciale, celle qui a eu lieu au dîner entre les chefs d'Etat et de gouvernement, c'est qu'elle a justement permis de mettre les choses sur la table pour ensuite chercher à les dépasser*" (emphasis added).

[24] A revealing glimpse of the kind of discussion taking place among the heads of government was given by the *El Pais* correspondent Carlos Yarnoz who got hold of the transcription of the debates at the Nice IGC summit and published extracts of it in his newspaper (*El Pais*, 16 December 2000, French translation in *Le Monde*, 20 December 2000, p. 17).

The work of the national delegations is coordinated by the *Presidency* and receives support from the Conference's *Legal Adviser* (the head of the Council's legal service)—both crucial actors in every IGC. The Presidency[25] faces the delicate task of fixing the agenda of each of the IGC meetings (at all three levels of the negotiation), of extracting from the various contributions a basis for common agreement which it submits in the form of Notes on specific subjects and general Reports on the state of negotiations prepared for each European Council meeting.[26] The Legal Adviser and his staff provide legal and drafting expertise which is often highly influential in closing off certain suggested routes, or bringing forward exquisitely fuzzy texts around which a compromise can be built.

In the shadow of the member state governments, one finds a whole army of more or less hidden *persuaders*, who do not have any formal say in the decision-making but attempt to convince national delegations by the force of their arguments. The most visible of these persuaders (but not necessarily the most influential ones) are the Commission and the European Parliament. Despite what a superficial reading of Article 48 EU Treaty might suggest, the Commission and the European Parliament can not prevent the governments from starting the revision process. They cannot, either, stop amendments which they dislike. They must rely on the power of persuasion which they can exercise on the governments. The Commission is best situated for this, as it is always represented in the negotiation room, until the very end at the concluding Summit. Accounts of the elaboration of the Single European Act note that the Commission (particularly its President Jacques Delors) was very influential in shaping the agenda through its White Paper on the Internal Market and continued to be a major player throughout the negotiations. Delors (and the Commission) was also an influential player in the Treaty negotiations on Economic and Monetary Union.[27] But, during the other recent IGCs, the Commission had only a minor impact on the negotiations.[28]

The same is true, *a fortiori*, for the European Parliament. The increase of its legislative powers over the years has not been matched by an increased formal role in the Treaty revision process. Although it may, on the basis of Article 48 EU, convey its opinion on the direction in which the Treaties should be changed, it has no formal power of assent or codecision. In the 1996 IGC, two representatives of the EP were for the first time allowed to attend, as observers, the official IGC meetings,[29]

[25] On the role of the Presidency in IGC negotiations, see the well-documented case study of the 1996–97 IGC by A-C Svensson, *In the Service of the European Union*, n. 17 above.

[26] For instance, during the first semester of 2000, the Portuguese Presidency produced twenty Notes for the IGC on various subjects (my own count from the documents made available on the IGC website) and drafted a Presidency Report for the European Council meeting of Feira in June.

[27] K Dyson and K Featherstone, *The Road to Maastricht*, n. 19 above, ch. 16.

[28] A Moravcsik, *The Choice for Europe. Social Purpose and State Power from Messina to Maastricht* (London: UCL Press, 1998) at 479–85.

[29] See M Petite, "The Treaty of Amsterdam", Harvard Law School Jean Monnet Papers 98–2, Introduction <www.jeanmonnetprogram.org/papers/98/98–2.html>. The text of the compromise laying down the manner in which the EP was to be involved in the negotiations was published in *Bulletin of the EU 3–1996*, nr. I.8.

but their political influence has not been important. There have been attempts to strengthen the influence of the EP in more indirect ways. During the Maastricht negotiations, the Italian and Belgian parliaments made a short-lived and ineffectual attempt to strengthen its position, by making their own ratification of the revision Treaty conditional upon its acceptance by the European Parliament.[30] But the EP was facing the simple choice of taking or leaving the Treaty as it had been agreed by the member state negotiators, and it chose to take it.

Then, there are some ghosts at the IGC table: actors who do not take part in the conversation, but whose views decisively weigh on the choices made by the negotiators, more so, often, than the views of the Commission and the European Parliament. Their indirect influence during the negotiation process derives from the "veto power" or interpretative influence which they may exercise *after* the conclusion of the negotiations and can be related, in the terms of international relations theory, to the fact that IGC's are "two-level bargaining games", in which the international actors are heavily constrained by their domestic politics.[31]

(a) The first of these "domestic players" in the IGC game are the *opposition parties* of most member states. Their views must be taken into account due to the need for special majorities in Parliament to approve important treaties and/or to approve the constitutional changes that have to precede such approval.[32] In some cases, the parliamentary majority may itself prove to be unreliable.[33]

(b) Other relevant actors are the *sub-state governments and assemblies* of Germany and Belgium who possess a collective (in the case of Germany) or individual (in the case of Belgium) veto right at the ratification stage, and who know how to make it weigh heavily on the negotiations.[34] In fact,

---

[30] For Belgium, see resolution of the Chamber of Representatives of 27 June 1991, *Gedrukte Stukken, Kamer*, 1990–91, nr. 1668/4, point 24.

[31] The "two-level games" model was first described by R O Putnam, "Diplomacy and Domestic Politics: The Logic of Two-Level Games" (1988) 42 *International Organization* 427. For a comparative study of the role of domestic "veto players" in the ratification process of the Amsterdam Treaty, see M Stoiber and P W Thurner, "Der Vergleich von Ratifikationsstrukturen der EU-Mitgliedsländer für Intergouvernementale Verträge: Eine Anwendung des Veto-Spieler Konzeptes" (2000) *Arbeitspapiere—Mannheimer Zentrum für Europäische Sozialforschung* Nr.27.

[32] The degree to which opposition party support is needed depends on the content of the revision Treaty (special majorities in national parliament may or may not be required) and on the composition of the parliament at the time of ratification. In the case of the Amsterdam Treaty, the governments needed additional parliamentary support for approval of the Treaty from non-government parties in no less than nine out of fifteen member states (M Stoiber and P W Thurner, "Der Vergleich", n. 31 above, at 31).

[33] Thus, in the UK, anti-Maastricht rebels inside the governing Conservative Party made parliamentary ratification of the Maastricht Treaty very difficult; see D Baker, A Gamble and S Ludlam, "The Parliamentary Siege of Maastricht 1993: Conservative Divisions and British Ratification" (1994) 47 *Parliamentary Affairs* 37.

[34] It seems that Chancellor Köhl's sudden reluctance to agree to proposed shifts from unanimity to qualified majority voting, in the final days before the Amsterdam summit, was due to pressure from the German *Länder*. In the most recent IGC, the *Länder* had originally threatened to use their veto if the negotiators would not take on board some of their claims (see M Borchmann, "Regierungskonferenz 2000—Länder nesteln an der Notbremse" 2000 *Europäische Zeitschrift für Wirtschaftsrecht*, 161). In the end, the *Länder* settled for a commitment, from the side of the federal

representatives of these two countries' subnational governments are also directly present at the negotation table, as part of their country's delegation.[35]

(c) IGC negotiators are increasingly concerned about the reception of the revision treaty by their *public opinion* at home. This is most obvious in the countries where a referendum must be called for reasons of constitutional obligation or political tradition; the most prominent example is Denmark where holding a referendum on European Treaty revisions has become a customary constitutional rule whose effects are highly unpredictable and which, therefore, considerably inhibits the Danish representatives' room for manoeuvre during negotiations.

(d) The governments of some member states must give a thought to their constitutional courts, who may declare the revision treaty to be wholly or partly incompatible with the national constitution as it stands. Declarations of unconstitutionality occurred for the Single European Act (in Ireland), for the Treaty of Maastricht (in France and Spain), and for the Treaty of Amsterdam (in France again). These constitutional decisions did not only, in the short term, require a constitutional revision to allow for ratification of the respective Treaties, but also set a long-term parameter of constitutionally acceptable Treaty reforms which government representatives at subsequent IGCs constantly have to keep in mind. The same effect was achieved by rulings of the German constitutional court and the Danish supreme court on the Maastricht Treaty which, while not having held that Treaty to be unconstitutional, have nevertheless fixed constitutional limits to later Treaty changes.

(e) A final, non-domestic, "hidden actor" is the European Court of Justice, the institution which, unlike the other supranational institutions, is not just the passive addressee of treaty revisions decided by others, but also has the general power to interpret the amending provisions and thereby shape them in sometimes unforeseen ways. The states have shown their awareness of this redoubtable power by excluding or limiting the power of the Court for some of the new fields of competence added in Maastricht and Amsterdam.

The Grammar of the Conversation: International Treaty Law

The contrast between IGC decision-making and ordinary European Union decision-making is perhaps least visible when the ministers of foreign affairs

government, to try to put the issue of "delimitation of powers" between the EU and the member states on the agenda for a next round of Treaty reform. This result was achieved in the Declaration on the Future of the European Union annexed to the Treaty of Nice ([2001] OJ C 80/85, point 5, first indent).

[35] For the Belgian practice in this matter, see H Bribosia, "La participation", n. 21 above, at 127–32.

discuss Treaty revision in the margin of an ordinary Council meeting. On such occasions, the ministers for foreign affairs (or their replacements), after dispatching the ordinary General Affairs Council business, transform themselves from members of the Council into "representatives of their governments at the Intergovernmental Conference".[36] However, this symbolic transformation has major political consequences. Suddenly, the Commission and the European Parliament, the ministers' troublesome interlocutors for normal EU business, become negligible sidekicks. It is not just that the national ministers, and their advisors, wear different hats when meeting in the Council or meeting in the IGC framework. Their behaviour and attitude is markedly different. They act, as the Germans say, as the *Herren der Verträge,* who are bound by nothing else than their respective national constitutional rules and by the rules of international treaty law; as "independent and sovereign states having freely decided . . . to exercise in common some of their competences".[37]

The dominant role of governments is compounded, and symbolised, by the fact that the rules governing the IGC process are those of the law of treaties as codified by the Vienna Convention. The EU Treaty revision process does not show any meaningful departure from the general rules on the amendment of treaties.[38] It is sometimes argued that the European revision treaties are not ordinary treaties of international law, because of the fact that the member states are legally bound to follow the procedure of revision fixed in Article 48 EU Treaty.[39] According to the general rules of international law, pre-determined procedures for treaty amendment may be set aside if all the states parties to the treaty agree to do so; this is sometimes called the "freedom of form" rule. In EU law, by contrast, the member states are bound to follow the rules for treaty revision as formulated in Article 48 EU Treaty. The ECJ affirmed this duty, a long time ago, in the *Defrenne* case,[40] and the states' practice in the decades since

---

[36] The press reports of Council meetings include, when appropriate, a brief account of the IGC ministerial sessions, but it is specified that these sessions were "held in the margins of the Council" (see, for example, the press report of 11 April 2000, 2254. Council—General Affairs, p. 10).

[37] A phrase used by the member state governments in the introductory part of the Decision on Denmark, adopted at the Edinburgh summit of 12 December 1992. This Decision, admittedly, was *not* a revision treaty but an agreement on the interpretation of a revision treaty (see D Curtin and R van Ooik, "Denmark and the Edinburgh Summit: Maastricht Without Tears: A Legal Analysis" in D O'Keeffe and P Twomey (eds.), *Legal Issues of the Maastricht Treaty* (Chichester: Chancery Law Publishing, 1994) 349); however, the member states would probably, and *a fortiori,* describe their own status when doing "real" Treaty revision work in equally if not more emphatically pre-eminent terms.

[38] See, for a detailed examination of this question, B de Witte, "Rules of Change in International Law: How Special is the European Community?" (1994) *Netherlands Yearbook of International Law* 299.

[39] See e.g. D Simon, *Le système juridique communautaire* (Paris: PUF, 1997), at 55: "les traités ne sont plus seulement des traités ordinaires, relevant des règles de révision du droit international général, mais la constitution de la Communauté, qui ne peut etre modifiée que selon les modalités fixées pour l'exercice du pouvoir constituant dérivé, c'est-à-dire en respectant les limites formelles imposées a la révision d'une constitution rigide."

[40] Case 43/75, *Defrenne,* [1976] ECR 480, par. 57.

Defrenne seems to show that they, indeed, accept the mandatory character of the Treaty revision procedures as laid down in the Treaties.

However, this procedure does not in any way affect the discretion of the member states as to the *substance* of the amendments. Some Community law authors have defended the view that there are so-called "material limits" to the changes which member states can make to the existing Treaties,[41] and have relied for that purpose on an enigmatic statement of the ECJ in Opinion 1/91 on the European Economic Area, but in my opinion there is no evidence that the member states have accepted any such substantive limits to their treaty-amending power.[42] The true protection of the *acquis communautaire* (and now also of the *acquis de l'Union*) lies in the common accord rule, which implies that all states must agree before they can turn back some of the integrative steps made on earlier treaty-making occasions. Thus, the attempts made by the UK government during the Amsterdam IGC to reduce some of the powers of the European Court of Justice were of no avail for lack of support from the other states,[43] and the idea, which is occasionally floated, of removing the Commission's quasi-monopoly of legislative initiative in EC matters, cannot be realised either, as long as some states staunchly defend the Commission's position (for reasons of their own, enlightened, national interest).

The international law character of Treaty revision has a number of practical legal consequences. It means that the states can use all the means provided by international law for achieving the desirable mix between "convergence" and "divergence". The member states have consistently refused to use the main tool which international law provides in this respect, namely the possibility to allow individual signatory states to make reservations to the treaty which was agreed in common. However, other tools have been frequently used, such as the adoption of common or separate Declarations to the text of a revision treaty, the adoption of an interpretative agreement, and, above all, the enactment of systems of differentiation of rights and obligations between groups of member states by means of special Protocols.

The international law character of Treaty revisions has more abstract, but potentially important consequences, as regards the possibility of collective

---

[41] J L da Cruz Vilaça and N Piçarra, "Y a-t-il des limites matérielles à la révision des traités instituant les CE?", (1993) *Cahiers de droit européen* 3; R Bieber, "Les limites matérielles et formelles à la révision des traités établissant la Communauté européenne", (1993) *Revue du Marché commun et de l'Union européenne* 343.

[42] My views on the alleged substantive limits to the states' revision power can be found in B de Witte, "International Agreement or European Constitution?", in J Winter et al. (eds.), *Reforming the Treaty on European Union—The Legal Debate* (The Hague: Kluwer Law International, 1996) 3, at 15–18. See also S Weatherill, "Safeguarding the Acquis Communautaire", in T Heukels, N Blokker, M Brus (eds.), *The European Union after Amsterdam—A Legal Analysis* (The Hague: Kluwer Law International, 1998) 153, at 167–8.

[43] Memorandum by the United Kingdom on the European Court of Justice, London, July 1996. See P J G Kapteyn, "The Court of Justice after Amsterdam: Taking Stock", in T Heukels, N Blokker, M Brus (eds.), *The European Union after Amsterdam—A Legal Analysis* (The Hague: Kluwer Law International, 1998) 139, at 142–3.

termination, or unilateral withdrawal of states. Finally, it continues to affect the domestic enforcement of the revision treaties. In many states (and contrary to the orthodoxy of the ECJ's supremacy doctrine) EC and EU law is applied on the basis of age-old constitutional doctrines about the domestic effect of international treaty law, and as long as primary EU law continues to take the form of international treaties, there is no clear need for national courts to move from that position.

The Main Subject-Matter of the Conversation: Constitutional Change

The international law framework, described above, is filled with constitutional content. There is no contradiction in this. An international treaty is the primary *instrument* used by states to organise their cooperation, and the choice of this instrument does not predetermine the content of the cooperation. Indeed, international treaties are remarkably flexible legal instruments that can contain a wide variety of contents. There is, thus, no obstacle against states choosing to elaborate a treaty that has constitutional objectives or a constitutional content.[44] Indeed, the treaty revisions have, so far, been the principal vehicles for "practical constitution-building"[45] in Europe.

This constitutional content exists at two levels. There is an openly constitutional content in the way the member state governments decide to replicate at the European Union level certain constitutional schemes and principles which are familiar to them at the national level. There is a growing literature on this form of "constitutionalisation of the treaties".[46] Obvious examples of such borrowing from the common constitutional tradition are the (half-hearted) incorporation of the fundamental rights tradition in the EU Treaty, and the gradual affirmation of the model of parliamentary government in the EC decision-making system. The IGC which was most openly constitutional in its choice of themes and in the organisation of its preparatory work was that of 1996–7. In its early stages, all the EU institutions and a specially convened "Reflection Group" of government representatives openly addressed the constitutional themes of citizenship, democracy, subsidiarity and transparency.[47] By contrast,

[44] See the distinction between *instrumentum* and *negotium*, as developed by A Pellet, "Les fondements juridiques internationaux du droit communautaire", *Collected Courses of the Academy of European Law*, Vol V, Bk 2 (1994) 193, at 217.

[45] J Shaw, "Process and Constitutional Discourse in the European Union", (2000) 27 *Journal of Law and Society* 4, at 18.

[46] See, among others, J Gerkrath, *L'émergence*, n. 1 above, at 301 *ff.*; P Magnette, "Entre parlementarisme et déficit démocratique", in M Telò et P Magnette (dir.), *De Maastricht à Amsterdam. L'Europe et son nouveau traité* (Bruxelles: Editions Complexe, 1998) 89; I Pernice, "Multilevel Constitutionalism and the Treaty of Amsterdam: European Constitution-Making Revisited?" (1999) *CMLRev* 703.

[47] For an analysis of the different views that were expressed at the time about these constitutional themes, see G de Búrca, "The Quest for Legitimacy in the European Union" (1996) 59 *Modern Law Review* 349.

the Nice IGC was very down-to-earth and broader constitutional issues were deliberately excluded from the agenda—but they returned with a vengeance after the Fischer and Chirac speeches of mid-2000 and prominently figure now as the main items for future discussion identified by the Nice Declaration on the Future of the European Union.

But there is also another, hidden or at least implicit, constitutional content of treaty revisions, namely the effects of Treaty changes on the internal constitution of each member state. The French Constitutional Council was right in pointing out that the new article in the Treaty of Amsterdam allowing, eventually, for an EC immigration policy to be made by qualified majority voting, directly affects the exercise of French national sovereignty.[48] Indeed, each and every transfer of legislative competences to the European Union affects the position of the national institutions and, very often, the internal division of powers between parliament and government. Also, any major change of the institutional balance between the European Union institutions reverberates in the legal orders of the member states and could be considered as a series of simultaneous adjustments of the fifteen constitutions of the member states. In some of these states, the constitutional relevance of EU revision treaties was recognised by the insertion of special "EU sections" in the Constitutions; France, Germany and Portugal did this after the adoption of the Maastricht Treaty. However, these "European sections" continue to stand apart from the well-worn "domestic" part of the constitution whose provisions are, very often, identical to what they were before the country joined the EC or EU. The most striking thing of all is that the texts of several member state constitutions (including that of a pro-integrationist country like the Netherlands) fail to make any mention whatsoever of the fact that the country is a member state of the European Union.

It should be acknowledged, though, that the IGC negotiators are not always fully aware of the implications of their "conversations" for the constitutional balance at the European or national level. The revision Treaties simply set a new scene on which a number of other actors then start a new constitutional play. As Jo Shaw puts it: "[A]t the conclusion of the IGC, the doors open to a much wider interpretive community comprising the EU institutions, national governments and other public bodies, judicial institutions at a variety of levels, social movements and interest groups, and even the wider "European' electorate and public opinion".[49]

Decline and Reform of the IGC Model

It has often been noted, particularly in the literature on the Maastricht and Amsterdam Treaties, that "an intergovernmental conference is not the best

---

[48] See S Boyron, "The French Constitution and the Treaty of Amsterdam: A Lesson in European Integration" (1999) *Maastricht Journal of European and Comparative Law* 169, at 177.

[49] J Shaw, "Process and Constitutional Discourse" n. 45 above, at 30.

forum for elaborating coherent solutions to complex institutional problems".[50]
In Neil Walker's words, an IGC "unhappily combines a narrow consultative
base, a protracted timescale and a procedure which encourages negative criticism rather than constructive debate".[51] The IGC format appears ill-suited for
elaborating constitutional rules, and seems increasingly unable to perform its
traditional role of delivering sophisticated and wide-ranging diplomatic break-
throughs.

One possible remedy is to broaden participation in, and increase the transparency of, the treaty revision process, particularly in its crucial negotiation
phase. In terms of transparency, some progress has been achieved in recent
IGCs. During the 1996–97 IGC, an internet site was established, in which many
(but not all!) the papers submitted by the delegations were made publicly available. The consecutive Presidencies of the conference published reports containing intermediary results of the negotiations. As Weatherill and Beaumont
delicately put it, the conference "attempted to maintain a level of transparency
commensurate with the delicacy of some of the negotiation".[52] In the most
recent IGC of 2000, a further improvement took place. Over the period between
1 February 2000 (when the IGC was started) and 12 December 2000 (on the eve
of the Nice summit), some 126 English-language documents[53] were posted on an
IGC website set up by the Council.[54] They emanated from the Presidency, from
member state delegations, from third states, from EU institutions and from the
IGC's legal adviser; together, they provide a comprehensive view of the docu-
mentary basis of the negotiations, although, as always, a number of confidential
"non-papers", minutes of bilateral meetings and internal notes of the single delegations were not made publicly available.

This increased transparency has not, so far, affected the full control exercised
by the member state governments over the negotiation agenda. Moreover, the
final part of the negotiation is invariably intransparent. As the Gordian knots
are being tied for the Heads of Government to cut at their final meeting, only a
small group of insiders is allowed to peep into the negotiation room; indeed, the
Heads of Government themselves have great difficulty, at their closing press
conferences, in remembering what exactly they have agreed during the night.

One radical way of attempting to change the nature of the constitutional conversation is to reject the IGC regime as utterly and irredeemably unsuited to the
task of drawing up a coherent constitutional future for the enlarged Europe.
The extreme alternative to the IGC is the old "Philadelphian" dream of a constitutional convention proclaiming the "United States of Europe". This model

---

[50] "Editorial Comments" (1997) 34 *Common Market Law Review* 1105, at 1108.

[51] N Walker, "European Constitutionalism and European Integration", [1996] *Public Law* 266,
at 281.

[52] S Weatherill and P Beaumont, *EU Law* (3rd edn., London: Penguin Books, 1999), p. 17.

[53] A certain number of documents were made available in English only, or in English and French
only. For example: 112 documents were published in French, 95 in Dutch, and 92 in Finnish.

[54] <http:/ue.eu.int/cig>.

was at the heart of Altiero Spinelli's European federalism,[55] although the constitutional document which the European Parliament adopted in 1984 on his initiative was not called "Constitution" but "Draft Treaty on European Union". A few years after that, in 1989, the constitutional convention model was proposed to, and overwhelmingly adopted by, the Italian people in a consultative referendum. This referendum conferred a mandate on the European Parliament for drafting a European Constitution to be submitted directly to the national parliaments, by-passing the intergovernmental negotiation stage. The EP willingly took up the invitation and approved, on 12 December 1990, a resolution on the constitutional basis of the European Union.[56] This was a fully elaborated text with a constitutional character which, however, was presented by the EP as merely the "basis" of the definitive draft Constitution which it was prepared to adopt once the member states had acknowledged its right to do so (Point 2 of the Resolution). The states never did, of course. On the contrary, they formally started, only a few days after the adoption of the Parliament's resolution, an IGC conducted along the traditional lines which was successfully concluded, one year later, at Maastricht. Since then, the idea of a European constitutional convention as an *alternative* mechanism to the IGC has turned, again, into a utopian scheme which is still occasionally proposed by academics of the federalist persuasion,[57] but is no longer officially promoted by any European or national institution.

A politically more promising idea seems to be that of grafting elements of the constitutional assembly model on the existing treaty revision process. A few years ago, Deirdre Curtin suggested that a forum, composed of the representatives of "civil society" drawn from across the Union, could be given a formal role *within the Treaty revision process*, including possibly the power to give final approval to the results of the formal governmental conference.[58] Surprisingly, the heads of government of the member states themselves decided to set into motion an embryonic constitutional assembly when they created, at the European Council of Cologne, a quadripartite *body*, composed of representatives of the EP, of national Parliaments, of the Commission and of the member state governments, to draft a Charter of Fundamental Rights for the

---

[55] See S Pistone, "Altiero Spinelli and the Strategy for the United States of Europe", reprinted in B F Nelsen and A Stubb (eds.), *The European Union. Readings on the Theory and Practice of European Integration* (Boulder: Lynne Rienner, 1994) 69; and A Bosco, "A 'Federator' for Europe: Altiero Spinelli and the Constituent Role of the European Parliament", *EUI Working Paper* RSC No. 94/19.

[56] [1991] OJ C 19/65.

[57] For a recent example, see D Rousseau, "Pour une constitution européenne", *Le Débat* n. 108, Janv.-févr. 2000, 54. The utopian character of his proposal is most visible in the suggestion that the Parliamentary Assembly of the Council of Europe would be the appropriate institution for taking the initiative for a constituent assembly (at pp. 64–5); see also the short manifesto "Pour une Constitution européenne", signed by D Rousseau and seven university professors from other European countries, in *Le Monde*, 5 May 1998.

[58] D Curtin, "Civil Society and the European Union: Opening Spaces for Deliberative Democracy?", (1999) Vol VII, Bk 1 *Collected Courses of the Academy of European Law*, 185, at 277.

European Union. The Body soon decided to call itself "Convention". Although it did not call itself a "*Constitutional* Convention", remained by and large within the limits of the mandate formulated by the Cologne European Council, and did not actually claim for itself the power to *adopt* the Charter (that was left to the political institutions of the EU[59] after the green light had been given by the European Council), the Convention acquired a high degree of institutional legitimacy, which made it virtually impossible for the member state governments to reject or even modify its proposals when they examined them at the Biarritz European Council of October 2000.

The relatively open and deliberative method of work adopted for drafting the Charter[60] became particularly attractive when contrasted with the bitter bickering that occurred, some months later, at the IGC summit in Nice.[61] In the text of the Declaration on the Future of the European Union, which is appended to the Nice Treaty, the governments admitted that there was a need for a "deeper and wider" reform debate than the one the IGC had been conducting. For this purpose, the governments agreed that the next IGC, scheduled for 2004, will have to be preceded by an open debate involving a large number of political institutions and wider groups in society. Although no direct reference is made to the "Convention method" in the Nice Declaration, it is very probable that a body resembling the Charter Convention will be put in place in December 2001 in order to prepare the ground for the next round of Treaty revision.

The attraction of this "convention model" lies in the way it broadens participation in the constitutional conversation and thereby allows a public *débat d'idées*,[62] and more specifically, in the fact that it provides a meaningful opportunity for the national parliaments to directly influence the drafting of a European constitutional text, in contrast with the essentially passive, or negative, role devoted to them in the traditional IGC regime.

Another improvement of the existing treaty revision mechanism may be needed in order to preserve the possibility of a meaningful conversation, namely the attenuation of the present rule of consensus-cum-unanimity decision-making. In Maastricht, Amsterdam and Nice, last-minute failure threatened, and the accord on revision was achieved each time at the cost of postponing or sidelining some of the more contentious issues. In a future European Union with an even larger membership, the consensus rule may become untenable altogether. A move away from unanimity towards some form of super-qualified

---

[59] Charter of Fundamental Rights of the European Union—Solemn Proclamation by the European Parliament, the Council and the Commission, [2000] OJ C 364/1.

[60] See G de Búrca, "The Drafting of the EU Charter of Fundamental Rights" (2001) 26 *European Law Review* 126.

[61] See the summary press report, "Nice Shambles Boosts Support for Convention", *European Voice*, 14–20 December 2000, p. 1.

[62] See J-V Louis, "Le modèle constitutionnel européen: de la Communauté à l'Union", in P Magnette and E Remacle (eds.), *Le nouveau modèle européen. Vol 1: Institutions et gouvernance* (Bruxelles: Editions de l'Université de Bruxelles, 2000) 31, at 45: "Une constitution n'est pas un texte qui résulte de l'accord unanime de délégués agissant sur instruction. Elle est le produit d'un débat d'idées sur des options majeures".

majority for treaty revision would be beneficial to the constitutional conversation: each country's views would still have to be taken seriously by the others, but single states would no longer be able to take the others hostage in order to achieve their narrow national interest. A shift away from the common accord requirement would not be equivalent to transforming the European treaties into a European Constitution; after all, there are many examples of international agreements which can be modified by a decision adopted by less than all the parties to the original treaty; but such a shift would be the condition for continuing, like before (and perhaps better than before), to insert constitutional content into an international treaty framework.[63]

---

[63] On the question of introducing a "superqualified majority" rule for Treaty revisions (accompanied perhaps by a partial opt-out for countries that would be overruled) see the report of the Robert Schuman Centre of the European University Institute: *Reforming the Treaties' Amendment Procedures. Second Report on the Reorganisation of the European Union Treaties submitted to the European Commission on 31 July 2000*, available on the IGC 2000 website of the European Commission: <europa.eu.int/comm/igc2000/offdoc/discussiondocs/index_en.htm>.

4

The Constitutional Structure of the European Union: Some Reflections on Vertical Unity-in-Diversity

DEIRDRE CURTIN AND IGE DEKKER

INTRODUCTION

As RECENTLY AS a few years ago it could be shown that regarding the existence and nature of a legal system of the European Union there was no clear legal picture at all and certainly no consensus of opinion.[1] In a contribution to the study of evolving European Union law the two present authors wrote together an article published in 1999 entitled "The EU as a 'Layered' International Organisation: Institutional Unity in Disguise" which presented what can perhaps now be regarded as reflecting an Utrecht approach to the nature of an evolving EU legal order.[2] This earlier article concentrated on two main questions: whether the European Union could be qualified as an international organisation in legal terms, and if so, whether its institutional legal system is developing in practice towards institutional unity, albeit in disguise. The main focus of the article was the European Union itself. We analysed the Union as a legal institution and defended the thesis that the Union is an international organisation with a unitary but complex character. This conclusion was based on an analysis not only of the EU treaties and other basic instruments, but also of the so-called legal practices, i.e. forms of legal action which are—explicitly or implicitly—employed in order to make the legal institution an operational entity. The analysis of the legal practices concerned mainly what the Union had done between 1993 and 1998 in the two new "pillars", the CFSP (Co-operation in Foreign and Security Policy) and the CJHA (Co-operation in Justice and Home Affairs). Three interconnected levels of Union activity were identified; namely, first, the international legal status of the Union, second the functioning of the main organs of the Union, and, third, the application

[1] For an overview and references, see D M Curtin and I F Dekker, "The EU as a 'Layered' International Organization: Institutional Unity in Disguise", in P Craig and G de Búrca (eds.), *The Evolution of EU Law*, (Oxford: Oxford University Press, 1999) pp. 83–5, 92–103; J Shaw, *Law of the European Union*, 3rd edn., (Basingstoke: Palgrave, 2000) Part I.
[2] D M Curtin and I F Dekker, n. 1 above, pp. 83–136.

of some fundamental principles and their effects on the legal protection of the citizens of the member states. The conclusion was that the legal system of the European Union as such was developing as an institutional unity but that this did not exclude the simultaneous creation of space for the development of a variety of sub-legal systems. Of course, some of these sub-legal systems already existed, such as the three "pillars", but also within these "pillars" additional sub-legal systems existed and could be further developed.

One of the remaining problematic aspects of the unity of the legal system of the Union is the relationship with the national legal order of the member states. Already at the level of principle the question is whether the complexly unitary legal system of the Union as such includes the national legal orders of the member states, and if that is the case how should we go about understanding the relationship between them? With regard to the European Communities the relationship with the national legal orders has already taken shape to a very considerable extent. Even if both legal systems, under the general overall umbrella of international law, must *qua* legal validity be considered as relatively independent one from the other they must nevertheless be considered as firmly intertwined through the operation of several general legal principles such as those relating to the applicability of EC law in the national legal orders and the principle of loyalty. However, it is not at all clear whether the same understanding can be said to apply to the relationship between the legal system of the Union and that of the member states. Some authors even defend the diametrically opposing view that the Union can only be understood in terms of a pure treaty regime and thus that within the Union there can only be horizontal relations between the "high contracting" parties.[3] But even if one accepts the view that the Union is more correctly to be understood as attracting legal personality in its own right—in particular in the shape of an international organisation—and it may accordingly be clear that the Union is a separate entity, that conclusion does not as such reveal the nature of its relationship with the legal orders of its member states. That latter—vertical—relationship can be framed either on the basis of the (classical) legal principle of the autonomy of the member states or on the basis of the (communautarian) legal principle of the unity of the legal systems of the organisations and its members.

In the present article we analyse the relationship between the Union legal system and the national legal systems from two perspectives. In the first place, we explore the angle of the structural principles concerning the validity and application of the Union's legal system in the national legal orders of the member states. It may be possible to refer to such structural principles as examples of "a-moral" principles in the sense that, from a normative point of view it does not independently matter whether there is a direct or indirect relationship between these two kinds of order. In using such terminology we do not mean to suggest

---

[3] This view is most clearly and consistently expressed in C Koenig and M Pechstein, *Die Europäische Union: Der Vertrag von Maastricht* (Tübingen: Mohr, 1995).

that the manner in which this legal relationship is structured cannot have far reaching consequences—for example, for the citizens in the member states—but such effect depends inevitably on the specific content of the rules at stake.

The second perspective we develop in analysing the relationship between the Union legal order and that of its member states relates precisely to some of the consequences for those citizens in the member states. In particular, we explore the question to what extent the member states can still be regarded as autonomous in the sense that they are free to go their own way with regard to the protection of their citizens. This relationship will be analysed mainly from the perspective of the principle of loyalty, as laid down in Article 10 of the EC Treaty, and we will look at the manner in which that principle is evolving and the important lessons that may be drawn concerning the nature of the relationship between the two systems. The principle of loyalty in the sense it is used here could possibly be referred to as a "moral" principle in the sense we indicated above since, from a normative viewpoint, it does make a difference whether the relationship in question is a direct or indirect one.

THE STRUCTURAL PRINCIPLES AND INSTITUTIONAL VERTICAL UNITY

Relations between legal systems

The theoretical starting point of our aforementioned analysis of the legal system of the European Union as a "layered" international organisation was the so-called "institutional theory of law".[4] This institutional approach still constitutes in our view the best possible theoretical framework for analysing complex modern legal systems such as those of the European Union and its member states. In particular, the theory has developed an expansive and at the same time quite precise view on the structures and content of legal systems and their functioning in practice. Although the theory is rooted in the tradition of legal positivism, it holds above all that a reduction of a legal system to duty-imposing norms of conduct is both theoretically and empirically untenable. Its central and intriguing question is "what kind of results stemming from human activity, can obtain legal validity as elements of the legal system".[5]

With regard to the issue of the relations between legal systems it is essential to realise that the institutional theory of law is "positivist" in the sense that it considers law as a system of primary and secondary rules which sets its own requirements for the validity of the legal system and of its elements, such as legal

---

[4] See N MacCormick and O Weinberger, *An Institutional Theory of Law, New Approaches to Legal Positivism* (Dordrecht: Reidel, 1986); O Weinberger, *Law, Institution and Legal Practice. Fundamental Problems of Legal Theory and Social Philosophy* (Dordrecht: Kluwer, 1991); D W P. Ruiter, *Institutional Legal Facts, Legal Powers and Their Effects* (Deventer: Kluwer,1993). See, also N MacCormick (ed.), *Constructing Legal Systems, "European Union" in Legal Theory* (Deventer: Kluwer, 1997).

[5] Ruiter, n. 4 above, p. 33.

rules and legal institutions. The concept of validity means a legal system (or its elements) *exists* in the "reality" of law because it is based on a higher legal system or, if the system itself is the highest legal order, on a hypothetical highest rule.[6] In other words, legal systems are systems of legal sub-orders that are connected to each other via validity relations. Thus, also according to the institutional theory of law, the unity of legal systems is in the first place expressed in terms of their sources of validity and in particular in how the validity of legal systems are related to each other (subsection below "Validity Relations of Legal Systems").

However, the outcome of the analysis of the validity relations between legal systems does not say much about other—more well known—structural aspects of the legal relations between two legal systems. These aspects concern in the first place the distinct concepts of "direct applicability" and "direct effect" of legal rules of one system in another legal system. The meaning and significance of these concepts are only partly determined by the way in which the validity relations between legal systems is structured. The same holds true for the issue of the supremacy of rules of one legal system over rules of another legal system. Whether a rule of one legal system has priority over a rule of another legal system does not follow from the mere fact that one legal system is of a higher—let alone, more encompassing—order than the other. For it is, for instance, possible that a higher legal system determines that decisions enacted by an organ of lower legal system have priority over decisions taken by an organ of the higher legal system. So, it is important to deal with the question of validity relations between legal systems separately from the questions concerning the direct applicability and the direct effect of legal rules and their supremacy over other legal rules (subsection below "Application Relations between Legal Systems").

Validity Relations of Legal Systems

As Kelsen pointed out many years ago, there are four conceivable kinds of validity relations between two legal systems, namely (1) both systems are as to their sources independent of each other; (2) system A derives its validity from system B; (3) system B derives its validity from system A; and (4) both systems are of the same value and relatively independent sub-systems of an overarching superior order.[7] The first option represents the well known dualist approach to the relationship

---

[6] We will not go into this problem of the formulation of—in Kelsen's terms—the *Grundnorm*, or—in the words of Hart—the ultimate rule of recognition. For an explanation and interpretation of this issue on the basis of the institutional theory of law, see, Weinberger, n. 4 above, pp. 132–9; Ruiter, n. 4 above, pp. 11–13.

[7] See, for the classic text, H Kelsen, *Das Problem der Souveränität und die Theorie des Völkerrechts: Beitrage zur einer reinen Rechtslehre*, (Aalen Scientia, 1960) p. 104; see also A Verdross and B Simma, *Universelles Völkerrecht, Theorie und Praxis* (Berlin: Duncker & Humblot, 1984) pp. 538–56. In writing this paragraph we used also W G Werner, *Het recht geworden woord* (Enschede, Twente University Press, 1995), pp. 154–65.

between distinct legal systems, whereas the other three options are the three possible variations of the monist view according to which both legal systems belong to *one* legal order. The instant question—which is hardly dealt with in European legal doctrine—is which of these four options provide the best explanation of the validity relation between the legal system of the European Union and those of the member states.

According to the *first* possibility, the classic dualist approach, the legal systems of the Union and the member states are completely independent—separate from each other—in the sense that they have different legal sources and thus also different legal subjects. The legal system of the Union provides rules for the member states (and for the functioning of the Union itself), whereas the legal system of the member states regulates the activities of their citizens and other private persons (and the functioning of the state itself). In other words, legally valid rights and duties of individuals can only be created under the national legal system of the member states. In the literature, this dualist construction is questioned in general with regard to the relation of international and national legal systems, both on theoretical and empirical grounds. Theoretically, the approach has, above all, problems in explaining the position of the state in relation to the national legal order, because the state, as the central subject of the international legal system, cannot *also* be a part of the national legal order. Obviously, this last consequence is difficult to reconcile with modern concepts of the rule of law, according to which the state is a legal subject of national law. Empirically, one can point to rules of positive international law that purport to bind private persons directly, without interference from national law. Under general international law, the most famous examples of such rules relate to the international criminal responsibility of individuals for international crimes. The legal system of the European Union—and in particular the legal system of the European Community—is a far richer field in this respect with treaty rules, regulations and decisions directly creating rights and duties for individuals and private legal persons. In the light of the jurisprudence of the European Court of Justice and legal doctrine, it is difficult to maintain that the validity of these legal acts is based on the national legal systems of the member states. The Community legal system itself provides for (secondary) rules on the formation, interpretation and implementation of Community law.

Given the fact that most of the aforementioned examples concern the legal system of the Community and not the Union, the question may be asked whether it is possible to reject the dualist vision on the validity relation with regard to Community law and national law, but accept it with regard to European Union law and national law. This contention seems to be difficult to reconcile with the unity of the legal system of the European Union as far as its validity is concerned. *This* unity seems to be firmly established with the introductory provision of the Treaty on European Union stating that the Union is based on the European Communities (Article 1 TEU) and the final provisions guaranteeing the unity of the legal system by the prescription of *one* amendment procedure for all the treaties on which the Union is based (Article 48 TEU) and the possibility of becoming a new member only of the Union as a whole (Article 49 TEU).

Now that we have established that the dualist approach to the validity relation between the legal system of the European Union and those of the member states raises serious objections, let us consider the three monist options distinguished above. According to the first option, the legal system of the European Union is—*qua* legal validity—the highest legal order implying that the national legal systems derive their validity from the Union legal system. Of course, one can see immediately that this explanation is not very plausible on historical grounds and leads to the rather absurd conclusion that the legal system of the member states is based on the Treaty on European Union.

The second monist option is that the national legal system(s) of the member states is (are) the highest legal order, of which the legal system of the European Union is one of the offspring. This option is, at least implicitly, probably the most common assumption about the source of the validity of the European legal system. The validity of the system is derived from the competence of the member states—or, in this respect, perhaps more appropriately, the High Contracting Parties—to establish this legal system by concluding the Treaty on European Union. According to the European Court of Justice, this option also seems to be the favourite explanation with regard to the European Communities.[8] However, this construction of the validity relation between the two legal systems is problematic as well. As the validity of the legal system of the European Union for each of the member states is only based on its own legal order, the consequence would be that the Treaty on European Union has not created *mutual* obligations between the member states at all![9] A national legal system as such cannot be a sufficient legal basis for the establishment of a valid *international* agreement between sovereign states. There has to be at least a rule "independent" from the national legal order according to which the expressed will by a sovereign state counts as a valid way to be bound by an international agreement. It follows that this option, according to which the national legal order is the highest one, cannot sufficiently explain the validity of the legal system of the European Union.

The analysis thus far leads automatically to the third monist solution as to the validity relations between legal systems. This solution must present the most

[8] See, for instance, Case 6/64 *Costa* v. *ENEL* [1964] ECR 585, in which the Court, *inter alia*, stated that ". . . the EEC Treaty . . . became an integral part of the legal system of the Member States . . .", and that the Member States have limited their sovereign rights by creating a Community having "real powers stemming from a limitation of sovereignty or a transfer of powers from the States to the Community . . .".

[9] The other possible basis for the primacy of the national legal order over the European Union legal system is that the highest rule is laid down in *one* of the national legal orders of the member states. However, this option leads to rather absurd consequences because not only the European legal system but also all the other national legal orders are in this case subordinated to the "highest" national legal order (for instance, the Irish or Dutch legal order).

plausible construction for the relation between the legal system of the European Union and those of the member states. According to this construction both legal systems are to be considered as equal and (relatively) independent legal sub-systems of the overarching international legal order. Both are based on international law and the validity of the Union's legal system is, in particular, grounded on the international customary rule of *pacta sunt servanda*.[10] The treaties establishing the European Union created—in the words of the European Court of Justice with regard to the European Community- "a new legal order in international law",[11] and this order has indeed an "autonomous" character.[12] However, the autonomy of the legal system of the Union concerns the legal systems of the member states and not the international legal order. On the contrary, the international legal order not only provides for the validity of the legal sub-systems, but also co-ordinates the relations between them. For instance, international treaty law provides that a state may not invoke its internal law as a justification for its failure to perform a treaty obligation, which, in principle, also applies to national constitutional law.[13] It is important to realise that this principle of (external) supremacy of Union law over national law does not follow as such from the validity relations between the two systems, because in that respect the systems are equal. The supremacy is based on a priority rule laid down in the overarching international legal order.

Application Relations between Legal Systems

The consequence of the view that the legal systems of the European Union and those of the member states are both part of a single, overarching legal order, is that *valid* legal rules of the European Union have to be accepted as legal *facts* by the member states. In other words, member states of the Union are not free to grant or to deny a valid legal rule of the Union its *validity* in its own legal order. The validity of European Union law can only be judged on the basis of the conditions set out in the legal system of the European Union (or in international law) and is not dependent on the (constitutional) law of the member states, even where it concerns its status in the national legal order.

However, at the same time it is important to underline that no other consequences can be attached, on logical grounds, to the unity of the legal systems of the Union and the member states insofar as this unity is shaped by their validity relations. As previously noted, the legal systems have, in principle, equal value and they are relatively independent of each other. In particular the validity relationship

---

[10] See, Art. 26 of the Vienna Convention on the Law of Treaties, 1969.
[11] Case 26/62 *Van Gend & Loos* [1963] ECR 1, 12.
[12] Case 6/64 *Costa* v. *ENEL* [1964] ECR 585.
[13] See Arts. 27 and 46 of the Vienna Convention on the Law of Treaties, 1969.

does not say anything about the following issues:[14] (1) Whether European Union law is directly applicable in the national legal order or not, meaning whether besides the national legislature other national authorities—such as regional or local administrations, and national courts—are competent to apply Union law as such; (2) Whether Union law is directly effective or not, meaning whether individuals may rely on provisions of Union law before their national courts; And (3), whether Union law has supremacy over national law in the event of conflict between both kinds of rules. The answers to these questions do not follow from the validity of Union law in the national legal systems of the member states, but depend on the relevant rules of international and national law.

As is well known, according to international law, states are, in principle, free to decide the way they apply and give effect to international law in their national legal orders. The consequence of this freedom is that, in practice, there are as many different ways in which the aforementioned issues are regulated as there are states.[15] For instance, with regard to the issue of applicability of international law in the national legal order, the national "solutions" vary between the situation in which international legal rules have to be transformed by the national legislature into national law before it can be applied by other national authorities,[16] and the situation in which, in principle, international legal rules are as such directly applicable by every national authority. This relatively anarchic situation is one of the reasons why the international legal system is often characterised as horizontal or decentralised. One can also say that institutional vertical unity between international law in general and the two hundred national legal systems is—apart from their validity relation—presumptively absent and, as far as it is present in practice, rests solely on the loyalty of the sovereign states.

The way to realise a more substantial relationship of institutional vertical unity between the international and national legal systems is to regulate the issues of applicability and effect in the international legal system. Such a regulation takes priority over national (constitutional) rules on the basis of the aforementioned customary rule that states may not invoke internal rules to justify breaches of treaty obligations.[17] The most well known example in this respect is, of course, the European Community legal order. Although an explicit regulation of the issues of applicability and effect of Community law in the national legal systems of the member states was barely discernible in the treaties

---

[14] See, Verdross and Simma, n. 7 above, pp. 550–4. For the application of these issues in the European law context, see, A Koller, *Die unmittelbare Anwendbarkeit völkerrechtlicher Verträge und des EWG—Vertrages im innerstaatlichen Bereich* (Bern: Stämpfli, 1971); J Winter, "Direct Applicability and Direct Effect, Two Distinct Concepts in Community Law" (1972) 9 *Common Market Law Review* 425; P Eleftheriadis, "The Direct Effect of Community Law: Conceptual Issues" (1996) 16 *Yearbook of European Law* 205; Shaw, n. 1 above, ch. 12.

[15] See, with further references, P Malanczuk, *Akehurst's Modern Introduction to International Law*, 7th edn., (London/New York: Routledge, 1997), pp. 63–71.

[16] Sometimes, such a system is also referred to as "dualist". However this is confusing because it can be applied within a monist relationship between distinct legal systems.

[17] See n. 13 above.

establishing the European Communities, the Court of Justice assumed that the founding fathers of the Communities had the clear intention that these issues in the end had to be settled by the Community institutions, and in particular, the Court of Justice, on the basis of some fundamental unwritten Community principles. There is no need to go into the far reaching significance of the *assertion* that the applicability and effect of Community law in the national legal orders are at least also questions of Community law.[18] It suffices here to say, on the basis of extensive analysis of both European and national jurisprudence, that Community law is in principle directly applicable and directly effective on a priority basis in the national legal orders of the member states, although not all the consequences of these structural principles are as yet fully developed or indeed fully accepted by the member states, in particular by some national courts.[19]

The question here is whether there is also such an institutional vertical unity between the legal systems of the European Union as such and those of the member states. This is in particular relevant with regard to the matters falling under the so-called "third pillar" of the Union—Police and Judicial Co-operation in Criminal Matters (PJC) in its truncated post-Amsterdam form—because these matters can affect the legal position of individuals quite substantially.[20] Insofar as the literature deals with this question, the answer is quite simply negative. It is assumed that the issues of applicability, effect, and supremacy have to be dealt with under the traditional rules of international law, meaning that these issues are solely regulated by the internal (constitutional) law of the member states.[21]

However, this conclusion seems to us to be premature. In the first place, the absence of an explicit regulation of the relationship between Union law and national law in the treaties is, in itself, as the Court of Justice has shown with respect to the Community legal order, not decisive with regard to the question whether Union law can be considered directly applicable or directly effective on

---

[18] See the literature mentioned at n. 14 above. For an excellent and recent overview of the development of some of the core concepts, see B de Witte, "Direct Effect, Supremacy, and the Nature of the Legal Order" in P Craig and G de Búrca (eds.), *The Evolution of EU Law* (Oxford: Oxford University Press, 1999), pp. 177–214.

[19] See, also P Craig and G de Búrca, *EU Law, Text, Cases and Materials* (2nd edn., Oxford: Oxford University Press, 1998), chs. 4, 5 and 6, in particular pp. 264–94.

[20] See, most recently, Council Framework Decision (2001/413/JHA) of 28 May 2001 on combating fraud and counterfeiting of non-cash means of payment ([2001] OJ L 149/1–4, 02.06.2001); and Council Framework Decision(2001/500/JHA) of 26 June 2001 on money laundering, the identification, tracing, freezing, seizing and confiscation of instrumentalities and the proceeds of crime ([2001] OJ L 182/1–2, 05.07.2001). Sometimes also decisions taken under the "second pillar" on the Common Foreign and Security Policy can affect individuals directly, such as the decision concerning "restrictive" measures against the Federal Republic of Yugoslavia which includes also a list of persons which will be not admitted in the territories of the member states. See pending cases T–349/99 and T–350/99 ([2000] OJ C79/35–36, 18.03.2000).

[21] See especially, de Witte, n. 18 above, p. 177, 185; L F M Besselink, "Tussen supranationaliteit en soevereiniteit: over het niet-communautaire recht van de Europese Unie", in *Europese Unie en nationale soevereiniteit, Staatsrechtconferentie 1997* (Deventer: Tjeenk Willink, 1997), pp. 125, 143–53; D M Curtin and R H van Ooik, *Revamping the European Union's Enforcement Systems with a View to Eastern Enlargement* (The Hague: WRR Scientific Council for Government Policy, Working Documents W 110, 2000), pp. 82–3.

a priority basis in the member states. It is generally recognised that the landmark judgments of the Court of Justice on the "own" legal nature of Community law were mainly based on "legal policy" (*rechtspolitieke*) considerations, in particular the "grand" objectives of the promotion of the effectiveness and uniformity of Community law and the legal protection of individuals. It is not clear why these objectives would, *a priori*, have lesser relevance in the other policy areas of the Union, such as for instance co-operation on criminal matters. However, the Treaty on European Union itself, it is said, excludes this line of reasoning. Before "Amsterdam" the argument was that the European Court of Justice had no jurisdiction in the second and third pillar of the Union. "Amsterdam" blunted the edge of this argument by creating a role for the Court under the third pillar on the basis of which it can give judgments on the validity and interpretation of certain legal acts of the Council.[22] However, with regard to the new forms of legal acts introduced by "Amsterdam" in the PJC chapter of the Treaty, namely "framework decisions" and other non-legislative "decisions", it was explicitly agreed that these acts "shall not entail direct effect".[23] Of course, this provision could restrict the significance of these legal acts, for the protection of the rights of individuals through the laying down of clear and precise obligations for member states. At the same time, this limitation has at least two other important consequences for the relation between Union law and national law. The first consequence has mainly an in-principle or theoretical significance; the second one could have also a more practical impact.

By the very act—exceptional in international treaty law in its explicit protection of national autonomy—of inserting a clause excluding the direct effect of certain types of legal acts, the member states have nevertheless in principle accepted that the regulation of the structural relation between Union law and their own legal systems has also become a matter of Union law itself. For the shaping of the institutional vertical legal unity this is of crucial importance, because the member states are no longer free to control this matter solely under their internal law.

Secondly, the exclusion of the direct effect of framework decisions and decisions implies that they are in principle directly applicable in the national legal orders, otherwise the exclusion makes no sense at all. If these legal acts were not directly applicable—in the sense that national courts are also competent to apply them—there would be no need to block the possibility that they may be invoked by individuals before a national court. The fact that framework decisions are in principle directly applicable implies, following the jurisprudence of the Court of Justice on the legal effects of Community law,[24] that they could have an "indirect effect" in the national legal systems. This principle of indirect

---

[22] See Art. 35 TEU.
[23] See Art. 34(2)(a)(b) TEU.
[24] See Case 14/83 *Von Colson*, [1984] ECR 1891; Case C–106/89 *Marleasing* [1990] ECR I–3061; Case C–91/92 *Faccini Dori* [1994] ECR I–3325.

effect, applied to Union law, would mean that all national authorities have the obligation to interpret national legislation and other measures as much as possible in the light of the wording and purpose of valid Union law.[25] In practice, national courts will also be expected to achieve the results laid down in the framework decisions. Because the subject of these (framework) decisions will often be criminal matters, it should also be noted that the Court of Justice has already imposed certain limitations on the application of the principle of indirect effect of Community law, which *mutatis mutandis*, it is argued, would also have to be applied to the indirect effect of Union law. In general, the obligation to interpret national law in conformity with Union law would be restricted by other general principles, such as the prohibition on retroactivity and the principle of legal certainty. More specific framework decisions would, for instance, not have indirect effect in criminal proceedings where they would cause the accused to be convicted where he would otherwise have been acquitted.[26]

In conclusion, it appears that there are not only strong arguments for the assertion that all valid Union law has to be accepted as legal fact by the Union's member states, but that, in principle, Union law is also directly applicable in the national legal orders of the member states. At least with regard to the framework decisions and other non-legislative decisions, effectively the most important legal instruments under the third pillar of the Union, it can be argued that, although their direct effect is explicitly excluded, they entail indirect effect, meaning that all national authorities have to interpret national law as much as possible in conformity with these decisions. This duty of interpretation is, according to the Court of Justice, based on the principle of loyalty, as laid down in Article 10 TEC, which will be the subject of the next section.

THE PRINCIPLE OF LOYALTY IN UNION LAW: AN EVOLVING "LEGAL PRACTICE"

The Message of Article 10 TEC

There is no doubt as a matter of international legal doctrine that the principle of good faith is a general principle of international law.[27] It is articulated most extensively in the context of the Charter of the United Nations where the requirement of acting in good faith is taken beyond the narrow confines of the Charter obligations and is extended successively to the obligations based on general international law and the law of treaties. In particular in the law of treaties, the general principle is applied to the relation between international and national law. As such, it is accepted that its content "combines moral ideas

---

[25] See on the principle of indirect effect and its relationship to the principle of direct effect, Shaw, n. 1 above, pp. 446–50; Craig and de Búrca, n. 19 above, pp. 198–206.

[26] See Case 80/86 *Kolpinghuis Nijmegen* [1987] ECR 3969.

[27] See A D'Amato, "Good Faith", in: 7 *EPIL* 107–9. J F O'Connor, *Good Faith in International Law* (Aldershot: Dortmann, 1991).

on correct action (honesty, seriousness, loyalty) and strictly legal contents (e.g. a ban on the abuse of legal rights)".[28]

In the legal order of the European Communities the principle of good faith has long been considered a classic general principle. It governs the vertical relationship with the legal and political orders of the member states and has evolved over the course of time into a pervasive duty on the political and legal orders of member states to co-operate in good faith.[29] That said, Article 10 TEC serves primarily as an interpretative provision and not as an independent source of law. The manner in which this principle of "sincere co-operation" or "loyalty" has been judicially interpreted makes it quite clear that the obligation imposed by Article 10 TEC is to be considered as a mutual obligation, owed by member states to the Community and *vice versa*. More broadly still, it has evolved from a duty of co-operation on the part of the member states to a multi-sided duty of loyalty and good faith in the vertical relationship between the Union and its member states and also among the member states themselves and among the Union institutions themselves.[30] Furthermore, many specific Treaty provisions are inspired by the principle of loyalty[31] and various judicial principles of the Community legal order have drawn heavily on the principle of loyalty for underlying inspiration.[32] Moreover, loyalty underpins the principle of mutual recognition as formulated by the Court of Justice in its *Cassis de Dijon* case-law,[33] a point made especially clear by the Court of Justice in *Vlassopoulou*.[34]

In the vertical system of interlocking legal systems the principle of mutual recognition plays a key role suggesting that each legal order recognises the autonomy and difference of the others but does so within mutually applicable limits. As an expression of mutual solidarity it requires all actors to take due account of the others' legitimate interests in the exercise of their own competencies and functions. Loyalty thus embraces the message that the EU legal system can be autonomous only to the extent it is accepted or mutually recognised by the other legal systems. As Amaryllis Verhoeven has eloquently phrased it: "The theory at

[28] B Simma, *The Charter of the United Nations, A Commentary* (Oxford: Oxford University Press, 1994), p. 93.

[29] See, for example, *The Duties of Co-operation of National Authorities and Courts and the Community Institutions under Art. 10 EC,* Proceedings of the XIX FIDE Congress (Helsinki, 2000) and further references cited in the Community Report.

[30] See further, A Verhoeven, *The European Union in Search of a Democratic and Constitutional Theory* (Unpublished PhD Thesis, University of Leuven, 2001).

[31] See, for example, Art. 234 TEC, obliging national courts to make references to the Court of Justice, and Art. 86 TEC, obliging member states to respect fully the Community rules with regard to, *inter alia*, state-owned enterprises.

[32] Among the best known examples is the principle that a state must make good loss and damage caused to individuals for breaches of Community law (Joined Cases 6/90 and 9/90, *Francovich* [1991] ECR I–5357).

[33] Case 120/78, *REWE* v. *Bundesmonopolverwaltung fur Brantwein* [1979] ECR 649. See further, P Oliver, *Free Movement of Goods in the European Community* (London: Sweet & Maxwell, 1996).

[34] Case C–340/89 *Vlassopoulou* [1991] ECR I–2357: "in so far as Community law makes no special provisions, the objectives of the Treaty and in particular the freedom of establishment may be achieved by measures enacted by the Member States, which under Art. 5 [now Art. 10] of the Treaty, must take all appropriate measures. . . .".

least is that the principle of loyalty ensures the autonomous operation of EU law but manages to do so in a non-hierarchical and potentially pluralist fashion. . . . In fact while Member States are, as actors within the EU legal system, tied to the principle of EU loyalty, they are under a similar duty of loyalty towards their respective national constitutions as well".[35] It is in the manner in which this tension may ultimately be resolved that lies the seeds of a deeper understanding of the nature and scope of the principle of loyalty as a "moral" principle of Union law.

From EU Normative Provisions to the Practice of Mutual Recognition

EU Normative Provisions

That the principle of loyalty is evolving into a general principle of Union law is underscored both by the normative provisions of the TEU itself and its "legal practices". For example, as regards the Union's external and security policy, Article 11, para 2, TEU requires that the member states support the Union's external and security policy "in a spirit of loyalty and mutual co-operation." Moreover, the member states have agreed to "refrain from any action which is contrary to the interests of the Union or likely to impair its effectiveness as a cohesive force in international relations" and the Council "shall ensure that these principles are complied with". Although the TEU is silent with regard to Union activity in the third pillar, it can quite easily be implied that similar loyalty obligations apply in that context. Article 43, paragraph 2, TEU for example, suggests that the relationship between "closer co-operation" law and "normal" EU law (in which the full quota of member states participate) is governed by the principle of loyalty.[36] The principle of loyalty thus applies in various forms and degrees across all the pillars and in all the spheres of Union activity.

It can be argued that the existence of a principle of mutual loyalty of legal systems pre-supposes in effect a requirement of homogeneity (or at least a certain degree thereof) in terms of basic (constitutional) values.[37] But the precise degree of homogeneity required in the relationship between the legal order of the EU and of the legal orders of its member states seems to be in continuous evolution. Since the Treaty of Amsterdam, Article 6, paragraph 1, TEU states that "the Union is founded on the principles of liberty, democracy, respect for human rights and fundamental freedoms, and the rule of law, principles which are common to the Member States". This provision arguably sets out the common constitutional principles that govern the relationships of loyalty in the EU and how they are to work. An example of the manner in which it can be given shape and

---

[35] n. 30 above.

[36] The principle of loyalty also informs the extension of the closer co-operation provisions to the second pillar in the new Treaty of Nice.

[37] See further, Verhoeven, n. 30 above.

form in a legislative context, involving a dialogue between the various levels of governance, is provided by recital 12 and Article 5 of the recently adopted Regulation on access to the documents of the European Parliament, Commission and the Council.[38]

At the same time a marked evolution has occurred in favour of EU rules providing the legal basis for interference by the EU as such in the member states democracy and fundamental rights affairs. This evolution has taken place both in the normative provisions of the EU and in its legal practices. Article 7 TEU (which has been procedurally refined by the Treaty of Nice) empowers the Council to take sanctions against a member state which violates in a serious and persistent manner the fundamental principles on which the European Union is founded. This implies that member states can be sanctioned in serious cases of human rights violations, even if these violations occur outside the scope of application of the EC Treaty.[39] A not dissimilar trend can be gleaned from the external relations context where the EU is imposing increasingly stringent "moral" requirements on non-member states when it provides development aid.[40]

A further example is provided by the Protocol on Asylum for the Nationals of the Member States of the EU (included by the Treaty of Amsterdam). The protocol establishes the principle that member states shall be regarded as constituting safe countries of origin in respect of each other for all legal and practical purposes in relation to asylum matters. Accordingly, a member state may only grant asylum to a national of another member state if certain conditions at the EU level are met. In other words, EU defined rules replace purely nationally defined ones and this provides a clear example of (potentially) far-reaching vertical enmeshment of the legal orders in question.

The Evolving "Legal Practice" of EU Mutual Recognition

In terms of "legal practice" the renewed lease of life which the principle of mutual recognition is experiencing outside classic internal market policy concerns is striking. The principle of mutual recognition in its classical EC reincarnation as an attempt to overcome market fragmentation resulting from differing standards adopted by member states, has been a cornerstone of the Community legal system for many years. It comes into play where, in the absence of harmonisation, a member state seeks to subject its goods (or services) from another member state to its own (indistinctly applicable) national rules, thereby constituting a barrier to trade. In such circumstances the principle of mutual recognition requires the host

---

[38] Regulation (EC) No 1049/2001, [2001] OJ L 145/43.

[39] See, in the case of sanctions imposed against Austria, B Bribosia et al., "Le controle par l'Union européenne du respect de la democratie et des droits de l'homme par ses Etats membres: à propos de l'Autriche" (2000) *JTDE* 61–4.

[40] See, in detail, M Bulterman, *Human Rights in the Treaty Relations of the European Community—Real Virtues or Virtual Reality?* (Antwerpen-Groningen, Oxford: Intersentia, Hart, 2001).

state to disapply its own national rules if the interests it seeks to protect through them are already met in an equivalent manner by the application of the rules of the exporting member state. In other words, whereas the principle of mutual recognition does not involve the transfer of regulatory powers to the European level, it nevertheless restricts the freedom of action of national governments (authorities) and obliges them to recognise and apply rules emanating from another member state (subject of course to caveats that certain minimum conditions are met).

In the Union context, in particular in the field of policy-making in police and judicial affairs, one can deduce the emergence and embedding of a principle of mutual recognition by the Union legislator (as opposed to the Treaty maker or the Court). This trend started in a sense in Title IV of the TEC, the newly imported title on immigration and asylum matters, and is now showing clear signs of spreading wider, to the third pillar *stricto sensu*. A striking example is the recently adopted directive on the mutual recognition of decisions on the expulsion of third country nationals.[41] The underlying principle is, in the words of Article 1 of the directive, "to make possible the recognition of an expulsion decision issued by a competent authority in one Member State . . . against a third country national present within the territory of another Member State". In other words, enforcing the decision by the issuing member state can be enforced in the member state by virtue of the principle of "mutual recognition". Moreover, the enforcing member state implements the decision according to its own law. The mutual recognition principle here entails that decisions taken in one member state should be accepted as valid in any other member state and put into effect on a reciprocal basis. In our view, this form of mutual recognition and enforcement constitutes a rather clear example of interlocking legal systems in pursuance of an overriding principle of loyalty at the EU level. As it has developed beyond its classical application in the field of goods, moreover, the principle of loyalty and of mutual recognition requires a more pro-active stance by the host state (from dis-application of its own rules in the original version to specific enforcement in the context of its own legal order).

In the emerging field of Union criminal law the beginnings of a principle of mutual recognition can also be detected. It was first mentioned in the conclusions of the European Council in Tampere in October 1999.[42] Andre Klip has called it a new variant of a type of "extrovert criminal law" which basically involves applying the criminal law of another member state in the enforcing member state.[43] In a Communication from the Commission to the European Parliament and the Council on the mutual recognition of final decisions in criminal cases (i.e. decisions that rule on the substance of a criminal case) the Commission placed considerable emphasis on the fact that in this context

---

[41] [2001] OJ L 150/147.

[42] <http://www.europa.eu.int/council/off/conclu/oct99/index.htm>.

[43] A Klip, *Nederlands strafprocesrecht en Europese harmonisatie* (Unpublished manuscript, Utrecht, 2001).

mutual trust is an important element: "not only trust in the adequacy of one's partners rules, but also trust that these rules are correctly applied". Moreover there is acknowledgement of the fact that mutual recognition must go hand in hand with approximation of laws.[44]

It is indeed fairly obvious that the principle of mutual recognition can only work well when there is considerable mutual trust between criminal justice systems.[45] That trust, in the words of the Council, is grounded, in particular, in the shared commitment of the member states to the principles of freedom, democracy and respect for human rights, fundamental freedoms and the rule of law (in other words on the common constitutional parameters as *per* Article 6 TEU).[46] In November 2000, the JHA Council adopted its "programme of measures" to implement the principle of "mutual recognition of decisions in criminal matters".[47] In adopting the programme, the Council met the deadline set at the Tampere summit (October 1999), where political agreement was reached on the use of the mutual recognition principle for integrating EU judicial systems. The programme is divided into four fields and comprises 23 far-reaching measures. Each measure has a priority rating for implementation, and each potentially requires specific EU legislation.

Mutual recognition comes in various shapes and may be sought at all stages of criminal proceedings, before, during or after conviction, but it is applied differently depending on the nature of the decision or the penalty imposed. In each of these areas the extent of the mutual recognition exercise is very much dependent on a number of parameters which determine its effectiveness, including the definition of minimum common national standards necessary to facilitate application of the principle of mutual recognition, for instance with regard to the competence of the courts. It is however no secret that the criminal justice systems of the member states display considerable divergence in procedures as well as in practice and culture. That is why there have been some calls recently for the parallel development of minimum procedural norms which the criminal justice systems must comply with. The Commission has announced in its most recent update to its "Scoreboard" in the field of Justice and Home Affairs that it intends to launch a Green Paper on the subject in 2002.[48] The understanding seems to be that European citizens must be given some countervailing (procedural and human rights) guarantees to counterbalance the operation of loyalty with regard to the enforcement of decisions in other member states. The suggestion is that the operation of a principle of loyalty in such sensitive fields as

[44] "Mutual Recognition of Final Decisions in Criminal Matters", Communication from the European Commission to the Council and the European Parliament, COM (2000) 495 final, 26.7.2000.
[45] "Programme of measures for the implementation of the principle of mutual recognition of decisions in civil and commercial matters", "A" Item Note from Coreper to Council, 13648/00, Justciv 130, 24.11.00.
[46] *Ibid.*
[47] *Ibid.*
[48] <http://www.europa.eu.int/comm/dgs/justice-home.pdf/com2001/278-en.pdf>.

criminal justice can only be effective and defensible if made subject to respect of certain EU imposed minimum parameters in procedural terms. In other words, all criminal investigations and all criminal procedures in all member states of the EU would have to fulfil the criteria of such minimum standards (which could then be regarded as part of the common constitutional standards as per Article 6 TEU). Moreover this approach necessarily implies that a given member state is free to apply a higher standard of protection. How this tension will work out in practice can only be the subject of speculation at this early stage of the debate in question.

Applying the Principle of Loyalty to EU Standards so as to Reduce Existing Rights of Citizens?

It has however not always been the case that a member state has been (or has felt itself to be) free to apply its own higher standards when the EC (EU) has legislated or taken action with regard to the formulation of standards of a penumbra of rights closely related to certain national constitutional "values" in the sense mentioned above. For example, in the *Metten* case we saw the Dutch *Raad van State* applying the provisions of the Council's Rules of Procedure (which were not considered to have direct effect) in order to pre-empt the more generous provisions of the Dutch Constitution on access to information.[49] The underlying rationale was one of loyalty to the Community institutions and their rules irrespective of quality and irrespective of their nature as directly effective rules or otherwise. Controversial as it undoubtedly was at the time it seems that, at least in the view of the Union institutions which participated in the co-decision procedure on the new regulation on access to information, the *Raad van State* indeed had this obligation even in the absence of direct effect of the relevant provision.

The newly adopted regulation on access to the documents of the European Parliament, Commission and Council appears to have been inspired by the line taken by the *Raad van State* in *Metten*.[50] Recital 15 states that: "even though it is neither the object or effect of this Regulation to amend national legislation on access to documents, it is nevertheless clear that, by virtue of the principle of loyal co-operation which governs relations between the Union institutions and the Member States, Member States should take care not to hamper the proper application of this Regulation and should respect the security rules of the institutions". One reading of the imperative fashion in which this recital is worded is that the principle of loyalty is employed so as to impose, in a one-track fashion, a requirement on member states to override their more extensive provisions

---

[49] *Alman Metten v. Ministry of Finance, July 7 1995 (Raad van State, afdeling administratie)*. See further, L Besselink, "Curing a Childhood Sickness? On Direct Effect, Internal Effect, Primacy and Derogation from Civil Rights" (1996) 3 *Maastricht Journal of European Law* 165.

[50] See n. 38 above.

of national law in cases of potential conflict. Moreover, the obligation of loyalty thus interpreted not only applies with regard to the substantive provisions of the regulation itself but also to the highly controversial (and certainly not directly applicable) rules of the Council regarding security.[51]

This example shows how the principle of loyalty of member states to the Union legal order is used by the decision-making institutions of the Union (Commission, Council and European Parliament) in order to ensure that fundamental principles of the national legal orders will not undermine an emergent fundamental principle of the Union legal order. In other words, the EU gives content and meaning to an evolving EU fundamental principle or civil right[52] in a more restrictive fashion than some of its member states and binds the member states in question and their citizens (who potentially see their rights reduced) by brandishing the principle of loyalty to pre-empt more favourable national (constitutional) rules. In effect, it seems that the minimum rule at the EU level overrides the maximum rule at the national level of some of the member states. Moreover, the principle of loyalty obliges the national courts in those circumstances to apply the EU rules in favour of the national rules.

An alternative approach which would have been more respectful of national traditions would have been to adopt a kind of subsidiarity principle which comes into play at the national level.[53] Where a fundamental right is better protected by the national standard national courts should also be allowed to apply that standard when EU action is at stake. In other words, the local maximum standard could prevail. As a result, the EU system of fundamental rights protection would be conceived in minimum terms only, in the same way as the European Convention on Human Rights. This approach could, however, lead to a situation where an EU measure would not be applied in some member states while being binding in its effect in other member states, a result which would affect adversely the uniformity and autonomy of EU law.

Recital no. 15 to the new access to documents regulation must be read in conjunction with its Article 5. This indicates just how and to what extent the scope of the regulation applies to documents authored by the three EU institutions in question even if the request for access is filed with the national authorities. Article 5 provides, in somewhat ambiguous language, that: "Where a Member State receives a request for a document in its possession, originating from an institution, unless it is clear that the document shall or shall not be handed out, the Member State shall consult with the institution concerned in order to take a decision that does not jeopardise the attainment of the objectives of this Regulation". In other words, the general rule is, that the member state consults

---

[51] Council Decision of 9 April 2001 on making certain categories of Council documents available to the public [2001] OJ L 111/29. The legality of this decision has been challenged before the European Court of Justice by the European Parliament.

[52] See further, the fascinating opinion by Advocate General Leger in Case C–353/99 P, *Council of the EU* v. *Hautala and others*, opinion of 10 July 2001, nyr and judgment of 6 December 2001, nyr.

[53] See for example, L Besselink, "Entrapped by the Maximum Standard: on Fundamental Rights, Pluralism and Subsidiarity in the European Union" (1998) 35 *Common Market Law Review* 629–80.

with the institution and that the rules of the Regulation prevail over national freedom of information rules. Whereas such a provision may indeed offer certainty and closes off certain undoubtedly irritating practices by some member states, it does not rule out all possibility of conflict, especially in the presence of national constitutional rules.[54] The point to emphasise here, however, is that pre-emption by EU rules seems to be effective even where no overriding interest in confidentiality can be upheld.

SOME CONCLUDING REMARKS

Our purpose has been to reveal and substantiate our claim that it is possible to speak of the evolving legal system of the European Union in terms of institutional unity both in terms of the (horizontal) international organisation itself and more particularly in terms of the relationship it enjoys in a vertical sense with the national legal systems of the member states. We have substantiated this conclusion by exploring those legal principles relating to questions of the legal validity of the EU rules itself and our understanding regarding their applicability in the national legal orders .We have concluded that on the basis of the rules laid down by the EU system itself (certain) Union law is capable of being directly applicable in the national legal orders and that, moreover, national judges and administrative authorities are under an obligation to give indirect effect to Union law. In addition we have attempted to explore the manner in which a principle of loyalty is taking shape at the level of the EU legal order itself as a key indicator of the intricate and evolving character of the relationship between the EU legal order and the national legal orders. With regard to the latter non-structural principle we have also sought to draw on actual examples in terms of legal practices and to demonstrate how this assists the process of conceptualising and evaluating the evolving vertical relationship between the legal orders in question.

In a sense, what may appear at times a rather abstract and theoretical exercise, of interest mainly to international and European lawyers and legal theorists, is also motivated by a concrete and practical desire to contribute to the ongoing debate about the future of Europe. After all, given the evolving reality of the European Union as such and the manner in which it has penetrated both social and legal understanding, why continue to obfuscate a relatively clear institutional reality by drawing elaborate distinctions between the Community legal order as such and the supposedly purely intergovernmental Union order (a social and legal fiction as we hope to have illustrated), thereby placing outside the range of common understanding the full constitutional significance of various important EU actors and processes? Moreover, does not the concept of institutional unity (both in a horizontal and vertical sense) contribute to a better

---

[54] See further, A Verhoeven, n. 30 above, 456 *et seq.*

understanding of the relationship between the various legal orders involved and so have a contribution to make in the post-Nice discussion on the manner in which powers must be shared across the various governance levels and applied in the various legal systems?

If anything has emerged from the debate on the future of the EU in recent months it is the overwhelming inability of the citizens in the various (existing and candidate) member states to understand what the EU as such is, what its tasks are, what the role of its institutions and various other actors and organs are and how this political system relates to their own national political and constitutional systems.[55] In our view it is in addressing the task of increasing understanding and rationalising the seemingly irrational and obtusely complicated that the real challenge lies in the coming months and years. And it is essential that the perspective of the citizen should ultimately assume central place and importance if we are genuinely to engage with the fact that at the beginning of the twenty-first century there is such widespread distrust in political institutions and politicians at all levels of our increasingly inter-connected societies.[56] That centrality of the individual is in our view enhanced by an approach which recognises and attempts to come to terms with the various levels of the multi-governance structure of the EU and its various intertwined legal systems as a complex institutional unity.

---

[55] See, in particular, the very useful and revealing *Perceptions of the European Union: A Qualitative Study of the Public's Attitudes to and Expectations of the European Union in the 15 Member States and the 9 Candidate Countries* (European Commission, June 2001).

[56] In this regard the long-awaited and much proclaimed *White Paper on European Governance*, COM (2001) 428 of 25 July 2001, published by the Commission can be regarded as a relatively weak and at times not very profound contribution to this critical and on-going debate.

5

Perspectives on Convergence Within the Theatre of European Integration

CAROLE LYONS[1]

INTRODUCTION

THERE IS A nice anecdote about a conversation between Samuel Beckett and James Joyce, who were friends in Paris in the 1930's; "Beckett was addicted to silences, and so was Joyce; they engaged in conversations which consisted often in silences directed towards each other, both suffused with sadness, Beckett mostly for the world, Joyce mostly for himself".[2] There are, after all, many different possible types of conversation; casual chats between friends, formal discussions in professional contexts, exchanges between priest and confessor or therapist and client, shouts in noisy cafés or whispers in hushed cathedrals, on telephones with no sight, in sign language with no words, and so forth. All of these, though, imply some exclusionary and closed dimension; there is a finite number of people who can take part in a (n effective) conversation, otherwise it ceases to be classed as such. The subject matter, whether static or fluid, is determined only by those taking part and while others may enter the conversation they do so only with the "permission" of the original participants. Furthermore, whatever the nature of the conversation it could also be said that in most, the body language, that is the imperceptible and unarticulated, non-verbal communication is more significant than the words (or signs) used.

The motif of "constitutional conversations" was chosen for this section of this collection in order to try and convey the extent to which constitutional law in Europe is affected by the constant dialogue between different levels of national, transnational and supranational polities. We had adopted the term "constitutional conversations" as signifying the various constructive ways in which national constitutional law and emergent EC/EU constitutional law are constantly being formed and re-formed under each other's influence. The idea was to explore how those constitutional conversations bring about degrees of convergence or divergence in constitutional law. This metaphor was intended to try and convey a sense of how in the complex judicial and political spaces, between

---

[1] With many thanks to Neil Walker for comments on an earlier draft.
[2] R Ellmann, *James Joyce* (Oxford: Oxford University Press, 1959) p. 661

national, transnational and supranational levels, constitutional conflict, compromise and consensus are negotiated leading to a level or levels of convergence in constitutional law in Europe. Bruno de Witte concentrates on the core of EC/EU constitutionalism by examining the processes of IGC negotiations and the methods by which Member State preferences and interests are mediated and converge in what he terms political conversations. National governments meet in intergovernmental formation to feel for footholds in the steep pathway that is the future of supranational integration. The chapter by Deirdre Curtin and Ige Dekker observes the process of convergence from a different perspective; their examination of the principles of loyalty and mutual recognition as underlying institutional unity in the EU demonstrates the subtle ways in which national laws are pressurised to converge under the influence of EU law. Both of these contributions go far beyond the usual focus of dialogue based analysis, namely, the ECJ-national court relationship. Though quite different in their separate approaches, the two chapters both throw light on the levels and methods of constitutional exchange within the EU polity. Both, too, address indirectly the extent to which these exchanges produce or are responsible for convergence within areas of European constitutional law. For de Witte, the high table of treaty negotiation is where future convergence is conceived, whereas for Curtin and Dekker it is the unstructured manner in which convergence flows from the operation of mutual recognition which is critically analysed.

Against this background, in this chapter, I suggest that the "conversation" metaphor may not be broad enough to encapsulate the complex nature of convergence within "the messy constitutional tapestry"[3] of the EU. Looking at particular instances of convergence, from a positive perspective, I see them as occurring within a system of plural and intermingling constitutional confluence within the European public law space in a manner that is more akin symbolically to a theatre of voices rather than a confined conversation. De Witte argues in his chapter that the IGC is "the closest thing to a constitutional conversation in Europe"; the analysis here suggests that the plurality of constitutional voices are expressed on a wider stage, which includes the IGC but which also draws in a much larger number of participants, the audience if you like. I chose this theatrical metaphor to convey some sense of the intricacy and complexity and dynamism of the way in which constitutional-type convergence is spontaneously generated in Europe.[4] The image of a theatre of voices allows us to imagine and see how parts can be played by many with many different "plots" or scenarios being developed simultaneously and not necessarily in any organised or focused manner. Many of the chapters in this collection lend substance to this image of a plurality of public law developments within the European legal order (Walker, de Búrca, Curtin and Dekker, Nic Shuibhne). Integration seen as a theatre of voices suggests the possibility of multiple scenarios, actors

---

[3] P Craig, "Constitutions, Constitutionalism, and the European Union" (2001) 7 *ELJ* 125 at 146.

[4] This is inspired in particular by the tradition of the "radical" French theatre, from Jarry, Artaud and Giradoux through to Peter Brook.

at many different levels, limited hierarchies, potential for open participation and a grouping of people governed by mutual interdependence, willingly accepted. With the overall framework of participation in European public law viewed thus as an active, open one, I consider how various voices have been expressed within it leading to what for the purpose of this collection is termed "convergence".

There are three broader, background themes which inform my discussion of convergence. First a brief word on terminology; what I understand and mean by the use of that term for the purpose of the argument here is, that within the realm of national and supranational public law of the EU, there is an ongoing process whereby those laws are mutually influenced which has resulted in shared or common principles. The Curtin and Dekker chapter reveals that such convergence does not always respect principles of democracy and accountability and the Legrand and Harlow chapters consider such elements of convergence to be undesirable and untenable from many perspectives. However, the approach in this chapter, while not ignoring the negative consequences, focuses on instances of convergence which can contribute to the legal order of the EU (including national legal orders) in a constructive and forward-looking way.

Secondly, this discussion of convergence attempts to delve beneath the seemingly rather fossilised, inhuman face[5] of legal integration and suggest the involvement and participation of actors at many different levels in the transnational judicial space. This leads me to suggest that there are, behind the curtain of the Treaties and the more formal operation of the EC/EU legal order, informal and sometimes imperceptible ways in which shared views, values and aspirations (a mentalité) are being formed. In other words, reading between the lines of the ordered[6], "hard text" of the process of (legal) integration, there is an evolving sense of a European common good which can be said to represent an emergent European (legal) culture.

Thirdly, in order to draw out this system of plural convergence I discuss recent cases and opinions from the ECJ. This jurisprudence seeks to demonstrate that, viewed through the lens of (positive) convergence, the relationship between the EU and the Member States (and other actors) is one of mutual respect and equality. By this I mean that convergence is not necessarily predicated on European Union institutional railroading of national values or culture or laws[7] but involves the EU judicial space absorbing national influences and building upon them rather than diluting them, respecting the national or local input. In identifying different variations of convergence within European public law, I argue that such instances contribute to and are an essential part of the foundations of a system of constitutional pluralism which is not (yet) tangible

---

[5] See I Ward, "Beyond Constitutionalism; The search for a European Political Imagination" (2001) 7 *ELJ* 24.

[6] P Legrand, ch. 12 in this volume.

[7] Although see Curtin and Dekker, ch. 4 in this volume for examples of this and also P Legrand for the contrary argument.

or easily defined but which is operative and working in unformed ways. In other words, the theatre of voices within the European constitutional space is very active without having a formal structured framework (normally but not necessarily a written constitution) to control it. I see the way in which convergence operates, with non-exclusive participation, with subtle recognition of common European principles, as a primitive early constitutionalism.[8] There are increasingly frequent calls for a written constitution for Europe and though these have largely specific political agendas, any committed project for such a document would need to be fully informed by the constitutional history and heritage of the Union. When the history books write of the formation of that constitution it will not be sufficient to mention the constitutional landmarks, the biased political support and say, thus was a constitution formed. For it to survive, it will be the fact there was underlying, often ignored and unarticulated support in the form of an allegiance to what the peoples of Europe shared which assured this. What is significant is that convergence is not viewed as an imposed, top down process; it is precisely a consequence of European legal culture, or common conceptions and shared values. Constitutionalism is a fragmentary and varied process. It is also a divisive process with tensions between the search for core principles and the trend towards establishing diversity and flexibility as having fundamental status.[9] Convergence is part of this process and there is no end point to such a process of convergence.[10] It is one of the constitutionalising forces which Neil Walker discusses.[11] These obviously include the well known constitutional beacons (such as *Van Gend* and *Costa*), but they also embrace the "small" cases in which the common and often unarticulated is given voice. In looking at some of the instances of convergence here I see a system of constitutional interactions and relationships operative both beneath and above the more formal and overt ones which are well recognised. They are part of the culture of constitutionalism in Europe, the underlying spirit of a European legal culture.[12] I see the convergent elements which I discuss here as an inherent part of constitutional practice within European law, as one of the many sources of the emerging constitution. They contribute to the gradual growth of an as yet unknown, unseen, and hard to imagine, constitutional formation of the future.[13]

---

[8] See N Walker, "Constitutionalism in a New Key", in G de Búrca and J Scott (eds.), *The EU and the WTO: Legal and Constitutional Aspects* (Oxford: Hart, 2001) and also, "The Idea of Constitutional Pluralism" (2002 MLR, forthcoming) arguing against a threshold definition which essentialises European constitutionalism.

[9] See further, G de Búrca and J Scott (eds.), *The European Constitution: between Uniformity and Flexibility* (Oxford: Hart, 2000).

[10] Comment by Z Bankowski, Symposium on European Public Law, Convergence or Divergence, Aberdeen, May 2000 and see further, Z Bankowski and E Christodoulidis, "The European Union as an essentially contested project" in Z Bankowski and A Scott (eds.), *The European Union and its Order* (Oxford: Blackwell, 2000) at p. 17.

[11] Ch. 13, below, note 37.

[12] The sort of common good referred to for example in the Preamble to the Irish Constitution 1937; see J M Kelly, *The Irish Constitution* (Dublin: Butterworths, 1980).

[13] *Ibid.*, p. 19 for a discussion of the gradual formation of the Irish Constitution.

These three themes, "positive" convergence, leading to a European culture, as part of early constitutionalism, form a broad theoretical framework for the analysis of the cases below. Beforehand, I consider some of the arguments raised against convergence.

ARGUMENTS AGAINST CONVERGENCE

Gunther Tuebner, in his analysis of the transplanting of good faith into British law by means of an EC Directive, argues that "foreign rules are irritants not only in relation to the domestic legal discourse itself but also in relation to the social discourse to which law is, under certain circumstances, closely coupled . . . [and that] the result of such a complex and turbulent process is rarely a convergence of the participating legal orders but rather the creation of new cleavages . . .".[14] He, like the others considered in this section, regards or deals with transplantation as a one way process, from outside in, into an established legal order. So, if we consider the question "are European legal systems converging?"[15], it implies we are trying to see to what extent the established individual European national legal systems have been or can be brought closer through the process of absorption or transplantation of influences and rules from each other. It is this view of (possible) convergence which has attracted most contrary argument. The negative consequences and/or impossibility ("transferred rules can only serve as an irritation" . . . etc.) of national legal systems successfully converging or effectively receiving outside or "foreign" legal rules is the focus of much of the debate. A different perspective on convergence, namely the manifestation and expression of shared values and principles, means it can be seen instead as a horizontal dynamic both between Member States and from Member State-to-EU. In other words, the locus of the convergence is not necessarily national legal orders but the wider EC legal order itself. Within the debate on the (im)possibility of convergence are arguments which, if inverted and viewed from another perspective, can expose it as a positive process, a consequence of a nascent legal culture or new ways of communicating and understanding through and with legal norms which is brought about by integration.[16] This is not to deny the obvious tensions which are caused as national legal orders either receive or resist outside rules in the necessary transformation they must undergo as part of the European legal order; there will be irritation and divergence as an inevitable part of this complex process. "European constitutionalism is inherently unstable"[17] and it is natural

---

[14] G Teubner, "Legal Irritants: Good Faith in British Law or How Unifying Law Ends Up in New Divergences" (1998) 61 *MLR* 11.

[15] See further, P Legrand, *Fragments on Law-as-Culture* (Deventer: WEJ Tjeenk Willink, 1999).

[16] See J Habermas, "Remarks on Dieter Grimm's 'Does Europe Need a Constitution?' " (1995) 3 *ELJ* at 305.

[17] See further, L Catá Backer, "Forging Federal Systems within a Matrix of Contained Conflict" (1998) Jean Monnet Papers, Harvard Law School, <http://www.law.harvard.edu/Programs/JeanMonnet/papers/98/98–4-.html>.

that suggestions of convergence will be met with opposition. But in the wider and longer term view of integration, degrees of convergence, whether organic and participatory, or involuntary and forced, are part of the creative conflict that results from the dialogue between legal orders in the EU.

Among the strongest of the voices against convergence is Pierre Legrand, whose work on this subject is well known.[18] In his chapter in this collection he, along with Carol Harlow, rails against what they both see as a kind of convergent fundamentalism sponsored and endorsed by order-seeking EC lawyers in search of coherence at all costs. But convergence does not flow only from the agents of a legal order but also from those who take active, day-to-day part in it. Secondly, I see the rather crude coupling of the local v the trans/supranational as in itself an artificially ordered view of the nature of the EC/EU legal order. Yet there is in fact much in both the Legrand and Harlow contributions which lends implicit support to a view of convergence in European public law that is not damaging to the national legal system and national cultures. Legrand sees the claims to convergence as leading to the covering up of the living process of society,[19] but convergence processes can be said to the contrary to give life to these processes. Convergence and the "textuality"[20] of the EC legal order are not necessarily at odds with each other but rather are each part of a more complex, interweaving of processes,[21] the implications of which can bring legal systems closer to each other without inevitable challenge. Ultimately, Legrand has a pessimistic and insular view of the potential of any convergence process, limited as it is to the absorption of influences from other legal systems. The key to understanding this view, and the alternative one, is perspective; Legrand views the national legal system and its "*loiness*" or distinctiveness from inside, looking out at and requiring protection from foreign influences. However, convergence within the fertile plurality of the EU legal order does not have to be limited to this one-way dynamic; national or local level values, cultures and laws also transplant to other legal systems, including that of the EU. In his evocation of loose but resilient cultural units,[22] Legrand implicitly denies the possibilities of this alternative perspective, as if European integration had not brought about any change whatsoever in the outlook of citizens' views on issues concerning the nature and operation of law,[23] whether national or supranational.[24] Just as much as he sees "Frenchness" behind French *lois*, there is no reason to believe

---

[18] See further, *supra* n. 15.

[19] P Legrand, ch. 12.

[20] *Ibid.*

[21] See also the Walker and de Búrca chs. in this collection on this point.

[22] P Legrand, ch. 12.

[23] See further, J L Gibson and G A Caldeira, "The Legal Cultures of Europe" (1996) 30 *Law and Society Review* 55.

[24] In *How Europeans See Themselves* (Luxembourg: European Commission, 2000), the "worries of Europeans" rank "loss of traditional values" rather low (13% worried) as compared to the environment (63%) or unemployment and crime (p. 41). Furthermore, in a survey of young Europeans, the loss of cultural diversity is also ranked very low compared to other "meanings" of European integration; 13% as opposed to 34% seeing the EU as representing "a better future" (p. 55).

that there is not an element of Europeanness behind ECJ decisions or Council Directives as an expression of an emergent "supranational sensibility". The narrow "convergence or not" lens is one way of trying to convey some of the essence of the nature of this sensibility. Yet Pierre Legrand himself nicely describes national sensibility in terms which could just as aptly be used to capture the sense of an evolving equivalent—a collective identity at supranational level; "less conscious, less formulated attitudes habits and feelings, or even unconscious assumptions, bearings and commitments" which are difficult to verbalise.[25] Ultimately, his argument works only if you accept that national (legal) cultures will eternally look inwards rather than outwards, a static view of European cultures in other words. But in the theatre of integration, the culture dynamic is not unidirectional and it is not only the main actors (member states, EU institutions) who have the potential to influence the action.

Carol Harlow's fundamental objection to viewing convergence of European public law in a positive light is based on the need to protect the local from universalising imperatives. In this she shares a certain amount of perspective with Curtin and Dekker and their analysis of the implications of mutual recognition for national principles. But it is quite hard to see precisely what is the source of the threat to Harlow's "local". She presents a vision of passive consent to elite action and specifically rails against Civil Codes and similar harmonising initiatives. Here, as in the case of the Legrand argument, I see the objections to convergence founded upon a somewhat constrained vision; European citizens do act within the European judicial space, they are not a passive, ignorant force. Sure, they do so in limited circumstances but, despite the borders, despite the persistence of the local as their most immediate trope, they share problems and also attitudes, beliefs and values with respect to law.[26] The problems, and therefore the solutions, cross borders and so the local cannot always provide judicial solace as it might once have. Gráinne de Búrca draws attention to this also in her chapter.[27] Finally, much of the Harlow argument draws attention to the over-activist ECJ and its role in the attempts to force convergence. Yet, an interesting element of arguments based on the role of the court and its over-inventive interpretations of the Treaty is that the latter have never been challenged before the Court itself. Parties involved in EC litigation have never sought to invoke the "illegality" of direct effect or supremacy or even Member State liability. These fundamental principles have gone unchallenged since their original expression by the ECJ. If that Court is seen by some as forcing "universalising imperatives", why have they not been questioned? Certainly, the fact that these principles have gone unchallenged is not an unqualified endorsement of closer integration and Union but it is a forceful argument for the threshold legitimacy of European legal culture. Harlow herself draws attention to the need for a legal system to be respected yet the unchallenged authority of the ECJ to pronounce fundamental

---

[25] P Legrand, p 234, note 37 citing R Williams.
[26] Gibson and Caldeira, *supra*, n. 23, p. 58.
[27] de Búrca, ch. 8, this collection.

principles points to a legal institution which is very much respected. If the ECJ is seen in some quarters as an instrument of illegitimate convergence then it is not apparent that this view is so widespread.[28]

Deirdre Curtin and Ige Dekker take a different approach to the dangers of convergence trend in their chapter.[29] Their piece shows how the (unified) EU legal order is bringing about convergence in subtle and unstructured ways. With the focus of most of the other contributions being on the EC legal order, this chapter takes us further along the convergence/divergence debate in examining the ways in which it might be emerging from the EU (rather than merely EC) legal order. The main emphasis of their paper is on the vertical relationship between the EU order and the member states and this is illustrated in two ways, both of which go to confirming in their view the reality of EU as legal order. Their development of a validity/application theory demonstrates how the EU order *per se* penetrates the member state orders while their analysis of the principle of loyalty exposes the ways in which national laws are affected (and are converging) as a result of allegiance to this principle. They are here expanding upon "a Utrecht approach" to the nature of the evolving EU legal order observed from the perspective of theory, treaty provisions and legal practices.[30] The developing institutional unity of the EU is seen as gradually emerging from EU and member states being intertwined through the operation of both legal principles and legal practices.

The way in which they introduce the element of convergence stems from their discussion of loyalty and the importance of mutual recognition within interlocking legal systems. Each order recognises the other's autonomy and difference but does so within mutually applicable limits. They assert that loyalty is evolving into a general principle of EU law which can be seen from treaties and legal practices of the Union: Article 11 and Article 43 TEU for example. The consequence of the operation of this loyalty to each other's legal systems presupposes homogeneity in terms of basic constitutional values, itself a process in continuous evolution. Thus, extrapolating, the suggestion is that convergence within the realm of constitutional law is being brought about because of the loyalty principle in EU law. Furthermore, EU rules now allow interference by the EU in member state democracy and fundamental rights. This occurs in the context of sanctions, Article 7 TEU, and also external relations and asylum. Because of the operation of mutual recognition, even when this does not involve the

---

[28] In *How Europeans See Themselves* (Luxembourg, 2000) the Court of Justice is "trusted" more than the Council of Ministers or the Commission with 45% of respondents tending to trust the ECJ. It is the second most trusted institution after the European Parliament. The more recently published, *Perceptions of the European Union* (European Commission, 2001), highlights however that "lack of knowledge" about the institutions [in general] is startling with often total ignorance of institutional mechanisms. The Court of Justice is, nonetheless, recognised more than the Council of Ministers which is not generally known (p. 9).

[29] Ch. 4.

[30] See further D Curtin and I Dekker, "The EU as a 'Layered' International Organization: Institutional Unity in Disguise" in G de Búrca and P Craig (eds.), *The Evolution of EU Law* (Oxford: OUP, 1999) p. 83.

transfer of regulatory powers to European level it does restrict the freedom of action of member state authorities and obliges them to apply rules from another member state. This is an example of how convergence in European legal systems can be brought about because of the (negative) influence of EC/EU law. The directive on third country nationals and the area of European Union criminal law are given as examples of the negative consequence of interlocked legal systems. Curtin and Dekker point out that it is imperative that citizens be given guarantees to counterbalance this operation of loyalty and its convergent effects. They discuss the Dutch *Metten* case in which the national court gave priority to EU rules over national standards, bound by the principle of loyalty. This would accord well with both Harlow and Legrand, fears for the protection of local laws and legal culture against EU imperatives; EC/EU law can have convergent effects which are damaging to well established national principles. As Curtin and Dekker point out, in a piece which strongly emphasises the need to increase citizenship understanding within the EU polity, such forced convergence can only have the effect of alienating citizens even further.

There are other sources voicing support for this general view of EC law as alienating and as intruding upon the local and upon national legal cultures. Ian Ward, for example, warns against the impoverished constitutionalism of EU law and its dehumanising effects.[31] He decries the lack of political affinity with the EU polity and its alienating jurisprudential discourse. Continuing in this vein, elsewhere, he has called for the need for narratives by which people can make sense of their condition and interpret their common life.[32] Both Legrand and Ward are articulating the problems of the alienation of the integration project but there is a fundamental difference in perspective; for Legrand, national legal culture is inherently and perpetually closed to any outside imports from integration. His view is that there is no possibility of seeing or creating a shared legal culture at EU level. Ward on the other hand, while deeply critical of current deficits of supranational law in particular, does not seem to deny scope for the emergence of something more positive in the future.

Neil Walker comments that Ward can be read as saying that "law [lacks] the sensibility to articulate and inculcate a new ethic of belonging".[33] This would imply that both unconverged and converged legal systems are fundamentally unable to appeal to the need for creating a "shared context of possible understanding"[34] or the type of commonality to which Ward refers. I discuss, in the next section, how this might be possible, *because* of the convergent potential of legal integration. Convergence does not necessarily equate with loss (of national culture, of local standards, of belonging, humanity); it can produce a positive gain as opposed to more frequently bemoaned losses. This may lie behind the

---

[31] I Ward (2001), *supra*, n. 5.
[32] I Ward, "Amsterdam and the Continuing Search for Community" in D O'Keeffe and P Twomey (eds.), *Legal Issues of the Amsterdam Treaty* (Oxford: Hart, 1998).
[33] N Walker, *supra*. n. 8, "The Idea of Constitutional Pluralism".
[34] J Habermas, *supra*, n. 16.

fact that member states have specifically never attempted to dam the flow of actual or possible convergence of their legal systems under the influence of EC/EU law. Precious and unique as their national legal cultures are and vital though national democratic standards are, in the real "constitutional conversation"[35] the actors often appear unthreatened by potential convergence. Equally, the Luxembourg Accords were never invoked to protect "vital" national cultural or democracy interests.[36] Member state governments seemingly are less threatened by convergence than the voices of difference suggest.

CONVERGENCE BEFORE THE COURTS

The essential argument of the previous section was that, contrary to some other voices in the debate, transplants do not have to be regarded as necessary irritants. To do so is too narrow a view of legal cultures generally but more so in the context of European legal culture, of European integration. The goals sought by communities, at national or supranational level, can have fundamental tensions and there is nothing unexpected about that. Equally, the reaction to and reception of the convergent effects of the EC/EU legal order are manifestly imbued with tensions and contradictions. Curtin and Dekker, in their effort to uncover some of the obfuscations of the EU legal order, use a magnifying glass to see it properly. In order to observe the multiple workings of convergence, an instrument more like a sensor or radar might be more appropriate at "measuring" the reality of converging legal systems as this is often not tangible or articulated in obvious ways. The process of convergence is just as amorphous in its many manifestations as national legal cultures can be. To take this point further, convergence born of a coming together of national cultures in a given context under the influence of and with the facilitation of the EU legal order, is just as complex and fluid as the legal systems which lie beneath. A few examples of recent decisions and Opinions from the ECJ may help us to "feel in the dark" for some of the various manifestations of convergence and transplanting, either way, member state to EU and vice versa.

The first is *Netherlands* v. *Council*[37] where the ECJ found that "the domestic legislation of most Member States enshrined in a general manner the public's right of access to documents held by public authorities as a constitutional or legislative principle". Secondly, take the recently delivered Opinion of AG Léger in *Council* v. *Hautala*.[38] In this case, concerning access to documents/information from the EC institutions, the Council appealed from the Court of First Instance decision, claiming that that Court misconstrued Decision 93/731, and sought to

[35] de Witte, ch. 3.
[36] P Craig, "Constitutions, Constitutionalism, and the European Union" (2001) 7 *ELJ* 125.
[37] Case C–58/94 *Netherlands* v. *Council* [1996] ECR I–2169.
[38] Case C–353/99 P *Council of the European Union* v. *Heidi Hautala*, appeal from the Court of First Instance, Opinion dated 10 July 2001 nyr, and judgment of 6 December 2001 nyr.

make a distinction between a right to information and a right of access to public documents. *Netherlands* v. *Council* did not concern, in substance, the nature of the right to, or principle of, access to documents in EC law. But the finding of shared attitudes in member states, accompanied by the Commission's study of comparative access to document rights, is the basis for Léger pointing out in his Opinion that this consensus amongst member state laws "reflects the strength and relevance of that right."[39] In a development paralleling the developments at EC level, a large number of states have amended their domestic legislation since 1996. This "convergence of national laws . . . constitutes a decisive reason for recognising the existence of a fundamental right of access to information held by Community institutions".[40] The AG goes on to emphasise that 13 out of 15 member states have a general rule on public right of access to information held by the administration and even though such rules are not identical, they demonstrate a "common conception in most of the Member States".[41] This reference to a common conception is in fact reminiscent of the kind of unarticulated, shared, mentalité to which Legrand refers. He does so for the opposite reason of highlighting the inevitable differences between the member states but here it is evoked as evidence of closeness amongst member state laws. As Léger recalls, such "convergence of constitutional traditions" suffices to establish the existence of a principle of a fundamental right at EC level without the need to draw on other European or international instruments. Indeed, he asserts that "it may suffice that Member States have a common approach to the right in question, demonstrating the same desire to provide protection" relying on *Hauer* and *Hoechst* to make this contention.[42] The existence of this common conception in Member State constitutional traditions leads the AG to state that " it appears natural to me to accept that there exists a principle of access to information held by the national public authorities and that that principle is such that it would engender an equivalent principle at Community level".[43] This leads him finally to two main contentions; first, that Community institutions should be subject to the same principle of access which is common to the member state institutions and, secondly, that transfer of sovereignty in specific fields should be accompanied by similar transfer of safeguards accorded to citizens.[44]

This Opinion by Léger concerns the construction of a fundamental principle in the EC legal order based upon recognising shared traditions and conceptions at member state level. The key tenet of his argument is that such shared

---

[39] Para. 54 of the Opinion

[40] Para. 55.

[41] Para. 58.

[42] Para. 69, Case 44/79 *Hauer* v. *Land Rheinland-Pfalz* [1979] ECR 3727 and Cases 46/87 and 227/88 *Hoechst AG* v. *Commission* [1989] ECR 2859.

[43] Para. 59.

[44] He also seeks the support of the provisions in the Charter of Fundamental Rights of the European Union, relying on the solemnity of its form and the procedure which led to its adoption to suggest that it is a privileged instrument for identifying fundamental rights and a source of guidance as to the true nature of the Community rules of positive law (para. 83).

traditions as to fundamental principle are a sufficient basis for the establishment of a similar principle at Community level. The consequence: convergence in national laws is the basis for a fundamental right in EC law. This is an example of what might be termed reverse "or bottom-up convergence"; it is the other side of the convergence coin as compared to the view of convergence taken in most debates on the subject. It is a positive perspective, viewing convergence as happening amongst member state laws, under the influence of or at the same time as a development in EC law, which in turn influences a development in Community law. However, such a view contrasts with Curtin and Dekker in this regard as they specifically highlight the area of access to information to show the negative effects of Community law. I expand on this further below.

A final point about the access to information story is that as well as providing an example of non-irritating convergence it also demonstrates an interesting trajectory from a moment of "political conversation" of the type which Bruno de Witte refers to in his chapter. The right of access to documents/to information began life as a political statement in the form of a Declaration attached to the Maastricht Treaty. This is a demonstration of the significance of the IGC process and how an EC "fundamental right" or principle can develop from a merely political product of that process into a full blown fundamental right; a relatively short journey, in fact, from politically influenced initiative via Court endorsement into acknowledgement as right. AG Léger in *Hautala* emphasises the importance of this consistent political will by the member states.[45] As he points out, Declaration No 17 is the first tangible act in which the Community acknowledged the general right of access to information. Of course, not all IGC initiatives are similarly successfully "implanted" in the body of EC law; EU citizenship occupies a grand and lofty position in the Treaty (Articles 18–22) but has yet to receive proper attention from either political or judicial institutions since its placing there.

In their analysis of the institutional unity of the legal order of the EU, Curtin and Dekker draw on the principle of loyalty, based on Article 10 EC, which they argue is "evolving into a general principle of Union Law".[46] There are two, independent, interesting aspects of this argument; first, that a loyalty principle/obligation can be traced in Union (as opposed to Community) provisions and, secondly, that the operation of a "general principle" can be extended to Union legislative activity and policies. This has wide ranging implications for the future judicial control and interpretation of the action of the Union. How loyalty works in this context is seen in "interference by the EU as such in member states democracy and fundamental rights"[47] and in the evolving legal practice of EU mutual recognition. This inevitably restricts the freedom of action of national governments and obliges them to recognise and apply rules

---

[45] Case C–353/99 P *Council of the European Union* v. *Heidi Hautala*, appeal from the Court of First Instance, Opinion dated 10 July 2001, para. 52 nyr.

[46] D Curtin and I Dekker, ch. 4.

[47] *Ibid.*

emanating from another member state. This might be said to be "enforced" convergence as opposed to voluntary or spontaneous convergence which works only if there is mutual trust in each other's systems. The positive implications of a theory of loyalty are not reciprocated in practice as it can operate as to reduce the existing rights of citizens. This "enforced convergence" via loyalty can have the result that member states feel unable to apply their own (higher) standards in the face of EC/EU provisions which are closely related to national constitutional values. Curtin and Dekker return to the access to information field, citing *Metten* as an example of a national authority/Court, in the face of convergence at EU level, applying EC rules in order to pre-empt the more generous provisions of the national constitution.[48] This position is implicitly endorsed more recently in the enactment of Regulation No 1049/2001 on Public Access to Parliament, Council and Commission Documents which specifically mentions the principle of loyal co-operation which should ensure that member states "do not hamper the proper application of the Regulation".

Both of these examples from access to information contrast in a marked way with Léger's Opinion in *Hautala*, and as Curtin and Dekker point out, suggest that the "principle of loyalty is employed so as to impose an obligation on member states to override their more extensive provisions of national law in case of conflict".[49] Loyalty is operating, they argue, so that fundamental principles of national legal orders will not undermine an emergent fundamental principle of the Union legal order".[50] This is what writers such as Legrand and Harlow are afraid of; the overriding of national constitutional values by binding principles of EU law. How does this possibly fit in with analysis of the type given by Léger? Is the latter an exercise in window dressing, hiding the reality of the convergence process? Or it is a matter of perspective; whichever way you look at it, convergence, even on precisely the same substantive issue can be seen as either positive or negative?

After Léger's arguments in *Hautala*, one might believe the relationship between convergence in national laws and fundamental principles of EC law to be quite clear and straightforward. The next case considered shows this not to be so. The recently decided *Jippes v. Minister van Landbouw*,[51] does present another example of what I would term (potential) positive convergence. It demonstrates also how a degree of convergence amongst member state laws can lead to the expression of a need to see that particular law or principle confirmed at Community level. It was a reference from the College van Beroep voor het bedrijfsleven (Adminstrative Court for Trade and Industry), in the Netherlands, which was dealt with by way of accelerated Article 234 procedure,[52] and addressed the question of the legality of the policy of slaughter to control

---

[48] *Metten* v. *Ministry of Finance*, July 1995 (Raad van State, afdeling administratie).
[49] Curtin and Dekker, ch. 4, p. 75.
[50] *Ibid.*
[51] Case C–189/01, decided on 12 July 2001 [2001] ECR I–5689.
[52] Art. 104a ECJ Rules of Procedure.

foot-and-mouth disease. Ms Jippes asked to have her animals[53] vaccinated rather than slaughtered. This request was denied by the Dutch agriculture ministry and Jippes appealed that decision to the referring court and raised an argument that the relevant Community law containing a vaccination ban was incompatible with the European Convention on the Protection of Animals kept for farm purposes. The relevant Community law on foot-and-mouth disease is Directives 85/511 and 90/423 which provide for the slaughter of animals in the case of a foot-and-mouth outbreak as well as emergency vaccination in specific circumstances as an exception to a slaughtering policy. These were supplemented by Decision 2001/246 dealing specifically with the Netherlands outbreak. The relevant animal welfare provisions are found in both international[54] and Community rules, the latter being Declaration No 24 and Protocol attached to the TEU.[55] Aside from the particular foot-and-mouth vaccination/slaughter issues, Jippes and the other appellants contended that the vaccination ban was contrary to what they termed was a general principle of animal welfare protection in Community law. As the Court summarised, this contention was based on the fact that "that principle forms part of the collective legal consciousness" [of the Member States].[56] The fact that animal welfare was not listed amongst the objectives of the Community should not, according to Jippes and the other appellants, affect its establishment as a general principle or, alternatively as "an interest to be taken into account in making a policy choice".[57] The question raised by the referring Court was whether such rule or principle forms part of the Community legal order.

The ECJ looked to various Community sources and found insufficient support for the establishment of animal welfare as a general principle of Community law. The lack of its inclusion amongst the Treaty objectives, no well-defined principle in the TEU protocol and Article 30's reference to the life of animals by way of exception only, led the Court to conclude that the need to ensure animal welfare is not to be regarded as a general principle of Community law. However, it is to be classed as an interest of the Community to be taken into account in the formulation and implementation of policy. The Court did not address the argument as to "collective legal consciousness" and in fact, to the contrary, draws attention to the differences which currently exist between the legislation of Member States as well as "the various sentiments harboured within those Member States".[58] In substance, it finds that the protection and health of animals *was* taken into account in the formulation of Community policy; i.e. both the general slaughter provisions and the specific Decision of 2001 were in fact aimed at improving the health of animals.

---

[53] Four sheep and two goats.

[54] The European Convention for the Protection of Animals kept for Farming Purposes.

[55] It is interesting to contrast the different paths of Declaration No 17 (access to information) and this Declaration.

[56] Para. 48 of the Decision.

[57] *Ibid.*, para. 54.

[58] Para. 79.

In dismissing the possibility of a general principle of animal welfare protection the Court does not develop any lengthy argument as to the differences which exist between member states or the meaning of "sentiments" as to animal welfare. It presents these differences and sentiments as a given without acknowledging the legitimacy of a contrary argument as to a shared, collective legal consciousness. Was it swayed by the economic implications of any positive endorsement of animal welfare as a principle? Was it the wrong case (involving only six endangered animals) or the wrong time, coming as it did in the middle of widespread foot-and-mouth outbreaks across the EU and the largely economic interest arguments raised by the six states intervening in the case? It is true that the denial of a general principle in this case was not primarily rooted in the assertion of differences in member states law and legal culture or culture as to animal welfare for only Community law sources in essence are examined. But the claim that animal welfare protection should be classed as a general principle formed the significant first part of the referring Court's questions founded on the appellants' claims as to collective consciousness. The ECJ is willing to draw, briefly, upon the position of animal welfare in member state laws and attitudes as part of the negative assessment of general principle but ignores that this might in any way feed into an opposing argument. The denial of general principle completely ignores the possibility of some element of collective legal consciousness which might affect this negative analysis. This approach contrasts in marked fashion with the arguments of AG Léger in *Hautala* and I compare the two positions further below.

But first a brief discussion of an interesting point made in a recent Opinion by AG Jacobs[59] in *Netherlands* v. *European Parliament and Council*.[60] The Netherlands was seeking to have Directive 98/44 (on the legal protection of biotechnology) annulled, its objection, in essence, based on "the notion that plants, animals and parts of the human body may be patentable",[61] raising six specific grounds for annulment, including subsidiarity and human rights. Recital 6 in the Directive refers to "*ordre public* and morality" and inventions are to be unpatentable if they offend either of these. The national patent office and courts are required by the Directive to look to ethical and moral principles recognised in a member state in order to determine whether *ordre public* is threatened. There is a history of this practice in Community intellectual property law; i.e. a refusal of registration if national public policy is offended, which refusal is subject to review by the EC. Nonetheless, national authorities may determine the scope of the concept of public morality in accordance with their own scale of values. But Jacobs in this Opinion, considering the issue of legal certainty of the Directive and whether public morality and *ordre public* are sufficiently clear, suggests that the limits of this, national or local discretion now be

---

[59] As in the Léger Opinion, the recently proclaimed Charter of Fundamental Rights is here also cited as if it were a potentially legally binding instrument.

[60] Opinion of AG Jacobs in Case C–377/98, 14 June 2001 nyr and judgment of 9 October 2001 nyr.

[61] Para. 10 of the Opinion.

revised and reviewed. "It may be that the ethical dimension of [patenting of biotechnology] is now more appropriately regarded as governed by common standards".[62] He relies for this on a decision of the Technical Board of Appeal of the European Patent Office in 1995. Morality was there defined as being founded on "the totality of the accepted norms which are deeply rooted in a particular culture".[63] This is a statement which would find acceptance with those who argue against convergence. But this is followed by the interesting statement, a glimmer of light on the obscure and complex recesses of the European culture question; "For the purposes of the European Patent Office, the culture in question is the culture inherent in European society and civilisation".[64]

The *Hautala* Opinion seems to suggest convergence working in reverse order whereas the Curtin and Dekker analysis of the same area of law suggests the very opposite, tangible evidence of one way, forced convergence, EU rules railroading national law and legal cultures. This is very far from the sensitive evocation of low level member state influence in IGC format germinating a general principle of wider access to information in citizen interest at EU level. From Léger, one might begin to see how a European culture might be said to exist; common or shared values being identified and located at national level and "transplanted" to EU level. Yet, the opposing view, as analysed by Curtin and Dekker demonstrates the insensitive, dehumanising, anti-citizen type overriding by the EU of national values, a "top-down" transplant bound to irritate. In further contrast, take Jippes seeking to impress upon the Court the need to recognise the existence of a general principle, relying like Léger, on a collective legal culture but the European Court of Justice effectively ignoring this. Finally, though, as seen in the recent *Netherlands* case, another European level judicial body has the courage and passion (in perhaps an unlikely context) to invoke European culture and civilisation and acknowledge the existence of a European culture. What is odd here is that such words would sound alien coming from the ECJ itself, natural home of such recognition which that Court might seem to be in principle.

The *Jippes* case is an example of an attempt to assert that convergence, or shared values should be recognised; the Opinion in *Hautala*, an analysis of how such shared local values can feed into the EC legal order (reverse convergence); *Metten* (and the new Regulation) a case of "negative" convergence, the realisation of "irritable" EC law; and finally, in the Jacobs Opinion we find the embodiment of the fears of those who are wary of convergence, in the simple statement of an Advocate General that there is a European culture and shared morality and values (mentalité) in Europe. In *Jippes*, a shared mentalité is evoked to try and prove a principle; in *Metten*, a principle is used to quash a local mentalité. In *Hautala*, it is member state's shared values which underpin and define a principle of access to information, yet under the Regulation, (and in other instances

---

[62] Opinion of AG Jacobs in Case C–377/98, 14 June 2001, para. 102,
[63] *Ibid.*
[64] *Ibid.*

given in Curtin and Dekker), "shared" laws are artificially imposed from another legal order. "Common conceptions" are preciously respected by Léger in *Hautala*, yet ignored by the ECJ in *Jippes*. There are, in other words, two co-existing, conflicting trends, the local defeated by EU loyalty leading to "involuntary" convergence, or, as against that, shared, converged values at local level called upon as the basis of (new) fundamental principles at EU level.

CONCLUSION

There is a tension in the EU legal order between the need to respect and preserve the specificities of the national legal systems, and the need to draw upon shared national values to authorise and legitimate supranational law. The question of the "desirability" of convergence amongst the national legal orders lies at the heart of this tension. What has been suggested in this chapter is that convergence need not have negative effects upon national legal systems and can, if shared values and attitudes are harnessed properly, lead to constructive effects in the wider EU legal order. My main contention has been that convergence of national rules does not have to be an irritant, does not have to offend either national democratic standards or national legal culture, and does not have to operate in such a way as to override long established national provisions. As other chapters in this collection have shown convergence can of course have the potential to do so and mine is not a thesis based on a blindly optimistic view of the process of convergence. However, convergence can be and is, already in cases, a positive, constructive process, which hints at the emergence of a European legal culture. The instances of bottom-up convergence which I have identified here contribute to a space of culture and principle which sits between and brings closer together national and transnational systems. Such convergent trends do not compensate for the lack of an adequate theory of democracy in a plural framework of governance[65] but can feed into its formation.

Central to the debate, and highlighted by Pierre Legrand in this collection, is the question of culture and legal culture. I have suggested in this chapter that it is essential to recognise the possibility and potential of a European legal culture in itself. Convergence occurs because of the existence of such a culture and at the same time helps to create and recreate its content. The emergent transnational judicial space allows actors at many levels to contribute to this process. However, there are inevitable tensions as I have shown above, between the effects of convergence on national legal orders and the way in which national legal orders can contribute to the EU legal order. Conflict and consensus— divergence and convergence—are destined to swim together eternally in this constitutional sea. This contradiction, and indeed this collection as a whole,

---

[65] N Walker, "All Dressed Up"(2001) *OJLS* 563, review article of J H H Weiler, *The Constitution of Europe* (Cambridge: CUP, 1999).

tends to suggest that it is necessary to accept some inevitable levels of complexity and confusion as part of more global, constructive process. The overall picture of converging legal systems which emerges is eventually more akin to a Jackson Pollock than to a serene, ordered Vermeer.

Part Three

The Administrative Law Dimension

6

Convergence and Divergence in Administrative Law

CHRIS HIMSWORTH

INTRODUCTION

IN THE BIG vision of the European Community or Union there has been an assumption, sometimes unspoken, of a strong role for law in its realisation. The law is the vehicle for the achievement of the common market and the other Community objectives and, by law, we mean law which has to be capable of being uniformly implemented and enforced across the whole territory of the Union. This is a uniformity of implementation and enforcement which has, of course, to be read subject to the possibility of variations in the content of the law created under the authority of an opt-out or other legitimate basis for differential treatment. Whatever the content, however, the underpinning of effective implementation and enforcement is assumed to be there. That assumption is, in turn, based on a reliance, where necessary, upon the role of national courts throughout the Community to apply Community law. If that assumption cannot be made, the legitimacy of the whole Community project falls to be challenged in the same way that any other project in governance is challenged where it falls short of compliance with core principles of the rule of law.

There is, of course, a long tradition now of doubting some or all these assumptions, of gnawing away at their principled or empirical underpinnings. It is humbling to appreciate that this is a critical activity which is about as old as the Community itself.[1] But it is, at the same time, valuable to revisit enduring questions—usefully restated in the tension between convergence and divergence—in the light of changing conditions. The expansion of Community functions and the enlargement of Community membership bring challenges that would have been unimaginable, I assume, to the Founders and, if they were asked their view, to their legal advisors. The Community of the Six was very different from that of the imagined Community of EU27 and one of the casualties of the changing Community must surely be the metaphors that have served to represent the behaviour of Community law in relation to national systems.

---

[1] E.g. J L Mashaw, "Federal Issues in and about the Jurisdiction of the Court of Justice of the European Communities" (1965) 40 *Tulane LR* 21.

There will have to be a bonfire of some of the old metaphors, including that of the incoming tide flowing into the national estuaries and rivers.[2] The image of the incoming tide is one which carries with it a deceptive illusion of natural inevitability unaffected by human failure or intervention. It also assumes a uniformity of tidal behaviour across a Community in which different geopolitical landscapes create quite different conditions in national estuaries and rivers.

A fundamental question which used to be asked from time to time in the academic literature was whether it is possible to deliver the content of a legal system supra-nationally imposed without recourse to a separate system of courts of its own creation.[3] The concept of Community courts scattered across the regions and states of Europe has probably, however, never had any political attractions and that is presumably the reason why it is a subject no longer discussed, but it would be a model usefully revived, if only hypothetically, if the difficult questions of ensuring compliance with EC law are to be seriously addressed. The EC is not alone in having to think of ways effectively to impose its laws on "alien" political and legal systems. Federations are in an analogous position and it is clear, for example, that the application of federal law across the United States has depended not solely on a supremacy rule and a supreme court but on those two features strongly supported by a system of federal courts.[4] There are further analogies with those systems familiar in the colonial era, but still continuing, in which imperial law was superimposed on the customary law of colonial territories. The question of how far a separate system of courts was essential to the successful implementation and enforcement of the law was an important issue.[5] The parallel does not, of course, end with the question of courts. General issues of reception and of transplants and their rejection have been matters for lively debate in that context as well.[6]

Within a general framework in which questions of convergence and divergence in EU27 are at issue, this paper first looks briefly (in Strategies of Convergence) at some of the familiar institutions and procedures relied upon to ensure a measure of convergence of implementation and enforcement across the broad range of EC law. Then (in The Special Function of National Administrative Law) the case is made for treating administrative law as a wholly separate category. The function of national administrative law in an EC context is so different from that of other bodies of national law that questions of national convergence should also be treated differently. Finally (in Conclusion) some concluding thoughts are brought together. We are under instruction from the UK

---

[2] Lord Denning in *Bulmer Ltd* v. *Bollinger SA* [1974] Ch 401 at 418.

[3] See e.g. M Cappelletti and D Golay, "The Judicial Branch in the Federal and Transnational Union: Its Impact on Integration" in M Cappelletti, M Seccombe and J Weiler (eds.), *Integration Through Law: Europe and the American Federal Experience* (Berlin: de Gruyter, 1986) Vol. 1, Bk 2, at p. 324 *et seq*.

[4] *Ibid*. p. 293 and see e.g. E McWhinney and P Pescatore, *Federation and Supreme Courts and the Integration of Legal Systems* (Heule: UGA, 1973).

[5] See e.g. A N Allott, *Essays in African Law* (London: Butterworth, 1960).

[6] See e.g. R B Seidman, *The State, Law and Development* (London: Croom Helm, 1978).

Prime Minister to be, if we wish, sceptical about the constitutional experiments of our time, but, on no account cynical, because cynicism is corrosive.[7] This is not a paper intended to be corrosively cynical but one which hopes to offer some healthily sceptical conclusions about the prospects for achieving the degree of convergence necessary to bring the project of implementation of EC law to fruition.

STRATEGIES OF CONVERGENCE

The general strategy for the implementation of EC law as it has emerged up to the period of the 15 member Union is familiar. There are two main elements. The first has been the doctrine of the supremacy of Community law carefully and persistently expanded by the Court of Justice. This has, of course, been a process which has attracted criticism. It has had its political detractors who have resented the resulting concentration of central authority at the hand of the unaccountable Court.[8] The reasoning used by the Court in its supremacy programme has been criticised and the Court was said, for a while, to have "run wild".[9] And, at the highest levels of constitutional abstraction, the supremacy asserted by the Court remains contested, with authority divided—for many, uncomfortably so—between the Community and national constitutional orders.[10]

For practical purposes below that level, however, the notion of supremacy drawn down from the EC Treaty and then developed by the ECJ and conceded by national courts is an essential element in the general promulgation of EC law. EC law trumps national law[11] and that principle is reinforced by the Court's expansive view of the impact of Directives[12] and further reinforced by its elaboration of state liability in the *Francovich* doctrine.[13]

The other essential element has been the procedural device of the reference to the Court under Article 234 EC. The supremacy doctrine spreads the net of Community law over all the national courts, high and low, of member states but then, in a system which lacks decentralised Community courts, Article 234 provides the vital link between the ECJ and the national systems. It provides the Court with most of its opportunities to expand the scope of its authoritative pronouncements on EC law and the compatibility of national law. The Court has depended upon references as pegs on which to hang the expanding

---

[7] The Prime Minister was speaking to MSPs about devolution but directing his remarks largely to the press.

[8] For recent discussion, see A Arnull, *The European Union and its Court of Justice* (Oxford: OUP, 1999), ch. 16 "Judging Europe's Judges".

[9] H Rasmussen, *On Law and Policy in the European Court of Justice* (Dordrecht: Nijhoff, 1986).

[10] See esp. N MacCormick, *Questioning Sovereignty* (Oxford: OUP, 1999).

[11] *Simmenthal* [1978] ECR 629.

[12] E.g. *Van Duyn* v. *Home Office* [1974] ECR 1337.

[13] *Francovich & Bonifaci* v. *Italy* [1991] ECR I–5357.

wardrobe of EC law but also, in combination with the doctrine of supremacy, as the mechanism, even if in a process of dialogue[14] for the imposition of its will. The integrity of the system comes to depend on the interaction of the two.

The reference is, however, a mechanism which has come under increasing strain. It must always have been a little improbable that a new legal order could be superimposed upon six diverse legal systems in reliance upon such a thin line of contact. There is something arrogant about the very idea that all that was necessary to create substantial economic and social change across a large part of the continent of Europe was a declaration of supremacy sustained by a single Community Court dependent upon references from national courts. Some recognition of the insufficiency of that provision is made in the supplementary procedural support given to sustaining the competition regime. That apart, however, and with the expansion of the Community and its competences, the strains on the reference system have become apparent. The Court itself has expressed its own concerns about the systemic stresses which are resulting from its growing work-load and the consequent delays in the handling of business.[15] The report of the (Due) Reflexion Group on the future of the judicial system of the Communities[16] has been presented to the Commission and the Commission itself prepared a paper on the reform of the Community courts in the run-up to the Intergovernmental Conference. The strains on the Court, especially in relation to its Article 234 business, figured significantly on the Conference agenda, and on the subsequent Treaty of Nice, signed in February 2001.

There will be a brief return to the possible impact of reforms in this area in my Conclusion but it will there be argued that, whatever their general effect, it is unlikely that the effect on administrative law, in particular, will be particularly significant. It is to the special situation of administrative law to which we turn in the next section.

THE SPECIAL FUNCTION OF NATIONAL ADMINISTRATIVE LAW

There are different reasons for the comparative study of administrative law, any of which may be associated with an interest in the convergence and divergence of systems. From a UK perspective, these have produced two-country comparisons, especially between England and France.[17] Then there have been many broader European comparative works,[18] including studies which have taken a particular interest in the processes of "cross-fertilisation" between systems[19]

---

[14] See e.g. Arnull n. 8 above, at 51.

[15] The Future of the Judicial System of the European Union: Proposals and Reflections (1999).

[16] Report by the Working Party on the Future of the European Communities' Court System, January 2000.

[17] As in L N Brown and J S Bell, *French Administrative Law* (5th edn., Oxford: Clarendon, 1998).

[18] E.g. J Schwarze, *European Administrative Law* (London: Sweet & Maxwell, 1992).

[19] J Bell, "Mechanisms for Cross-Fertilisation of Administrative Law in Europe" in J Beatson and T Tridimas (eds.), *New Directions in European Public Law* (Oxford: Hart, 1998).

which may, in turn, produce a convergence of rules and principles. But different reasons for entering the field produce different points of focus and outcomes. For some, the emphasis may be primarily historical and, for others, there may be a particular interest in distinctions between the civilian and common law styles.

As must be already clear, the particular focus adopted here is on administrative law as one of the principal variables in the processes of implementation and enforcement where, in the use of "indirect administration",[20] the Community relies upon the institutions of the member states. In doing so, it relies on that complex mix of the administrative and judicial institutions which have been designed or have emerged largely to serve national (or sub-national) purposes rather than those of the Community. They are assumed mainly to continue to serve national rather than Community purposes; to be resourced largely on the basis of their national functions; and to be subject to work-loads and other pressures (with consequences for inefficiency or delay) which again are largely national in origin. Included within these national systems are not only the processes which would routinely be characterised as administrative (within which there is, in any event, great variation between states) but also the points of overlap between the administrative and the judicial where the accountability of national administration is not measured solely by reference to tribunals and courts applying established standards of judicial review but also by reference to principles of civil liability in tort or delict (a *very* difficult interface in contemporary UK law[21]) and responsibility to ombudsmen, financial auditors and to the domestic political system, whether central, regional or local. Nor is the assessment of a national system to be confined to the procedures for accountability and control of government agencies. Also important are the powers of enforcement available, for instance, within the ambit of the criminal law. It may be that there are political sensitivities about the content of national criminal law and national control of systems of criminal prosecution but they are matters which plainly cannot be ignored in an overall assessment of the functioning of administrative law, broadly viewed.

Relevant to all of these procedures are, of course, the rights of individuals and, perhaps to a greater extent, of pressure groups and the like to initiate or to intervene in administrative or judicial procedures to ensure compliance with the law, whether on their own behalf or in some wider public interest. A system which offers little such opportunity will, all other things being equal, provide less assurance that the standards imposed by the law, whether domestic or EC, will be upheld. All of these considerations produce obvious questions about the diversity of national systems, based on the interaction of a variety of characteristics

---

[20] See e.g. C Harlow, "Codification of EC Administrative Procedures? Fitting the Foot to the Shoe or the Shoe to the Foot" (1996) 2 *European Law Journal* 5–25.

[21] See e.g. P P Craig, *Administrative Law* (4th edn, London: Sweet & Maxwell, 1999) ch. 26; P Craig and D Fairgrieve, "*Barrett*, Negligence and Discretionary Powers" [1999] *PL* 626.

within those systems, which in turn have consequences for the capacity of national systems to deliver a coherent product across the Community.

As an aside, it is interesting to trace a parallel here between the national variations within the EC and, on the other hand, variations between the legal systems within the United Kingdom, in particular between England and Scotland. Devolution from July 1999 under the Scotland Act 1998 has increased the scope for variations in administrative law between the two systems, with important consequences for the implementation of UK-level policy. Even before the arrival of devolution, however, there were interesting signs of variation in practice. The Scottish courts have, on a number of occasions, declared that, when they engage in the judicial review of administrative action, the grounds of review are substantially the same as those invoked by the English courts.[22] On the other hand, there are clear variations in matters of procedure, for which separate provision is made, and the remedies which may be awarded by the Court of Session. The law on *locus standi* has appeared to diverge quite sharply between the two jurisdictions, with the Court of Session taking a more restrictive view of access, in particular for representative organisations.[23] In the English High Court, the point has quite explicitly been taken that an application for judicial review brought by Greenpeace against the decision of a minister would be treated very differently in the two jurisdictions.[24] Another point of divergence with practical consequences has been in the willingness of the courts to grant interim remedies in certain types of challenge to immigration decisions. In this case, it has been the Court of Session which has taken the more "generous" view and granted interim liberation in circumstances where the equivalent remedy would not have been available in England.[25]

The impact of these instances of difference between the operation of the two systems should not be overstated. No one would suggest that they are evidence of a breakdown in the effective implementation of the law in the two jurisdictions. They are, however, pointers to the potential for differences where reliance is placed, for purposes of implementation and enforcement of the law, upon two operationally different legal systems. Another example is that of the different operation in the two jurisdictions of the systems of criminal prosecution. In England and Wales, it is common practice for public authorities to take direct responsibility for prosecutions in the criminal courts in respect of offences in areas where they have administrative responsibility. They are not obliged to involve the Crown Prosecution Service and local councils are, for instance, competent to prosecute on their own behalf offences under consumer protection legislation. In Scotland, however, there is a virtual monopoly of criminal prosecution by the

---

[22] For discussion, see e.g. C M G Himsworth, "Public Law—In Peril of Neglect?" in H L MacQueen (ed.), *Scots Law into the 21st Century* (Edinburgh: W. Green, 1996).

[23] *Ibid.*

[24] *R* v. *Secretary of State for Scotland, ex parte Greenpeace*, (High Court, England) 24 May 1995, unreported.

[25] See Himsworth n. 22 above.

Crown Office and procurator fiscal and it is almost certainly largely for this reason that, whereas the Environment Agency in England prosecutes extensively in respect of environmental offences, the Scottish Environment Protection Agency initiates many fewer prosecutions. The environmental legislation itself may be virtually identical but prosecution practice (and, it should be added, sentencing practice in the courts) is very different.[26]

These are differences which may be expected to increase in the new period of devolution. Practically all aspects of the Scottish legal system—the court system, and, for most purposes, Scottish private law (including procedural law and, interestingly, judicial review) and Scottish criminal law—are legislatively devolved to the Scottish Parliament.[27] If it wished to do so, the Parliament could make deliberate changes to the law of procedure and remedies which might be much greater than those which have emerged so far in ways which have been more accidental than deliberate. This may, of course, be treated as a perfectly natural consequence of devolution. There should be nothing unexpected about greater diversity of practice. The interest may develop, however, around the consequences of any such diversity for the implementation of those policy areas which remain reserved to the Westminster Parliament and the UK Government. These include immigration and many aspects of the regulation of economic, fiscal, social security and employment matters. It is in these areas that there will be a continued dependence by the UK authorities upon the devolved police and prosecution services and upon the devolved court system.

And it is here that this discursus into UK devolutionary preoccupations may be seen to be quite directly relevant to the starting point in EC law. The parallel is not absolutely precise. Differences between the ways in which competences are divided in the two regimes and, in particular, the ways in which the "upper" tier of authority may take action to override the "lower" and in which the regimes are supervised by the courts are all significant. The comparison is, however, useful in its reminder of common problems. Indirect administration by the EC through national legal systems shares many common elements with the United Kingdom's administration of reserved matters in reliance upon a devolved legal system it can no longer directly control or can do so only with great, probably heavy-handed, difficulty.[28] There are common problems of cross-cutting competences. The division of competences by reference to policy area collides with a division based on different "legal system" criteria which makes it impossible for either to operate cleanly. Inevitably, they intrude on each other and produce discomfort. Either the implementation of Community or reserved policy must suffer because of its reliance upon an incompatible domestic enforcement system or it must intrude further into that system, demand special procedures to suit the implementation of specific policies and,

---

[26] See e.g. C Smith, N Collar and M Poustie, *Pollution Control: the Law in Scotland* (Edinburgh: T & T Clark, 1997) pp. 40–7.

[27] Scotland Act 1998, ss. 9, 126 (4), (5).

[28] Formally, the power to legislate for the whole of the UK on any matter is retained, s. 28(7).

thereby, disrupt the integrity and coherence of the system in the member states or in a devolved Scotland, as the case may be, in the achievement of its wider purposes.

Whether we are considering the problems of implementation of law and policy across the EC or, in reserved areas across the (asymmetrically) devolved conditions of the United Kingdom, we now have an understanding of the distinctive demands placed upon the systems of public administration and of administrative law which are called upon to deliver the policy outcomes. However finely tuned may be the content of the substantive law, its implementation is turned over to the rude mechanics of national legal orders whose tools, techniques and training make for delivery which, when viewed from the "centre", is clumsy and variable in character. Although not fully examined and its effect unquantified, this phenomenon is well recognised. Problems were, for instance, identified in the EC Commission's communication on "Implementing Community Environmental Law" in 1996.[29] Implementation across the Community was made difficult not just because of the inherent complexity of policy and law in the environmental area but also because of the devolution to member states (and often to decentralised agencies within member states) of the practical application and enforcement of the law.[30] Direct enforcement by the Commission was not practical and much depended, therefore, upon inspection operations by member states and then the ways of dealing with environmental complaints and the manner of their investigation. Above all, the role of national courts was crucial. Access to justice, the Commission said, is generally sufficiently ensured, as it is in other fields, if powerful economic interests are at stake. Enforcement will be encouraged by economic operators with sufficient resources to fight for enforcement. This is not, however, necessarily the case for ecological interests and enforcement therefore mainly rests with public authorities and is dependent on their powers, resources and goodwill. It is necessary too that these efforts of public authorities should be supplemented by those of non-governmental organisations.[31] This is an interdependence reinforced by the proposals recently made by the Commission for the enforcement of a new scheme for environmental liability across the Community.[32] The rules on access to the courts become crucial.[33]

The same paper concedes that there is no possibility that the resources of time and personnel which are available to the Commission and to the Court of Justice will ever be sufficient to take over the functions of national courts which are, in any event, better placed to take into account the particular legal, administrative and environmental context in each member state. They are also better placed to grant interim measures.[34]

---

[29] COM(96) 500.
[30] *Ibid*. para. 9.
[31] *Ibid*. paras. 36, 37.
[32] White Paper on Environmental Liability, COM (2000) 66.
[33] *Ibid*. para. 4.7.
[34] COM (96) 500 para. 41.

They may indeed be "better placed" for the task in these respects, but we are forced to return to the question of whether they can ever be relied on to use their powers to best effect for Community purposes. The standard combination of supremacy and Article 234 has offered little reason for optimism about the scope of the Court to impose its will in this area. The content of the substantive law (whether environmental or whatever) is not the issue and the Court has tended to adopt a rather relaxed approach to standards of enforcement by national courts.[35] It is a latitude enhanced by an inappropriately one-dimensional view of the meaning of "judicial protection" in a Community context. If the task of supervising the performance of national courts is to be taken seriously, it will not often be sufficient for the ECJ merely to establish a base or floor level of "protection". Under an environmental code, for instance, both environmental interests and polluters have rights, and decisions must be made which strike the correct balance between the two. Minimum protection of the rights of one or the other is an insufficient and inappropriate standard.[36]

If there are reasons to be rather pessimistic about the prospects for the convergence of the practice of administrative law because of initial signs of divergence and the apparent lack of capacity of the ECJ to rectify the situation, there are also some arguments, on the other hand, that tendencies in the direction of convergence may be developing for other reasons. It can, at least, be argued that there are developments across the European jurisdictions towards greater uniformity in the grounds of judicial review, in part because of the adoption of principles applied by the ECJ, because of the impact of principles derived from the ECHR, and also perhaps because of other processes of "cross-fertilisation".[37] There is a related group of arguments, perhaps just a sub-set of the first, that, if the adoption by national courts of peculiarly EC doctrine in those areas to which EC law applies might open up a "gap"[38] within national systems between EC administrative law and the rest, there are signs that national courts will tend to seek to close that gap by expanding the scope of EC doctrine into other sectors.

On both these matters there are, however, strong reasons for suspending judgment. In the first place, the evidence for convergence of grounds of review tends to be very selective. In the United Kingdom there has been, for instance, a concentration upon the theme of proportionality (or disproportionality) as a ground of review which could usefully be developed along lines more clearly established in many European jurisdictions and in EC jurisprudence itself.[39] This has, however, inevitably been a stalking horse for the broader case for increased judicial power in administrative law and for a shift from narrower

---

[35] See e.g. Arnull, n. 8 above, ch. 5.

[36] C M G Himsworth, "Things Fall Apart: The Harmonisation of Community Judicial Procedural Protection Revisited" (1997) 22 *European LR* 291.

[37] J Bell, n. 19 above.

[38] W van Gerven, "Bridging the Gap between Community and National Laws: Towards a Principle of Homogeneity in the Field of Legal Remedies" (1995) 32 *CMLRev* 679.

[39] See especially E Ellis (ed.), *The Principle of Proportionality in the Laws of Europe* (Oxford: Hart, 1999).

vires-based grounds of review.[40] It has also been closely linked to the case for more rights-based doctrine.[41] With the arrival of the Human Rights Act 1998, however, there is at least room for the suggestion that, with incorporation achieved, the impetus for the spread of proportionality as a general ground of review may now fall away. Proportionality was essential to the project of implied incorporation. Statutory intervention has greatly reduced its campaigning significance.[42] It should also be observed that, although in the very long run the 1998 Act may be interpreted as a sign of convergence in the direction of ECHR compliance, it also illustrates the fact that the specific method used for the "incorporation" of the Convention can produce substantial diversity in its application. Paradoxically the variation of method used may, in practice, make incorporation the cause of greater divergence than of convergence. It is fairly clear that the full implementation of the Human Rights Act from 2 October 2000 will, in due course, produce sharp differences in the practice of UK courts. It is much less clear that these will be in the direction of convergence with other EC jurisdictions where the style and degree of recognition of Convention rights may be quite different.[43]

Secondly, if there is selectivity in the treatment of grounds of review, there is apparently an even greater selectivity in the choice of evidence for the closing of "gaps" within national systems. It is strange how influential have been the dicta in the one case of *M* v. *Home Office*[44] and it is extremely difficult, in the light of the rather crude methodology adopted, to determine how far general conclusions may be drawn about the narrowing or widening of "gaps" in this context.

Thirdly and perhaps most importantly of all, any enquiry into the greater convergence of doctrine on the grounds of review ignores the point already stressed that, in the seamless web of the practice of administrative law, the substantive grounds are only one, perhaps rather small, element. *Even if* a single concept of proportionality were given approval across all the EC jurisdictions, that concept would have to make its way in systems which remain better characterised otherwise by the extent of their diversity. What if one is not granted *locus standi* to assert an observed disproportionality of administrative behaviour? What if the rules of a chosen member state impose strict time limits within which review must be sought? What if, on the other hand, practical conditions in a state's courts mean a delay of years? What if the rules on admissibility of evidence differ—generally or, in particular, say in relation to public interest immunity? What if remedial provision is insubstantial? What if orders go unrecognised by state institutions or unenforced against them? What if the balance of reliance upon

---

[40] See e.g. L Jowell and A Lester, "Proportionality: Neither Novel nor Dangerous", in J L Jowell and D Oliver (eds.), *New Directions in Judicial Review* (London: Stevens, 1988).

[41] M Hunt, *Using Human Rights Law in English Courts* (Oxford: Hart, 1997).

[42] C M G Himsworth, "La proporcionalidad en el Reino Unido" (1998) 5 *Cuardernos de Derecho Publico* 273–286.

[43] C A Gearty (ed.), *European Civil Liberties and the European Convention on Human Rights: A Comparative Study* (The Hague: Kluwer, 1997).

[44] [1994] 1 AC 377. For detailed discussion, see P Legrand's contribution to the present volume.

legal and political remedies or upon court and ombudsman remedies produces a quite different context within which specific substantive rules are required to operate? If these are questions which reasonably can be asked about the implementation and enforcement of indirect administration in a Community of fifteen, how much more significant will they be in EU27?

CONCLUSION

If the special function of national systems of administration law in the implementation of EC law has been correctly identified and if the potential for dysfunctionality of these systems in the aim of securing uniformity of provision does indeed raise the problems discussed, it is necessary to consider possible "solutions". There are perhaps six:

1. The first is to confront the issue of diversity head-on and to deny that there is any difficulty. This may take two different but related forms. It may first be argued that the initial assumption that the EC project is one which inherently demands a very high degree of uniformity of legal implementation and enforcement is simply wrong. However, such an argument must surely be unacceptable. It would certainly surprise those who either administer or are subject to the core regimes of the Community, whether in the fields of competition, fishing, or agriculture. Assumptions about the uniformity of the rigour of their implementation are built into those regimes. A second approach concedes the general validity of the need for uniformity but then insists on a balancing of uniformity against national variations in practice which are to be justified and indeed celebrated in the name of some special form of subsidiarity. Once again, this approach takes different forms. Either the national variations seem to take on an intrinsic or essential character deriving from fundamental differences between legal systems,[45] but this is an approach which has to deny or has no explanation for the important changes which *have* been wrought across widely different systems and to convergent effect. The alternative is to argue not that essential characteristics of legal systems deny the possibility of change but that the differences should be accorded respect in the name of a legal pluralism which parallels political pluralism. This also, however, seems unacceptable. The variations it may produce are too haphazard and unpredictable to be accommodated within a system which, overall, pays respect to the rule of law.[46] To return to the UK devolution analogy, if immigration law is reserved to Westminster, the implementation of that law cannot sensibly and consistently be devolved, in the name of pluralism, to the different component parts of the United Kingdom. To do so would be to undermine the reservation. Similarly, if at the EC level, the

---

[45] P Legrand, "European Legal Systems are not Converging" (1996) 45 *ICLQ* 52–81.
[46] See e.g. S Gustavesson, "Why not Focus on the Real World Issues?", in U Bernitz and P Hallström (eds.), *Principles of Justice and the European Union* (Stockholm: Juristförlaget, 1995).

political and constitutional commitment has been made to ensure the administration of a Community-wide programme, this cannot simply be subject to the vicissitudes of local variations in national legal systems.

2. A second response would be to look to the reforms of the procedures of the Court of Justice designated by the Treaty of Nice, in particular the provisions extending the preliminary reference jurisdiction to the Court of First Instance and allowing the establishment of specialist panels.[47] On the face of it, however, even a redesigned and more efficient reference procedure and the provision of direct Community-level judicial oversight in limited areas would be ill-equipped and insufficient to deal with the procedural and remedial questions raised by defects in the supervision of indirect administration.

3. Thirdly, a much greater Community power to intrude into national systems of administrative law could be contemplated—but the logistical and political problems involved in anything resembling a Community-wide code must be unimaginably great.

4. Another response would be to rely on a much more optimistic assessment than that presented earlier in this paper of the prospects for some sort of natural alignment of state practice and thus of uniformity of outcomes.

5. A retreat from reliance upon indirect administration and national courts would remove the problem in its present form. This would imply, however, a less ambitious forward programme in these areas of Community activity where a substantial reliance has been placed upon national implementation thus far. It would be an enlarged but much shallower Community.

6. If, however, the Community retains its ambitions for both enlargement and the depth of its economic and social programmes, there may yet come the day when the notion of a separate system of federal-style Community courts will have to be taken seriously. There may be a need for the Community's own judicial troops on the ground?

---

[47] See new Arts. 225–225a TEC.

7

Towards Homogeneity in the Field of Legal Remedies: Convergence and Divergence

TON HEUKELS AND JAMILA TIB

INTRODUCTION

IN THE COURSE of the last decade the legally complex and politically sensitive issue of convergence and divergence in the field of legal remedies has attracted increasing attention.[1] The debate basically concentrates on two obvious, but apparently contradictory issues:

(a) the need for a uniform and coherent application of Community law, inherent in the doctrines of supremacy and direct effect,[2] versus subsidiarity and respect for the alleged procedural autonomy of member states;[3]

This contribution is based on a presentation of Ton Heukels during the May 2000 Aberdeen Conference on convergence and divergence in European public law. The views expressed are strictly personal.

[1] See e.g. A Biondi, "The European Court of Justice and certain National Procedural Limitations: not such a tough Relationship" (1999) 36 *CML Rev* 1271–87; R Craufurd Smith, "Remedies for Breaches of EC Law in National Courts: Legal Variation and Selection" in P Craig and G De Búrca (eds.), *The Evolution of EU Law* (Oxford: OUP, 1999), 287–320; C Harding, "Member State Enforcement of European Community Measures: The Chimera of 'Effective' Enforcement" (1997) 4 *MJ* 5–24; C M G Himsworth, "Things Fall Apart: the Harmonisation of Community Judicial Procedural Protection Revisited" (1997) 22 *EL Rev* 291–311; M Hoskins, "Tilting the Balance: Supremacy and National Procedural Rules" (1996) 21 *EL Rev* 365–77; F Jacobs, "Enforcing Community Rights and Obligations in National Courts: Striking the Balance" in J Lonbay and A Biondi (eds.), *Remedies for Breach of EC Law* (Chichester: Wiley, 1996) 25 *et seq.*; CN Kakouris, "Do the Member States possess judicial procedural 'autonomy'?" (1997) 34 *CML Rev* 1389–412; E Szyszczak, "Making Europe more relevant to its Citizens: Effective Judicial Process" (1996) 21 *EL Rev* 351–64; W Van Gerven, "Bridging the Gap between Community and National Laws: Towards a Principle of Homogeneity in the Field of Legal Remedies?" (1995) 32 *CML Rev* 679–702; J Schwarze (ed.), *Administrative Law under European Influence—On the Convergence of the Administrative Laws of the EU Member States* (London: Sweet & Maxwell, 1996) and J Jans, R De Lange, S Prechal, P Widdershoven, *Inleiding tot het Europees bestuursrecht* (Nijmegen: Ars Aequi Libri, 1999).

[2] Case 6/64 *Costa* v. *ENEL* [1964] ECR 1255, Case 106/77 *Simmenthal* [1978] ECR 629, Joined Cases C–143/88 and C–92/89 *Zuckerfabrik Süderithmarschen* [1991] ECR I–415, Joined Cases C–46/93 and C–48/93 *Brasserie du Pêcheur* [1996] ECR I–1029.

[3] Art. 5 (ex Art. 3) EC, as refined in the Protocol on Subsidiarity and Proportionality, [1997] OJ C 340/105. *Cf.* also Case C–120/97 *Upjohn* [1999] ECR I–223, para. 32 and Case C–326/96 *Levez* [1998] ECR I–7835, para. 18.

(b) the much advocated need for legislative and judicial restraint versus the need for European citizens to be able to enforce equal substantive rights granted to them under Community law through equivalent legal procedures at the national level.

The delicate balance to be struck appears equally obvious: effective application and enforcement of Community law through domestic legal remedies by individuals—their vigilance[4] having contributed so much to the progressive development of fundamental doctrines such as the requirement of consistent interpretation[5] and state liability for violation of EC law[6]—need to be reconciled with and fit into the still significantly divergent systems of judicial protection at member state level. Underlying this interaction, meanwhile, are two widely accepted concepts, namely "*dédoublement fonctionnel*" and the national courts performing, at least to some extent, the role of "*juge de droit commun*".[7]

More recent legal as well as political developments highlight the importance of the "convergence/divergence-debate" in the field of legal remedies even more acutely. First, there is the fact of imminent enlargements, likely to result in a European Union of 25–30 members, all with their own legal traditions and differing perceptions on the relationship between domestic law and international law. If we add to this the pressures, needs and new mechanisms associated with flexible co-operation,[8] it appears that not only the uniform application, supremacy and direct effect of Community law might be endangered;[9] in addition, the Community's reliance on effective judicial enforcement through national legal procedures might be challenged. Furthermore, the Treaties of Maastricht and Amsterdam have introduced some new provisions that are of (in)direct relevance to the issues under consideration. It is well-known that the Union is based on the principles of subsidiarity, the rule of law and respect for the national identities of its member states.[10] Just as important is the

---

[4] Case 26/62, *Van Gend & Loos* [1963] ECR 3.
[5] Case 14/83 *Von Colson and Kamann* [1984] ECR 1891, Case C–53/96 *Hermes* [1998] ECR I–3603, para. 28, Case 106/89 *Marleasing* [1990], ECR I–4135. See in general T Heukels, "Richtlijnen gemeenschapsrechtconforme interpretatie: nieuwe internationale dimensies" (1997) 40 *NJB* 1845–50 and *idem*, "Von richtlinienkonformer zur völkerrechtskonformen Auslegung im EG-Recht: Internationale Dimensionen einer normhierarchiegerechten Interpretationsmaxime" (1999) 3 *ZEuS*, 313–33.
[6] Joined Cases C–6/90 and C–9/90 *Francovich*, [1991] ECR I–5357, *Brasserie du Pêcheur*, n. 2 above, Case C–265/95 *Commission* v. *France* [1997] ECR I–6959.
[7] Kakouris, n. 1, at 1393.
[8] See e.g. Art. 65 EC, and Arts. 43–45 TEU juncto Art. 11 EC.See also *clausulae* A–P of the 2000 Nice Treaty.
[9] Himsworth, n. 1 above, at 310 and S Prechal, "Community Law in National Courts: The Lessons From *Van Schijndel*" (1998) 35 *CML Rev* 681–706, at 685.
[10] *Cf.* Art. 2, last paragraph, TEU *juncto* Art. 5 EC, as well as Arts. 6 (1), which can be regarded— at least to some extent—as a codification of the Court's ruling in Case C–334/89 *Commission* v. *Italy*, [1991] ECR I–93, and 6 (3) TEU. According to the Protocol on the Application of the Principles of Subsidiarity and Proportionality, [1997] OJ C 340/105, the subsidiarity principle should be respected by "each institution", including the Court of Justice. See, however, also Art. 135 EC,

self-proclaimed goal of the Union to establish gradually and maintain an area of freedom, security and justice, which entitles the Community, *inter alia*, to adopt certain measures in the field of judicial co-operation in civil matters, including the promotion of the compatibility of the rules on civil procedure applicable in the member states.[11] Finally, the Protocol on subsidiarity and proportionality should be mentioned. This 1997 Protocol, while stressing the need for proper and effective enforcement of Community law, requires the Community legislator, when considering the adoption of Community measures, to take due care to respect "the organisation and working of Member States' legal systems".[12] This provision clearly illustrates, that national procedural law may be influenced— or, some would argue, compromised—not only by the Court's case law, but also equally by (harmonising) measures of the Community's legislator.

The main aim of this contribution is to provide a summary overview of the interaction between Community law and national procedural law. Two perspectives will be at the core of this analysis: the impact of the Court's case-law on national systems of judicial protection (pp. 113–22) as well as legislative measures adopted by the EC institutions aimed at (partly) harmonising national procedural law (pp. 122–7). This summary analysis will provide a framework for identifying some basic trends towards convergence and/or divergence in the field of judicial remedies, that serves to indicate the challenges ahead in this fascinating, yet complicated and controversial domain of Community law (pp. 127–8).

TWO BASIC TRENDS IN THE CASE LAW OF THE COURT OF JUSTICE

The basic principle underlying the Court's case law on the interaction between Community law and national procedural law is an obvious one: *ubi ius, ibi remedium*. Yet, it was only in the mid 1980's that the Court explicitly stated that the existence of a remedy of a judicial nature against any decision of a national authority refusing the benefit of a Community right should qualify as "essential in order to secure for the individual effective protection for this right", reflecting "a general principle of Community law which underlies the constitutional traditions common to the Member States" also inherent in Articles 6 and 13 ECHR.[13]

according to which EC measures in the field of customs co-operation shall not concern "the national administration of justice".

[11] Art. 2, fourth indent, TEU in conjunction with Arts. 61, esp. (c), and 65, esp. (c), EC. See also points 38–39 of the conclusions reached by the Presidency of the European Council in Tampere on 15/16 October 1999.

[12] Points (6) and (7) of the Protocol on the Application of the Principles of Subsidiarity and Proportionality, [1997] OJ C 340/105. See also point (2), according to which the application of the principles of subsidiarity and proportionality "shall not affect the principles developed by the Court of Justice regarding the relationship between national and Community law". This reservation appears to include the Court's jurisprudence on legal remedies, discussed below.

[13] Case 222/86 *Heylens* [1987] ECR 4097, para. 14, confirmed in Case C–1/99 *Kofisa Italia* [2001] ECR I–207 para. 46, where the Court expressly refers to "the right to effective judicial protection". It follows from Case C–97/91 *Borelli* [1992] ECR I–6313, that the principle of effective judicial protection extends to all substantive rights granted by Community law.

Obviously, the principle of effective judicial protection not only requires member states, if necessary, to introduce legal remedies in order to ensure individuals proper access to justice in order to vindicate their rights derived from Community law. Equally, it presupposes that European citizens are fully aware of the grounds that led national authorities to deny their directly effective Community rights.[14] Consequently, not only the self-evident principle of "access to court", but also the general duty to give reasons is a logical corollary to the general and wider principle of effective judicial protection.[15] Against the background of the multifaceted principle of effective judicial protection, the Court of Justice had and took ample opportunity to develop carefully and progressively a jurisprudence on the interaction between Community law and national procedural law. Two apparently separate trends appear to characterise the Court's case law.

On the one hand, the Court has gradually developed, as from 1976, its famous so-called "*Rewe*-doctrine". This doctrine acknowledges the crucial, supportive function of national procedural law for the effectuation of substantive Community law rights; highlights and respects, in the absence of Community harmonising measures, "national procedural autonomy"; and sets, in exceptional cases, only minimum limits to the unrestricted application of national procedural law in cases of judicial enforcement of Community rights.[16]

In contrast, the second trend in the Court's jurisprudence is characterised by a communautarisation of important parts of domestic procedural law, whereby certain doctrines that belonged, to a greater or lesser extent, to the traditional domain of member states were, so to speak, transferred into autonomous Community law doctrines. The Court's famous jurisprudence on member state liability for violation of Community law offers a perfect example of this trend, if by no means the only significant one.[17] In this context, and in contrast to the "*Rewe*-doctrine", national procedural autonomy appears to be largely eclipsed, being mainly confined to questions such as rules on (in)admissibility, evidence and the amount of compensation to be awarded.

These two lines of jurisprudence are briefly outlined below, as they form a cornerstone, albeit by no means an uncontroversial one, of the interaction between Community law and national procedural law.

---

[14] Case 222/84 *Johnston* [1989] ECR 1651, para. 12, *Heylens* n. 13 above, para. 17 and Case C–340/89 *Vlassopoulou* [1991] ECR I–2357, para. 22.

[15] See, however, the Court of Appeal, 8 May 1998, R v. *Secretary of State for the Environment, Transport and Regions, ex parte Anthony Marson*, [1999] 1 CMLR 268, apparently denying the existence of a general duty to state reasons concerning acts of the administration that come within the scope of Community law.

[16] Case 33/76 *Rewe* [1976] ECR 1989.

[17] See pp. 119–22 below. The Court's case law on interim measures constitutes another example. See e.g. Case C–92/89 *Zuckerfabrik Süderdithmarschen* [1991] ECR I–415 and Case C–465/93 *Atlanta Fruchthandelsgesellschaft* [1995] ECR I–3761.

THE "*REWE*-DOCTRINE": CHARACTERISTICS AND APPRAISAL

From the *Rewe*-judgment in 1976 onwards, the Court of Justice, while continuing to hold that, in principle, national procedural rules and rules on sanctions are to apply to Community law based claims, consistently laid down two important constraints on this approach:

(a) that those national rules, when applied to cases in which Community law rights are invoked, may not be less favourable than those governing similar domestic claims (principle of equivalence),[18] and

(b) that such national rules may not render virtually impossible or excessively difficult the exercise of rights conferred by Community law (principle of effectiveness).[19]

In twenty-five years of case law, these cumulative minimum requirements have been applied to a wide variety of cases, including the reliance on time limits and limitation periods in order to avoid or limit Community law based claims,[20] the reimbursement of national charges levied contrary to the requirements of Community law,[21] national rules on evidence,[22] sanctions[23] and the question of the extent to which a national court is under a Community law obligation to apply directly effective provisions of EC law of its own motion.[24]

---

[18] E.g. Case 33/76 *Rewe* [1976] ECR 1989, Case 45/76 *Comet* [1976] ECR 2043, Case 61/79 *Denkavit* [1980] ECR 1205, Case 68/79 *Just* [1980] ECR 501 and Case 222/86 *Heylens* [1987] ECR 4097.

[19] *Rewe*, n. 16 above, *Comet*, n. 18 above, confirmed in Case 199/82 *San Giorgio* [1983] ECR 3595, Case C–208/90 *Emmot* [1991] ECR I–4269, Case C–212/94 *FMC* [1996] ECR I–389, Case 312/93 *Peterbroeck* [1995] ECR I–4599, Case C–260/96 *Spac* [1998] ECR I–4997, Case C–228/96 *Aprile* [1998] ECR I–7141 and Case C–326/96 *Levez* [1998] ECR I–7835. See also T Heukels, "Concretiseringen van de 'Rewe-jurisprudentie': minimumharmonisatie langs jurisprudentiële weg", (1999) 7/8 *NTER* 197–202.

[20] For example *Emmot*, n. 19 above, Case C–338/91 *Steenhorst-Neerings* [1993] ECR I–5435, Case C–309/85 *Barra* [1988] ECR 355 and Case C–240/87 *Deville* [1988] ECR 3513.

[21] Case 68/79 *Just* [1980] ECR 501, Case 811/79 *Ariete* [1980] ECR 2545, Case 826/79 *Mireco* [1980] ECR 2559, Joined Cases C–279–281/96 *Ansaldo* [1998] ECR I–5025 as well as Joined Cases C–10/97–22/97 *IN.CO.GE '90* [1998] ECR I–6307.

[22] Case C–343/96 *Dilexport* [1999] ECR I–579, *San Giorgio* n. 19 above, *FMC* n. 19 above, Case 109/88, *Danfoss* [1989] ECR 3199, Joined Cases 331/85, 376/85 and 378/85 *Bianco et Girard* [1988] ECR 1099.

[23] According to established jurisprudence, national sanctions designed to effectuate EC law have to be proportional, dissuasive and effective. See e.g. Case 14/83 *Von Colson en Kamann* [1984] ECR 1891, Case 68/88 *Greece Maize* [1989] ECR 2965, Case C–265/95 *Commission* v. *France* [1997] ECR I–6959 and Case C–348/96 *Calfa* [1999] ECR I–11. Cf. also Art. 280 EC.

[24] Joined Cases C–430/93 and C–431/93 *Van Schijndel* [1995] ECR I–4705 and Case C–312/93, *Peterbroeck* [1995] ECR I–4599, (1996) 33 *CML Rev* 1420–6, (with annotations by T Heukels). See as regards the question whether and to what extent national administrations may be under an obligation to apply EC-law *ex officio* the pending case *Kühne & Heitz NV* (2001), 1/2 *NTER* 29–35.

Despite the great number of occasions in which the "*Rewe*-criteria" were invoked before and confirmed by the Court,[25] a violation of either the principle of equivalence or the principle of effectiveness was only found to exist in a relatively limited number of cases. For example, infringements of the principle of equivalence were established in cases where the national legislature had introduced, subsequent to a Court's ruling in which national law was declared incompatible with Community law, new procedural rules specifically intended to limit the possibilities of bringing proceedings for repayment of charges levied contrary to EC-law.[26] A violation of the principle of effectiveness was found to exist in such prominent cases as *Emmott*,[27] *Peterbroeck*,[28] *Dilexport* and *Comateb*[29] as well as in *Hoechst*[30] and *Preston*.[31]

The "*Rewe*-test" has some specific characteristics. Obviously, the criteria applied by the Court of Justice do have the nature of minimum requirements, introducing a kind of minimum harmonisation of national procedural laws through creeping jurisprudence without interfering in an unnecessary manner with "national procedural autonomy"[32] (so-called negative convergence). Consequently, once the *Rewe*-test is satisfied, divergences in national procedural law remain unaffected. Moreover, the principles of effectiveness and equivalence are, at least in principle, of a horizontal nature; meaning that they apply regardless of whether national administrative, civil, criminal or other procedural rules are at issue. Finally, the "*Rewe*-test" appears attractive in its simplicity and legal *rationale*, namely to promote the uniform application of Community law, and thus to strengthen the enforcement of its primacy and direct effect.[33]

Simplicity, however, is not synonymous with predictability. Indeed, one of the main and repeated criticisms of the Court's case law in this respect is that, though perhaps attractive in their simplicity, the exact scope, meaning and impact of the principles of equivalence and effectiveness remain far from clear and predictable.[34] An illustration of this is that it took the Court, initially proceeding on

---

[25] See, more recently, e.g. Case C–88/99 *Roquette Frères*, 28 Nov. 2000, nyr., paras. 20/21, Case C–78/98 *Preston* [2000] ECR I–3201, para. 31 as well as Joined Cases C–397/98 and C–410/98 *Hoechst*, 8 March 2001, nyr., para. 85, all with further references.

[26] Case 240/87 *Deville* [1988] ECR 3513, *Barra* n. 20 above, para. 19. See, more recently, e.g. *Dilexport*, n. 22 above, paras. 37 and 39 as well as Case C–231/96 *Edis* [1998] ECR I–4951, para. 24.

[27] *Emmott*, n. 19 above, as confirmed in Case C–326/96 *Levez* [1998] ECR I–7835. See also T Heukels, n. 19 above.

[28] n. 24 above.

[29] *Dilexport*, n. 22 above, paras. 52–4, Joined Cases C–192/95 and C–218/95 *Comateb* [1997] ECR I–165. See also e.g. Joined Cases 331/85, 376/85 and 378/85 *Bianco et Girard* [1988] ECR 1099, para. 12 as well as Case C–228/98 *Dounias* [2000] ECR I–577, paras. 58–61.

[30] Joined Cases C–397/98 and C–410/98, *Hoechst*, 8 March 2001, nyr., esp. paras. 85, 96 and 107.

[31] Case C–78/98 *Preston* [2000] ECR I–3201, paras. 40–45.

[32] Kakouris, n. 1 above, at 1395–6, Szyszczak, n. 1 above, at 351–63 and Van Gerven, n. 1 above, at 694.

[33] *Cf.* in general W van Gerven, "Of Rights, Remedies and Procedures" (2000) 37 *CML Rev* 501–36.

[34] Biondi, n. 1 above, at 1277–80, Himsworth, n. 1 above, at 310 and Prechal, n. 9 above, at 689–90.

a case by case basis, nearly twenty years to begin to clarify the general scope and implications of the principle of effectiveness. In 1995, the Court stated in the much-discussed *Peterbroeck* case:[35]

"[. . .] each case which raises the question whether a national procedural provision renders application of Community law impossible or excessively difficult must be analysed by reference to the role of that provision in the procedure, its progress and its special features, viewed as a whole, before the various national instances. In the light of that analysis the basic principles of the domestic judicial system, such as the protection of the rights of the defence, the principle of legal certainty and the proper conduct of the procedure must, where appropriate, be taken into consideration".

It took the Court even longer—until 1998—to find the opportunity to address in a more general way the complicated question, in the context of the principle of equivalence, as to how it should be assessed whether Community law claims are treated less favourably than similar claims under domestic law. More specifically, the Court stressed in *Levez* that the principle of equivalence requires that the rule at issue be applied without distinction, whether the infringement alleged is of Community law or national law, where the purpose and cause of action are similar, without, however, obliging member states to extend their most favourable rules to all actions brought. As regards the case before it, the Court asserted:[36]

"[. . .] the national court [. . .] must consider both the purpose and the essential characteristics of allegedly similar domestic actions. Furthermore, whenever it falls to be determined whether a procedural rule of national law is less favourable than those governing similar domestic actions, the national court must take into account the role played by that provision in the procedure as a whole, as well as the operation and any special features of that procedure before the different national courts".

Peterbroeck, *Levez* and similar judgments, such as the rulings in *Edis*, *Ansaldo* and *Dilexport*,[37] were welcomed and criticised alike by commentators.[38] Some felt that the Court took due care of the particular characteristics underlying the national procedural provisions of Belgian and Italian law and welcomed the introduction of more detailed elements to be taken into account when applying the "*Rewe*-test".[39] Others, however, emphasised that the Court's jurisprudence not only appeared to be inconsistent in some respects, but also accused the "*Rewe*-doctrine" of being too complicated and opaque to be applied properly by most domestic courts, who are, as a rule, only occasionally

[35] Case C–312/93 *Peterbroeck* [1995] ECR I–4599, para. 14.
[36] Case C–326/96 *Levez*,[1998] ECR I–7835, paras. 41–44, with reference to Case C–231/96 *Edis* [1998] ECR I–4951, para. 36, Case C–261/95 *Palmisani* [1997] ECR I–4025, paras. 34–38 and Case C–431/93 *Van Schijndel* [1995] ECR I–4705, para. 19. Confirmed and refined in Case C–78/98 *Preston* [2000] ECR I–3201, paras. 49 and 56–63.
[37] *Cf*. esp. the rulings of 15 Sept. 1998 in Joined Cases C–279/96, C–280/96 and C–281/96 *Ansaldo* [1998] ECR I–5025 and Case C–231/96 *Edis* [1998] ECR I–4951.
[38] Biondi, n. 1 above, at 1277, Himsworth, n. 1 above, at 307–10, Hoskins, n. 1 above, at 365.
[39] E.g. Craufurd Smith, n. 1 above, at 299.

confronted with the Community law principles of equivalence and effective-ness.[40] Moreover, the Court was criticised for applying the "*Rewe*-test" itself, instead of leaving the assessment of national procedural rules in the light of Community law in a particular case to the national judiciary, who might be con-sidered to be better equipped for this task. Such an approach would, it was added, also do justice to the division of competence between the Court of Justice and domestic courts.[41]

Indeed, despite their appealing simplicity and horizontal scope, the actual application of the "*Rewe* criteria" by an "ordinary" national court appears highly complex. The overall impression is that the national judiciary are hardly given any detailed and decisive clues as to how to apply the principles of equiv-alence and effectiveness in a particular case. For example, how should the crite-ria developed in *Peterbroeck* be weighted? Is there any hierarchy between these criteria, or are they of equal—and interrelated—value? Is it not true that nearly every provision of national procedural law can be justified by reference to such general principles as legal certainty?[42]

In short, the national judiciary is obliged to apply an apparently simple Community law test; in many cases, however, a national court may face a puz-zling, if not confusing, range of sometimes vague legal guidelines that should be applied when being called to decide whether a national procedural rule is violating the principle of equivalence and/or effectiveness. Foreseeability and clarity, two criteria rightly and repeatedly imposed by the Court on Community legislation,[43] appear not yet fully consolidated within the development of the "*Rewe*-doctrine". Consequently, further clarification appears of great importance. This appears even more urgent, if it is taken into account that non-application or incorrect application of the principles of equivalence and/or effectiveness may even in exceptional circumstances trigger a member state's liability for violation of Community law.

STATE LIABILITY AND INTERIM MEASURES:
TRENDS TOWARDS COMMUNAUTARISATION

Originally, the minimum requirements of the *Rewe*-test also governed the doc-trine of state liability for violation of Community law as well as the criteria for the adoption of interim measures suspending the application of national rules implementing EC law. Consequently, questions of state liability and interim measures were originally governed by domestic law, subject to the principles of

---

[40] Craufurd Smith, n. 1 above, at 292, Biondi, n. 1 above, at 1276 and Van Gerven, n. 1 above, at 692.

[41] Szyszczak, n. 1 above, at 351.

[42] Hoskins, n. 1 above, at 375.

[43] Compare e.g. Case T–115/94 *Opel Austria* [1997] ECR II–39, para. 124, Case C–325/91 *France* v. *Commission* [1993] ECR I–3283, para. 26 and Case C–30/89 *Commission* v. *France* [1990] ECR I–691, para. 23.

effectiveness and equivalence.[44] From 1990 onwards, however, the Court's jurisprudence is characterised by a remarkable and rapid change from respect for national procedural autonomy towards communautarisation.

State Liability

In the field of state liability for violation of Community law, this change of perspective started with the famous *Francovich*-ruling and was further developed in well-known judgments such as *Brasserie du Pêcheur*, *British Telecom*, *Hedley Lomas* and *Dillenkofer*.[45] As a result, in general terms member states may be held liable for a violation of Community law provisions intended to confer rights on individuals when a sufficiently serious breach of EC law lies at the origin of the damage allegedly incurred.[46] Consequently, the substantive conditions determining a member state's liability for violation of EC law are henceforth of a Community law, and not of a national law nature. The interaction with and assimilation to the conditions governing the Community's non-contractual liability under Article 288(2) EC are obvious, and the underlying *rationale* is also the same in both cases: whenever individuals suffer damage from a violation of Community law, compensation should be awarded according to similar criteria, regardless of whether a Community institution or a member state authority has caused the damage sustained.

It should be noted that the regime thus created for member state liability for violation of EC law retains a minimalist character; the Court's jurisprudence does not prevent the national legislature or judiciary from introducing or maintaining a higher level of judicial protection for the benefit of individuals.[47] It should, moreover, be stressed that issues such as causation, the establishment of the actual amount of compensation and the determination of the public authority of the member state concerned which should fulfil the obligation to make reparation still remain a matter for domestic law, subject of course to the *Rewe*-test.[48] In other words, the Court's case law does not lead to complete harmonisation.

[44] Esp. Case 6/60 *Humblet* [1960] ECR 559 and Case 60/75 *Russo* [1976] ECR 45, para. 9.

[45] Joined Cases C–6/90 and C–9/90 *Francovich* [1991] ECR I–5357, *Brasserie du Pêcheur*, n. 2 above, Joined Cases C–178, C–179, C–188, C–189 and C–190/94 *Dillenkofer* [1996] 3, Case C–392/93 *British Telecom* [1996] ECR I–1654 and Case C–5/94 *Hedley Lomas* [1996] ECR I–2553. See e.g. T Heukels, "Het Dillenkofer-arrest: tweesporenbeleid of synthese?" (1997) 1/2 *NTER* 28–32.

[46] See in general e.g. D Waelbroeck, "Treaty Violations and Liability of Member States: The Effect of the Francovich Case Law" in T Heukels and A McDonnell, n. 51 below, 311–38 and T Tridimas, "Member State Liability in Damages for Breach of Community Law: an Assessment of the Case Law" in J Beatson and T Tridimas (eds.), *New Directions in European Public Law* (Oxford: Hart, 1998) 11–33.

[47] E.g. *Brasserie*, n. 2 above, para. 66.

[48] *Brasserie*, n. 2 above, paras. 67 and 83. *Cf.* also Case C–302/97 *Konle* [1999] ECR I–3099, paras. 63–64, confirmed in Case C–424/97 *Haim* [2000] ECR I–5123, paras. 27–34. See as regards the potential practical impact of the Court's case law e.g the *Factortame* judgment of 28 Oct. 1999 of the House of Lords, [1999] 3 WLR 1062. *Cf.* also A Cygan, "Defining a Sufficiently Serious Breach of Community Law: the House of Lords casts its Nets into the Waters" (2000) 25 *EL Rev* 452–59.

This revolutionary jurisprudence of the EC Court has not only triggered approval, but also (sometimes vehement) criticism from politicians and academics alike. For example, the Court was accused of exercising an unfounded form of judicial activism,[49] relying on an insufficient legal basis, i.e. Article 10 EC in conjunction with the ominous proclamation that the principle of state liability for violations of Community law is a principle inherent in the EC Treaty itself.[50] Likewise, the Court's assumption that there is a general principle both in Community law and in the national law of the member states according to which an unlawful act or omission gives rise to an obligation to make good the damage caused, was labeled "an unsubstantiated sweeping statement".[51] Moreover, it is well known that during the negotiations on the Amsterdam Treaty it was proposed, albeit in vain, to limit some of the potential implications of the *Francovich/Brasserie*-doctrine.[52]

Interim Measures

A trend similar to the developments concerning state liability for violation of Community law can be discerned as regards the question of which conditions govern the award of interim measures against national rules implementing EC law. The Court's case law in this respect is basically characterised by two stages.

The first stage is marked by the famous *Factortame I* ruling, according to which national courts are under a duty to set aside any national procedural rule that forms the sole obstacle for granting interim relief in case of national measures implementing Community law.[53] Clearly, the underlying, albeit implicit, premise still was that the award of interim measures basically was governed by national procedural rules, provided that both the *Rewe*-criteria were duly respected.[54]

In the 1991 *Zuckerfabrik Süderdithmarschen* case, however, a second major step was taken.[55] Having found that the conditions concerning the suspension

[49] See in general e.g. T Tridimas, "The Court of Justice and Judicial Activism" (1996) 21 *EL Rev* 199–210.
[50] *Francovich*, n. 6 above, paras. 35–7, recently confirmed in Case C–150/99 *Stockholm Lindöpark* [2001] ECR I–493, para. 36, with extensive references to earlier Court rulings.
[51] A Barav, "State Liability in Damages for Breach of Community Law in the National Courts" in T Heukels and A McDonnell (eds.) *The Action for Damages in Community Law* (London: Kluwer Law International, 1997) 363–408, at 374.
[52] See e.g. *Agence Europe*, 16 Mar. 1996, No. 6689, at 3. *Cf.* also G Betlem, "The King can do no wrong: State liability for breach of European Community law in the post-*Francovich* area", http://webjcli.ncl.ac.uk, at 11.
[53] Case C–213/89 *Factortame I* [1990] ECR I–2433, para. 23, confirmed in Case C–1/99 *Kofisa Italia*, 11 Jan. 2001, nyr., para. 48. See e.g. N Gravells, "Effective Protection of Community Law Rights: temporary Disapplication of an Act of Parliament" [1991] *Public Law* 180.
[54] See e.g. implicitly P Craig and G de Búrca, *EU Law* (2nd edn., Oxford: OUP, 1998) 222, who explain the *Factortame* ruling on the basis of the Court's previous rulings that national rules governing the grant of remedies should not be such as to render the exercise of a Community right impossible or ineffective.
[55] Joined Cases C–143/88 and C–92/89 *Zuckerfabrik Süderdithmarschen* [1991] ECR I–415, paras. 14–21.

of enforcement of administrative measures may vary from member state to member state and, consequently, may jeopardise the uniform application of Community law, the Court formulated four cumulative criteria to be respected by the national judiciary when being called upon temporarily to suspend national rules implementing EC law. In brief, there must be serious doubts as to the validity of the Community measure concerned, the case must be referred to the Court of Justice under Article 234 EC,[56] there must be urgency as well as a threat of serious and irreparable damage to the applicants and, finally, due account must be taken of the Community's interests.[57] Several subsequent judgments have confirmed and clarified these principles, which reflect established jurisprudence now.[58] The result is that the criteria governing the award of interim measures against national measures implementing Community law come very close to those developed by the Court in the case of interim measures against acts of the EC institutions under Articles 242 and 243 EC.

Common Features

The Court's rulings concerning state liability and interim measures do have some interesting common features. In both instances, formerly typically national law doctrines that were only marginally influenced by Community law through the application of the *Rewe*-criteria have now been transformed into autonomous Community law doctrines (so-called positive convergence). Consequently, trends towards communautarisation have superceded respect for national procedural autonomy to the benefit of a uniform application of Community law and the effective enforcement of Community law rights. Likewise, the Court has taken its own jurisprudence on the Community system of judicial protection as a predominant source of inspiration. In the case of state liability according to the *Francovich/Brasserie*-doctrine there is an obvious assimilation to the conditions governing the Community's non-contractual liability under Article 288(2) EC.[59] Similarly, a clear convergence can be distinguished between the regime established by Articles 242 and 243 EC, on the one hand, and the conditions allowing national courts to grant interim measures against national acts implementing EC law, on the other hand.[60] The underlying assumption is obvious. As the Court

[56] Obviously, only the EC Court can declare a Community measure invalid. *Cf.* Case 314/85 *Foto-Frost* [1987] ECR 4199.

[57] *Zuckerfabrik Süderdithmarschen*, n. 2 above, para. 33.

[58] See esp. Case C–465/93 *Atlanta Fruchthandelsgesellschaft* [1995] ECR I–3761 and Case C–68/95 *T. Port* [1996] ECR I–6065.

[59] *Cf.* also A Barav, "State Liability in Damages for Breach of Community Law in the National Courts" (1996) 16 *YEL* 87; P Craig, "Once More unto the Breach: the Community, the State and Damages Liability" (1997) 113 *LQR* 67 and W Van Gerven, "Bridging the Unbridgeable: Community and National Tort Laws after Francovich and Brasserie" (1996) 45 *ICLQ* 507.

[60] See for further details e.g. A Barav, "Omnipotent Courts" in D Curtin and T Heukels (eds.) *Institutional Dynamics of European Integration* (Dordrecht: Nijhoff, 1994) 265–302; D Oliver, "Interim Measures: Some Recent Developments" (1992) 29 *CML Rev* 7 and Pappadias, "Interim Protection under Community Law before the National Courts" (1994) 2 *LIEI* 153.

held in the recent *Bergaderm*-ruling, "[t]he protection of rights which individuals derive from Community law cannot vary depending on whether a national authority or a Community authority is responsible".[61]

As a logical consequence, the margin of discretion for national courts has diminished. Needless to say, both trends towards communautarisation are in marked contrast with the aforementioned *Rewe*-doctrine, which mainly focuses on respect for national procedural autonomy.

LEGISLATIVE HARMONISATION: A PATCHWORK-APPROACH?

Parallel to the growing case law of the Court of Justice concerning national legal remedies, legislative acts of the Community institutions have increasingly encroached upon national procedural law. This is clearly reflected in the "*Rewe*-test" itself, which is only held to be applicable "[i]n the absence of Community rules on this subject [. . .]".[62] Obviously, this reservation is based on the premise that the Community is competent to establish its own harmonised system of procedural law by means of secondary law. Indeed, as early as 1964 the Community felt the need to give migrant workers and their family members adequate legal remedies in the state of residence, and provided in Directive No. 64/221 that they should have "the same legal remedies [. . .] as are available to nationals of the State concerned in respect of acts of the administration".[63] Roughly two trends appear to dominate the Community's efforts to improve judicial protection at the national level, namely; (a) the partial harmonisation of diverging national systems of judicial protection through standard clauses concerning access to justice and; (b) the establishment of coherent, specific and more detailed procedures in sector-specific areas.[64]

Many directives reflect the cautious efforts of the Community to harmonise national procedural law. Often, such directives intend to secure that administrative decisions of national public authorities to the detriment of individuals

---

[61] Case C–352/98 P *Bergaderm*, [2000] ECR I–5291, para. 41, confirming *Brasserie*, n. 2 above, para. 42. Similarly as regards interim measures *Süderithmarschen*, n. 2 above, paras. 16–20, and *Atlanta Fruchthandelsgesellschaft*, n. 17 above, paras. 20–24.

[62] Case 33/76 *Rewe* [1976] ECR 1989, para. 5, *inter alia* confirmed in Case 45/76 *Comet* [1976] ECR 2043, para. 13, Case 68/79 *Just* [1980] ECR 501, para. 25 and Joined Cases C–6/90 and C–9/90 *Francovich* [1991] ECR I–5357, para. 42. Equivalent expressions include "[i]n the absence of relevant Community provisions" and "in so far as no provisions of Community law are relevant". See e.g. Joined Cases C–46/93 and C–48/93 *Brasserie du Pêcheur* [1996] ECR I–1029, paras. 83 and 90 as well as Case 265/78 *Ferwerda* [1980] ECR 617, para. 10.

[63] Third consideration of the Preamble and Art. 8 of Dir. No. 64/221 of 25 Feb. 1964 on the co-ordination of special measures concerning the movement and residence of foreign nationals which are justified on grounds of public policy, public security or public health, [1964] OJ 117–19. See also Art. 9 of this Dir.

[64] See for a more detailed analysis Jans and De Jong, "Interne harmonisatie van rechtsbeschermingsclausules in het secundaire gemeenschapsrecht?" (1999) 2 *RegelMaat* 73–83.

are properly motivated[65] and/or that aggrieved individuals have the opportunity to avail themselves of effective legal remedies under domestic law.[66] An example may be found in Directive No. 90/313, stating that any one who considers that his request for information on the environment has been unreasonably refused or ignored, "may seek a judicial or administrative review of the decision in accordance with the relevant national legal system".[67] Similarly, Directive No. 76/207 prescribes that all persons who claim to be victims of gender discrimination in the field of employment, should be able "to pursue their claims by judicial process after possible recourse to other competent authorities".[68] Occasionally, directives require the member states to provide for some form of accelerated judicial review, in order to facilitate reliance by individuals on Community law rights.[69] Other directives may state that, in particular circumstances, a person "shall be informed of the remedies available to him under the laws in force in the Member States and of the time limits allowed for the

[65] Comp. e.g. Art. 14 of Dir. No. 70/156 of 6 Feb. 1970 on the type-approval of motor vehicles and their trailers, [1970] OJ L 42/1 ("shall state in detail the reasons on which they are based") and Art. 12 of the amending Dir. No. 92/53 of 18 June 1992, [1992] OJ L 225/1. *Cf.* also Art. 5(5) of Dir. No. 80/215 of 22 Jan. 1980 on animal health problems affecting intra-Community trade in meat products, [1980] OJ L 47/4, Art. 9 of Dir. No. 98/5 of 16 Feb. 1998 to facilitate the practice of the profession of lawyer on a permanent basis in another Member State, [1998] OJ L 77/36, Art. 11 of Dir. No. 99/36 of 29 April 1999 on transportable pressure equipment, [1999] OJ L 138/20 and Art. 10 of Dir. No. 2000/14 of 8 May 2000 on the approximation of the laws of the Member States relating to the noise emission in the environment by equipment for use outdoors, [2000] OJ L 162/1.

[66] E.g. Art. 8(2) of Dir. No. 89/48 of 21 Dec. 1988 on a general system for the recognition of higher-education diplomas, [1989] OJ L 19/16, states: "A remedy shall be available against this decision, or the absence thereof, before a court or tribunal in accordance with the provisions of national law". Nearly identical Art. 12(2) of Dir. No. 92/51 of 18 June 1992 on a second general system for the recognition of professional education and training to supplement Dir. No. 89/48, [1992] OJ L 209/25, and Art. 9 of Dir. No. 98/5 of 16 Feb. 1998 to facilitate the practice of the profession of lawyer on a permanent basis in another Member State, [1998] OJ L 77/36.

[67] Art. 4 of Dir. No. 90/313 of 7 June 1990 on the freedom of access to information on environment, [1990] OJ L 158/56. *Cf.* also Arts. 12 and 22(3) of Dir. No. 73/239 of 24 July 1973 on the co-ordination of provisions relating to the taking-up and pursuit of the business of direct insurance other than life insurance, [1973] OJ L 228/3, according to which Member States "shall make provision for a right to apply to the courts", Art. 7 of Dir. 96/57 of 3 Sept. 1996 on energy efficiency requirements for household electric refrigerators, freezers and combinations thereof, [1996] OJ L 236/36 and Art. 33 of Dir. No. 2000/12 relating to the taking up and pursuit of the business of credit institutions, [2000] OJ L 126/1.

[68] Art. 6 of Dir. No. 76/207 of 9 Feb. 1976 on the implementation of the principle of equal treatment for men and women as regards access to employment, vocational training and promotion, and working conditions, [1976] OJ L 39/41. Similarly, Art. 6 of Dir. No. 79/7 of 19 Dec. 1978 on the progressive implementation of the principle of equal treatment for men and women in matters of social security, [1979] OJ L 6/24, and Art. 8(1) of Dir. No. 91/553 of 14 Oct. 1991 on an employer's obligation to inform employees of the conditions applicable to the contract or employment relationship, [1991] OJ L288/32. *Cf.* also Art. 23(5) of Dir. No. 89/552 of 3 Oct. 1989 on the co-ordination of provisions concerning the pursuit of television broadcasting activities, [1989] OJ L 298/23 (disputes as to the exercise of the right of reply should be subject to judicial review), Art. 9 of Dir. No. 98/49 of 29 June 1998 on safeguarding the supplementary pension rights of employed and self-employed persons moving within the Community, [1998] OJ L 209/46, Art. 7a of Dir. No. 98/50 of 29 June 1998 amending Dir. No. 77/187 on the approximation of the laws of the Member States relating to the safeguarding of employees' rights in the event of transfers of undertakings, business or parts of business, [1998] OJ L 201/88.

[69] E.g. Art. 18(1) of Dir. No. 2000/31 of 8 June 2000 on electronic commerce, [2000] OJ L 178/1.

exercise of such remedies".[70] However, sometimes, and somewhat curiously, it is added that the directive concerned shall not affect the current domestic system of remedies against decisions of public authorities.[71] Legal bases used in this respect are, *inter alia*, Articles 37,[72] 40,[73] 46(2),[74] 47,[75] 55,[76] 94,[77] 95,[78] 175[79] and/or 308 EC.[80]

In principle, Community harmonising measures may contribute to transparency and coherence in the field of national procedural rules. However, in as far as harmonising Community acts merely express the basic principles of access to justice and the duty to state reasons, they basically just confirm what already follows from the *Heylens* ruling. There the Court held the principle of effective judicial protection and the duty to state reasons to be autonomous general principles of a constitutional nature that apply in any case in which individuals seek to invoke Community rights in national courts, regardless of whether they are embodied in secondary law.[81] Moreover, it would be mistaken to conclude from the insertion of standard clauses in directives concerning access to justice that member states would retain complete freedom as to the method of its realisation; instead, this apparent procedural autonomy is limited by the traditional and self-evident "*Rewe*-criteria", as discussed above.[82]

More detailed and sector-specific (partial) harmonisation of national procedural laws may be found in fields such as consumer protection and pub-

---

[70] Such a so-called "*Rechtsmittelbelehrung*" is e.g. provided for in Art. 14 of Dir. No. 70/156 of 6 Feb. 1970 on the approximation of the laws of the Member States relating to the type-approval of motor vehicles and their trailers, [1970] OJ L 42/1, Art. 5(5) of Dir. No. 80/215, n. 65 above, Art. 12 of the amending Dir. No. 92/53 of 18 June 1992, [1992] OJ L 225/1 as well as in Art. 11 of Dir. No. 93/44 of 14 June 1993 amending Dir. No. 89/392 on the approximation of the laws of the Member States relating to machinery, [1993] OJ L 175/13. In Case C–120/97 *Upjohn* [1999] ECR I–223, para. 28, the Court interpreted Art. 12 of Dir. No. 65/65 on the approximation of provisions laid down by law, regulation or administrative action in relation to proprietary medicinal products as requiring "[. . .] the Member States to provide for decisions to be open to challenge by way of legal proceedings".

[71] For example Art. 6(1) of Dir. No. 80/215, n. 65 above.

[72] Dir. No. 80/215, n. 65 above.

[73] Dir. No. 89/48, n. 66 above, the supplementing Dir. No. 92/51, n. 66 above, and Dir. No. 98/5, n. 65 above.

[74] Dir. No. 64/221, n. 63 above.

[75] Dir. No. 73/239, n. 67 above, Dir. No. 89/48, n. 66 above, the supplementing Dir. No. 92/51, n. 66 above, Dir. No. 98/5, n. 65 above, and Dir. No. 2000/9 of 20 March 2000 relating to cableway installations designed to carry persons, [2000] OJ L 106/21.

[76] E.g. Dir. No. 89/48, n. 66 above, and the supplementing Dir. No. 92/51, n. 66 above. See also Dir. No. 89/552, n. 68 above.

[77] Dir. No. 70/156, n. 65 above, Dir. No. 80/215, n. 65 above, and Dir. No. 98/50, n. 68 above.

[78] Dir. No. 92/53, n. 65 above, Dir. No. 93/44, n. 70 above, Dir. No. 99/44 of 25 May 1999 on certain aspects of the sale of consumer goods and associated guarantees, [1999] OJ L 171/12 and Dir. No. 2000/14, n. 65 above.

[79] E.g. Dir. No. 90/313, n. 67 above.

[80] Dir. No. 76/207, n. 68 above, and Dir. No. 79/7, n. 68 above.

[81] Case 222/86 *Heylens* [1987] ECR 4097, with reference to Case 222/84 *Johnston* [1986] ECR 1651. This conclusion is clearly supported by Case C–97/91 *Borelli* [1992] ECR I–6313.

[82] Jans and de Jong, n. 64 above, at 78.

lic procurement. As regards consumer protection, mention may be made of Directive No. 84/450 concerning misleading advertising. Persons and organisations regarded under national law as having a legitimate interest in prohibiting misleading advertising may take legal action against such advertising and/or bring such advertising before an administrative authority. Specific provisions concern, *inter alia*, the nature of claims and procedures (e.g. order of cessation or interim relief) as well as evidence and the burden of proof.[83] Other prominent examples in the field of consumer protection are to be found in the directives concerning product liability, package travels, unfair terms in consumer contracts and injunctions for the protection of consumers' interests.[84] The directive on product liability concerns important issues, such as the introduction of a system of liability without fault on the part of the producer, reversal of the burden of proof, contributory negligence of the injured person, joint liability and the introduction of a uniform period of limitation for bringing an action for compensation, as well as rules governing its suspension or interruption.[85]

In the field of public procurement, one can point to Directives No. 89/665 and No. 92/13. Both introduce more detailed rules concerning, *inter alia*, the suspensive effect of procedures concerning allegedly wrongful public tenders, interlocutory proceedings, evidence and the award of damages.[86] However, due account is taken of "the specific nature of certain legal orders by authorising the Member States to choose between the introduction of different powers for the review bodies which have equivalent effects".[87] Another striking example, this time in the field of equal treatment, is provided by Directive No. 97/80, which provides for detailed rules concerning the reversal of the burden of proof in gender discrimination cases.[88]

---

[83] *Cf.* Arts. 4–6 of Dir. No. 84/450 of 10 Sept. 1984 concerning misleading advertising, [1984] OJ L 250/17, as amended by Dir. No. 97/55 so as to include comparative advertising, [1997] OJ L 290/18. See also Art. 12 of Dir. No. 92/28 of 31 March 1992 on the advertising of medicinal products for human use, [1992] OJ L 113/13.

[84] Dir. No. 85/375 of 25 July 1985 concerning liability for defective products, [1985] OJ L 210/29 as amended by Dir. No. 99/34 of 10 May 1999, [1999] OJ L 141/20, Dir. No. 90/314 of 13 June 1990 on package travel, package holiday and package tours, [1990] OJ L 158/59, Dir. No. 93/13 of 5 April 1993 on unfair terms in consumer contracts, [1993] OJ L 95/29 and Dir. No. 98/27 of 19 May 1998 on injunctions for the protection of consumers' interests, [1998] OJ L 166/51. See also Commission Recommendation No. 98/257 of 30 March 1998 on the principles applicable to the bodies responsible for out-of-court settlement of consumer disputes, [1998] OJ L 115/31.

[85] Compare Arts. 1, 5 and 8 of Dir. No. 85/375, n. 84 above.

[86] Dir. No. 89/665 of 21 December 1989 relating to the application of review procedures to the award of public supply and public works contracts, [1989] OJ L 395/33, and Dir. No. 92/13 of 25 Feb. 1992 on the procurement procedures of entities operating in the water, energy, transport and telecommunications sectors, [1992] OJ L 76/14.

[87] *Cf.* e.g. the 7th consideration of the Preamble of Dir. No. 92/13, *ibid.* Likewise consideration 8 of the Preamble to Dir. No. 98/27, n. 84 above: "the specific features of national legal systems must be taken into account to every extent possible by leaving Member States free to choose between different options having equivalent effect."

[88] Dir. No. 97/80 of 15 Dec. 1997, [1998] OJ L 14/6.

Most of the directives mentioned here are, in whole or in part, based on Article 94[89] or 95 EC.[90] The frequent use of Article 95 EC as a legal basis for specific provisions indicate that it is intended to establish a certain degree of minimum harmonisation of national procedural law.[91] In other words, member states are not precluded *a priori* from retaining or adopting provisions with a view to ensuring more extensive judicial protection for individuals coming within the scope of the directives concerned. Again, however, should member states decide to maintain or introduce a higher level of judicial protection, such autonomous national procedural measures remain subject to the aforementioned "*Rewe*-criteria".

For the sake of completeness, it should be noted that Community regulations may also have a (in)direct bearing on national procedural rules. Such influence may be rather minimal, in that only some elementary rules of judicial protection are expressed. For example, Regulation No. 2913/92 establishing the Community Customs Code basically provides for a right to appeal against decisions of the national customs authorities in administrative and, subsequently, judicial procedures as well as the possible suspension of the disputed decision.[92]

Quite detailed rules relating to national procedural rules are, however, contained in the Regulation on the Community trade mark. This regulation obliges member states to designate courts as "Community trade mark courts" in first and second instance, determines their exclusive jurisdiction, and provides fairly precise rules as to, for example, counterclaims, sanctions, provisional measures and the presumption of validity.[93] Interaction may, however, also occur the other way around. Thus, it is provided that the Community Trade Mark Office shall, in the absence of procedural provisions in the relevant Community acts, "take into account the principles of procedural law generally recognised in the Member States".[94] Even the principle of equivalence, as developed in the Court's established case law, appears to be codified in this context: "[. . .] a Community trade mark court shall apply the rules of procedure governing the same type of action relating to a national trade mark in the Member State where it has its seat".[95]

Even though some basic trends might be discerned in the Community's efforts to harmonise national procedural rules, it appears difficult to distinguish a

[89] E.g. Dir. No. 84/450, n. 83 above, and Dir. No. 85/374 of 25 July 1985 on the approximation of the laws, regulations and administrative provisions of the Member States concerning liability for defective products, [1985] OJ L 210/29.
[90] Such as Dir. No. 89/665, n. 86 above, Dir. No. 92/13, n. 86 above, Dir. No. 92/28, n. 83 above, Dir. No. 98/27, n. 84 above, Dir. No. 97/55, n. 83 above, and Dir. No. 2000/31, n. 69 above.
[91] For example, Art. 7 (1) of Dir. No. 84/450 as amended by Dir. No. 97/55, both n. 83 above, as well as Art. 8 of Dir. No. 90/314, n. 84 above, and Art. 7 of Dir. No. 98/27, n. 84 above.
[92] Reg. No. 2913/92 of 12 Oct. 1992, [1992] OJ L 302/1.
[93] See esp. Arts. 90–104 of Reg. No. 40/94 of 20 Dec. 1993 on the Community trade mark, [1994] OJ L 11/1. *Cf.* also Arts. 94–107 of Reg. No. 2100/94 of 27 July 1994 on Community plant variety rights, [1994] OJ L 227/1.
[94] *Ibid.*, Art. 79. The analogy with Art. 288(2) EC appears obvious. Similarly Art. 81(1) of Reg. No. 2100/94, n. 93 above.
[95] *Ibid.*, Art. 97(3). Likewise Art. 103 of Reg. No. 2100/94, n. 93 above.

coherent overall policy underlying the Community's activities. Rather, the impression is one of fragmentation and of an *ad hoc*-approach. Obviously, *ad hocery* has the merit of avoiding fundamental discussions—and controversies— on matters of principle, including the creeping loss of external competence for member states that is inherent in the process of harmonisation at the Community level by virtue of the *ERTA* doctrine. On the negative side, however, it becomes more and more difficult to establish, if such were desirable, a more coherent and transparent Community law framework for embedding national procedural rules.[96] One may wonder whether, given the current stage of harmonisation and integration and having regard to the principle of subsidiarity, it should not be a priority to take up the difficult challenge to discuss the expediency, legal possibilities and legal limits of harmonisation of national procedural laws.[97]

CONCLUDING REMARKS

This brief *tour d'horizon* clearly demonstrates that the combined effect of both Community harmonisation measures and the case law of the Court of Justice is a growing "communautarisation" of national procedural law. This trend is characterised by two approaches, i.e. the gradual replacement of national procedural rules by Community law standards (e.g. the *Francovich/Brasserie*-approach) and the creation of Community minimum standards imposed on national procedural law (e.g. the *Rewe*-approach). The first one can be typified as positive convergence, whereas the latter rather reflects tendencies towards negative convergence. As shown above, both phenomena can also be found in Community legislative efforts to harmonise national procedural law. The result appears to be a clear tendency towards homogeneity and convergence in the field of legal remedies.

Homogenising tendencies, however, do not exclude divergence. On the contrary, approaches such as in *Rewe* leave ample scope for divergence in the field of legal remedies above the minimum level of protection required by Community law. Similar considerations apply to the *Francovich/Brasserie*-doctrine, in as much as it does not prevent member states from maintaining or introducing a higher level of judicial protection. Moreover, the aforementioned trends towards "communautarisation" of national procedural law benefit only claims based on Community law and do not extend to claims solely based on national law. Consequently, the problem of so-called "double procedural

---

[96] It should be noted that, in some cases, "harmonisation" is subjected to the regime of the third pillar. See e.g. Arts. 61(e) EC *juncto* Arts. 29(e) and 31(e) EU.

[97] The complexity of such an effort is clearly demonstrated by similar projects undertaken in the field of civil law. See especially O Lando and H Beale (eds.), *Principles of European Contract Law*, Parts I and II (London: Kluwer Law International, 2000), H Koziol (ed.), *Unification of Tort Law: Wrongfulness* (London: Kluwer Law International, 1998) and J Spier and F D Burnelli (eds.), *Unification of Tort Law: Causation* (London: Kluwer Academic, 2000).

standards" may arise: the judicial enforcement of Community law rights may have to be treated more favourably under national procedural law than the enforcement of equivalent claims solely based on domestic law.[98] Obviously, Community law does not oppose such "reverse discrimination" in the field of judicial protection.[99] From the perspective of the individual seeking judicial redress, however, it may be legitimately questioned whether Community rights are by definition more important than rights claimed under national (constitutional) law. Why, for example, should it make a difference whether an individual invokes the Community law principle of equal pay under Article 141 EC Treaty, or the like principle inherent in domestic law or, alternatively, Article 26 of the UN Convention on Civil and Political Rights (1966)? So-called spontaneous harmonisation, i.e. the voluntary extension of Community solutions, either by the national legislator or by a member state's judiciary, to similar situations belonging solely to the domain of domestic law, might be a technique to overcome this dichotomy. It can, however, hardly offer a structural solution since it is ultimately based on the willingness of national authorities.[100]

Finally, it appears difficult to discern a coherent overall policy underlying the Community's efforts to harmonise national procedural rules. Rather, the picture is one of an *ad hoc* approach. One may, therefore, wonder whether, given the current stage of harmonisation and integration, it should not become a priority to take up the difficult challenge to discuss the expediency, legal possibilities and legal limits of harmonisation of national procedural laws, having due regard to the principle of subsidiarity and the relationship between the first and the third pillar of the European Union.[101]

---

[98] *Cf.* also Caranta, "Learning from Neighbours: Public Law Remedies Homogenization from Bottom up", (1997) 4 *MJ* 220.

[99] Craufurd Smith, n. 1 above, at 297.

[100] In the area of administrative law, already in 1992 J Schwarze (*European Administrative Law* (London: Sweet & Maxwell, 1992), at 1436) demonstrated that it is "difficult to prove that the administrative law of the European Community has also influenced the administrative laws of the Member States in areas of exclusive national competence, that is, apart from the implementation of Community law". See as regards Dutch law, Widdershoven, "Interne harmonisatie binnen de Nederlandse rechtsbescherming onder invloed van de Europese rechtspraak" (1999) 2 *RegelMaat* 84–98, at 91. An example of such upgrading of domestic judicial protection has been achieved with regard to the remedy of interim relief by the House of Lords' decision in *M.* v. *Home Office* [1994] AC 377, [1993] 3 All ER 537.

[101] See e.g. Art. 61 (e) EC in conjunction with Art. 29 *et seq.* EU.

Part Four
The Human Rights Dimension

<h1 style="text-align:center">8</h1>

Convergence and Divergence in European Public Law: The Case of Human Rights

GRAINNE DE BÚRCA*

INTRODUCTION

GIVEN THAT THE theme of this book is one which seeks to explore convergences and divergences in European public law, an obvious way of situating the subject of human rights within that framework would be to consider whether the legal and political conceptions of human rights protection within and across member states of the EU are converging under the influence of the European Convention on Human Rights, the evolving human rights jurisprudence of the European Court of Justice, and more recently and speculatively, the EU Charter of Fundamental Rights. The inquiry of this chapter, however, is situated at a prior stage, in considering the extent to which a human rights "system" is in fact emerging at the European level. Its focus is primarily on the EU, rather than on the ECHR or on the relationship between those systems.[1] As far as the Convention on Human Rights is concerned, it is certainly possible to point to a degree of formal convergence, most obviously manifested in its eventual incorporation by all of the EU member states including recently the UK and Ireland. But to consider seriously the impact of the Convention norms and of the jurisprudence of the Strasbourg Court on EU member states would entail a more complex inquiry, examining not only the extent to which national laws and practices have been adapted in order to achieve a degree of conformity with those norms, but also the extent to which such implementation, transposition or absorption of norms might be occurring in ways which are quite distinctive and specific to the various national legal systems.

The focus of this chapter instead is on the EU dimension of the subject. In the field of human rights, the question whether some degree of convergence of

* Thanks are due to many of the participants at the conference held in Aberdeen in May 2000 for their suggestions and comments, and in particular to Carol Harlow and Neil Walker.
[1] Some of these issues are considered in the chapters by Paul Beaumont and Niamh Nic Shuibhne in the present volume.

national law is taking place under the influence of EU law presupposes that there are relevant norms at EU level which could cause national legal systems to converge in this respect. Yet, in the field of human rights (even taking into account how vague the contours of that subject may be) the role and relevance of the European Union remains contested and confused. Unlike some other fields of administrative and constitutional law, the legal foundations of the EU's competence to adopt human rights norms and its position as an actor in that field are uncertain. From one perspective, it could be said that the EU's influence on the nature and content of human rights norms within member states is at best a derived and indirect one, since the human rights principles recognised within EU law are actually drawn from the ECHR and from the national legal systems in the first place. However, the position is more complex than this. While there is clearly—as there is in various other fields of administrative law—some kind of reciprocal relationship between the development of legal principles within the EU legal system and within member states' legal systems, the EU is arguably developing what might be called an autonomous, rather than a parasitic or purely derivative human rights competence. How the norms and principles which are articulated by the EU will be shaped, and whether and how they are likely to influence the national legal systems remains to be seen. But my current focus is on examining the emerging basis for and nature of a distinctive European Union human rights policy, rather than tracing the subsequent question of its influence on national systems.

There are a number of contested premises underlying this chapter, which I will set out here but without attempting to defend them in any detail within the constraints of this particular forum. First, in contrast to the chapter of Paul Beaumont, which poses certain challenges to the discourse and concept of human rights, the principle of equal human dignity is accepted here as the normative foundation on which the international human rights regime, and in turn the emergent EU regime (however weakly developed), is based. Secondly, the fairly stark dichotomisation which sometimes characterises debate on the EU, in which the EU is posited essentially as an elite-driven liberal trade regime while the nation state is presented as the only legitimate site of pluralist democracy, is rejected. Thirdly, the depiction of politics as a deliberative public sphere, with "human rights" contrasted as a set of categorical legal constructs which privilege the judicial role, is rejected. The argument proceeds instead from a number of other premises, to which I will return at the end of the paper. Firstly, that the legal category of "human rights" whether as the subject of policy-making or in the context of adjudication provides a language which can draw participants into a debate rather than closing off or pre-empting dialogue. Secondly, that the nation state and the EU remain to some extent as distinct but overlapping and interlocking sites of decision-making, which represent differing balances between a range of values and policies. Thirdly, that there is also an emergent transnational political space—albeit as yet rather undeveloped—in Europe within which debate, contestation and decision-making can take place without the existence of pre-political conditions of social and cultural homogeneity. Fourthly, that it is no longer for citizens to choose *between* national, supranational or transnational political sites and structures of governance, because in a globalising economic environment, failure to engage other than with those situated within the nation state does not remain a viable option. It is not a simple choice between culturally situated specific national laws and abstracted technocratic supranational EU laws, but rather the existence of a much more complex and plural system of national and transnational governance needs to be acknowledged.

Beginning from these premises, the aim of the chapter is to consider whether, given the existence of the ECHR and the national systems of human rights protection, it is either necessary or legitimate for the EU to foster human rights norms, and to develop an autonomous human rights policy of its own.

For the purposes of conceptual clarity, four broad dimensions or elements of the subject can be traced. (i) The first element is the EU dimension, in the sense of whether the EU as an entity should develop a set of human rights norms governing its own institutions and actions. (ii) The second is the national/member state dimension, in the sense of whether the EU should develop a set of human rights norms governing the institutions and actions of member states. (iii) The third is the specifically judicial dimension in terms of the desirability or need for a degree of EU-level judicial monitoring of human rights norms; (iv) and the fourth is the broader policy dimension in terms of the desirability or need for positive EU legislative and other measures in the field of human rights. A slightly different way of conceptualising the last two elements would be in terms of the somewhat unrefined but nevertheless useful distinction between negative and positive policy-making. While judicial monitoring and "negative" legal protections certainly overlap, they are not co-terminus, and similarly positive policy-making and legislative decision-making are not identical. As the adoption of the Charter of Fundamental Rights shows, this is a positive legal instrument in the sense of having been adopted as a general measure (and by an interesting and novel constitutional process), but one which can at the same time be presented as a largely "negative", constraining rather than enabling legal instrument.[2] Further, judicial decision-making in the human rights field is certainly not always purely negative, in the sense of monitoring public action for conformity with clearly fixed limits, but frequently entails direct and positive policy consequences.[3]

[2] This is certainly the view expressed by the legal secretariat of the Community institutions which assisted in drafting the Charter, see CHARTRE 4111/00, 20 Jan. 2000, and it is also reflected to some extent in Art. 51 of the document, which specifies that the Charter "does not establish any new power or task for the Community or the Union, or modify powers and tasks defined by the Treaties". See also the view of Fritz Scharpf "European Governance; Effective and Legitimate?", paper delivered at a workshop on Global Governance at the EUI, Florence 7 April 2001, where the Charter is presented as a constraint on EU action rather than an enabling document.

[3] See, for an interesting recent example of the justiciability of economic and social rights, *Government of South Africa and others* v. *Grootboom and others Constitutional Court—* CCT11/00 2001 (1) SA 46 (CC) 4 Oct. 2000 and the comment by C Scott and P Alston "Adjudicating Constitutional Priorities in a Transnational Context: A Comment on Soobramoney's Legacy and

The *first* (and least controversial) combination of the four elements outlined above is that of the first and the third, i.e. providing for European judicial review of the EC/EU and its institutions to monitor their observance of human rights norms. Even this subject, however, is not uncontested particularly in relation to the judicial body which should be competent to supervise: whether the European Court of Justice, the European Court of Human Rights, both or others.[4] A *second* combination which is also somewhat contested, partly on grounds of uncertain legal competence, is that of the first and the fourth elements, the EU and positive (including legislative) policy: i.e. whether the EU can and should enact human-rights protective norms to govern its own institutions and policies. A third and fourth set of combinations are, however, generally perceived to be the most problematic, and they raise the issues of convergence and divergence which are the central themes of this book in a more direct and pointed way. The *third* combination is that of elements two and three, i.e. whether some kind of EU-level judicial monitoring of member state action for compliance with human rights norms within the fields of EC/EU law is appropriate. The *fourth* combination is of elements two and four, i.e. whether it is necessary and legitimate for the EU to enact policy measures of a specific or general kind, which are binding on or legally relevant within member states, with the aim of promoting human rights. This chapter touches to some extent on all of these dimensions and combinations, but the main focus will be on the latter two combinations and particularly on the fourth. The third can already be said loosely to exist, in the shape of the Court of Justice's claim that member states are bound, within the sphere of EC law, to respect the general principles and fundamental rights which are part of their common constitutional traditions.[5] This claim is now backed up not only by Article 6 of the Treaty on European Union and the ECJ's jurisdiction under Article 46 TEU in that respect, but also to some extent by Article 51 of the Charter on Fundamental Rights proclaimed at Nice in December 2001, which declares (albeit as yet in a non-binding way and which therefore does not of itself confer any jurisdiction on the ECJ) the member states to be bound by the rights set out in the Charter "when they are

---

Grootboom's Promise" (2000) 16 *South African Journal on Human Rights* 206. Contrast the views of A Von Bogdandy who critiques the proposal for a strong EU human rights policy founded on the indivisibility of positive and negative rights, or, to use a different kind of language, the indivisibility of civil-political and social-economic rights: "The European Union as a Human Rights Organization: Human Rights and the Core of the European Union" (2000) 37 *CML Rev* 1307 at 1314–16.

[4] See E Bribosia, "La protection des droits fondamentaux" in P Magnette, (ed.), *La Constitution de l'Europe* (Bruxelles: Bruylant, 2000), I Canor. "Primus Inter Pares: Who is the Ultimate Guardian of Human Rights in Europe?" (2000) 25 *EL Rev* 2, T King "Ensuring Human Rights Review of Inter-Governmental Acts in Europe" (2000) 25 *EL Rev* 79 and K Lenaerts "Respect for Fundamental Rights as a Constitutional Principle of the European Union" (2000) *Columbia JEL* 1, 9–18 and also "Fundamental Rights in the European Union" (2000) 25 *EL Rev* 575.

[5] See generally, Case 5/88, *Wachauf* [1989] ECR 2609, Case C–260/89 *ERT* [1991] ECR I–2925, Case 292/97 *Kjell Karlsson*, [2000] ECR I–2737.

implementing Union law".[6] Consequently, the primary focus here will be on the question whether, and if so why, the EU should pursue an active EU-wide human rights policy or programme through law.

The subject of EU human rights action is one in respect of which, paradoxically, there has been a great deal of discussion but few concrete measures, and particularly not relative to the bulk of EU legislative activity. There are many reports and official documents and there has been a good deal of discussion, but relatively little until recently by way of concrete policy measures. Further, there have been a number of developments, outlined below, which suggest that the legal powers and basic competence of the EU to act within its own borders in the field of human rights are substantially restricted, forming an interesting contrast to the more enthusiastic claims for the EU's external human rights role and responsibility.[7]

A closer look at the rather technical-sounding "legal competence" question entails asking what it means to say the EU lacks competence to adopt "internal" human rights norms (including those applying to its own member states), and seeking an understanding of why it is the case that whereas promotion of human rights is claimed and asserted as a conscious objective of EU foreign policy, there remains an express reluctance to adopt a positive, legally and constitutionally grounded, internal Community human rights policy. The second issue then is to examine whether there is a more principled justification for that apparent position—which has often been criticised as a form of hypocrisy on the EU's part in refusing to do "at home" what it insists upon for others abroad.[8] The question

---

[6] For discussion of the ambiguities of this particular formulation, see G de Búrca "The drafting of the EU Charter of Fundamental Rights" (2001) 26 *EL Rev* 126. See more generally, B de Witte "The Past and Future Role of the ECJ in the Protection of Human Rights" in P Alston, M Bustelo and J Heenan (eds.), *The EU and Human Rights* (Oxford, Oxford University Press, 1999).

[7] See, for example, the deliberate and predominant emphasis on external policy in the first and the second EU Annual Human Rights Reports of 1999 and 2000, and less formally in various speeches and statements by Chris Patten in his capacity as the EC's External Relations Commissioner. See also the Commission Report on the Implementation of Measures Intended to Promote Observance of Human Rights and Democratic Principles in External Relations for 1996—1999 COM(2000)726. On the external dimension of EU human rights policy more generally, see B Brandtner and A Rosas "Trade Preferences and Human Rights", E Riedel and M Will "Human Rights Clauses in External Agreements of the EC", M Kamminga "Holding Multinational Corporations Accountable for Human Rights Abuses: A Challenge for the EC", A Clapham "Where is the EU's Human Rights Common Foreign Policy, and How is it Manifested in Multilateral Fora", B Simma, J Aschenbauer and C Schultze "Human Rights Considerations in the Development Co-operation Activities of the EC" and M Nowak "Human Rights 'Conditionality' in Relation to Entry to, and Full Participation in, the EU" which form various chapters in the collection of P Alston, M Bustelo and J Heenan (eds.), n. 6 above.

[8] In the first "EU Human Rights Discussion Forum" held in 1999 apparently in order to bring together NGOs and other members of civil society for the purposes of debate, the coherence of the external and internal dimensions of EU human rights policy (as well as its coherence "across pillars") was one of the key questions discussed. See the report of the First EU Human Rights

is, in other words, whether the EU needs a proactive, legally supported internal human rights policy for itself and its member states, or whether there are reasons to argue that this would be neither necessary nor legitimate. Insofar as an internal human rights policy of this kind seeks to develop a set of legal norms, shared by all of the member states and to which their policies are to be aligned, it is a move towards legal convergence in this field.

There is a constant tension between the economic power of the EU, its expanding size and status as an international player and the responsibilities and expectations which that generates, on the one hand, and the internal and constitutional forces of restraint on the other. The latter can be seen in the repeated calls for clearer limits to the powers and competences of the EU over the past ten years, but more clearly than ever in the context of the high-level political debate on the constitutional "finalité" or otherwise of the EU during and after the Nice Intergovernmental Conference. It was also seen reflected, for example, in the cautiously drafted competences of the previous two treaties of Maastricht and Amsterdam (such as the provisions on education, health and culture) and in the promotion of subsidiarity as both a political and a legal principle. The most recent and most explicit demonstration of the desire for constitutional restraint and limits, however, is evident in the fact that one of the key items on the "post-Nice agenda" for discussion in the 2004 IGC, having been included in the Declaration on the Future of the Union attached to the Nice Treaty, is "how to establish and monitor a more precise delimitation of powers between the European Union and the Member States, reflecting the principle of subsidiarity".[9]

The political anxiety which is manifested in this rather unexpected high-level debate on the *finalité politique* of the EU reflects the fact that, despite its growing power and strengthening identity as a political as well as an economic organisation, the European Union remains an ambiguous entity which eludes satisfactory definition, whether in conceptual, legal or constitutional terms. If the EU is conceived of as a special interest organisation or association, the starting point for analysis is to ask what its function or purpose is, what its powers are and what it is designed to achieve. If, on the other hand, it is conceived of as a constitutional polity, the assumption is that its function is a more general one of political ordering and government. Conceptually speaking, the EU still lies somewhere between these two paradigms, which explains something of the complexity and uncertainty of (quite apart from the anxiety over) its powers and functions. It reflects and contains elements of a special interest organisation,

Discussion Forum, <http ://europa.eu.int/comm/dg1a/human_rights/intro>. See also generally the Comité des Sages Report, *Leading by Example: A Human Rights Agenda for the EU for the year 2000* (Florence: EUI, 1998), and more recently A Williams "Enlargement of the Union and Human Rights conditionality: a policy of distinction?" (2000) 25 *EL Rev* 601.

[9] For further discussion see G de Búrca "Setting Constitutional Limits to EU Competence?" Robert Schuman Centre Forum paper, EUI 2001, and B de Witte and G de Búrca "The Post-Nice Delimitation of Powers", RSC policy paper 2001.

and in its inception as the Coal and Steel Community it most closely fitted this paradigm. However, as it has evolved and grown it has developed characteristics, powers and an institutional form which are those of a more developed, although inchoate and partial constitutional polity.

At present, the constituent European Treaties do not contain a great deal, particularly not of an enabling or empowering nature, on the subject of human rights. Since the Community legal system—as confirmed by Article 5 EC (ex Article 3b) is a system of limited, attributed competence whereby all legal powers must be traced back to the constituent treaties, this fact could appear to provide a fairly decisive answer to the question whether the EC has policy competence to act in the field of human rights. However, the issue does not end there for a number of reasons. First, as is very well known, the ECJ has long declared respect for fundamental human rights to be part of the Community legal system, binding both on the EC institutions when they act and also on the member states when they are acting within the field of EC law.[10] This development was not just with the support of but at the instigation of member state courts, since it was seen not as an expansion of Community competence but as imposing normative limits on the EU's own powers by subjecting them to human rights values. This unwritten catalogue of rights has been held to be a kind of negative constraint[11] on EU lawmaking and policymaking, but it remains open-ended—inspired by the ECHR, by national constitutional traditions and by other international treaties which the states have signed—even after the proclamation of the (as yet non-binding) EU Charter of Fundamental Rights, which draws on and partly incorporates this "catalogue". The ECJ jurisprudence from which it originated had already, prior to the Charter's adoption, been politically approved and a kind of loose codification of the case law was enshrined in the form of Article 6 of the Treaty on European Union. Article 6 declares that the Union is "founded on" the principles of liberty, democracy and respect for human rights and fundamental freedoms. Whether the newly drawn-up Charter of Rights will eventually be incorporated into the Treaties remains to be seen, either at the 2004 IGC or later, but there is no doubt that its formal incorporation would be likely to have a significant effect on the legal basis for Community competence in the field of human rights, whatever disclaimers and qualifications the Charter itself may contain in this respect.

In addition to the principles developed in the case law and confirmed by later acts of political approval, the two clearest and most concrete legal bases in the

---

[10] See A Clapham, "A Human Rights Policy for the European Community" (1990) 10 *YBEL* 309; P Craig and G de Búrca, *EU Law* (2nd edn., 1998) ch. 7.

[11] The uneasy relationship between negative restraints and positive powers, between restraining and enabling norms, particularly in the context of "rights", has been apparent in this context. Even under the ECHR, a classically liberal set of entrenched rights, for example, it has been clear that "negative" duties not to restrict certain fundamental rights can also be held to impose positive obligations on states to enact measures to protect those rights.

Treaty for EC action in the field of human rights are Article 177 (formerly 130u, existing since the Maastricht Treaty) concerning development policy agreements, and Article 13 (in existence since the Amsterdam Treaty) going beyond the gender equality provisions of Articles 3(2) and 141 EC to allow for other forms of anti-discrimination legislation to be adopted by the Community legislature. Finally, Article 7 TEU, most recently amended in the Nice Treaty, contains a less explicit but pregnant Treaty provision with potential to justify significant European Union intervention in the field of human rights within its member states.[12] This article, which follows the commitment of the EU and its member states in Article 6 TEU to respect human rights and fundamental freedoms, provides for the possibility of suspending the rights of a member state which is found to be in serious and persistent violation of these principles. Although the implications of the existence of this apparently drastic sanction were not seriously considered until the fracas over the coming into power of the FPÖ in Austria, they were made somewhat more explicit in the amendment of Article 7 by the Nice Treaty, so that the power of the EU to investigate the internal policies of any member state so as to monitor compliance with human rights is now spelt out more clearly.

All of the above—the legal principles developed and extended by the Court, the formal legal bases in development policy and anti-discrimination, the commitments in Article 6 and the powers in Article 7 TEU, and the promise of the recent Charter—would appear to add up in legal-constitutional terms to a significant degree of competence in the field of human rights. However, this reality co-exists with a considerably more cautious "official" or institutional view of the limits of the Community's human rights competence, in particular in the internal sphere, and it is this tension which requires further explanation and understanding.

A first restraining influence is normally traced to the ruling given by the Court of Justice in Opinion 2/94, in which it declared that the Community lacked competence to accede to the European Convention on Human Rights.[13] One reading of the case is to say that it provides a fairly conclusive answer (particularly given the Court's constitutional role in interpreting the extent of Community powers under the Treaty) to the effect that, apart from its specific external development policy powers, the Community has no real powers or competence to act in the field of human rights, the provisions of the Treaties are exhaustive of the powers of the Community and there is no power given by any explicit Treaty provision to enact general rules in the field of human rights. However, quite apart from the subsequent changes introduced by the Amsterdam and Nice Treaties, to leave it at that would be to ignore the obvious room for inter-

---

[12] According to Von Bogdandy, n. 3 above, the standard used by the Union to monitor the performance of member states must "leave considerable space for autonomous human rights regimes in the Member States" (2000) 37 *CML Rev* at 1319.

[13] *Opinion 2/94 on accession to the ECHR* [1996] ECR I–1759.

pretation left by the Court in its Opinion,[14] particularly in relation to a question which the Court neither expressly accepted nor rejected, *viz.* whether the protection of human rights is in itself an independent objective of the Community (thus bringing Article 308 of the EC Treaty into play). It would also ignore the obvious fact that when legal texts are open-ended and ambiguous, as is the case with many parts of the EC and EU treaties including those which mention human rights, including the residual powers clause of Article 308, the question whether the Community has competence cannot plausibly be characterised as a "technical" legal one. Rather it is both a political question which centres on the willingness of the various legal and political actors involved to develop and defend a human rights policy, and a more philosophical question concerning the justification for an entity such as the EU developing or not developing such a policy. Once the simple assumption that whether or not the EC/EU is currently justified in developing and promoting a European human rights policy is a relatively straightforward matter of formal legal competence has been rejected, the way is clear to explore more closely the basis for the opposition to the EC exercising law-making powers in its "domestic sphere" in pursuit of human rights goals. Put in another way, it becomes possible to ask why an EU-led degree of convergence in human rights norms is considered to be constitutionally undesirable.

It is apparent from a number of official EC texts that the institutional response to Opinion 2/94 and to developments since then—including the Charter—has been a cautious one, emphasising the limits to the Community's competence in the human rights field, and warning against any attempts to erode the constitutional limits to its powers.[15] This cautious approach to internal legal competences in particular is exemplified by the opinion given by the Council legal service on the proposed Commission regulation on democratisation and human rights in 1997.[16] It is apparent also in Article 51 of the Charter on Fundamental Rights, cited above, which provides (regardless of whether it

---

[14] This can be seen in the differing views expressed in the many commentaries published on the Opinion—see e.g. J H H. Weiler and S Fries, "A Human Rights Policy for the European Community and Union: the Question of Competences" in P Alston *et al.*, n. 6 above; N Burrows (1997) 22 *EL Rev* 58; G Gaja (1996) 33 *CML Rev* 973; S Peers (1998) 35 *CML Rev* 539; and A Dashwood and A Arnull in CELS Occasional Paper no. 1, and C Vedder, (1996) *Europarecht* 309.

[15] When it was proposed to establish the Vienna Monitoring Centre on Racism and Xenophobia by a legal Regulation in 1997, the Economic and Social Committee—no sceptic as to the social role of the Community more generally—warned as to the inadequacy of Community legal competence to do so. See [1997] OJ C 158/9.

[16] See the discussion of this opinion in J H H Weiler and S Fries, "A Human Rights Policy for the European Community and Union: the Question of Competences" n. 14 above. The proposal in question subsequently evolved and was adopted in 1999 as two separate regulations with different legal bases in the Treaty, one on development cooperation and the second on other forms of cooperation. See Regs. 975/1999 and 976/1999, [1999] OJ L 120/1, 8. Now, however, by virtue of an amendment proposed by the Nice Treaty, a new Article 181a will be added to the EC Treaty, providing an explicit legal basis for such non-development-orientated cooperation agreements, which expressly provides that Community policy in this area shall contribute to the objective of respecting human rights and fundamental freedoms.

eventually becomes binding or not) that the Charter does not establish any new power or task for the Community or the Union, or modify any of the powers and tasks defined by the Treaties. The explanatory memorandum to the Charter emphasises this fact further.[17] In other words, the Charter is presented not as any source of or basis for positive legislative action, but simply as a codified or supplemented form of what already exists under ECJ jurisprudence: i.e. a broad set of standards against which EU and member state action within the scope of existing EU policies and powers is to be judged. This formula—that human rights instruments are not to create new areas of Community policy—can also be seen even in the relatively bold provision of Article 13 EC, which provides that action to combat discrimination based on a range of grounds can be adopted only "within the limits of the powers conferred on the Community by the Treaty". The curious tension reflected in this provision which simultaneously confers power on the EC to adopt and promote human rights and yet seems to reaffirm the *existing* limits of Community powers under the Treaties is another reflection of the ambivalence and uncertainty over the existence and scope of an internal EU human rights policy. But it is clear that it is the member states—in their drafting of provisions of the Treaty—and the Council either in legislative instruments or through its legal advisers, which express the most cautious view as to the existence, scope and legal basis for such a policy. And, in contrast, the institution which has consistently claimed and advocated in its reports and resolutions a strong internal human rights competence and responsibility for the EC and EU is the European Parliament, in particular when it was the least powerful in both legal and political terms.

"INTERNAL" VERSUS "EXTERNAL" HUMAN RIGHTS POLICY

At the same time, there appears to have been a contrast between the official restrictiveness and caution in relation to EC human rights competence in the "internal" domain on the one hand, and the institutional willingness to claim and to exercise a human rights mandate, including through the use of legal instruments, in the external domain. External influence, it might be concluded, was seen to be more acceptable than internal convergence of human rights norms. In the first European Union Annual Report on Human Rights adopted in 1999, the Council declared, although without explaining why, that "the Report concentrates on the EU's external relations". The report readily mentioned that the protection of human rights was an objective of the then Common Foreign and Security Policy, contrasting with the circumspection in relation to

---

[17] CHARTE 4473/00, 11 Oct. 2000. The relevant explanatory note to Art. 51 reads "Paragraph 2 confirms that the Charter may not have the effect of extending the competences and tasks which the Treaties confer on the Community and the Union. Explicit mention is made here of the logical consequences of the principle of subsidiarity and of the fact that the Union only has those powers which have been conferred upon it. The fundamental rights as guaranteed in the Union do not have any effect other than in the context of the powers determined by the Treaty."

the internal sphere and specifically with the debate sparked by Opinion 2/94 as to whether the protection of human rights is in fact an objective of the *Community* or not. "The development and consolidation of democracy and the rule of law, as well as respect for human rights and fundamental freedoms feature among the key objectives of the EU's Common Foreign and Security Policy in Article 11 of the TEU".[18] The report did nonetheless go on to say that the picture "would not be complete without at least making a reference to EU action related to developments in the EU area. Therefore, an introspective look at one specific theme will be included. In this edition, the theme . . . is racism". The contrast between the treatment of external and internal policy in the report is quite stark, but this is not merely a consequence of the way in which the Council chose to present the facts contained in it.

The "one specific theme" concerning internal EU human rights policy which the report examined was in fact by far the strongest example which could have been presented at the time, since it was the one area of autonomous human rights activity pursued in which strong legal instruments were available, within the EU. Even before Article 13 of the EC Treaty was added by the Amsterdam Treaty, the area of racism and xenophobia within the Union had received a degree of political attention and in 1997 the Monitoring Centre on Racism and Xenophobia was established by a Council Regulation.[19] Apart from that and the longer-established sex equality policy which derived originally from the market rationale of harmonising competitive conditions between the member states, but which has expanded considerably through the mainstreaming project pursued by the Community,[20] the only other acknowledged internal human rights policy was in a measure of funding provided to NGOs and certain other social assistance initiatives through dedicated budget lines.[21] These softer human rights policies were not aimed at producing convergence in a strong sense, other than loosely in the sense of the kinds of projects which the Commission chose to support and to fund across member states, with the requisite element of partnership between different states. Further, while it is evidently the case that many areas of "internal" EU policy raise distinct human rights concerns—policing, refugee and asylum law, and employment law for example—this does not amount to the same thing as the EU having a proactive,

---

[18] First Annual Report <http://europa.eu.int/comm/external_relations/human_rights/doc/report_99_en.pdf>.

[19] This, despite the Economic and Social Committee's doubts, was based on Arts. 284 and 308 of the EC Treaty, see Reg. 1035/97, [1997] OJ L 151.

[20] See for discussion, M Pollack and E Hafner-Burton, "Mainstreaming Gender in the European Union" (2000) 7 *Journal of European Public Policy* 432.

[21] The practice of funding significant "non-pilot" projects, including NGOs working in areas of social exclusion and poverty, under a dedicated budget heading but without any other legal basis was condemned by the ECJ in its 1998 decision C–106/96, *UK v. Commission* [1998] ECR I–2729. The implications of this judgment for external "human rights and democratisation" funding, which was introduced in 1994 under the B7–70 budget heading, led ultimately to the adoption of the two regulations on human rights and democratisation in development policy and other aspects of cooperation policy in 1999, based on Arts. 177 and 208 respectively. See n. 16.

autonomous competence to promote and protect human rights. Thus the Council's "introspective look" at "one specific theme" in its first report was somewhat misleading in so far as it might have suggested that this was merely one small part of a comprehensive internal human rights policy.

On the other hand, this is not to say that the Council in the first report was not also cautious about the legal basis for external policy instruments promoting human rights.[22] The report argues that conditionality clauses in external agreements[23] do not themselves make human rights a field of policy within such agreements, but merely make respect for human rights an essential element of the agreement.[24] On the other hand, the report asserts in various places the importance attached to human rights issues in external relations, for example in the negotiations with various African states within the context of the Lomé Convention, and in the suspension of trade preferences for Myanmar as a result of their forced labour practices.

The second report, published in 2000, clearly reflects a greater awareness of the criticisms made about the disparity between the external and internal dimensions of the EU's human rights activities, and makes express reference to the "Leading by Example" *Comité des Sages* report and to the conclusions of the first EU Human Rights Discussion Forum,[25] declaring that "the European Union is aware that it must begin by applying to itself the principles for which it stands". The first section explains that "although its contents are primarily focused on the external activities of the EU and its role on the international stage, this second report also includes a substantial section devoted to human rights within the European Union". This time, the field of anti-racism is not the only topic within the internal section, but also social exclusion policy, "security and justice" and gender mainstreaming, as well as some of the actions (e.g. to combat violence and human trafficking) and funding initiatives in the field of women's and children's rights. Nonetheless, it is still the case—without any explanation offered as to why—that the report declares the external activities of the EU to be its primary focus. Further, the cautious approach to internal human rights competence

---

[22] The Council was influenced here, clearly, by the cautious India Cooperation agreement judgment of the ECJ in C–268/94 *Portuguese Republic* v. *Council* [1996] ECR I–6177, given by the Court shortly before Opinion 2/94, which dealt very cautiously with the limits of the role of human rights in development policy, which was one of the only areas at the time where the Treaty clearly specified such a role.

[23] It is interesting to note that in certain areas of internal EU distributive policy such as in the context of the structural funds, a form of conditionality clause can be found. but these have not so far been general human rights clauses, rather environmental and equal opportunities clauses

[24] "The human rights clause does not transform the basic nature of agreements which are otherwise concerned with matters not directly related to the promotion of human rights. It simply constitutes a mutual reaffirmation of commonly shared values and principles, a precondition for economic and other cooperation under the agreements, and allows for and regulates suspension in cases of non-compliance with these values. Such a clause thus does not seek to establish new standards in the international protection of human rights. It merely reaffirms existing commitments which, as general international law, already bind all States as well as the EC in its capacity as a subject of international law".

[25] See n. 8 for the Sages report and the Discussion Forum. The Council's Second Annual Human Rights Report was published on 9 Oct. 2000.

clearly persists—reference is made at the outset to "the fifteen" member states rather than to the EC/EU, the report begins by reiterating the legal bases for action, and throughout there is considerably greater emphasis placed on external responsibilities rather than internal matters with only 13 out of 73 pages devoted to human rights issues within the Union.

Given this greater willingness to present human rights as an actual objective of EU foreign policy and given also the readier range of instruments—such as the regular practice since 1995 of including human rights clauses in external agreements, including trade, development and association agreements[26]—which have been adopted in the external field, a more convincing explanation for the cautious and reserved approach in the internal sphere is needed if the more basic allegation of double standards is to be avoided.[27] Otherwise the practice of the EU might be seen to reflect more than a shade of the colonial practice of the UK, which inserted Bills of Rights into the independence constitutions of former colonies while refusing to adopt one itself. A more credible explanation needs to be found for the difference between the justification and scope of the EU's role as an international actor on the one hand, and the justification and scope of its "internal" role on the other. The concepts of parallelism and coherence in the context of EU external relations remain vague and insufficiently developed, and the question whether the internal and external policies of a polity should mirror one another remains open to question.

The rather crude response of the fourteen member states to the Jörg Haider controversy in 2000, when the very right-wing Austrian freedom party came into government, led some to question whether the EU required a less extreme mechanism for policing internal human rights standards than that existing under Articles 6 and 7 TEU. In particular, attention focused on the question whether the EU should have the power and the instruments to deal with the situation where a member state which is not guilty of a serious and persistent violation of human rights, is nonetheless responsible for policies which are considered to undermine or breach the basic human rights norms to which all EU member states have committed themselves. As far as "severe and persistent" violation of the principles of Article 6 TEU by a member state is concerned, as intimated earlier the formal mechanism for dealing with such a situation has already been the subject of amendment in the Nice Treaty, in the light of proposals put forward during the Intergovernmental Conference both by the

---

[26] It can be argued, in this context, given the exclusivity of Community competence in external trade, that since member states have lost the power to pursue human rights aims through their own external trade policies, there is a strong justification for the EC to do so. I am grateful to B de Witte for this point. On the other hand, criticism was voiced at the first EU Human Rights Discussion Forum 1999 that human rights policy was largely confined to projects funded under the B7–70 initiative and was not at all fully integrated into policies across the pillars and across the different dimensions of foreign policy.

[27] See e.g. A Williams "Enlargement of the Union and Human Rights conditionality: a policy of distinction?" (2000) 25 *EL Rev* 601. A Von Bogdandy, n. 3 above, suggests that in order to avoid appearing as an imperialist power in its foreign policy, the EU should limit its policy in relation to third states to countering grave human rights violations, (2000) 37 *CML Rev* 1319.

Austrian and by the Belgian governments. Following those changes, the Council under Article 7 TEU may, rather than engaging in an ex post investigation, determine that there is a clear *risk* of a serious breach by a member state of the principles of Article 6(1), and it may address "appropriate recommendations" to the state in question. Evidently, one of the lessons learned from the awkwardness and uncertainty revealed by the situation involving the Austrian sanctions, was that more attention needed to be paid to the procedures preceding and following the determination of a risk of breach. The Nice Treaty changes require the Council to hear the member state concerned before it makes a determination of this kind, and (in a retrospective constitutionalisation of the practice eventually adopted on an *ad hoc* basis in the case of Austria, with the appointment of a three-person commission to report on the situation) it may call on "independent persons to submit within a reasonable time limit a report on the situation in the Member State in question". However, it remains the case that there is no mechanism for ascertaining, pointing out, or responding to, human rights violations of a less grave nature which are committed or permitted by member states. Despite the recommendations of the three-person committee which reported on Austria,[28] which picked up on the recommendation made by the Comité des Sages in the *Leading by Example* Report, no monitoring or reporting system on human rights issues has been proposed or established. The suggestion to extend the Vienna monitoring centre beyond the fields of racism and xenophobia has not been followed up, and some doubts as to its usefulness given the other mechanisms for reporting on human rights within the EU (e.g. national courts, ombudsmen, the ECHR, UN reports) were raised in the First Human Rights Discussion Forum report.[29]

This focuses attention squarely on the question whether the EU needs an "internal" human rights policy. Should the EU possess its own legitimate constitutional mechanisms for dealing with violations of the set of human rights values to which member states have committed themselves? Should the treatment of the travelling community in Britain, or the condition of psychiatric prisons in France, for example, be the subject of EU concern? Or would this, as well as adding an unnecessary extra layer of monitoring, constitute an unjustifiable violation of what remains of national sovereignty and an overreaching of the legitimate limits of its powers and role by the EU? Armin Von Bogdandy, in an article which aims to respond to the Leading by Example report of the *sages* in 1999, and the chapter by Alston and Weiler in the accompanying volume,[30] sets out a series of arguments against a strong human rights policy.[31] He begins by contrasting two positions, stating that whereas human rights at present mainly

---

[28] The report of the so-called "three wise men", M Aahtisaari, J Frowein and M Oreja, on the EU's sanctions against Austria, in Sept. 2000.

[29] See p. 33 of the report, cited at n. 8 above.

[30] P Alston and J H H Weiler "An 'Ever Closer Union' in Need of a Human Rights Policy" in P Alston, M Bustelo and J Heenan (eds.), *The EU and Human Rights* (Oxford: Oxford University Press, 1999).

[31] A Von Bogdandy, n. 3 above.

operate as a *limit* on the European legal system, the argument for a human rights policy would mean that human rights would *determine* that system.[32] Positing the debate in this polarised way, however, avoids engagement with the more complex reality of EU law and policy at present, whereby human rights principles and instruments form a limit on certain policies, an integral part of other policies (e.g. the current proposals on family reunification), and the core, proactive element of others (e.g. the anti-discrimination measures). While some of his argument seems to be premised on an ordo-liberal conception of the EU legal and political order, as in his promotion of first-generation negative, judicially protected rights rather than positive social and economic rights as the legitimate core of human rights, other parts are more nuanced and suggest an openness to the human rights main-streaming philosophy underpinning the Alston/Weiler report. Towards the end of his paper, for example, he appears sympathetic towards some kind of mainstreaming approach in that he leans towards the vision of "human rights as normative orientation and foundation for the whole of social relations in the polity" rather than the vision of "rights as safeguards against sovereign intrusion without any further plan of how society should develop".[33] However, he is careful to distance this "quest for reconstruction of the supranational legal order on a human rights basis" from that of one which would seek to realise progressive social rights, and ultimately he remains agnostic about whether the EU should seek to "reconstruct" itself, as he puts it, in this way.

THE CASE FOR AN EU HUMAN RIGHTS POLICY

One of the main positive arguments, to date, in favour of a comprehensive internal human rights policy, has been the argument from credibility or coherence. In other words, since the EU claims to make human rights promotion an important element of its external policies, in development, trade, foreign and security policy etc., it should equally develop a clear human rights policy in the internal sphere if the accusation of hypocrisy and incoherence is to be avoided. On the other hand, to say that the development of a "domestic" EU human rights policy would lend credibility to foreign policy is no real argument in favour of developing such a domestic dimension, and indeed it could beg the question whether there should be an external human rights policy in the first place. One obvious response is to assert that since protection for basic human rights is an important aspect of social justice, and since the EU's origins as a common market have resulted in an excessive policy focus on trade over time, this historic neglect of important aspects of the social and human dimension within what is now such a powerful and complex polity should be corrected. As far as an internal human rights system which would effectively monitor the EU institutions

---

[32] *Ibid.*, p. 1308.
[33] *Ibid.*, p. 1334.

themselves is concerned, the desire to demonstrate the (current) existence of such a system was clearly what lay behind the political impetus to draw up an EU Charter of Fundamental Rights, rather than the desire to develop a new set of rights binding on the *member states*.[34] The aim of constraining and orienting the actions of the EU institutions themselves (the first and second combinations of elements in the matrix set out at the beginning of this chapter) has always been less controversial than the attempt to create such a system for the member states (the third and fourth combinations). This is at least in part because all member states already have their own systems for the protection of human rights, and the Council of Europe and the ECHR provide a monitoring and partial enforcement system for all EU and Council of Europe member states.[35] It raises the question why the EU should add an extra layer to those which already exist. The idea behind the subsidiarity principle in the EC Treaty is that the EU should not take action when this is not "necessary" at European level and in particular when the aims of the action can be better achieved by the member states individually.

There are a number of dimensions to this question. On the one hand, as the extensive literature on the subject of the EU and the ECHR clearly reveals, there is a range of arguments to be made both against and in favour of ECJ jurisdiction over member state action within fields of EU law and policy which is claimed to violate the human rights standards to which all states are allegedly committed under the TEU. Few question the need for some kind of supranational judicial monitoring of states human rights records, however, and the issue normally centres on identifying the appropriate institution—whether in Strasbourg or in Luxembourg or in a specially constituted judicial tribunal—to undertake that task in the context of the EU.[36]

More problematic, however, is the fourth and final combination of the elements set out at the start of the chapter, in other words the development of a positive internal policy competence (therefore necessarily affecting the states as well as the EU itself) in the field of human rights. From a legal point of view, as indicated above, there are a number of Treaty provisions which could facilitate such a policy, and the likely evolution of the Charter of Fundamental Rights into a more significant legal instrument also militates in this direction. From a policy point of view, the argument for coherence and avoiding hypocrisy and the argument concerning the need to correct its excessive market orientation support the exercise by the EU of an internal human rights competence. More convincingly, and this will be explored further below, it can be argued that the human rights tensions or problems which have been created or contributed to by the EU's

[34] See "The drafting of the EU Charter of Fundamental Rights", n. 6 above.

[35] See for a nuanced discussion of the different issues arising in relation to the potentially overlapping jurisdiction of the ECJ and ECHR in relation to alleged member state breaches of human rights, J H H Weiler, "Fundamental Rights and Fundamental Boundaries: On the Conflict of Standards and Values in the Protection of Human Rights in the European Legal Space" in *The Constitution of Europe* (Cambridge: Cambridge University Press, 1999) ch. 3.

[36] See e.g. the literature cited in nn. 4 and 30.

market integration project, place an onus on the EU to develop policies to remedy or redress them.[37] This goes further than the "correcting" argument above—it is not merely that the EU should develop a more human or social dimension in order to become more than purely a market, but that there are specific problems to which the market integration project gives rise which call for action: the increase in racism that accompanies movements of persons across borders, for example, or the problems of social exclusion which are exacerbated by various market policies. This is partly a version of the neo-functionalist argument—that integration within certain sectors spills over into others and leads to the perceived need for concerted action in these also, but it goes further than asserting that policy integration in one field creates problems which need to be rectified in another. Rather the argument is that joint or unified policy action in a particular field will operate more smoothly and positively if there is also coordination and cooperation within other fields which may be affected by the former. It is less a strictly functional argument from necessity and more a normative argument about the better operation of the polity.

These legal and policy arguments do not in themselves, however, answer the question whether a stronger internal human rights policy is either necessary or legitimate: in other words, whether an attempt at further convergence in such matters is actually desirable. Fritz Scharpf's work, although it does not touch specifically on questions of human rights promotion or policies, is concerned more generally with the legitimacy of positive policy competence exercised at EU level (as he terms it, the issue of positive rather than negative integration), and particularly with the question whether social welfare and market correcting policies can legitimately and effectively be pursued by the EU.[38] He argues that in general the EU as a polity—in the absence of the thick collective identity which is taken for granted in national democracies, and given the absence of a sufficient European public or political space—lacks input legitimacy ("government by the people"). Like the German Bundesverfassungsgericht in its Maastricht judgment, he does not actually rule out the possibility that a stronger political identity may ultimately form within the EU,[39] but in the absence of such an identity-based input legitimacy, he argues that European policies can only be legitimated primarily by an interest-based output legitimacy ("government for the people"),

[37] This, arguably, was the original foundation for some of the equality and non-discrimination policies developed by the EC, from the earlier sex equality policy to the more gradually emerging race discrimination policy, and justifications for the enactment of the new Art. 13 EC have been couched also in these terms: that some of the economic and social problems caused by the removal of barriers between states and the liberalisation of trade give rise to a need for more centralised or at least co-ordinated anti-discrimination norms.

[38] See in particular F Scharpf, *Governing in Europe: Effective and Democratic?* (Oxford: Oxford University Press, 1999).

[39] In this sense Scharpf's position is less categorical that of Giandomenico Majone, in that Scharpf does not argue for the maintenance of the EU as a primarily regulatory and administrative entity, but he clearly sees the possibility or desirability of a more social and political Europe being dependent on the development of a thicker form of collective identity at the European level. On the other hand, the likelihood of enlargement certainly increases pessimism about this prospect.

accompanied by minimal institutional safeguards. This particular version of Joseph Weiler's "no demos" thesis bases the primary legitimacy of EU policy-making on its functional capacity to solve problems requiring collective solutions which can apparently not be solved through individual action or market exchanges. In such circumstances, Scharpf would argue, a much thinner form of constituency is required to justify EU-type institutional arrangements for collective action. The practical focus of his work is on the legitimacy of EU "positive integration" measures in fields such as environmental, social and competition policy, but the reasoning could equally be applied to the positive dimensions of a non market-making field like the promotion of human rights, as expressed in the EU's anti-discrimination norms and monitoring of racism, the funding of NGOs, and policies of mainstreaming, in terms of exploring the justification for EU action in this field.

On Scharpf's view, given his perspective on the "demos" question, EU distributive, market-correcting policies of this kind cannot readily be justified unless the problem-solving capacity of states is inadequate. If his analysis is accepted, could it plausibly be argued that the EU is in fact a more effective problem solver in this field? One of the suggestions made above is that there are problems—of migration, racism, and social exclusion, for example—which are generated by EU market integration, and which arguably require a trans-national or at least a coordinated response across Europe. And on the other hand there are arguably "human rights" issues raised by the growing multi-culturalism of an expanding geographic entity which, even if not generated by market integration nor requiring transnational action, would at least benefit from the coordination and mutual learning of a European response and might facilitate the more harmonious development and operation of other policies.

More fundamentally, however, recent critiques of Scharpf's analysis point out the problematic nature of his distinction between input and output legitimacy.[40] It has been argued that there is a basic tension between his initial notion of democratic legitimacy as being connected to the idea of moral justification, and the apparent abandonment of this idea when it comes to the elite-led imposition of welfare policy choices which are "interest-based". Why the "thinner" community/constituency should accept the interests which are identified and imposed as being in the substantive welfare interests of that community is not clear. Further his concept of input legitimacy seems based on a pluralist idea of the feeding in of relatively fixed preferences, so that compliance with an outcome which contradicts those preferences requires the positing of a thick collective identity. A more deliberative conception of democracy, according to

---

[40] O Gerstenberg, "Proceduralisation of Law and the Transformation of Adjudicative Functions in the EC and the WTO", (2002) *ELJ*, forthcoming. For an earlier discussion of Scharpf's thesis, see O Gerstenberg and C. Sabel "Directly Deliberative Polyarchy: An Institutional Ideal for Europe" in C Joerges (ed.), *Good Governance and Administration in Europe's Integrated Market* (Oxford: Oxford University Press, 2002).

Oliver Gerstenberg, would collapse the distinction between input and output legitimacy. On this analysis the emergence of transnational problem-solving fora and an incipient form of transnational democracy could also render the distinction between market-making and market-correcting policies less salient. Gerstenberg's argument is an attractive and optimistic one which holds out the promise of a justification for transnational action which does not depend on more traditional and essentialist accounts of social identity and solidarity, but which perhaps lends itself to the opposite criticism that its strong constructivist faith overlooks some of the undeniable cultural barriers to law's capacity to engineer radically new forms of collective solidarity.

It may be contended, however, that a more confident and comprehensive EU human rights policy could provide the possibility for an intermediate approach between the pessimism of a Scharpfian analysis and the risk of a prematurely optimistic assessment of transnational democracy in Europe. The instruments and language of human rights provide a framework which is both sensitive to notions of identity and yet at the same time contains transformative and even identity-(re)constitutive possibilities. Some of the strong democratic critiques of human rights discourse which have most salience in the context of the state apply with considerably less force to the novel, non-demotic context of the EU,[41] and the spaces created by the "regulatory gap" identified by Scharpf and others between positive policy-making at national level and the apparently more technocratic negative trade integration conventionally pursued at European level, lend themselves to be filled by novel or adapted forms of law and policy-making.

Arguably, an EU commitment to a clear human rights policy could provide a legal and conceptual framework through which different norms and claims can be articulated and adjudicated, and through the use of policy instruments such as mainstreaming,[42] the financing and empowerment of social groups and NGOs,[43] as well as through more conventional instruments like the recently adopted anti-racism Directive.[44] Although this Directive seems on its face to be a more traditional regulatory instrument containing a set of prohibitions and standards to be adopted by the member states, it actually reflects in various ways a more facilitative, procedural and participative character. Apart from the fact that it identifies itself as a "framework" directive, designed to put into effect the principle of equal treatment on grounds of racial or ethnic origin, and as a

---

[41] See N Walker "Human Rights in a Postnational Constitutional Order: Reconciling Political and Constitutional Pluralism" in T Campbell, K Ewing and A Tomkins (eds.), *Sceptical Essays on Human Rights* (Oxford: Oxford University Press, 2001).

[42] Mainstreaming is advanced in the EU in the area of gender equality, and to a lesser extent in the environmental field, but the broader policy of mainstreaming human rights which is being advocated and to some extent pursued within other international institutions has not been adopted or seriously discussed in the EU context other than in the context of its external democratisation programmes and policies.

[43] This being the practice which was thrown into doubt by the challenge brought before the ECJ by the UK in C–106/96, *UK v. Commission* [1998] ECR I–2729, see n. 21.

[44] Council Dir. 2000/43 EC of 29 June 2000. [2000] OJ L 180/22.

minimum harmonisation directive which does not prevent stronger forms of positive action or protection on the part of member states, its remedial provisions (which are probably the most important in practical terms) allow for a variety of alternatives to be adopted including conciliation. Secondly, the directive provides that states should foster social dialogue between both sides of industry with a view to encouraging their promotion of equal treatment, and also that they should encourage dialogue with relevant NGOs.[45] Implementation of the Directive in the context of collective bargaining can be left to the social partners, at their request, and in its reporting on the application of the Directive, the Commission is required to seek the views of the social partners, the relevant NGOs and the European Monitoring Centre on racism and xenophobia. More generally, the new and general Treaty-based anti-discrimination instrument most recently added to paragraph 2 of Article 13 EC by the Nice Treaty, explicitly provides for the adoption of facilitative rather than harmonisation measures, in setting up a mechanism for the adoption of "supportive" action in relation to national anti-discrimination measures.[46]

These examples by no means exhaust the potential of a rights-sensitive approach for the promotion of a broad-ranging social and political dialogue. Rather, they are given by way of illustration, as emergent tendencies to support the more general proposition being advanced here that the discourse and instruments of human rights—which can be seen both as a substantive policy field, a dimension of all policy fields, and as a set of mechanisms—could provide a framework in which the novel democratic possibilities of the new transnational European arena could be tested and developed.

---

[45] To cite the relevant provisions in full, Arts. 11 and 12 provide that:

Art. 11 1. Member States shall, in accordance with national traditions and practice, take adequate measures to promote the social dialogue between the two sides of industry with a view to fostering equal treatment, including through the monitoring of workplace practices, collective agreements, codes of conduct, research or exchange of experiences and good practices.

2. Where consistent with national traditions and practice, Member States shall encourage the two sides of the industry without prejudice to their autonomy to conclude, at the appropriate level, agreements laying down anti-discrimination rules in the fields referred to in Art. 3 which fall within the scope of collective bargaining. These agreements shall respect the minimum requirements laid down by this Directive and the relevant national implementing measures.

Art. 12 Dialogue with non-governmental organisations Member States shall encourage dialogue with appropriate non-governmental organisations which have, in accordance with their national law and practice, a legitimate interest in contributing to the fight against discrimination on grounds of racial and ethnic origin with a view to promoting the principle of equal treatment.

[46] The new Art. 13(2) provides "By way of derogation from paragraph 1, when the Council adopts Community incentive measures, excluding any harmonization of the laws and regulations of the Member States, to support action taken by the Member states in order to contribute to the achievement of the objectives referred to in this Article, it shall act in accordance with the procedure referred to in Art. 251".

9

Human Rights: Some Recent Developments and Their Impact on Convergence and Divergence of Law in Europe

PAUL BEAUMONT

INTRODUCTION

THE EUROPEAN UNION has some problems with human rights. The Court of Justice has created a negative competence, since the 1970s, to decide that Community acts are unlawful because they are in breach of human rights as developed by that Court. The Court is influenced by the constitutional traditions of the member states and the European Convention on Human Rights in developing those rights but is bound by neither. Until 1 May 1999 the Court had no legal basis for this course of action but the entry into force of the Treaty of Amsterdam on that date made the provision in the Treaty on European Union concerning human rights justiciable for the first time. That provision, however, simply codifies the common law position in leaving it to the Court of Justice to determine what constitutes a fundamental right.

This paper will address some of the relevant questions in this field:

—Should the European Community adopt legislation in the field of human rights?
—Should the European Court of Justice continue to assert that it is not bound by the decisions of the European Court of Human Rights? What place does distinguishing between the two jurisdictions have in ensuring a healthy diversity in European human rights protection?
—Should the European Court of Justice interpret provisions of the EC Law in a particular way to fulfil its view of the priorities in the Treaty based on its protection of fundamental human rights?
—Should the European Court of Justice construe provisions of EC Law contrary to the textual indications of those provisions in order to protect fundamental human rights as perceived by the European Court of Justice?
—Should the European Court of Human Rights review the compliance of European Community Law with the European Convention on Human Rights?

LEGISLATIVE COMPETENCE OF THE EUROPEAN COMMUNITY

Weiler and Fries have argued for a Community power to make human rights legislation based on the existing Treaty competences.[1] It is uncontested that the Community has competence in the field of development co-operation to contribute to "respecting human rights and fundamental freedoms" in developing countries.[2] Weiler and Fries argue from some case law of the European Court of Justice that there are signs that the Court expects Community institutions to take certain positive action to comply with fundamental rights. In addition they argue that the fact the Court exercises jurisdiction in relation to fundamental rights in the entire field of Community law justifies the Community institutions in dealing with human rights across the same entire field. However the main weakness of this argument is that it asks the Court to pull itself up by its own bootstraps. The Court did not have an explicit negative Treaty based competence to strike down Community acts as contrary to its own notions of human rights until the Treaty of Amsterdam gave it such a negative competence on 1 May 1999.[3] As is well known the Court developed such a competence, without ever justifying its legal basis for doing so, from the case of *Stauder* v. *Ulm* onwards,[4] at least partially as a defence against the supremacy of Community law being rejected in some member states. It is no business of the Court to impose positive duties on the Community institutions, still less member states, to uphold human rights. The fact that there is at least one isolated dicta where

[1] J H H Weiler and S C Fries, "A Human Rights Policy for the European Community and Union: the Question of Competence", Harvard Law School, Jean Monnet Paper, 1999 and in P Alston (ed.), *The EU and Human Rights* (Oxford: Oxford University Press, 1999) 147–65.

[2] See Art. 177(2) EC (ex 130u(2)), discussed in Case C–268/94 *Portugal* v. *Council* [1996] ECR I–6177. E Fierro makes an interesting case, building on the work of Weiler and Fries, for extending human rights clauses to Community agreements with third States that are not limited to development co-operation, see "Legal Basis and Scope of the Human Rights Clauses in EC Bilateral Agreements: Any Room for Positive Interpretation?" (2001) 7 *European Law Journal* 41–68. As argued below, the present author believes that if a shift of competence away from member states to the Community is to take place in the field of human rights, which he does not favour, it should be done by an amendment to the EC Treaty rather than by using an expansive construction of existing Treaty competences in Arts. 177 and 308 EC as suggested by Fierro and by Weiler and Fries. He is comforted that a Council Legal Service opinion of 16 Oct. 1997 that is cited by Fierro at p. 44 but due to its confidential nature has not been seen by this author, apparently took a restrictive view of the Community's competence to pursue a human rights policy.

[3] The Treaty of Amsterdam amended Art. 46 TEU so that the powers of the Court of Justice of the European Communities apply to "Art. 6(2) TEU with regard to action of the institutions, insofar as the Court has jurisdiction under the Treaties establishing the European Communities and under this Treaty". Art. 6(2) TEU, which had been introduced by the Treaty of Maastricht as a nonjusticiable provision, is in the following terms: "The Union shall respect fundamental rights, as guaranteed by the European Convention for the Protection of Human Rights and Fundamental Freedoms signed in Rome on 4 Nov. 1950 and as they result from the constitutional traditions common to the Member States, as general principles of Community law". The Treaty of Nice makes no changes to this provision.

[4] Case 29/69 [1969] ECR 419. See P Craig and G de Búrca, *EU Law* (2nd edn., Oxford: Oxford University Press, 1998), ch. 7 and S Weatherill and P Beaumont, *EU Law* (3rd edn., London: Penguin, 1999) 284–90, 434, and 443–5 and the works cited for further reading in those books.

it may have suggested doing so[5] does not make it legally competent or acceptable. Such positive duties are bound to be based on blatant judicial activism and therefore fall foul of many important principles which could be characterised as human rights if one was convinced that it was helpful to characterise all issues of policy and principle in these terms. The Court by creating positive duties to uphold particular human rights would be creating retrospective law because individuals have no way of anticipating this in advance. The Court would be undermining the democratic process by asserting its world-view over that of the Community institutions or member states. The Court would be increasing its own power at the expense of more accountable institutions. The Court would be centralising more policy decisions in the Community.

It might be argued that the Community institutions and the member states have accepted positive duties to uphold a very wide catalogue of human rights by the Solemn Proclamation during the European Council meeting at Nice on 7 December 2000 of the Charter of Fundamental Rights of the European Union.[6] Certainly this Charter is solemnly proclaimed by the European Parliament, the Council and the Commission. However, it cannot bind those institutions because it was accepted by those who proclaimed it that the document was not legally binding. Its status was expressly put on the table for consideration in the process leading up to the next Intergovernmental Conference to be convened in 2004.[7] It certainly cannot bind the member states even though the Charter is addressed to them "when they are implementing Union law". The member

---

[5] Para. 40 of Case 68/95 *T. Port* [1996] ECR I–6065.

[6] [2000] OJ C 364/1. For commentary see K Lenaerts and E De Smijter, "A 'Bill of Rights' for the European Union" (2001) 38 *CML Rev* 273; G de Búrca, "The drafting of the European Union Charter of fundamental rights" (2001) 26 *EL Rev* 126; N Walker, "Protection of Fundamental Rights in the European Union: The Charter of Fundamental Rights," in P Cullen and P A Zervakis (eds.), *The Post-Nice Process: Towards a European Constitution* (Baden-Baden: Nomos Verlag, 2001).

[7] See Declaration 23 adopted by the Nice Intergovernmental Conference at [2001] OJ C 80/85. The Laeken/Brussels European Council in December 2001 is to agree on a declaration "containing appropriate initiatives for the continuation" of the process of "a deeper and wider debate about the future of the European Union" drawing on a wide range of discussions between the Community political institutions, national parliaments, and "all those reflecting public opinion" in considering, *inter alia*, the "status of the Charter of Fundamental Rights". There will be pressure to introduce the Charter into the Treaty structure because the Declaration goes on to say that the IGC convened in 2004 will address the items mentioned in the Declaration, including the status of the Charter, "with a view to making corresponding changes to the Treaties". Lenaerts and De Smijter, n. 6 above, at pp. 299–300, are not convincing in arguing that the Charter is part of the *acquis communautaire* and is a "legally enforceable text". The authors dismiss the views of those member states who were clearly opposed to the granting of binding legal status to the Charter as "political". The authors are determined to see a European constitution—arguing that the Charter will "stimulate a process that should result in a Constitution for the European Union" and that the Charter could be the "Bill of Rights" of the European constitution in a way similar to the US constitution (p. 300). It seems that their political goal is clouding their legal judgment. The European Constitution, if it is to be built at all, can only be built by due process of law. That requires the consent of all the member states in accordance with their proper constitutional processes. The Charter of Rights has not had that consent. Some member states are opposed to the Charter having legally enforceable status and their views should be respected if the European constitution is to be built on secure foundations. Soft law should not be deemed to be hard law because the authors happen to like, for political reasons, the contents of the soft law.

states could only be bound by the Charter if it was stated to be legally binding and the process for its adoption involved its acceptance by the same constitutional requirements as must be satisfied in each member state when that state agrees to accept amendments to the EC and EU Treaties contained in Treaties that emerge from intergovernmental conferences like the Treaties of Maastricht, Amsterdam and Nice. Clearly the Charter of Rights does not create any new legislative competence in human rights for the Community or the Union and this is expressly recognised by the Charter in Article 51(2).[8]

The prospect of the Charter being given binding legal status in the European Union by the next intergovernmental conference is worrying.[9] There are 50 Articles giving unqualified rights to people on such diverse issues as human dignity, right to life, protection of personal data, freedom of the arts and sciences, the right to engage in work, non-discrimination, the rights of the child, the right to collective bargaining, the right of access to a free placement service, the right to good administration, and a prohibition on double jeopardy. The rights are often stated in a simple and categorical way, e.g., "Everyone has the right to respect for his or her private and family life, home and communications". The implication is that all the rights are equally important. The constraint on these individual rights in the interests of society as a whole or other individuals is left to one very general paragraph in the Charter, Article 52(1), which provides that:

> "Any limitation on the exercise of the rights and freedoms recognised by this Charter must be provided for by law and respect the essence of those rights and freedoms. Subject to the principle of proportionality, limitations may be made only if they are necessary and genuinely meet objectives of general interest recognised by the Union or the need to protect the rights and freedoms of others".

The Community's political institutions and the member states when implementing Union law are given very little guidance from this provision as to when it is acceptable to limit one of the rights in the Charter and the final decision on the legality of such a limitation is with the European Court of Justice. Nothing in the wording of the Charter sets any limits on judicial power in this context. It is quite possible for the Community courts (ECJ and CFI) to allow no deference to the policy choices which the political institutions and the member states will inevitably make on a regular basis in limiting individual rights and freedoms. The Charter leaves it open for the few wise judges in Luxembourg to impose their values and policy choices on the political institutions and member states as to what limitations on rights are "necessary", as to what "objectives of general interest the Union" recognises,[10] as to whether the measures taken "genuinely"

---

[8] "This Charter does not establish any new power or task for the Community or the Union, or modify powers and tasks defined by the Treaties".

[9] This is a view shared by Pierre Pescatore, a former judge of the European Court of Justice, who describes the Charter as a "spurious document" and hopes it will remain non-legally binding, see "Guest editorial" (2001) 38 *CML Rev* 265 at 268.

[10] Art. 2 TEU does set out objectives for the Union but these are very general and give little guidance to a Court as to when any of them might justify limiting the rights proclaimed in the Charter.

meet those objectives, and whether the measures are needed "to protect the rights and freedoms of others". The Court of Justice has at present an unconstrained power to strike down the acts of the political institutions or the member states which are in violation of the Community's fundamental rights because the Court of Justice is the sole arbiter of what constitutes a fundamental right in terms of the "general principles of Community law".[11] It might be argued that it is better to replace a judicially developed power with one given binding status by the next IGC that puts at least the minimal constraints on judicial development that Article 52(1) does. However, it should be possible for the member states to constrain judicial power more clearly than Article 52(1) currently does and if the political will is not there to do so it would be better not to legitimise a virtually unconstrained power on the Court of Justice to strike down the acts of Community political institutions and member states. The scope of the Court's power of judicial review would be wider than that clearly permitted by Article 6(2) of the TEU, the basis of review would not be adequately limited and the intensity of review would be undefined. Member states should not write such generous blank cheques to a few unelected judges in Luxembourg who are appointed primarily for their skills in Community law rather than their expertise on human rights or public policy.

---

[11] Art. 6(2) TEU might be said to impose an implied limit on the Court's power to determine the scope and content of "fundamental rights" in that the sentence "The Union shall respect fundamental rights . . . as general principles of Community law" contains what can be read as a limiting clause on what constitutes "fundamental rights" between commas in place of the three dots. That clause says "*as* guaranteed by the European Convention for the Protection of Human Rights and Fundamental Freedoms signed in Rome on 4 Nov. 1950 and *as* they result from the constitutional traditions common to the Member States" (emphasis added). Therefore the inclusion in the Charter of Rights of rights going beyond the European Convention on Human Rights and the constitutional traditions which are genuinely common to the member states could be said to constitute a significant increase in the power of the Court of Justice to exercise judicial review in this area if the Charter were to be given binding legal force at the next IGC. Lenaerts and De Smijter, however, argue, n. 6 above, at 280–1 that "all rights enumerated in the Charter are either listed in the EC Treaty or belong to the Member States' common constitutional traditions *sensu lato*". But they concede that the Charter "goes beyond the fundamental rights recognized so far by the Court of Justice" (at 280). They accept that the novelty of the Charter is in listing "social rights" but contend that they are part of the common constitutional traditions of the member states even though the Court of Justice has made no such finding thus far. The authors imply some doubt as to "what extent the Court will be ready to enforce respect for this politically sensitive set of fundamental rights" (at 280). It is surely highly debatable as to whether all of the rights listed in the Charter which are not derived from the European Convention on Human Rights are part of the common constitutional traditions of the member states. Given the absence of a clear notion of what comes within the UK constitution it is impossible to be categorical about these matters in the absence of a European Court of Justice decision. This author is of the view that nothing in Chapter IV of the Charter is part of the "constitutional traditions" of the UK. Some so called rights are obscure and would be regarded as a matter of policy which is open to change by different governments, e.g. Art. 29 of the Charter states that "Everyone has the right of access to a free placement service". Furthermore, it is worth noting that Advocate General Jacobs had given an Opinion in 1999, before the existence of the Charter, that a right to free collective bargaining was not a Community fundamental right, see Case C–67/96 *Albany* discussed in the text below. Therefore it can be argued that its elevation to a right in Art. 28 of the Charter extends the scope of Community fundamental rights—unless the Court is wise enough to ignore the Charter on this matter.

Weiler and Fries argue that the Community should adopt human rights legislation across the whole spectrum of Community law in order to improve access to justice. However, the issue of access to justice is about specific procedural rights and does not need to be dressed up or clothed in the theological language of rights. Member states and the Community have to make difficult public spending choices about how much scarce public resource should be spent on the Court system, on legal aid, on alternative dispute resolution, on legal education, etc. There is no reason to require the same policy choices to be made in all the legal systems of the European Union. After all our right to good health care and a decent environment may be just as important as access to justice—frankly more important—but calling those things rights gives us no handle on how much Governments should spend on each and what should happen when these and other rights conflict. Some limited cross-border issues might require measures on access to justice under Title IV of the EC Treaty but it adds little or nothing to dress that up in the rhetoric of human rights. There is a good case for giving individuals better standing to challenge the legality of Community acts in the Community courts but this requires a Treaty amendment to Article 230, not some new human rights legislation.

In terms of legal bases for human rights legislation Weiler and Fries identify three. First, in order to tag human rights concerns on to any substantive area of Community competence, they say that: "the duty and right of non-discrimination and equality is at the core of all other human rights and can provide a broad platform for a human right policy". Why should this be the case? Discrimination happens every day in life, e.g. academically excellent students are admitted to study postgraduate law degrees at the University of Aberdeen but academically weak students or even those who are good but not good enough are not admitted. Some discrimination is acceptable and other types of discrimination are not. Thus merit based discrimination is acceptable but race based discrimination is not acceptable unless you subscribe to the view that positive discrimination in favour of certain races is necessary in order to help people overcome the merit based hurdles. Whether and when discrimination is acceptable is a complex and debatable question not easily reduced to the language of rights. As for "equality" the writers probably mean equality of opportunity or equal pay for equal work but not equality of outcomes otherwise we would all be able to fly business class when crossing the Atlantic (or none of us would). It is just the fashionable liberal philosophy of the recent past which has elevated these two ideas of "non-discrimination and equality" to be the core of all other human rights. I would argue instead, in a deeply unfashionable way, that the core human right—if compelled to use such language—is freedom of religion. All individuals should be free to make the most important life choice—whether or not to worship God and follow the lifestyle prescribed by God. Once that choice is made then the precepts laid down by God will reveal the best way to live life on earth. This may involve deciding that the religious community should be free to discriminate and practice inequalities untrammelled by state interference in the form of courts or legislatures seeking to uphold human rights. So religious communities should be free to decide that priests and rabbis can only be male and to decide that people who have sexual relations with people to whom they are not married cannot be priests and rabbis. So human rights are rhetorical and conceal the true divisions based on philosophy, religion and policy priorities. It is better to deal with these divisions openly rather than through the prism of human rights which seems to be ideologically loaded towards a maximalist liberal outcome.[12]

Secondly, Weiler and Fries argue for the use of Article 95 (ex 100a) of the EC Treaty on the harmonisation of laws in the internal market as the legal basis for measures on human rights. This would harmonise the legitimate human rights limits that could be put on internal market freedoms by member states. Is this a good idea? The authors recognise that it should perhaps be subject to the principle of subsidiarity and then note in a footnote that this principle would not operate once a measure had been adopted and not at all if the Commission's view of its exclusive competence in this area were to prevail.[13] This highlights the problem with the suggestion. At the latest once a Community competence has been exercised the member states cease to have competence and therefore what is currently within the territory of legitimate policy debate in Edinburgh or London or Barcelona or Madrid becomes a matter only for Brussels. Human rights becomes yet another device for centralisation of power in the Community. The other problem is that once the Community has exercised

---

[12] In fact part of this policy debate has been put into the Community arena by the insertion of Art. 13 of the EC Treaty by the Treaty of Amsterdam that gives the Community power to legislate to combat discrimination on various grounds including religion, sex and sexual orientation. The balance between the religious freedom of churches and other religious groups to form themselves in accordance with the teachings of their religion and the rights of individuals not to be discriminated against on grounds of religion, sex or sexual orientation in employment by such churches and religious groups was the subject of vigorous debate and is legislated for in Art. 4 of Council Dir. 2000/78/EC, [2000] OJ L 303/16, see P Beaumont, "Christian Perspectives on the Law: what makes them distinctive?" in A Lewis and R O'Dair (eds.), *Law and Religion, Current Legal Issues* Vol 4 (Oxford: Oxford University Press, 2002) 529–546 and P Beaumont, "Christianity and Law Reform: A Living Tradition" in *The Law and Christian Ethics* (Edinburgh: Saint Andrew Press, 2001) 88–104. The legislative balance is far from perfect and too much is decided at Community level that would be better left to national law to demonstrate proper respect for subsidiarity. However, the balance between religious freedom and non-discrimination also needs to be addressed in a way that limits the powers of the judges who have to apply that balance to individual cases. This is something the Charter of Rights singularly fails to do because it makes no attempt to deal with the difficult questions that arise when rights clash. Religious groups should be permitted to employ only people of that religious group and to restrict employment to those members of that religious group who are prepared to make a serious effort to live up to the sexual standards required by the teachings of that religious group. The Community, however, by imposing its values of sexual and sexual orientation non-discrimination in the private sphere of employment relationships is in danger of preventing religious groups from being true to their teachings. These religious groups are not just, so-called, cults but mainstream Jewish, Christian and Muslim groups. This has the undesired consequence of prioritising non-discrimination over religious freedom. See generally C Harlow below at 221–3.

[13] Advocate General Jacobs stated in para. 81 of his opinion of 14 June 2001, in Case C–377/98 *Netherlands* v. *European Parliament and Council*, that "the Community has exclusive competence in the approximation of national rules concerning the establishment and functioning of the internal market". The Court of Justice did not comment on this issue, judgment of 9 Oct. 2001, in giving a superficial subsidiarity analysis (paras. 30–33).

internal competence in any area it then obtains external competence.[14] This would mean that in those areas within the Community where human rights are harmonised it would become the prerogative of the Commission rather than the member states to negotiate externally on these human rights issues. The Commission simply does not have the resources or expertise to do this. The last Commission was forced to resign due to the report of independent experts. One of the main findings of that report was that the Commission did too many things with too few resources and did not accept responsibility for its actions.[15] The resources have not been increased and the reforms of the Commission have a long way to go. It is surely irresponsible to suggest that the Commission should take on more responsibilities and that it is in the best position to promote human rights or to represent the Community externally in this sphere.

Thirdly, the authors maintain that the Community can use Article 308 (ex 235) of the EC Treaty to legislate on most human rights issues provided it:

> "respected the current institutional balance, which avoided formal accession to the ECHR, which left intact the definition of the material contents of rights and their Community autonomy and which, critically, scrupulously remained within the field of Community law, would not and could not be considered of 'constitutional significance' in the sense used by the Court in Opinion 2/94".

This analysis is based on a reading of Opinion 2/94.[16] That case concerned whether Article 308 could be the legal basis for the Community to accede to the European Convention on Human Rights to which the Court gave a negative answer.[17] It does not of course determine whether or not the Community can use Article 308 to make any legislation on human rights. However it does affirm the principle of conferred powers and the vital fact that Article 308 "cannot serve as a basis for widening the scope of Community powers beyond the general framework created by the provisions of the Treaty as a whole and, in particular, by those that define the tasks and the activities of the Community".[18] Therefore the Community could only use Article 308 to legislate on human rights if this was one of the tasks and activities of the Community set out in Articles 2 and 3 of the EC Treaty. It is not. Therefore Article 308 should not be used as a legal basis for legislation on human rights. That is not to say that the Community institutions should not respect human rights when legislating on other matters. As things stand if they do not do so the legislation is in danger of being struck down by the Court. Once again the problem with the Weiler and Fries solution is that it departs from the principle of conferred powers and gives

---

[14] A doctrine developed by the Court of Justice since Case 22/70 *Commission* v. *Council (ERTA)* [1971] ECR 263, see Weatherill and Beaumont, n. 4 above, 366–72.

[15] See Weatherill and Beaumont, n. 4 above, 1059–64.

[16] [1996] ECR I–1759.

[17] See P Beaumont, "The European Community Cannot Accede to the European Convention on Human Rights" (1997) 1 *Edinburgh Law Review* 235.

[18] Para. 30 of Opinion 2/94.

the Community institutions a legislative power which the member states have not given them in the EC Treaty. This is a matter still within national competence.

Relationship with the European Convention on Human Rights

The Court of Justice reiterated in the *Emesa Sugar* case that the European Convention on Human Rights is not binding on the European Court of Justice but that it has "special significance" in the development of the Court's own concept of fundamental rights.[19] The Court, however, skilfully managed to conclude that the fact that the parties are not allowed to comment on the Advocate General's Opinion is not a breach of Article 6(1) of the European Convention on Human Rights even though the European Court of Human Rights had ruled that the right in Article 6:

> "means in principle the opportunity for the parties to a criminal or civil trial to have knowledge of and comment on all evidence adduced or observations filed, even by an independent member of the national legal service [in the French version. 'magistrat independant'], with a view to influencing the court's decision".[20]

The Court of Justice engaged in some old fashioned distinguishing. It pointed out that an Advocate General in the Court of Justice has the same status as the Judges, not an independent member of the legal service, and when he gives an Opinion:

> "it constitutes the individual reasoned opinion, expressed in open court, of a Member of the Court of Justice itself. The Advocate General thus takes part, publicly and individually, in the process by which the Court reaches its judgment, and therefore in carrying out the judicial function entrusted to it. Furthermore, the Opinion is published together with the Court's judgment. Having regard to both the organic and the functional link between the Advocate General and the Court . . . the . . . case law of the European Court of Human Rights does not appear to be transposable to the Opinion of the Court's Advocates General".[21]

The Court of Justice is avoiding problems with Article 6(1) by stressing the judicial nature of the Advocate General's Opinion. However, it is by no means

[19] See Case C–17/98 *Emesa Sugar (Free Zone) NV* v. *Aruba*, Order of the Court of 4 Feb. 2000, para. 8 citing Case C–260/89 *ERT* [1991] ECR I–2925, para. 41. See also Case C–274/99 *Connolly* v. *Commission*, judgment of 6 Mar. 2001, para. 37.

[20] *Ibid.* at para. 6. Quoting para. 33 of *Vermeulen* v. *Belgium* 1996–I ECHR Reports of Judgments and Decisions 224. That Court had decided that the *avocat général* from the *procureur général's* department at the Belgian Court of Cassation gave an objective opinion in advising the Court but that the failure to allow the parties to respond to that opinion was a breach of Art. 6(1).

[21] Case C–17/98, Order of 4 Feb. 2000 at paras. 14–16. Followed by the Court in Case C–265/97P *VBA* v. *Florimex, VGB and Commission*, judgment of 30 Mar. 2000 at para. 63.

certain that if the European Court of Human Rights were able to decide the issue that it would take the same view. The Advocate General is institutionally a member of the Court of Justice but the Opinion is not analogous to a normal judicial opinion in that it is not binding on anyone. The Advocate General plays no part in the deliberations of the Court so it is perfectly possible to take the view that it is unfair on the parties to the case to be unable to respond to the Advocate General's Opinion before the Judges decide the case. It is interesting that the Court gives a back-up reason for not allowing routine responses to an Advocate General's Opinion—though it does contemplate that it may reopen the oral procedure in certain circumstances—that has nothing to do with a fair trial in the individual case but everything to do with the quality of justice offered by the Court. The Court was worried about the increase in the length of the procedure before the Court which is exacerbated by the "special constraints inherent in Community judicial procedure, connected in particular with its language regime".[22] The Court has a point. Already the Court's procedures take too long and act as a denial of justice and a deterrent to national courts referring cases for preliminary rulings. It is a legitimate viewpoint that the Advocate General's Opinion is the first phase of the judicial process and not the last but one phase of the hearing. Why should a central body, the European Court of Human Rights, decide on such fine questions about how civil proceedings are conducted in protecting the very vague notion of "a fair and public hearing within a reasonable time by an independent and impartial tribunal established by law" set out in Article 6(1) of the Convention? Much more judicial restraint is required if the minimum guarantees provided by the text are not to be transformed by judges into their conception of a detailed blueprint for a fair trial that must be applied throughout Europe (see Harlow, 218–9 below).

Pro-Human Rights Interpretation

In *Schroder*,[23] a three judge Chamber of the Court of Justice stated that the prohibition on discrimination on the ground of sex is a fundamental human right. The Court decided that the "social" objective of Article 141 (ex 119) EC should take priority over the economic objective in order to promote fundamental rights. One of the problems with this kind of approach is that it rather arbitrarily elevates the importance of some rights over others. Why is it more important for social reasons to prevent sex discrimination than it is for economic reasons to prevent companies in some countries from gaining an unfair advantage by not having to pay women the same as men? If the net result of prioritising the former is that people lose their jobs because the employer cannot afford the

---

[22] Case C–17/98 at para. 17.
[23] Cases C–50/96 and C–270–271/97 *Deutsche Telekom AG* v. *Schröder* etc. (3 judge decision) [2000] ECR I–743.

higher salary bills and decides to relocate the whole business to a part of the Union in which this higher obligation is not in force then how have social rights been advanced?[24] Is the right to a job not just as important as the right not to be sexually discriminated against? Is not the problem with a rights based approach that it tends to promote those rights which are justiciable, like equal pay for men and women, over those which are not, like the right to a job? Of course the relationship between levels of employment and equal pay requirements is far more subtle than the above might suggest. The point is that judges should be wary of second guessing the text of Community law by superimposing some hierarchy of fundamental rights which, however well intentioned, may not achieve its intended purpose.

It is interesting that the earlier eleven judge decision of the European Court in the *Albany* case[25] avoided a human rights analysis. Perhaps this was because Advocate General Jacobs had convincingly shown in his Opinion that there is no human right to free collective bargaining, and that even if there was it could still be subject to restrictions imposed by Community competition rules in the public interest.[26] Instead, he engaged in a contextual interpretation of the Treaty which led the Court to prioritise social policy objectives over competition law objectives as follows:

> "It is beyond question that certain restrictions of competition are inherent in collective agreements between organisations representing employers and workers. However, the social policy objectives pursued by such agreements would be seriously undermined if management and labour were subject to Article 85(1) of the Treaty [now Article 81(1)] when seeking jointly to adopt measures to improve conditions of work and employment".

> "It therefore follows from an interpretation of the provisions of the Treaty as a whole which is both effective and consistent that agreements concluded in the context of collective negotiations between management and labour in pursuit of such objectives must, by virtue of their nature and purpose, be regarded as falling outside the scope of Article 85(1) of the Treaty [now Article 81(1)]."[27]

Too much should not be read into one three judge Chamber decision in *Schröder*. The two cases discussed above show that the Court is capable of using human rights justifications when it finds them useful and ignoring them when it does not. It seems to take a pragmatic approach. The Court seems intent on

---

[24] Admittedly this could not happen in the context of the cases in hand because the obligation is retrospective relating to a period before the mid 1970s.

[25] Case C–67/96 *Albany International BV* v. *Stichting Bedrijfspensioenfonds Textielindustrie* [1999] ECR I–5751.

[26] Opinion of 28 Jan. 1999 at paras. 132–63.

[27] Court judgment, paras. 59–60. Advocate General Jacobs had argued against removing collective agreements from the scope of Community competition law and instead suggested a limited immunity: "collective agreements between management and labour concluded in good faith on core subjects of collective bargaining such as wages and working conditions which do not directly affect third markets and third parties are not caught by Art. 85(1) of the Treaty [now Art. 81(1)]." (para. 194 of his Opinion).

promoting the Treaty's social objectives over those of its economic and competition objectives but does not feel compelled to use human rights arguments to achieve this. The Court should follow its own example in the *Grant* case[28] and not only avoid using human rights reasoning as a method of extending Community competence but also avoid using it as a pretext for distorting the interpretation of the Treaty. The Court would be well advised to hold the different objectives of the Treaty in creative tension rather than to give total priority to one objective over the other.

The Court of Justice, Sixth Chamber, in the *BECTU* case,[29] classified the right to paid annual leave set out in Directive 93/104 as a "social right"[30] and rejected the UK Government's contention that the Directive permitted member states to have a qualifying period of employment—13 weeks in the UK—before a person becomes entitled to paid annual leave because "Member States are not entitled to make the existence of that right [paid annual leave], which derives directly from Directive 93/104, subject to any preconditions whatsoever".[31] Article 7(1) of the Directive states that "Member States shall take the measures necessary to ensure that every worker is entitled to paid annual leave of at least four weeks in accordance with the conditions for entitlement to, and granting of, such leave laid down by national legislation and/or practice." The Court of Justice construed the "in accordance" clause restrictively saying it refers "only to the arrangements for paid annual leave adopted in the various Member States".[32] The Court did not expressly refer to the Charter of Rights, unlike the Advocate General,[33] but its use of the phrase "social right", rather than entitlement under the Directive, and its reasoning that a restriction on a "right" cannot deny its existence could have been influenced by the Charter and the Advocate General's references to it. Article 31(2) of the Charter states that every worker has a right to "an annual period of paid leave" and Article 52 of the Charter states that any limitation on the rights in the Charter must "respect the essence of those rights and freedoms". The Directive creates an entitlement to four weeks paid annual leave but the "conditions for entitlement" are a matter for national law. Thus it is reasonable to assume that the Council was leaving some discretion to member states as to "entitlement" to leave and not just the "arrangements" for leave. As a matter of policy it may be better that all workers should be entitled to paid

---

[28] Case C–249/96 *Grant* v. *South-West Trains Ltd* [1998] ECR I–621, see Weatherill and Beaumont, n. 4 above, 158–9 and 289–90.

[29] Case C–173/99 *The Queen* v. *Secretary of State for Trade and Industry, ex parte Broadcasting, Entertainment, Cinematographic and Theatre Union (BECTU)* [2001] ECR I–4881.

[30] *Ibid.* at para. 47.

[31] *Ibid.* at para. 53.

[32] *Ibid.* at para. 53.

[33] The Advocate General referred to the Charter of Rights at paras. 26–28. He conceded that the Charter "is not in itself binding" but "in proceedings concerned with the nature and scope of a fundamental right, the relevant statements of the Charter cannot be ignored" and should be used as a "substantive reference point". The Sixth Chamber may have diplomatically declined to refer expressly to the Charter but it would be unwise to assume that they ignored it. Indeed the rights reasoning in the judgment suggests that they did have it in mind.

annual leave even when they only work for a few weeks (though it may deter short term employment e.g. of students during the summer vacation) but is that clearly what was agreed by the Council in adopting Directive 93/104?

In *BECTU* the Court used the language of social rights to give a maximalist interpretation to a specific entitlement in a Directive. In the challenge by the Netherlands to the validity of Directive 98/44 on the legal protection of biotechnological inventions Advocate General Jacobs[34] refers to certain provisions of the Charter of Rights which were relied on as part of the argument that the Directive is contrary to Community fundamental rights, but decides that human rights protection need not only be built into the Directive but can be inherent in other provisions of national law. The Directive is concerned with patent law and any dangers it may present to "human dignity" (Article 1 of the Charter) and "free and informed consent" in the fields of medicine and biology (Article 3(2) of the Charter) are avoided by the restrictions inherent in the Directive and also by provisions of national law outside the arena of patent law. So Advocate General Jacobs succeeds in upholding the validity of Community law without requiring the Directive in and of itself to guarantee that the rights he refers to in the Charter will not be violated. He avoided any analysis of Article 52 of the Charter—analysis which would seem to require an exposition of how the essence of the Charter rights are safeguarded in this field by law. By his approach Advocate General Jacobs rightly exposes one of the weaknesses of the Charter structure. Community law is not a complete system but rather a part of the national law of each of the member states. It is not sensible to assume that human rights protection must be built in to every instrument of Community law, as Article 52 of the Charter would imply, because the appropriate protection, e.g. the right to free and informed consent in the fields of medicine and biology, is really an area within national law and should not be communautarised just in order to deal with human rights issues. The alternative approach implied by the Charter would create a huge increase in Community competence by the back door method of requiring Community human rights protections in areas previously, and adequately, regulated by national law.

In the eleven judge decision of the European Court of Justice in *Krombach*,[35] the Court acknowledged that Article II of the Annexed Protocol to the Brussels Convention on its own terms and in the light of earlier case law of the European Court of Justice "clearly seeks to deny the right to be defended without appearing in person to persons who are being prosecuted for offences which are sufficiently serious to justify this".[36] However, the Court of Justice relied on case law of the European Court of Human Rights[37] to show that in criminal proceedings

---

[34] Case C–377/98 *Netherlands* v. *European Parliament and Council*. opinion of 14 June 2001, see paras. 185–215.
[35] Case C–7/98, *Krombach* v. *Bamberski* [2000] ECR I–1935.
[36] Para. 41. The Court cited para. 12 of its own decision in Case 157/80 *Rinkau* [1981] ECR 1391.
[37] Para. 39 referring to *Poitrimol* v. *France* (1993) Series A No. 277–A, *Pelladoch* v. *Netherlands* (1994) Series A No. 297–B, and *Van Geyseghem* v. *Belgium*, [GC], no. 26103/95, ECHR 1999–I, 129.

the accused has the right to be represented by a lawyer in court even if he or she does not attend the hearing in person. The Court of Justice concluded that "a national court of a Member State is entitled to hold that a refusal to hear the defence of an accused person who is not present at the hearing constitutes a manifest breach of a fundamental right".[38] Applying this principle in the context of the public policy exception in the Brussels Convention to the requirement to recognise and enforce judgments from other member states the Court decided that:

> "recourse to the public-policy clause must be regarded as being possible in exceptional cases where the guarantees laid down in the legislation of the State of origin and in the Convention itself have been insufficient to protect the defendant from a manifest breach of his right to defend himself before the court of origin, as recognised by the ECHR. Consequently, Article II of the Protocol cannot be construed as precluding the court of the State in which enforcement is sought from being entitled to take account, in relation to public policy, as referred to in Article 27, point 1, of the Convention, of the fact that, in an action for damages based on an offence, the court of the State of origin refused to hear the defence of the accused person, who was being prosecuted for an intentional offence, solely on the ground that that person was not present at the hearing".[39]

The danger with this approach is that the relatively tightly circumscribed concept of public policy in private international law[40] is now opened up to be equated with a human rights exception. Where human rights is given a narrow construction this is not problematic.[41] It is a dangerous problem if an expansive approach is taken to human rights, both in terms of the spread of issues regarded as human rights and the level of detail encompassed by human rights. A classic example is the idea that a right to a fair trial in Article 6 of the European Convention on Human Rights includes a right to access to justice which in turn includes a positive requirement on the State to provide legal aid.[42] This tendency of the European Court of Human Rights to turn classic civil and political rights guaranteeing fair treatment in court into an economic right to be aided to take a case to court is very European and, perhaps, rather outdated in its thinking.

---

[38] Para. 40.

[39] Para. 44.

[40] See N Enonchong, "Public Policy in the Conflict of Laws: A Chinese Wall Around Little England?" (1996) 45 *ICLQ* 633–61; A Anton with P Beaumont, *Private International Law* (2nd edn., Edinburgh: W Green/SULI, 1990) 101–6.

[41] Indeed I have argued for public policy to protect human rights in the context of evidence to the Special Public Bill Committee of the House of Lords, see *Private International Law (Miscellaneous Provisions) Bill [HL], Proceedings of the Special Public Bill Committee*, House of Lords Paper 36, Session 1994–95, 75–76. The particular problem then was the risk of the freedom of expression of writers in UK newspapers being restricted by the application of a foreign law to a tort or delict action in the UK if that foreign law, for example, made it a tort or delict to criticise a member of the government. It would, in my opinion, be legitimate to invoke the human right of freedom of expression as a public policy justification for not applying a foreign law that was designed to protect foreign leaders from any press criticism.

[42] See *Airey* v. *Ireland*, judgment of 9 Oct. 1979 (no. 32), 2 EHRR 305.

Imagine the consequences if judgments in the United States and many other countries in the world that have little or no provision for legal aid were routinely refused recognition because the party objecting to the judgment was denied legal aid in the original court hearing? This would undermine the proposed Hague Convention on Jurisdiction and Enforcement of Judgments in Civil and Commercial Matters.[43]

It is interesting to contrast the decision in *Emesa Sugar* with that in *Krombach* given just a few weeks later. It may be that the reason that the Court upheld a human rights argument based on Article 6 of the ECHR in *Krombach* but not in *Emesa Sugar* is simply on account of the more glaring and serious violation of the Article in the former than in the latter. Of course a more cynical explanation is that the Court found national breaches of human rights easier to castigate than its own breaches. Another gloss has been put on *Emesa Sugar* by the Sixth Chamber in Case C–50/96 *Deutsche Telekom AG v. Schröder*.[44] The three judges in the Sixth Chamber emphasised that the Court can, of its own motion, on a proposal from the Advocate General, or at the request of the parties, under Article 61 of its Rules of Procedure re-open the oral procedure after the Advocate General's Opinion "if it considers that it lacks sufficient information, or that the case must be dealt with on the basis of an argument which has not been debated between the parties" and that this system exists "precisely in deference to Article 6 of the ECHR and to the very purpose of every individual's right to adversarial proceedings and to a fair hearing within the meaning of that provision".[45] If the Sixth Chamber is right then it is encouraging parties to seek a reopening of the oral procedure whenever the Advocate General's Opinion is based on an idea or ideas not canvassed by the parties in the oral procedure. In such circumstances if the Court were to deny a request to reopen the oral procedure it would seem to be in breach of Article 6 of the ECHR on the Sixth Chamber's reading of *Emesa Sugar*. If this case by case approach is adopted rather than the view that the Advocate General is giving a judicial opinion and therefore the parties have no right under Article 6 to comment on it then the Court of Justice may be able to avoid a clash with the European Court of Human Rights and more readily justify its support for Article 6 in *Krombach* and its *de minimis* approach to it in *Emesa Sugar*.

In *Mannesmannröhren-Werke AG v. Commission*,[46] the Court of First Instance was asked by the applicant to rule that the Commission's investigative

---

[43] See the preliminary draft Convention of Oct. 1999 and the Interim Text from the Diplomatic Conference of June 2001 <http://www.hcch.net>. In the drafting of that Convention it is explicitly recognised that parties can only expect equal treatment with persons habitually resident in the State where legal aid is sought (Art. 32). It would be contrary to the intention of the Convention to deny recognition to a judgment on the basis that a foreign party should be given legal aid when a local person has no such entitlement because in the country of the foreign party legal aid is a human right.

[44] n. 23 above.

[45] *Ibid.*, para. 22. Two of the three judges in this case (Hirsch and Ragnemalm) were members of the Court in *Emesa Sugar* but the rapporteur in Case C–50/96 (Schintgen) was not and this may account for the interesting emphasis on what to draw out of *Emesa Sugar*.

[46] Case T–112/98, [2001] ECR II–729.

powers in the field of competition law under Regulation 17 are limited by Community fundamental rights as set out in Article 6(1) of the European Convention on Human Rights. In particular that Article 6 gives the applicant a right not to incriminate itself by positive action and therefore undertakings should not be put under pressure by the Commission to disclose documents and other facts which might lead to them being found in breach of competition law and being subject to heavy financial penalties.[47] The Commission accepted that the European Court of Human Rights has held that in a matter covered by Article 6 of the Convention a natural person has a right to maintain silence or to decline to give evidence against him or herself.[48] However, the Commission argued that Article 6 of the Convention was not applicable to the Commission in the context of their preliminary competition policy investigations as it was not acting as a court, the applicant was a legal person, the investigations did not lead to criminal penalties and, in any case, it would be impossible for the Commission to apply Community law on restrictive agreements and practices if undertakings were not required to furnish information that might incriminate them.

The Court of First Instance did not analyse the case law of the European Court of Human Rights (indeed it pointedly stated that the European Convention on Human Rights "as such is not part of Community law"[49]) and only addressed the Commission's last "in any case" argument. It decided to follow the established case law of the Court of Justice and of itself in deciding that "the Commission is entitled to compel an undertaking to provide all necessary information concerning such facts as may be known to it and to disclose to the Commission, if necessary, such documents relating thereto as are in its possession, even if the latter may be used to establish, against it or another undertaking, the existence of anti-competitive conduct".[50] It is noteworthy that the Court of Justice case law relied on predated the case law of the European Court of Human Rights relied on by the applicant. Furthermore, the Court of First Instance decided that an "absolute right to silence" goes beyond what is "necessary to protect the rights of defence of undertakings, and would constitute an unjustified hindrance to the Commission's performance of its duty under Article 89 of the EC Treaty (now, after amendment, Article 85 EC) to ensure that the rules on competition within the common market are observed".[51] The Court of First Instance gave a more limited right to silence. An undertaking would be required to give only factual information in a Regulation 17 investigation and would not be required to provide answers which might involve an admission on

---

[47] Case T–112/98 at paras. 36–7 relying on the European Court of Human Rights judgment of 25 Feb. 1993 in *Funke* (Series A, no. 256–A).

[48] *Ibid*. at para. 49.

[49] *Ibid*. at para. 59.

[50] *Ibid*. at para.65 relying on Case 374/87 *Orkem* v. *Commission* [1989] ECR 3283, para. 34, Case 27/88 *Solvay* v. *Commission* [1989] ECR 3355, and Case T–34/93 *Société Générale* v. *Commission* [1995] ECR II–545, para. 74.

[51] Case T–112/98 at para. 66.

its part that it was party to an agreement liable to prevent or restrict competition.[52] The Court of First Instance refused the applicant's request to re-open the oral procedure in order for the Court to take account of the Charter of Rights. The CFI decided that the Charter was irrelevant because it was adopted after the contested measure.[53]

The decision of the Court of First Instance shows that there are limits to the extent to which the Community courts are willing to follow the jurisprudence of the European Court of Human Rights. The rights of defence, as set out in Article 6(1) of the European Convention on Human Rights are limited by overriding EC Treaty objectives in achieving fair competition in the common market. However, Article 6(1) of the Convention is not drafted in such a way that it permits the rights contained in it to be limited for any policy reason except in relation to restricting publicity surrounding a trial. Nonetheless Regulation 17 was interpreted restrictively by the Court of First Instance to prohibit the Commission from requiring undertakings to go beyond providing factual information and documents. This restrictive interpretation was to protect the rights of defence to some extent. The fact that the European Convention on Human Rights is not part of Community law *per se* gives the Community courts the freedom to decide how broad its own doctrine of fundamental rights is and when that doctrine is limited by overriding Community policy objectives. By avoiding an absolutist approach to the right to silence the Court is able to give a restrictive interpretation to the application of Regulation 17 to favour human rights to a certain extent but is not compelled to effectively repeal parts of that Regulation on human rights grounds.

In two important recent decisions of the European Court of Justice on the Community's Staff Regulations the Court has decided that the decisions taken under the Regulations were not contrary to human rights and that no change to the interpretation of the Regulations was required.[54] In *D and Sweden* v. *Council*,[55] the full Court of 15 judges decided that a Council of European Union official of Swedish nationality who had registered his homosexual partnership under Swedish law (which treats such partnerships as equivalent to marriage for purposes of employment benefits) was not "a married official" for the purposes of the Staff Regulations and therefore not entitled to a household allowance. The Court, upholding the decision of the Court of First Instance, took the view that the interpretation of the phrase "married official" in the Staff Regulations

---

[52] *Ibid.* at paras. 67, 71 and 79.

[53] *Ibid.* at para. 76.

[54] In Case C–270/99P *Z* v. *European Parliament*, Advocate General Jacobs gave his opinion, 22 Mar. 2001, that Art. 6(1) of the European Convention on Human Rights does not apply to delays in disciplinary proceedings under the Staff Regulations because they are of an administrative rather than judicial nature (para. 62). However, in para. 61 he refers to case law of the European Court of Human Rights which supports the view that "disputes concerning disciplinary measures imposed on civil servants do not fall wholly outside the scope of Art. 6(1) of the Convention". This issue was not decided by the Sixth Chamber, judgment of 27 Nov. 2001.

[55] Cases C–122/99P and C–125/99P, judgment of 31 May 2001.

was a matter for independent Community interpretation and could not be referred to national law. The Court decided that any change to the Staff Regulations to give household allowances to homosexuals in a registered partnership should be done by the Community legislature and not by the Court.[56] The Court was struck by the fact that when the Staff Regulations were adopted in 1998 Sweden had asked for registered partnerships to be included but instead the Community legislature instructed the Commission to study the consequences of such a change, particularly the financial ones.[57]

The human rights argument before the Court of Justice was rather marginal.[58] D argued that under Article 8 of the European Convention on Human Rights he had a right to protection of his family life that included having the civil status accorded to his homosexual relationship in Sweden upheld by the Community so as to ensure that no incorrect data about his status be communicated by the Community to third parties.[59] The Court dealt with this argument very succinctly by saying that the Community's refusal to give D a household allowance did not affect his civil status but rather his relationship with his employer, and that the information would not be transmitted by the employer to third parties outside the Community administration.[60]

In *Connolly* v. *Commission*,[61] the Court of Justice considered at some length[62] whether Connolly's rights to freedom of expression had been limited by his employer, the Commission, in preventing him from publishing a book that contained insults about members of the Commission and indicated strong opposition to economic and monetary union. The Court analysed Article 10 of the European Convention on Human Rights on freedom of expression and considered whether the Commission's decision to prevent publication was justifiable within the meaning of Article 10(2) of the Convention because it was necessary in a democratic society for the protection of the rights of others. In this case the "others" referred to are the citizens who depend on their civil servants carrying out their tasks in the public interest. The Court of Justice gave a rather detailed exposition of the case law of the European Court of Human Rights on freedom of expression as it applies to civil servants, noting in particular that that Court

---

[56]   Case C–125/99P at para. 38.
[57]   *Ibid.* at para. 32.
[58]   Broader questions had been dealt with by the Court of First Instance, Case T–264/97 *D* v. *Council* [1999] ECR–SC I–A–1 and II–1, but were not considered by the Court of Justice on appeal. The CFI had, on the basis of the case law of the European Court of Human Rights and that of the Court of Justice in Case C–249/96 *Grant* [1998] ECR I–621, held in paras. 28–30 of its judgment that the Council was under no obligation to regard as equivalent to marriage, for the purposes of the Staff Regulations, the situation of a person who had a stable relationship with a partner of the same sex. The CFI in paras. 39–41 had also decided that Art. 8 of the European Convention on Human Rights does not include within the meaning of respect for family life long term homosexual relationships.
[59]   *Ibid.* at para. 58.
[60]   *Ibid.* at para. 59.
[61]   Case C–274/99P, judgment of 6 Mar. 2001.
[62]   *Ibid.* at paras. 37–65.

had given member states a margin of appreciation in deciding whether civil servants' freedom of expression can be restricted on one of the grounds in Article 10(2) and that the application of the article varies depending on the nature of the duties performed by the civil servant and his or her place in the hierarchy. Connolly was quite a high grade civil servant employed by the Commission to implement economic and monetary union, a key EC Treaty objective and Commission policy. Therefore the Court of Justice decided that preventing him from publishing a book that fundamentally opposed the policy he was employed to implement was a necessary restriction on Connolly's freedom of expression while he remained an official of the Community.

It is arguable that in this case the Court of Justice was willing to embark on a detailed analysis of Article 10 of the European Convention on Human Rights and the European Court of Human Rights case law thereon because it gives sufficient flexibility for the Court of Justice to arrive at the decision that upheld the Commission's treatment of Connolly.[63] Given that Connolly was arguing against the single currency and had been sacked by the Commission, it gave comfort to the Community institutions (which includes the Court of Justice) to be able to analyse the European Court of Human Rights case law in some detail to show that they were not biased against Connolly and that they wanted to take his human rights seriously, while demonstrating nevertheless that his rights had not been breached.

JUDICIAL COMPETENCE OF THE EUROPEAN COURT OF HUMAN RIGHTS OVER EUROPEAN UNION LAW

In *Matthews* v. *United Kingdom*,[64] the European Court of Human Rights decided that it could review the compliance of primary European Community law with the European Convention on Human Rights. It also found that the UK had breached Article 3 of Protocol No.1 to the European Convention on Human Rights by not allowing Ms Matthews, a Gibraltar resident, any opportunity to vote in the elections to the European Parliament in June 1994. In doing so it decided that the European Parliament constitutes "part of the 'legislature' of Gibraltar for the purposes of Article 3 of Protocol No. 1".[65] This was an overwhelming decision of fifteen votes to two. The dissenting minority[66] followed the stance of the substantial majority of the European Commission of Human Rights, eleven votes to six, that "the role of Article 3 is to ensure that elections take place at regular intervals to the national or local legislative assembly". This

---

[63] The Court was following the example of the Advocate General, R-J Colomer, opinion of 19 Oct. 2000, paras. 4–28.

[64] [GC], no. 24833/94, ECHR 1999–I, 251, noted by H Schermers (1999) 36 *CML Rev* 673–81 and T King (2000) 25 *EL Rev* 79–88. See also the broader and very stimulating piece by I Canor, "Primus Inter Pares. Who is the Ultimate Guardian of Fundamental Rights in Europe?" (2000) 25 *EL Rev* 3–21.

[65] Para. 54 of the judgment.

[66] Judges Sir John Freeland and Jungwiert.

view was reinforced by reference to the *travaux preparatoires* of the Protocol. The most telling remark of the dissent for the purposes of this chapter was that:

> "by confining the ambit of the provision to bodies within the domestic area and excluding any supranational representative organ, it avoids the uncertainty and invidiousness involved in analysis by an outside body of the characteristics of such an organ, which as experience has shown are likely to be neither straightforward nor static".[67]

The majority judgment has some very far reaching statements about the role of the European Parliament in the European Community. It asserts that:

> "the European Parliament represents the principal form of democratic, political accountability in the Community system . . . which derives democratic legitimation from the direct elections by universal suffrage, [and] must be seen as that part of the European Community structure which best reflects concerns as to 'effective political democracy' ".[68]

These are highly controversial assertions. Surely the Council is in practice much more politically accountable than the European Parliament. Members of the European Parliament are often elected by a small proportion of the electorate; have no clear political mandate because the electorate are predominantly voting on national political issues in accordance with the popularity of those political parties nationally and not on the basis of the issues at stake in the Community legislative process; have little or no accountability to the electorate because performance in the Parliament and the way in which they vote on particular issues is unlikely to have much if any bearing on the prospect of re-election; and their work is largely ignored or misunderstood by those who elect them because it is largely ignored by the media. The Council, on the other hand, is made up of members of the executive in each of the member states. Almost all of them are elected in national parliamentary elections in which there is a high turnout and in which the voters are choosing a government whose broad policies are known to the electorate. The national governments are accountable to their people in national elections as well as to their fellow members of the national parliaments, and are in the constant glare of media exposure. In addition, the Council is supported by the collective expertise of fifteen national civil services as well as the small Council Secretariat. The technical expertise to support the European Parliament is minimal. Thus consultation with experts, interest groups and the population as a whole is conducted more systematically by the Commission and the governments of the member states (in preparation for the Council and its various Working Parties) than by the European Parliament.

One could go on, but the crucial point is that the European Court of Human Rights' assertion that the Parliament is the part of the European Community structure which "best reflects" concerns as to "effective political democracy" is

---

[67] Para. 3 of the dissent.
[68] Para. 52 of the judgment.

not uncontentious. Frankly, it is also irrelevant as the only issue before them was whether the European Parliament could be described as "the legislature" for Gibraltar. The Court of Human Rights no doubt realised that if it simply decided that the European Parliament was "the legislature" for the purposes of Article 3 of Protocol No. 1 by an analysis of the European Parliament's legislative powers rather than its democratic credentials it would logically have to conclude that the body with more legislative power in the European Community, the Council, is also "the legislature".[69] This would of course lead to the absurd situation where the European Court of Human Rights decides that the citizens of the European Union have a right to "free elections at reasonable intervals by secret ballot" in relation to the Council of the European Union. By this process a concern for human rights would lead to the complete dismantling and restructuring of the supranational institutions of the European Community to make them fit the world of 1950 in which only national legislatures made legislation. So instead the Court of Human Rights comes to the contentious and surprising conclusion that the nearest thing to a legislature in the European Community is the European Parliament, because it looks democratic and has some legislative power, whereas by implication the Council of the European Union is not a legislature because although it does have real legislative power it does not look (directly) democratic. The key to being the legislature is not the ability to legislate but rather being directly elected. So the right to free elections to the legislature is turned on its head and instead if a body is freely elected it must be a legislature.

It would have been far wiser for the Court to conclude that Article 3 of Protocol No. 1 is restricted to national legislatures. If supranational legislatures are to be covered the Contracting States should specifically agree to this in a Protocol. The European Court of Human Rights instead sees itself as the supreme European legislature by construing the Convention as a "living instrument"[70] and regarding it as its duty to make the Convention fit the modern world of international institutions with legislative powers. However this will not do. Even in 1950 the Security Council of the United Nations had power to make binding laws (economic sanctions on States that were guilty of aggression) but it would be ridiculous to say that people in Europe have their fundamental rights abused by the lack of democratic elections to the Security Council. The drafters of the Convention in 1950 knew that there were multiple legislatures in some national systems, that there were some signs of bodies with legislative power in the international community, and that there could well be in the future many more such bodies internationally. Thus Article 3 refers to "the legislature" not "a legislature" or "a legislative body". After all, in most national systems governments have significant legislative powers, particularly to make secondary

---

[69] In para. 7 of the dissent the two judges say: "In fact, of the institutions of the Community it is the Council of Ministers which performs the functions most closely related to those of a legislature at national level."

[70] Para. 39 of the judgment.

legislation,[71] and therefore the drafters must have consciously attempted to exclude them from the scope of Article 3.

The European Court of Human Rights also exposes its own weakness in *Matthews*. It compels the UK to pay some of her legal costs but it can do nothing to ensure that Gibraltar residents will be able to vote in European Parliament elections. This will require unanimity among the fifteen member states of the European Union to change the primary EC law which governs elections to the European Parliament. Is it likely that Spain will allow Gibraltar people to be represented in the European Parliament as anything other than a small part of a Spanish constituency?

The European Court of Human Rights would do well to tolerate more divergence in the methods by which bodies with legislative powers are held accountable to the people in modern democracies rather than forcing them to fit the classic model prescribed by Article 3 of Protocol No. 1 which was geared for the lower house of the national parliament.[72] It can only do this if it gives a very narrow construction to the phrase "the legislature" in Article 3 of the First Protocol.

CONCLUSION

The Charter of Fundamental Rights of the European Union is not legally binding and should remain so after the next Intergovernmental Conference. Legally binding human rights provisions should be a matter for member states except in the limited sphere of development co-operation. The alternative of widening Community competence is deeply worrying not only because of its extended interference with the national democratic prerogative over internal affairs but also because any legislation on human rights in the Community creates external Community competence (thereby giving the overstretched and largely unaccountable Commission even more to do badly) and further damages the individual's ability to influence public policy through democratic processes. Binding human rights legislation in the European Community is a step too far in convergence of European public law.

It is possible to hold out the vision of human rights as the tool by which the Court of Justice can become not only the interpreter of the EU Constitution (the primary treaties) but the controller of the validity of the Constitution. Iris Canor has argued that the European Court of Justice should consider reviewing primary Community law (the EC Treaty and other acts of the representatives of the Governments of the Member States which have Treaty status) in order to ensure its compatibility with fundamental human rights and at least be prepared to give "indirect effect" to fundamental rights by interpreting the EC Treaty consistent

---

[71] As does the Commission of the European Community. Should it be subject to direct elections?

[72] After all the House of Lords in the UK has always been a part of the UK legislature but, as yet, has never been the subject of democratic election.

with fundamental rights so far as possible.[73] Such temptation to the judges in Luxembourg to play God should be resisted. It would be blatant and unacceptable judicial activism.[74]

What does the small sample of recent cases on human rights which have been analysed in this paper tell us about convergence and divergence of law in Europe? The most radical decision of the European Court of Justice, *Krombach*, in which the Court goes against the textual indications of the provision under scrutiny through reliance on human rights actually allows for more divergence in the laws in Europe. It permits member states not to recognise a judgment coming from another member state on public policy grounds when there is a breach of human rights even if that breach was anticipated in the terms of the Community instrument. A strict construction of the instrument might have led to a decision preventing diversity and forcing recognition of the judgment. However, the Court could have protected diversity without getting tied up in equating human rights with public policy. The Court could have contented itself with saying that public policy is to be interpreted strictly and only used in exceptional cases.[75] Instead it tried to square the circle of saying that states can "determine, according to their own conceptions, what public policy requires" but "the limits of that concept are a matter for interpretation of the Convention" which is to be done by the Court of Justice.[76] The Court cannot predict in advance all the various matters that might be regarded as public policy in each member state so it is absurd to suggest that it can formulate the outer limits of public policy without interfering in what a particular member state might regard as a matter of public policy. By definition public policy is a national concept and is a safety valve to protect strongly held norms in a particular society. It is a mistake to attempt to internationalise it by equating it with standards in the European Convention on Human Rights. In some respects these human rights values may be far narrower than traditional public policy[77] and in other respects human rights arguments may lead to a significant broadening of the use of public policy in private international law. It should be for the national courts in member

[73] n. 54 above, at pp. 7–8.

[74] See Weatherill and Beaumont, n. 4 above, 193–201 for a brief account of unacceptable judicial activism. For more detailed accounts see H. Rasmussen, *On Law and Policy in the European Court of Justice* (Rotterdam: Martinus Nijhoff, 1986) and *European Court of Justice* (Copenhagen: GadJura, 1998).

[75] As it had previously done in Case 145/86 *Hoffmann* v. *Krieg* [1988] ECR 645, para. 21 and Case C–78/95 *Hendrikman and Feyen* v. *Magenta Druck & Verlag* [1996] ECR I–4943, para. 23.

[76] *Krombach* at para. 22.

[77] Certainly this was the view of the drafters of the Hague Convention on International Child Abduction of 1980 who worked hard at the Diplomatic Conference to reverse a decision to include a public policy clause in favour of a human rights clause on the basis that the latter would be less likely to be used as a justification for refusing to return a child who had been wrongfully removed or retained from the country of their habitual residence, see P Beaumont and P McEleavy, *Hague Convention on International Child Abduction* (Oxford: Oxford University Press, 1999), 137–8 and 172–6. However, things have moved on since 1980. The human rights of children grew with the UN Convention on the Rights of the Child and may grow further in a way that could make them as broad or broader than some national public policy in the area.

states to determine what constitutes public policy in that state and for those states to decide whether, and when, to use human rights arguments as a support for concluding that something is contrary to public policy.

The decision of the Court of Justice in *Schröder* tolerates unequal treatment of Community nationals and the distortion of competition in the single market that goes with it in order to promote the human right which prohibits discrimination on the ground of sex. In doing so it promotes diversity from one member state to another but interferes fundamentally in the internal affairs of a state by saying that if it partially implemented Article 119 (now 141) EC before that provision was given direct effect by the European Court in the *Defrenne* case[78] then individuals in that state should get their full Article 119 rights. On the other hand in states which did not partially implement Article 119 individuals are left with no rights in relation to the period prior to the *Defrenne* case. Had the European Court retained the original focus of the Community on equal treatment of Community nationals in a cross border context it would have more easily allowed for divergence by saying that in the pre-direct effect period it is a matter for the national law in each member state to determine what rights a woman had to equal pay and equal treatment. By focusing on human rights the Court reaches the slightly bizarre conclusion that it is a human right under Community law that in some member states women and men should be given equal pay and equal treatment while in other member states no such human right under Community law arises. This produces a forced divergence of law in Europe in relation to a period that would have been better left entirely to national decision-making.

Albany is a case in which the Court eschewed human rights reasoning and coincidentally arrived at a result which creates more divergence in European law by exempting agreements arrived at in collective bargaining between employers and employees from the scope of the Community's competition policy. The decision may be a good one because it promotes divergence and because it helps to reduce the already unmanageable workload of the Commission in dealing with competition cases.

Emesa Sugar may just be a skilful case of distinguishing the case law of the European Court of Human Rights on Article 6(1) of the European Convention on Human Rights rather than a rebellion by the European Court of Justice against compliance with the case law of that Court on the Convention. Such distinguishing may on occasions be necessary because the supranational framework of the European Community may not always neatly fit the norms of the European Court of Human Rights in interpreting the European Convention on Human Rights which was designed to apply to traditional states. This becomes evident from an analysis of the European Court of Human Rights' decision in *Matthews* in which the European Parliament is squeezed into the box marked

---

[78] Case 43/75 *Defrenne* v. *Sabena* [1976] ECR 455; see Weatherill and Beaumont, n. 4 above, at 351. In *Defrenne* the European Court had deliberately decided not to give retrospective effect to its decision that Art. 119 (now 141) EC had direct effect in relation to equal pay for men and women.

"legislature" in the European Convention on Human Rights. The Community legislature is of course a combination of the Commission, Council and European Parliament—should they all be directly elected? The European Court of Human Rights should allow for some diversity on human rights by not supervising the work of the European Community. It should acknowledge that it has no jurisdiction over the Community because the latter has not acceded to the Convention and accept that the Convention is ill-suited as currently drafted for application to the Community.

The decision in *Mannesmannröhren-Werke AG* shows that distinguishing of European Court of Human Rights' decisions may have its limits. In that case the Court of First Instance avoided an analysis of the decisions of the European Court of Human Rights and the distinguishing suggestions given by the Commission. Instead it chose to set out an autonomous Community standard for a less than absolute right to silence in the context of Commission competition policy investigations under Regulation 17. This has the merit of seeking to guard against being forced to adopt a different position in the future if the Court of Human Rights were to reach a decision that removes the basis on which the distinguishing was done. It has the disadvantage of leaving the Community exposed to accusations that it is failing to uphold human rights. The Community legislature should debate the restrictions that human rights should impose on Commission investigations under Regulation 17 and amend the Regulation to impose the appropriate limits on Commission action. The European Court of Human Rights should be careful not to read too much detail into the very vague wording of Article 6 of the European Convention on Human Rights, which makes no mention of a right to silence—absolute or restricted— or of a right to reply to findings of an independent lawyer appointed to give an objective opinion on the case prior to the Court's judgment, and thereby limit too much the discretion of legislatures in deciding the appropriate level of protection to give to the defendant in a particular context. A degree of healthy divergence is to be welcomed and the minimum standards in Article 6(1) should not be set too high and should not be imposed uniformly on all types of cases.

10

The European Union and Fundamental Rights: Well in Spirit but Considerably Rumpled in Body?

NIAMH NIC SHUIBHNE[1]

"How are you?"
"I am well in body although considerably rumpled up in spirit, thank you, ma'am", said Anne gravely. Then aside to Marilla, in an audible whisper, "There wasn't anything startling in that, was there?"

Anne of Green Gables
L. M. Montgomery[2]

INTRODUCTION

IT IS SOMEWHAT paradoxical that alongside the seemingly extensive trend in favour of codifying human rights at national and international levels, considerable attention is drawn concurrently to residual gaps in protection from the perspective of groups and of individuals, and on how best, and at what level of governance, these disparities should be redressed. As a public authority with the capacity to impinge on the rights and freedoms of individuals, the European Community is affected intrinsically by these concerns, heightened at present by debate on the future of the EU Charter of Fundamental Rights—promulgated by solemn declaration of the European institutions at Nice in December 2000. Given that this chapter was conceived as a response to those of Beaumont and de Búrca, its scope is necessarily coloured by the ideas raised therein. It should be noted at the outset that their arguments proceed from inherently different ideological premises. This can perhaps be best explained by stating first that, at present, Community institutions and member states (or more appropriately, emanations of the member states, in so far as they are administering EC law or restricting Community freedoms) are bound by fundamental rights principles as they have been recognised by the Court of Justice, and to the extent to which

---

[1] Thanks, yet again, to Robert Lane and Christine O'Neill.
[2] (London: Harrap & Co., 1925), 75.

this duty has been codified in the Treaties.[3] This position has been reaffirmed in the Charter.[4] Both Beaumont and de Búrca discuss various questions, including the legal competence of the EU to act in the field of human rights, in both an internal and external sense, and the relationship between the Luxembourg and Strasbourg courts; but while de Búrca takes as her starting point the view that fundamental rights protection within and by the EU is an inherently good thing, before going on to explore the limits of Community/Union competence in this domain, Beaumont challenges that very assumption, questioning the basic tenets of human rights discourse *per se*. And so, while de Búrca asks where EU fundamental rights protection might be going in the future, Beaumont seeks to call into question its very legitimacy in the first place. These considerably disparate theses will first be examined briefly. It is not the intention of this chapter simply to restate the substantive arguments made by both authors; rather, some general themes that have been raised in their papers will be commented on, to set the background for the main thesis of this contribution i.e. that the way in which we think about EU involvement in human rights protection is arguably at a new threshold once again, taking into account the considerable and shifting reach of contemporary Community and Union law.

THE EU AND FUNDAMENTAL RIGHTS: JUSTIFYING A JURISDICTION

Since the vast majority of academic writers tend to bemoan the limitations to and restrictions on fundamental rights protection by and within the European Community, Beaumont's stance to the contrary represents a viewpoint not often voiced. And certainly, he raises some legitimate questions and concerns. But it is difficult to resist the conclusion that the ethos of his chapter seeks too thinly to challenge the validity of an entrenched phenomenon, and one that is far broader than its embodiment in the EC context in any case. Objections raised to Community competence in the fundamental rights sphere include charges of judicial activism and the idea that procedural rights deriving from access to justice do not need to be "dressed up" in the language of rights. While it is undeniable that the Court of Justice introduced the terminology of fundamental rights to Community law,[5] and perhaps more significantly, moulded the consequences of their protection into the Community legal order, the motivation behind this development can be traced (at least in part) to the need to establish the supremacy of EC law, a fact acknowledged by Beaumont; but as de Búrca has

---

[3] The jurisprudence of the Court of Justice in this field is discussed throughout this chapter. As regards Treaty provisions, see in particular Arts. 6(2) and 7 TEU and Art. 177(2) EC.

[4] See Art. 51(1) of the EU Charter of Fundamental Rights (Charte 4487/00, Brussels, 28 Sept. 2000).

[5] See, most notably, Case 29/69 *Stauder* v. *City of Ulm* [1969] ECR 419 at 419, para. 7; note the contrasting stance adopted by the Court in earlier decisions, including Case 1/58 *Stork* v. *High Authority* [1959] ECR 17, Cases 36–38, 40/59 *Geitling* v. *High Authority* [1960] ECR 523 and Case 40/64 *Sgarlata* v. *EEC Commission* [1965] ECR 215.

noted, the Court's action on this point was made at the instigation of the courts
of certain member states in the first place. And crucially, the approach of the
ECJ was endorsed explicitly by a Joint Declaration of the Parliament, Council
(and so by inference, the Member States) and Commission, issued on 5 April
1977.[6]

So the Court did not act alone. It was obliged initially to react to what was
effectively a constitutional dispute, in the absence of solutions from the "political" institutions or from the member states themselves directly, who sought
neither to revoke nor curb the evolution of the Court's logic. In reality, the Joint
Declaration represents their retrospective complicity, at the very least. As to the
"dressing up" of legal rights in the rhetoric of fundamental or human rights, the
difference between "legal" and "human" rights probably becomes most critical
in the realm of enforcement, tied as it is to the extent to which rights can be
implemented as a check against the exercise of public authority. In this context,
the relationship between rights and duties of enforcement occupies a prime place
in academic debate.[7] The primary advantage of establishing that rights are fundamental or human rights—as opposed to legal claims rooted in the realm of
administrative or social organisation—is that they then lie outwith the discretionary arena of administrative policy to a far greater extent. More specifically,
recognition and implementation would not be so dependent on the potentially
inconstant will of policy makers. The significance of this distinction cannot be
overstated, given that a supportive political environment is frequently elusive. A
key question habitually posed is whether rights or duties are then deemed
"prior": does a claim become a right only *because* we can identify a corresponding duty of implementation, or does that duty stem from the prior status of the
claim as a right? Rights can be ascribed to (or said to inhere in) the basic yet
abstract notions of humanity, dignity and freedom; and indeed, at least ten of the
fifteen EU member states have enshrined this very tenet to some degree in their
constitutions.[8] But the plain fact is that rights are virtually meaningless without
corresponding recognition and implementation. So however the rights/duties
debate is resolved in terms of priority, both the existence and realisation of
"duty" remain crucial. What is most relevant for present purposes is that the
attachment of duty takes fundamental rights beyond the usually discretionary

---

[6] [1977] OJ C 103/1.

[7] See especially, W N Hohfeld, *Fundamental Legal Conceptions*, (Westport: Greenwood Press,
1964) and J Raz, *The Morality of Freedom* (Oxford: Clarendon Press, 1986), both of which have
generated an abundance of related commentary.

[8] See the following provisions of the member state constitutions: Art. 23 (Belgium), Art. 1
(Germany), Art. 2 (Italy), Art. 11 (Luxembourg), Art. 2 (Greece), Section 1 (Finland), Preamble
(Ireland), Art. 1 (Portugal), Art. 10 (Spain) and Art. 1 (Sweden). The Preamble to the French
Constitution refers to the "Rights of Man" while those of both the Netherlands (Art. 1) and Austria
(Art. 7) refer to the principle of equality for all nationals. Part VIII of the Danish Constitution
guarantees a number of "Individual Rights" but the source of these rights is not stated expressly.
The United Kingdom does not have a written constitution, but the UK government has provided
recently for the incorporation of elements of the ECHR into domestic law (via the 1998 Human
Rights Act).

province of administrative or legal rights. Here, the terminology is not just rhetoric. There remains, of course, a whole host of difficulties with the alternative construction of rights as fundamental or human rights, and with attempts to ascertain both the nature and scope of rights from, as noted, often abstract "higher" sources. But on balance, it is still a preferable starting point when one considers the relative ease with which otherwise purely "legal" rights can be distorted, even revoked, at the political level—a scenario that contradicts a core rationale behind the enforcement of human rights in the first place.

Beaumont goes on to assert that the idea of equality is not an appropriate grounding for human rights policy given that we discriminate every day. But the achievement of "equality" does not require non-discrimination in an absolute sense; as an underlying principle, similar situations should be treated similarly, but differences in treatment are typically open to justification on objective grounds;[9] in some circumstances, and somewhat ironically, striving for equality of treatment in an unqualified or blanket sense can actually perpetuate *in*equalities. Neither is it sufficient to disregard discrepancies in the philosophy and practice of human rights as the disguised reality of religious difference and division; almost a century of international progress in the human rights arena has striven precisely to overcome adherence to such divisions, and to develop principles to be adhered to irrespective of whether someone has chosen to follow (a particular) religion or not. Closely associated with these arguments is the idea of elevating some rights above others in a hierarchical priority. In the EC context specifically, Beaumont challenges the propriety of bypassing the member states' unilateral constructions of public policy via the device of homogenous "Community" fundamental rights. The notion of prioritising fundamental rights raises a myriad of significant questions in a general sense. Are some rights inherently (and so justifiably) more fundamental than others? This construct would allow for a hierarchy of rights that might run, for example, from abolition of the death penalty, to freedom of thought and belief, to securing due process in criminal proceedings, and finally, to the enjoyment of social and cultural rights. Listing rights in this way necessarily implies a priority of order, which cannot always be determined objectively and thus brings the issue of value judgments into play.

A related consideration is that different rights will invariably clash with one another. The balancing of conflicting rights is a task undertaken in both legal and political realms on a continual basis but it is inevitably one that, again, hinges on the notion of priority. Rights are also balanced against other (often somewhat blurry) interests—usually societal, e.g. the requirements of the common good or of public policy, but also economic and political interests. Ultimately, who should decide which rights take precedence? Add to this the very real danger that differentiating between "types" of rights could lead to varying commitments in

---

[9] This reflects the approach of the Court of Justice to non-discrimination in a general sense; see for example, Cases 103 and 145/77 *Royal Scholten Honig* [1978] ECR 2037 at 2072, paras. 26–27.

terms of enforcement and implementation, or even to the belief that norms at the "lower" end of the scale do not really constitute rights at all. Squaring these varying priorities and interests takes on even keener significance in the EC domain. A core rule of interpretation is that the ECJ will balance fundamental rights claims against limits set by the overall objectives of the EC Treaty but not to the extent that the substance of the right in question is impaired.[10] The Court restated this principle most recently in *Karlsson*:[11]

> "[I]t is well established in the case law of the Court that restrictions may be imposed on the exercise of fundamental rights, in particular in the context of a common organisation of the market, provided that those restrictions in fact correspond to objectives of general interest pursued by the Community and do not constitute, with regard to the aim pursued, disproportionate and unreasonable interference undermining the very substance of those rights."

But examination of the Court's case law demonstrates that while it focused initially on economic and social rights, as might be anticipated given the objectives laid down originally in the EEC Treaty, a broader agenda encompassing civil and political rights has evolved in keeping with the gradual extension of Community competence, the expansion of Treaty objectives and the emphasis on administrative and procedural fairness that characterises the majority of contemporary claims invoking EC law arguments.

More contentiously, the perceived subordination of nuclear (domestic) constitutional values has sparked virulent debate among academic commentators, characterised most notably by the charge that the Court of Justice does not take its fundamental rights jurisdiction seriously;[12] the circumstances leading to the Court's decision in *Grogan* provide a particularly striking example of where morals and economics collide.[13] In the vein of the "public policy" argument outlined by Beaumont, Phelan has recommended modification of the "exceptionless supremacy doctrine", giving precedence to adjudications by national constitutional courts on "basic principles concerning life, liberty, religion and the family" while maintaining the primacy of EC law for economic and social rights.[14] Moreover, he considers that this teleological approach conforms especially well

---

[10] See Case 4/73 *Nold* v. *Commission* [1974] ECR 491 at 508, para. 14 (". . . these rights should, if necessary be subject to certain limits justified by the overall objectives pursued by the Community, on condition that the substance of these rights is left untouched.") This approach is exemplified by Case 44/79 *Hauer* v. *Land Rheinland-Pfalz* [1979] ECR 3727 (see especially 3750, para. 32).

[11] Case C–292/97 *Karlsson and others*, judgment of 13 April 2000, not yet reported, para. 45.

[12] J Coppel and A O'Neill, "The European Court of Justice: Taking rights seriously?" (1992) 29 *Common Market Law Review* 669–92; responded to by J H H Weiler and N J S Lockhart, " 'Taking rights seriously' seriously: The European Court of Justice and its fundamental rights jurisprudence" (1995) 32 *Common Market Law Review* 51–94 and 579–62.

[13] Case C–159/90 *SPUC* v. *Grogan* [1991] ECR I–4685; see D R Phelan, "Right to Life of the Unborn v. Promotion of Trade in Services: The ECJ and the Normative Shaping of the European Union" (1992) 55 *Modern Law Review* 670–89 and G de Búrca, "Fundamental Rights and the Reach of EC Law" (1993) 13 *Oxford Journal of Legal Studies* 283–319. See also, Coppel and O'Neill, n. 12 above, 685–9, and Weiler and Lockhart, n. 12 above, 597–605.

[14] Phelan, n. 13 above, 688–9.

with the principle of subsidiarity, enshrined (since Maastricht) in the EC Treaty.[15] But this solution fails to appreciate the very problem epitomised in *Grogan*, that the severance of values into neatly distinct constitutional and economic boxes is just not always possible. The gulf that exists between according competences to the EC and accepting their implementation at supranational level reflects a simmering unease that is also relevant here, given the clash of deeply rooted national values with fledgling "Community" versions, the contingent threat to national sovereignty, the uncertain scope of fundamental rights within the Community legal order and the inevitable reaction of mainly civil law member states to what is perceived as bald judicial activism, more usually associated with the common law tradition.

There are valid questions to be discussed here; but "returning" competence to the member states wherever issues take on a fundamental rights slant is neither practical nor desirable. Furthermore, the impression of Community/member state competition in this context is misplaced. As Weiler and Lockhart have expressed succinctly, ". . . human rights issues do not necessarily pit the Community against Member States: human rights issues typically will pit the individual against public authorities [rendering] artificial in many instances the notions of *Member States* v. *Community* institutions."[16] What court, in truth, will consider cases before it in a legal vacuum? Legal decision-making is in fact a complex formula, taking into account policy considerations, values and objectives; acknowledgement and application of this fact is something of a present-day legal trend, the impact that the Human Rights Act will have on UK decision-making being the most current domestic example at the time of writing. The Court of Justice, as a contemporary decision-making forum, is no different, and to expect it so to be results in the application of standards far above and beyond those operating in other (domestic) courts.

Finally, Beaumont addresses the complex relationship between the European Court of Justice and the European Court of Human Rights. The European Convention on Human Rights and Fundamental Freedoms (ECHR) was first referred to specifically by the ECJ in *Rutili*.[17] But the ECJ has always pointed out that it is not bound by the Convention in a substantive sense and, in turn, is not bound either by the jurisprudence of the European Court of Human Rights; in other words, the ECJ looks at fundamental rights *principles* as distinct from the substantive *provisions* of the ECHR. The realisation of this distinction in

---

[15] See Art. 5 EC, second paragraph; see also the Protocol on the Application of the Principles of Subsidiarity and Proportionality, attached to the EC Treaty.

[16] Weiler and Lockhart, n. 12 above, 621.

[17] Case 36/75 *Rutili* [1975] ECR 1219 (in *Nold*, the Court (at 507, para. 13) had declared that ". . . international treaties for the protection of human rights, on which the Member States have collaborated or of which they are signatories, can supply guidelines which should be followed within the framework of Community law.") In Cases 60, 61/84 *Cinéthèque* v. *Fédération Nationale des Cinémas Français* [1985] ECR 2605, the ECJ noted that it had no power to assess the compatibility of domestic law with the ECHR in an area that fell solely within national jurisdiction; see more recently, Case C–299/95 *Kremzow* v. *Austria* [1997] ECR I–2629.

practice has enabled the ECJ sometimes to go beyond the extent of protection accorded under the Convention, a development that has engendered criticism in terms of the risk of incoherence between the Community interpretation of a given right and that of the European Court of Human Rights.[18]

How can this inter-organisational relationship best be organised? It has been argued from many quarters that the EC should accede to the ECHR, thus establishing a clear hierarchy as regards judicial interpretation of the Convention and, in turn, enhancing the accountability of the Community itself.[19] This solution does not really solve the underlying issue, however, that is to say, the proper interpretation of extra-Convention principles, or the granting of additional protection over and above that actually codified in ECHR provisions. In any case, the ECJ's Opinion on accession thwarted the momentum of this debate; the Court held that accession to the ECHR by the European Community would only be possible following a Treaty amendment, given the constitutional significance attached to entering a "distinct international institutional system".[20] There is nothing to prevent *any* party to the Convention, whether a state or the Community if it should ever accede, from introducing measures that strive to implement *greater* protection that that offered by the Convention. The standards set by any international instrument represent a lowest common denominator (settled upon after an often contentious negotiating procedure) and not the last word on the acceptable benchmark of rights protection; this is expressly provided for in Article 53 ECHR.[21] But the relationship between the EC and the Council of Europe is a peculiar one, calling into question issues that simply do not arise in the context of state parties.

The debate on accession has moved forward somewhat and is now framed by the Charter of Fundamental Rights of the European Union, Article 52(3) of which reserves for Union law the possibility of providing "more extensive protection" than that laid down by the ECHR. Aside from institutional tensions sparked by differing Court of Justice/Court of Human Rights interpretations, perhaps the more serious issue here, from the perspective of individuals, is the unpredictability that results as a consequence of the ECJ's interpretative approach, which raises serious concerns in the domain of legal certainty and legitimate expectations. This is especially relevant when a "new" fundamental right is raised in the EC context, even where that right is protected already under

---

[18] See D Spielman, "Human rights case law in the Strasbourg and Luxembourg courts: Conflicts, inconsistencies and complementarities", in P Alston (ed.), *The EU and Human Rights*, (Oxford: Oxford University Press, 1999) 757–80.

[19] The advantages of EC accession to the ECHR were recently restated by the House of Lords Select Committee on European Union in its *Report on the EC Draft Charter of Fundamental Rights*, Eighth Report (London: The Stationery Office, 2000), paras. 15–17, 96–112, 136–143 and 154.

[20] Opinion 2/94, [1996] ECR I–1759 at 1789, para. 34; see also, S O'Leary, "Accession by the EC to the ECHR: The Opinion of the European Court of Justice", (1996) 4 *European Human Rights Law Review* 362–277.

[21] Art. 53 ECHR provides that "[n]othing in this Convention shall be construed as limiting or derogating from any of the human rights and fundamental freedoms which may be ensured under the laws of any High Contracting Party or under any other agreement to which it is a Party."

the Convention. The inevitable level of doubt generated here is yet another reason why the advent of the Charter, as a specific catalogue of "EC rights", needs to be taken seriously. As submitted at the outset, Beaumont's critique of EC involvement in human rights seems to go more to the heart of the international human rights creed in general terms, questioning its appropriateness as a check against (member state) public authority. Certainly, there are problems both with the identification of human rights norms and more specifically with their translation into legal rules. In truth, perhaps the most astonishing thing about human rights protection at an international level is that it both exists and works at all. But it does. That there are ongoing difficulties and shortfalls within this system is not reason enough to undermine its basic legitimacy; the way forward is not only to raise these concerns and to grapple with them, but to do so from a constructive outlook.

WHERE TO FROM HERE? THE LIMITS TO EU COMPETENCE IN FUNDAMENTAL RIGHTS

Having grounded her paper in the assertion that international human rights norms are derived from the concept of human dignity, de Búrca asks in effect whether the human rights policy of the EU should be extended beyond its present parameters. This question is pitched against the backdrop of multi-layered governance, given that a discrete and "proper" locus for all decision-making that affects the rights and freedoms of individuals is not really a contemporary probability. De Búrca first frames the question in a bipartite manner, asking whether a convergent, internal EU human rights code—one that would, in effect, precede member state human rights policies over and above the implementation of EC law—is either legitimate *or* necessary, although she does later argue that both considerations merge together to some extent. She gives a theoretical and nuanced assessment of how far an EU human rights policy should go and is at least favourable to its application to the "problems" generated by EU market integration.

It is perhaps not only desirable that the Community should have human rights obligations in the sphere of "problems" of its own making; it is arguably a responsibility that flows from its definite, if indefinable, character as a governing public authority. But this conclusion requires us seriously to contemplate just what problems *are* caused or contributed to by the realisation of EC market integration and to measure, in turn, the capacity of an EC policy to react sufficiently to the apparent fluidity of that very concept. A corollary of this argument is that the impact of EC market integration can raise anomalies in the treatment of comparable situations within a member state, in that a national of that state will sometimes be in a less favourable position than a national of another member state—a glitch that is usually referred to as "reverse discrimination".

Consigned traditionally to the realm of Community oddity, are instances of reverse discrimination likely to intensify in light of the expanding reach of EC law? And moreover, even if this is likely, is it actually relevant to the scope of EC fundamental rights protection? These issues will now be addressed in turn.

THE REACH OF EU LAW: A SHIFTING BOUNDARY

It is arguable that one of the key lessons to be learned from the wealth of academic writing on EC integration is that as a process, it still eludes comprehensive explanation. We have access to a vast corpus of work that has both discovered and deserted spillover, and that has generated a profusion of "isms", all of which make sense individually; and yet the sum of these various parts does not quite solve definitively either the rationale behind or ultimate ambition of the Community reality.[22] In consequence, as already alluded to above, attempting to define the range of issues generated by market integration is arguably an impossible task; and the further such matters arise outwith the core content of EC economic policy, the fuzzier and more mangled the boundaries between EC and member state competence become. On the one hand, the circumstances in accordance with which a Community element can be attached to any particular situation—take, for example, the provision of cross-border services in the digital age, or the daily reality of transnational movement for a considerable majority of EU citizens—seems virtually infinite, so that the point at which (ultimately) the Court of Justice sets boundaries can seem arbitrary as against taking EC law to its "logical" conclusion. The Court's decision in *Singh* is a particularly thorny example of this very question, and is discussed further below.[23]

On the other hand, it is a fact that the way in which EC law impacts on the rights and freedoms of individuals has intensified dramatically since the inception of the Community via the Treaty of Rome; but perhaps more importantly, this continues to occur in still significant leaps. Early views that the concept of EU citizenship was nothing more than a meaningless restatement of limited, pre-existing rights reserved for Community workers could not have predicted the way in which its breadth would be animated by the Court of Justice,

---

[22] See M Holland, *The Community Experience*, (London: Pinter, 1993); W Wallace (ed.), *The Dynamics of European Integration*, (London: Pinter, 1990); N Walker, "European Constitutionalism and European Integration" (1996) *Public Law* 266–90; and D Chalmers, "Judicial Preferences and the Community Legal Order" (1997) 60 *Modern Law Review* 164–99, all of which outline both the evolving debate and associated concepts. See more recently, the essays collected in Z Bankowski and A Scott (eds.), *The European Union and its Order: The Legal Theory of European Integration* (Oxford: Blackwell, 2000).

[23] Case C–370/90 *R* v. *Immigration Appeal Tribunal and Singh*, ex parte *Secretary of State for the Home Department* [1992] ECR I–4265.

most notably in *Martínez Sala*;[24] and the rights to freedom of movement and
residence in their more general incarnation may yet be bolstered further by the
Charter of Fundamental Rights.[25] In *Angonese*, the Court of Justice carefully
affirmed what may have long been suspected but had never been declared
(judicially) outright—that the prohibition of discrimination on grounds of
nationality contained in Article 39 EC was horizontally directly effective.[26] And
the "communitarisation" via the Amsterdam Treaty of a significant chunk
of the Third Pillar, creating what is now Title IV EC, has, as the House of
Lords Select Committee has observed, generated ". . . greater scope than
hitherto for EU actions and policies to impinge on individual rights and
freedoms".[27]

In other words, as the range of aspirations set down in the EC Treaty and
TEU come more variously to the fore, the impact on both the nature and substance of EC integration will have to be honed correspondingly, leading us to
revise once again what we mean by "market integration" and, in turn, how we
are then to define and match the corresponding scope of EC fundamental rights
jurisdiction. On the surface it might seem that tying this competence to issues
generated by market integration is a means by which EU human rights policy
might be limited, but the ambiguities inherent in that linkage are themselves
problematic. Not only does the application of EC law relate to an immense
array of possible issues and circumstances, but its content, even in substantive
terms, is subject to persistent variation via both Treaty reform and, perhaps
more ominously for present purposes, the jurisprudence of the Court of Justice.
What has been especially significant about the most recent batch of EC law
developments is that they have the potential to impinge significantly on individuals. Which causes us now to ask: just how tenable is it to maintain the distinction between situations that trigger the application of "Community"
fundamental rights and those that do not? This question is related to the idea
that certain issues are "purely internal" from the perspective of the member
states, an arguably unsettled ECJ construction that will now be examined, in the
specific light of fundamental rights and reverse discrimination.

---

[24] Case C–85/96 *Martínez-Sala* v. *Freistaat Bayern* [1998] ECR I–2691 (see especially, paras.
23–24 of the Opinion of Advocate General Jacobs); for case comment and analysis, see S Fries and
J Shaw, "Citizenship of the Union: First steps in the European Court of Justice" (1998) 4 *European
Public Law*, 533–59 and S O'Leary, "Putting Flesh on the Bones of European Union Citizenship"
(1999) 24 *European Law Review* 68–79.

[25] See Art. 45 of the EU Charter of Fundamental Rights.

[26] Case C–281/98 *Angonese* v. *Cassa di Risparmio di Bolzano SpA*, judgment of 6 June 2000, not
yet reported, at para. 39; see R Lane and N Nic Shuibhne, (case comment) (2000) 37 *Common
Market Law Review* 1237–47.

[27] House of Lords Select Committee, Eighth Report, para. 25; see Art. 2 TEU, the new Title IV
EC and Title VI TEU. See also, P Twomey, "Constructing a Secure Space", in D O'Keeffe and
P Twomey (eds.), *Legal Issues of the Amsterdam Treaty* (Oxford: Hart, 1998) 351–74.

CURIO OR CRISIS? (THE RISE OF) REVERSE DISCRIMINATION

It is first important to state here what this chapter does *not* assert i.e. that there are no situations which can be deemed "purely internal" to the member states. While it has been argued that the reach of EC law has extended and continues to extend in a not insignificant way, the arguments presented here do not go so far as to advocate that no province of national regulation should be untouched by the EC Treaty; so in terms of respective competences, the scope of this chapter is limited to the specific domain of fundamental rights protection, to whether or not there should be a "general" EC competence in that sphere. Obviously, even this would require a huge shift in political culture, as well as in the Community's legal framework. And the matter can be turned back once again to de Búrca's questioning of whether such a development would be either legitimate or necessary. It was argued above that the reasoning prescribed against a more general human rights jurisdiction—so as to retain its association with market integration—is not so straightforward in any case; the definitional difficulties identified cannot be so easily discounted. But consideration of the "purely internal" principle, which is in effect the inverse of the "market integration" limitation, brings into focus also the position regarding nationals of a member state who lose out simply because they have not, in most basic terms, moved anywhere (or have not moved at all, but have watched television broadcasts, for example, from other member states) and thus have not activated any Community rights. Instances of reverse discrimination have been recognised as something of a rare if unfortunate side-effect of the fact that the Community does not have jurisdiction over matters purely internal to a member state, as a justifiable casualty of the more pressing need to establish and preserve a member state's "hands off" domain. But as the reach of Community law extends still further—most recently, as pointed out above, into discrimination by private employers—the reserve of matters that are "purely internal" ebbs in tandem; and it is likely that both awareness and instances of "reverse" discrimination will increase in volume and significance as a result. Viewed in this light, and against a general background of fundamental rights protection, does different treatment of similar situations that is hinged solely on nationality remain (objectively) justifiable? The principal difficulty here is that what are highlighted or revealed by Community standards are disparities in the protection of individuals at *national* level as compared to that available for nationals of other member states who are in comparable situations, and not gaps in the Community regime itself.

In its early jurisprudence, the Court of Justice wove a tacit acceptance of the fact that a member state can discriminate against its own nationals into its exposition of the "purely internal" principle.[28] But how can we reconcile this acceptance of

---

[28] Case 136/78 *Ministère Public v. Auer* [1979] ECR 437 and Case 175/78 *R v. Saunders* [1979] ECR 1129; *cf.* Case 115/78 *Knoors v. Staatssecretaris van Economische Zaken* [1979] ECR 399. For analysis of these decisions, see S Kon, "Aspects of reverse discrimination in Community law" (1981) 6 *European Law Review* 75–101.

"reverse" discrimination with the ethos of non-discrimination that has shaped the rationale behind its underpinning of Community law more generally? Given that only situations connected to Community law can be caught by the Community conception of equal treatment, there is no clash in substantive or legal terms;[29] but the principle that similar situations should not be treated differently undergoes something of an ideological battering, at least, when we add the proviso that this may not necessarily hold true by reason of the very distinction so abhorred by the Treaty, and indeed the Court, in the first place—that of nationality. It is not wholly convincing that upholding the "purely internal" member state reserve amounts to an objective justification in and of itself when the consequences borne by the individuals affected are brought to the fore. How this stands up to scrutiny in the ambit of fundamental rights is considered below; but first, the coherence of more recent ECJ jurisprudence on the scope of the "purely internal" principle should be addressed.

In *Singh*, the Court of Justice ostensibly retained the need for the applicant to establish a connection between his circumstances and Community law; but it is arguable that the tenuous quality of the connection actually accepted marks a departure in itself. The applicant was a non-Community national married to a British national, challenging a decision that refused him leave to remain indefinitely in the United Kingdom.[30] After their marriage in England, Mrs Singh had exercised her Treaty right to work in another member state and was accompanied there by her husband (in accordance with Directive 68/360[31]). Both returned subsequently to the United Kingdom where Mrs Singh re-established herself (in her own member state) as a self-employed person within the meaning of Article 43 EC; but did her husband enjoy a right of residence with her in the UK in accordance with Directive 73/148?[32] The United Kingdom submitted that at this point, the Singh's situation was (re)governed by national law; but the ECJ countered as follows:[33]

> "[T]his case is concerned not with a right under national law but with the rights of movement and establishment granted to a Community national by Articles [39 and 43] of the Treaty. These rights cannot be fully effective if such a person may be deterred from exercising them by obstacles raised in his or her own country of origin to the

[29] On this point, see E Cannizzaro, "Producing 'reverse discrimination' through the exercise of EC competences", (1997) 17 *Yearbook of European Law*, 29–46 at 38–9, who argues that while "[i]t does not seem unreasonable to infer that the Treaty obliges both the European Community and Member States to exercise their concurrent competences . . . so as to avoid unjustified disparity of treatment in situations that are materially identical" (38), there are problems with the grounding of such an inference in either Art. 10 EC or some general unwritten principle of equality.

[30] The decision of the Immigration Appeal Tribunal related to the fact that a decree *nisi* of divorce had been pronounced against the applicant in proceedings brought against him by his wife; and the marriage was subsequently dissolved. But for the period of time under consideration for the purposes of the Art. 234 reference, the Singhs were still lawfully married (see the judgment of the ECJ at 4292, para. 12).

[31] [1968] JO L257/13.

[32] [1973] OJ L172/14.

[33] *Singh*, pp. 4294–3, paras. 23–4.

entry and residence of her spouse. Accordingly, when a Community national who has availed himself or herself of those rights returns to his or her country of origin, his or her spouse must enjoy at least the same rights of entry and residence as would be granted to him or her under Community law if his or her spouse chose to enter and reside in another Member State."

The Court focused, therefore, on preventing the inculcation of what could be described as a deterrent national climate, biased *against* the exercise of Treaty rights; and in the same case, Advocate General Tesauro remarked that there was nothing "paradoxical or illogical" about the fact that someone who could not satisfy the requirement that there be some connection with Community law so that these rights of entry and residence might be activated would be required to leave the member state in question.[34] But consider the following argument put forward by Cannizaro:[35]

> "It is difficult to perceive the rationale of a solution that would impose restraints on Member States in the treatment of some citizens only, depending on a very formal element, like that of having once—and perhaps in a situation unconnected with the case at stake—availed themselves of the rights and freedoms of the Treaty. If we apply this argument, we must conclude that a subject who has exercised the right to free movement and worked abroad for a certain time will enjoy, once back in his home country, every right afforded by EC law relating to free movement. This conclusion could be justified only by a need to provide citizens of the national state with minimal standards in order to allow them to come back and stay in their home country on a basis of equality with foreign workers. But if we adopt this line of reasoning, there is logically no ground for excluding from the enjoyment of the same provisions those citizens who never exercised the right of free movement".

The emphasis in *Singh* on the need to avoid discouraging the exercise of Community rights in the first place does not really fit with placing weight instead on the (arguably more specific) needs of resettled workers *after* re-establishment. And what remains unclear is not only the threshold at which it will be accepted that a Community right has been exercised, but the extent to which it will be held to have a bearing on the circumstances that have somehow come before the Court. Would the Court's answer in *Singh* have been different had the couple *not* established themselves within the meaning of Article 43 EC on their return to the United Kingdom? The fact that both Articles 39 and 43 EC were relevant to their situation (albeit at different times) seems, in a cumulative sense, to be decisive on logical terms, but that this is necessarily the case cannot be implied from the judgment. Certainly, the rights exercised under both provisions were conjoined by the ECJ in *Singh*, but that does not necessarily presage a situation involving workers only. And it does not seem that such a conclusion could be derived either from the Court's decision in

---

[34] *Singh*, Opinion of Advocate General Tesauro, p. 4287, para. 15.
[35] Cannizaro, n. 29 above, 43.

Uecker and Jacquet, discussed below.[36] It is true that Article 43 contains a possible textual loophole, in that it refers merely to "establishment of nationals of *a* Member State in the territory of *another* Member State", which could arguably cover Mrs Singh's returning from Germany to the United Kingdom;[37] but the ECJ did not tie its decision to, or ever raise, this point at all.

The factual circumstances in *Angonese* presented an opportunity for the Court to clarify either the expanse of or limitations to its line of reasoning in *Singh*, but it was an opportunity not taken. The enduring significance of *Angonese* is likely to be its declaration that Article 39 is directly effective both vertically *and* horizontally. The applicant, an Italian national, challenged the means by which a private employer in the autonomous Italian province of Bolzano required evidence of linguistic competence in German to be satisfied as a precondition for entry into an employment competition; just one certificate of competence issued by the public authorities in Bolzano (the "*patentino*") was specified as acceptable. In order to establish a connection with Community law, the applicant submitted evidence of his studies through the medium of German at a university in Austria; but at the material time, these studies had not led to the award of a degree, meaning that the applicant did not possess a formal diploma or certificate of qualification. This issue formed the basis of the opinion of Advocate General Fennelly; he took as his starting point the reasoning derived from *Knoors* and subsequent jurisprudence i.e. that ". . . account can only be taken of time spent studying abroad in the exercise of Community-law rights if it results in a relevant diploma or recognised training—a condition not satisfied in the present case, as the applicant's studies in Vienna had no connection with banking. . . ."[38] He then analysed subsequent decisions on the mutual recognition of qualifications, notably *Bouchoucha*[39] and *Kraus*[40]. But on the facts before him in *Angonese*, the Advocate General concluded that:[41]

> "[L]eaving aside for the moment the fact that the applicant had not completed his studies, it is of primary importance, in my view, that while those studies can be characterised as a type of vocational training within the meaning of [Article 150 EC], they were, none the less, quite remote in content both from the banking post for which the applicant wished to be considered and from the certificate of bilingualism required of candidates for that post . . . [T]he facts as found by the national court do not suggest

---

[36] Joined cases C 64 and 65/1996 *Land Nordrhein-Westfalen* v. *Kari Uecker; Vera Jacquet* v. *Land Nordrhein-Westfalen* [1997] ECR I–3171.

[37] On this point, see Case 136/78 *Ministère Public* v. *Auer* [1979] ECR 437 at 449, paras. 20 *et seq.*; *cf.* the Opinion of Advocate General Warner at 455. See more recently, Case C–19/92 *Kraus* v. *Land Baden-Württemberg* [1993] ECR I–1663.

[38] *Angonese*, Opinion of Advocate General Fennelly, para. 9, relying on Case 115/78 *Knoors* v. *Secretary of State for Economic Affairs* [1979] ECR 399; see also Council Dir. 64/427, 7 July 1964, [OJ Spec. Ed., Series I, 1963–1964, 148], regarding recognition of periods of relevant work experience for certain trades.

[39] Case C–61/89 *Criminal Proceedings against Bouchoucha* [1990] ECR I–3551.

[40] Case C–19/92 *Kraus* v. *Land Baden-Württemberg* [1993] ECR I–1663.

[41] *Angonese*, Opinion of the Advocate General, para. 28.

any link between the nature of those studies and the employment sought by him in Bolzano or the condition imposed for access to that employment."

So the Advocate General advocated an extension of the general rules on mutual recognition, stating openly that he had not attached "particular importance" to the fact that the applicant had not completed his studies at the material time.[42] Applying his own substantive test, however, he did not find an appreciable Community element given the particular facts of the case. Had the Court chosen to follow the reasoning of the Advocate General, the decision would have amounted to a significant advance in the jurisprudence on the mutual recognition of qualifications more generally—and not necessarily a welcome one— from the perspective of coherence. But by noting somewhat opaquely that it was ". . . far from clear that the interpretation of Community law . . . has no relation to the actual facts of the case or to the subject-matter of the main action",[43] the the ECJ rejected a claim on the inadmissibility of the reference. And that, as far as the Court was concerned, was entirely the end of the "purely internal" matter. Some cautioning against a broad application of *Singh* could be implied from the Advocate General's remarks in *Angonese* that ". . . short educational exchanges or even periods of as little as one day spent abroad as a tourist could, *quite arbitrarily*, enable a person to invoke Community-law rights against his own Member State."[44] But again, this issue did not fall to be considered by the Court; and it is arguable equally that to draw a line under the activation of Community rights at the point suggested by the Advocate General would itself appear "arbitrary" in light of *Singh*.

It is unlikely that the Court will be able to evade these questions in a case referred recently within the ambit of the provision of services, however. In *Carpenter*, the non-Community spouse of a British national is claiming a right of residence with him in the United Kingdom given that he provides services in other member states from time to time.[45] The eventual decision in this case will hopefully provide some sorely lacking clarity on the embryonic expansion of the "appreciable Community element" test that can be derived from *Singh*; and in any case, the Court will be called upon to justify either its extension or its limitation of the ambit of service provision and derivative rights.

What is clear at this point is that the stance of the Court has shifted markedly from its earlier reasoning in cases like *Knoors* and *Saunders*, and the "purely internal" principle seems already less stalwart as a result. The interest of legal certainty comes down in favour of far more coherence than has been forthcoming. This is reinforced by the fact that uncertainties as to the scope of Community law in the sense discussed here invariably involve the rights and freedoms enjoyed by individuals. But the whole debate is compounded still

[42] *Ibid.*, para. 33.
[43] *Ibid.*, Judgment of the Court, para. 19.
[44] *Ibid.*, Opinion of Advocate General Fennelly, para. 9.
[45] Case C–60/00 *Carpenter* v. *Secretary of State for the Home Department*, pending; for the questions put to the Court of Justice see [2000] OJ C122/14.

further by adding the parallel consideration of reverse discrimination into the equation; if the reach of Community law is extending on the one hand, while the ways in which a connection to Community law are becoming less stringent on the other, then the difference in treatment accorded to individuals still outwith this sphere becomes less and less tenable.

If the argument is framed in terms of "gaps" in protection from the perspective of individuals, there are, in reality, three responses that could be made. First, we could simply live with the anomalies, reasoning that the advantages ascribed to consistency of treatment and the uniform application of Community law simply do not require to be stretched to this extent. In effect, this is what we do at present. But questions raised above about the (in)coherence of the "purely internal" rule in ECJ jurisprudence, the expanding reach of EC law and its impact on the rights and freedoms of individuals and, most significantly for present purposes, the corollary supposition that occurrences of reverse discrimination will increase as a result, cannot be dismissed so readily; in other words, identifying and remedying inequalities in protection boils down to considerably more than the sheer neatness of uniformity. There is also a question of public perception here. Where instances of reverse discrimination are highlighted in the public domain—as they have been in Scotland and the UK more generally on the question of Scottish university fees, for example—the typical conclusion is not that EC law "gives" certain rights to nationals of other member states over and above those available domestically, but that the Community has somehow deprived home nationals of the benefit in question. While this is not actually true, it is a common misunderstanding. In any case, is it rational to say to an aggrieved complainant that things would be different if only, for example, s/he had that diploma from another member state rather than from their own? If Mr Angonese had never studied abroad, then he could not have challenged the structure of linguistic examinations in Bolzano; and the irony is that although his substantive claim succeeded before the ECJ, he is not likely to be able to benefit at all himself.[46] But he *has* ensured that a national of any other member state in a similar position in future will benefit from his efforts. It is just not adequate to proclaim that instances which generate reverse discrimination are matters of "purely internal" concern for the member state in question, and leave things at that. But the idea of a wholly centralised or "absolute" EU human rights policy is equally unfeasible; as already suggested, it is simply erroneous to argue that all member state issues must necessarily become Community issues, and this quite aside from the deep-seated social, cultural and political objections likely to emerge against such a radical move in the first place.

The third option, then, is that while the gaps in protection might be identified via the application of EC law, the member states should themselves take on board a responsibility to "trade up to the Community standards",[47] a proposition still

---

[46] See Lane and Nic Shuibhne, n. 26 above, 1243.

[47] R C A White, "A Fresh Look at Reverse Discrimination" (1993) 18 *European Law Review* 527–32 at 532.

loaded with acute political sensitivity. It is persuasively arguable that while various discrepancies might be highlighted via cases with a Community dimension, it is the member states that should look more carefully, then, at their domestic rules. The catalytic influence of the EC on this process would still be remarkable in itself; but leaving the responsibility for actual change at member state level skirts around more difficult competence and sovereignty questions necessarily associated with attempts to manipulate domestic protection mechanisms more directly. Can responsibility be justified, however? Because even at this diluted or derived level, the fact remains that domestic member state standards would still be "traded up" to their Community counterparts, generating something of an indirect harmonisation process.

In the context of the free movement of goods, Advocate General Mischo has argued that "[r]everse discrimination is clearly impossible in the long run within a true common market, which must of necessity be based on the principle of equal treatment. Such discrimination must be eliminated by means of the harmonisation of legislation."[48] Writing later in time, White hinged his justification on a different premise, by referring to the concept of EU citizenship.[49] And it has already been noted that the true implications of citizenship have since begun to unfold in the Court of Justice. While *Martínez Sala* is the authority usually cited in this context, it is instructive here to look also at the Court's decision in *Bickel and Franz*, the implications of which themselves give rise to the possibility of reverse discrimination.[50] Relating once again to the particular linguistic arrangements in Bolzano, the ECJ accorded to an Austrian tourist and a German worker the right to have criminal proceedings against them in that region conducted through the medium of the German language, a right reserved typically for residents of Bolzano only and not available to Italian nationals in general. The Court acknowledged that establishing the rules of criminal procedure is generally within member state competence, but stated that the fundamental principle of non-discrimination on grounds of nationality (contained in Article 12 EC) and the overriding Community principles on freedom of movement set legitimate limits to these internal legislative procedures. Advocate General Jacobs submitted that the extension of non-discrimination to cover criminal proceedings arising in the course of the exercise of free movement was particularly appropriate in light of EU citizenship.[51] He declared that it was still open to member states to justify advantages reserved to nationals on grounds unrelated to nationality, but that it was becoming ". . . increasingly difficult to see why Community law should accept any type of difference in treatment

---

[48] Joined cases 80 and 159/85 *Nederlandse Bakkerij Stichting* v. *EDAH* [1986] ECR 3359 at 3375.

[49] White, n. 47 above, 532.

[50] Case C–274/96 *Criminal Proceedings against Bickel and Franz* [1998] ECR I–7637.

[51] The Advocate General made some especially strong remarks on the fundamental nature of Union citizenship and on the relevance of non-discrimination to citizenship at p. 7645, paras. 23–24; see, in the same vein, the earlier Opinion of the same Advocate General in Case C–168/91 *Konstantinidis* v. *Stadt Altensteig, Standesamt & Landratsamt Calw, Ordnungsamt* [1993] ECR I–1191 at 1211–12, para. 46.

which is based purely on nationality, except in so far as the essential characteristics of nationality are at stake, such as access to a limited range of posts in the
public service or the exercise of certain political rights."[52] Again, the irony that
instances of reverse discrimination *are* grounded in nationality comes to the
fore.

In *Uecker and Jacquet*, the Court pulled together the "purely internal" principle and the increasing momentum and implications of the European Union
(and citizenship specifically), reaching the following conclusion:[53]

> "[A] member of the family of a worker who is a national of a Member State cannot
> rely on Community law to challenge the validity of a limitation on the duration of his
> or her contract of employment within that same State when the worker in question has
> never exercised the right to freedom of movement within the Community . . . [T]he
> national court asks whether the fundamental principles of a Community moving
> towards European Union still permit a rule of national law which is incompatible with
> Community law because it is in breach of Article [39](2) of the Treaty to continue to
> be applied against its own nationals and their spouses from non-member countries. In
> that regard, it must be noted that citizenship of the Union . . . is not intended to extend
> the scope *rationae materiae* of the Treaty also to internal situations which have no link
> with Community law . . . Any discrimination which nationals of a Member State may
> suffer under the law of that State fall within the scope of that law and must therefore
> be dealt with within the framework of the internal legal system of that State".

This interpretation confirms that as things stand at present, the Court of Justice
simply could not make any other decision—although, the advance evident in
both *Martinez Sala* and *Bickel and Franz* has come about in the interim. Is the
ethos of free movement becoming bigger than its expression in the Treaty? At
the very least, establishing an "appreciable" Community element seems to be
swaying more towards the simple fact of movement and is less tied to showing
a more substantive or material connection; *Singh* is especially illustrative here,
and *Carpenter* may prove ultimately decisive. But the Court's stance in *Uecker*
does not mean that the issue cannot be addressed at the political level, from the
motivation of changing the legal framework; nor does it deny a catalytic EC
influence even if the locus of change remains ultimately at member state level.
Taking the essence of the internal market and citizenship arguments together,
there is already a strong and cumulative base from which the legitimacy of continuing to ignore the reverse discrimination anomaly can be called into question.
And surely arguments grounded in fundamental rights protection for individuals throughout the Community add all the more appreciably to this?

---

[52] Case C–168/91 *Konstantinidis* v. *Stadt Altensteig, Standesamt & Landratsamt Calw,
Ordnungsamt* [1993] ECR, pp. 7645–6, para. 27.
[53] *Uecker and Jacquet, op. cit.* n. 36, pp. 3189, 3190, paras. 19, 22–23.

CONCLUSION

Both the shifting boundaries of EC law and the likely increase in instances of reverse discrimination make the exclusion of Community standards more difficult to sustain even in spheres governed legitimately by internal regulation and, moreover, will make resulting anomalies in protection more difficult to explain to the individuals concerned. That these gaps in protection should be filled by a centralised EC fundamental rights policy is not necessarily the appropriate inference; but a re-examination of national standards on a whole plethora of issues (most likely in the domains of employment and immigration) seems inevitable. And the catalytic role of the EC in this context is itself significant. The impact of EC law on individuals is a changing and multifaceted force, and one that is coloured by varying codes of fundamental rights protection. Where the standard of protection available on a given issue diverges depending on whether the individual is dealing with his/her own member state or with another member state by virtue of having activated a Community element for the situation at issue, disparities in treatment can come to the fore. It has been argued that it is not feasible to counter either that discrepancies of this kind should be ignored or that a Community dictum should shape all national rules so that they conform to Community requirements for all cases.

However, if a member state responsibility that flows from but is not strictly governed by Community requirements can be identified, then that may well be an effective and pragmatic way to proceed. This idea was reflected to a certain extent in the "concentric circles" model of EC human rights competence developed by Lenaerts almost a decade ago, where the nucleus of rights protection is constituted by implementation of the ECHR, leading outwards to general principles of law, rights based on Union citizenship and, finally, "aspirational" fundamental rights—envisaging here a new competence for the EC as ". . . the supervisory structure for the protection of fundamental rights in areas which substantively continue to belong to the sphere of powers of the Member States (and without the Community itself having any specific normative power in this respect)."[54] Lenaerts' construction allowed for a relatively flexible vision of fundamental rights protection—alongside and not in place of both the existing *acquis communautaire* and evolving developments such as the EU Charter of Fundamental Rights—that could work especially well in subject areas that are politically sensitive, or as regards claims the realisation of which is both demanding of resources and inherently subject to localised variation. Moreover, the envisaged structure would have considerable advantages from the perspective of individuals, given that primary responsibility is correctly placed on national authorities (meaning more tangible results at national level). As cautioned, however, a defined catalytic

---

[54] K Lenaerts, "Fundamental rights to be included in a Community catalogue" (1991) 16 *European Law Review* 367–390, 389.

function for the EC in this way demands more than an amended legal framework; it would be naïve to underestimate the extent of the required corresponding shift in political culture. It seems, then, that the label of "aspiration" was chosen most wisely.

Part Five

The Public/Private Dimension

11

Voices of Difference in a Plural Community

CAROL HARLOW*

In trying to redefine itself, Europe is forgetting and ignoring its cultural history.

Jacques Derrida

INTRODUCTION

THE STATEMENT OF intention by the European Council at Tampere to promote greater cooperation in the domain of Justice and Home Affairs placed "co-ordination" of our national criminal justice systems squarely on the EU agenda.[1] Work was also authorised, and has now been completed, on the drafting of an EU Charter of Rights.[2] Both are steps in the direction of legal unity. In addition, many civil lawyers would agree with Heinz Kotz that[3]

> "a serious effort must be made to develop a common core of European legal principles and rules, to engage in the construction of a European legal *lingua franca* . . . and thus to lay the basis for what will be needed when the time is ripe to undertake the project of a European Civil Code".

---

* I have had the help of many colleagues in arriving at the final version of this paper, presented at seminars at the University of Florence, at LSE, at Bristol University and at the University of Aberdeen. I should like to thank all my critics. Special thanks go to Keith Vincent, my assiduous researcher, and colleagues Damian Chalmers, Pavlos Eleftheriadis, John Griffith, Imelda Maher, James Penner and Richard Rawlings for detailed comments. This version was completed in December 2000.

[1] Conclusions of the Finnish Presidency, Tampere, Doc 200/99 (15–16 June 1999).

[2] Authorised by a decision of the European Council at Cologne, 3–4 June 1999, activated by the Tampere European Council, 15–16 June 1999. The concluded Charter was adopted within the framework of the Nice Summit of Dec. 2000, although not incorporated into the Nice Treaty which resulted from the Intergovernmental Conference concluded at Nice or otherwise given the force of law. See, Solemn Proclamation of the European Parliament, the Commission and the Council of 7 December 2000, [2000] OJ C346/1.

[3] H Kotz, "Towards a European Civil Code", in P Cane and J Stapleton (eds.), *The Law of Obligations, Essays in Celebration of John Fleming*, (Oxford: Clarendon Press, 1998), pp. 243–4.

This common core of principles, popular with comparative lawyers, is coming to be called the *ius commune*.[4] Many EC lawyers[5] see the European Union as the *forum conveniens* for the *ius commune*. They believe that it is already emerging and should be encouraged to emerge through the convergence of national legal systems inside the framework of the European Union.

In contrast, this chapter draws support from the contrary signals given by the concept of subsidiarity introduced at Maastricht and reiterated at Amsterdam.[6] It sets out to present the counter-argument for diversity and legal pluralism within the EU, the emphasis throughout being on public and procedural law. The argument rests on the belief that a pluralist Europe is not inconsistent with a commitment to internationalism. Cultural diversity is valuable in its own right and is a basic strength of the European enterprise, providing a valuable genetic store of cultural experience, essential as a foundation for constitutional and legal experiment and as a yardstick against which to measure the infant institutions of the EU. The need for diversity is indirectly recognised in the Preamble to the TEU, which confirms the desire of the Masters of the Treaties "to deepen the solidarity between their peoples while respecting their history, their culture and their traditions". This commitment is reflected in the Charter of Human Rights, which proclaims respect for "cultural, religious and linguistic diversity".[7] In the Treaty of Amsterdam we find a specific reference to legal culture, requiring "care [to] be taken to respect well established national arrangements and the organisation and working of Member States' legal systems".[8]

In modern liberal democracies which acknowledge the need for limited government, the authority of the judiciary is traditionally justified in terms of the rule of law, a principle with which lawyers tend naturally to empathise strongly. This inclines them to read arguments for democracy as an argument for legislative sovereignty in its narrowest and least reflective sense. The rule of law clearly forms an essential element of liberal democracy and plays its part in providing the theoretical basis for an independent judiciary but it forms only one side of a balanced constitution or debate about a balanced constitution. This chapter is premised on the ideal of pluralist democracy, seen as the best, though also the

---

[4] For discussion and explanation of the *ius commune*, see B Jackson, "Legal Visions of the New Europe: Ius Gentium, Ius Commune, European Law", in B Jackson and D McGoldrick (eds.), *Legal Visions of the New Europe,* (London: Graham and Trotman, 1993).

[5] Notably W van Gerven, "Bridging the Gap Between Community and National Laws: Towards a Principle of Homogeneity in the Field of Legal Remedies?" (1995) 32 *CML Rev* 679 and "Bridging the Unbridgeable: Community and National Tort Laws after *Francovich* and *Brasserie*" (1996) 45 *ICLQ* 507. See also R Caranta, "Judicial Protection Against Member States: A New Jus Commune Takes Shape" (1995) 32 *CML Rev* 703.

[6] Treaty of Amsterdam, Protocol on the Application of the Principles of Subsidiarity and Proportionality. On the history of differentiation, see C-D Ehlermann, "Differentiation, Flexibility, Closer Co-operation: The New Provisions of the Amsterdam Treaty" (1998) 4 *European Law Journal* 246.

[7] Art. 22 of the Charter of Fundamental Rights of the European Union, Charter 4487/1/00 Rev 1 (10 Oct. 2000).

[8] Treaty of Amsterdam, Protocol on the Application of the Principles of Subsidiarity and Proportionality, para. 7.

most demanding, form of government that contemporary society has to offer. For the purposes of the argument, a simple but robust definition of democracy has been adopted as a form of popular political self-government with "the people of a country deciding for themselves the contents of the laws that organize and regulate their political association".[9] In this chapter, the political components of democracy have been stressed, though the author accepts that the balance of power in modern constitutions is typically more complex. The true position is reflected in the Preamble to the TEU, where the member states confirm their "attachment to the principles of liberty, democracy and respect for human rights and fundamental freedoms and of the rule of law", a formulation not changed at Amsterdam. It should be noted that liberty and democracy here take precedence over respect for human rights and fundamental freedoms and the rule of law.

Underlying the argument of this chapter are two further assumptions. First, law is seen not merely as a toolkit of autonomous concepts readily transferable in time and space, but as a cultural artifact embedded in the society in which it functions. This conception of law is discussed in the next section. Secondly, the paper maintains that a legal system is part of the governmental arrangements of a given state or society. A legal system is not and never can be "autonomous" in the sense of lying outside the system of governance, though this is not to deny the judicial independence demanded in modern European constitutions, which often finds expression through the doctrine of separation of powers. (In any society whose constitution is written, the distinction will be self-evident).

Neither "harmonisation" nor "convergence", which bear broadly the same meaning, are terms of art and in this chapter they are distinguished. The term "harmonisation" is here reserved for a conscious and negotiated process of harmonisation, culminating in a rulemaking procedure or legislative act. The European Commission has in the past sponsored several efforts at legal harmonisation, notably in the area of consumer protection law and products liability.[10] Latterly, however, the Commission—perhaps more sensitive to the problems of harmonisation in a wider and more divergent Community—has been more selective; rather than attempt broad, general harmonisation, it has sought agreement on specific action in limited areas: a common law of remedies inside the public procurement directives, for example.[11] Attempts made to arrive at a codification of European civil law[12] and the law of judicial procedure have so far had negative outcomes. Indeed, the Storme Commission, the semi-official body set up under the sponsorship of the European Parliament to harmonise procedural law and to draw up a "European Judicial Code", ultimately

---

[9] F Michelman, "Brennan and Democracy: the 1996–97 Brennan Centre Symposium Lecture" (1998) 86 *California Law Review* 399, 400.

[10] EEC 93/13 Dir. on unfair terms in consumer contracts and EEC 85/374 Dir. concerning liability for defective products.

[11] EEC 89/665 Dir. on Remedies.

[12] A Hartkamp et al. (eds.), *Towards a European Civil Code* (Dordrecht: Kluwer,1994).

concluded that the basic distinction in European legal systems between adversarial and inquisitorial procedures was "so deeply enshrined in the respective legal cultures as to make harmonisation practically unfeasible".[13]

The term "convergence" can be used in several senses. It may simply denote the coming together of legal systems through mutual interest and common development, often perceived as an inevitable part of the process of "globalisation". The cumbersome phrase "cross-fertilisation",[14] is really a better way of expressing this process. But in the context of the EU, convergence may also denote the process of harmonisation of national legal principles and procedure brought about by the jurisprudence of the European Court of Justice. In this paper, the term "vertical convergence" is used to convey judicial intervention of this type. "Vertical convergence", which draws on the doctrine of precedent to impose common principles or common rules of interpretation through the rulings of superior courts, has been seen by the ECJ as lying very much at the centre of its role. The boldest example to date of this type of judicial harmonisation is perhaps the case of member state liability, imposed by the ECJ in *Francovich*[15] for failure correctly to transpose EC Directives. While many EC lawyers accept vertical convergence as unexceptional and well within the remit of a superior court,[16] others would certainly question its legitimacy.[17]

To the ECJ, "horizontal divergence" in the sense of variance between the legal principles and procedures of the member states, is often problematic. But in ironing out discrepancies, an equally difficult problem of horizontal divergence may be passed to national courts. This occurs when rules applicable in different areas of domestic law diverge because of the introduction of a principle of EC law which is out of synchronisation with the existing rules of the domestic legal system. This gap creates a quandary for a national judiciary charged with maintaining so far as possible the integrity of the domestic legal system. The standard reaction of EC lawyers to problems of horizontal convergence is to treat them simply as a question of "levelling up" to a common EC standard, generally assumed to be "higher law" in both senses of the phrase. The fallacy of the "levelling up" concept is discussed below (pp. 218–21).

---

[13] M Storme, "General Introductory Report", in M Storme (ed.), *Rapprochement du Droit Judiciare de l'Union Européenne* (Rotterdam: Martinus Nijhoff, 1994), p. 63.

[14] See J Beatson and T Tridimas (eds.), *New Directions in European Public Law* (Oxford: Hart, 1998).

[15] Joined Cases 6, 9/90 *Francovich and Bonafaci* v. *Italy* [1991] ECR I–5357. And see Joined Cases C 46/93 and C 48/93 *Brasserie du Pêcheur SA* v. *Germany*; *R* v. *Transport Secretary ex p. Factortame (No 4)* [1996] ECR I–1029.

[16] A Toth, "The Authority of Judgments of the European Court of Justice: Binding Force and Legal Effects", in N MacCormick and R Summers (eds.), *Interpreting Precedents: a Comparative Study* (Aldershot: Dartmouth, 1997).

[17] T Hartley, "The European Court, Judicial Objectivity and the Constitution of the European Union" (1996) 112 *Law Quarterly Review* 95. The classic attack is by H Rasmussen, *On Law and Policy in the Court of Justice* (Rotterdam: Martinus Nijhoff, 1986).

Law and Democracy

Explanations of European governance were at first largely grounded in international relations theory, notably neofunctionalism and intergovernmentalism, where democracy is not a special concern.[18] Legitimacy was not really in issue in the era of so-called "tacit consent", when the European project was seen as essentially an affair of elites who could rely on a docile public to support their decisions uncritically, including the low visibility decisions of the Court of Justice.[19] Elite government at Community level was seen as validated by representative democracy at national level.[20] It is important to note that this was the prevailing political culture at the time when the doctrine of supremacy was shaped (below, pp. 214–17).

When the Community was first perceived as possessing a "democratic deficit", this was largely defined in terms of the absence of representative institutions at EC level. Only after direct elections were conceded in 1979 did attention turn from representation to the problem of sovereignty as manifested in the EP's lack of sovereign lawmaking powers. Significantly, both variants on the theme of representative democracy were under discussion in the formative years when the ECJ was forging the basic constitutional principles of the Community; both were reflected in some of the Court's most ambitious jurisprudence of the period; and both are compatible with integrationism (below, pp. 212–14). The robust definition adopted in this paper of popular democratic government is incompatible both with the notion of legitimation through the doctrine of "passive consent" and with elite government, even in the modified two-tier theory of European democracy, whereby popular democracy at national level justifies elite governance in the Community.

Today the argument has shifted. Models of deliberative and participatory democracy are increasingly fashionable.[21] These are of course consonant with pluralism; they could flourish in a federal Europe endowed with strong representative institutions and traditions, or a "Europe of the Regions". Popular or populist democracy also contains a notion of inclusivity: as Scott puts it, "the

[18] M Horeth, "No Way Out for the Beast? The Unsolved Legitimacy Problem of European Governance" (1999) 6 *Journal of European Public Policy* 249.

[19] D Obradovic, "Policy Legitimacy and the European Union" (1996) 34 *Journal of Common Market Studies* 191.

[20] S Andersen and T Burns, "The European Union and the Erosion of Parliamentary Democracy: A Study of Post-Parliamentary Governance", in S Andersen and K Eliassen (eds.), *The European Union: How Democratic Is It?* (London: Sage, 1996).

[21] P Craig,"Democracy and Rule-making Within the EC: An Empirical and Normative Assessment" (1997) 3 *European Law Journal* 105; D Curtin, *Postnational Democracy: The European Union in Search of a Political Philosophy* (Dordrecht: Kluwer, 1997) and " 'Civil Society' and the European Union: Opening Spaces for Deliberative Democracy?" in *Collected Courses of the Academy of European Law*, vol VII, Bk 1, (Oxford: Oxford University Press, 1998) p. 185.

modern republic is an inclusive republic which seeks to render audible and effective all the voices of difference emanating from within the polity".[22] This, however, necessitates provision not only of machinery for representation but also of pathways for direct public participation in policy- and decision-making. To some theorists of European governance, participatory proceduralism can be used strongly to promote pluralist democracy;[23] in practice, however, it contains a powerful bias towards elitism or forms of corporate governance in which interest groups obtain a stranglehold on policy. The "constitutionalisation" of administrative procedures also creates its own problems, as discussed below (pp. 218–21).

This chapter suggests that arguments for the convergence of European legal systems are tacitly based on elitist theories of European government and originate in the doctrine of passive consent. At Community level, the relocation of power has typically been achieved through a judge-made construction—to which national and European judiciaries have contributed—of constitutional norms imposed on the democratic institutions of governance in the name of public law. Thus the effect of a "unified system of judicial protection" throughout Europe could be at least as significant as harmonisation of procedural criminal law through the sprouting *Corpus Juris* project.[24]

What we are seeing is a variant of the "open flank" argument, according to which democratic deficit at European level, or shifts in the balance of power between European and national institutions, impact unfavourably on democratic government at national level. Daniel Wincott calls this the "perversion" of European democracy by the two-tier system of European governance, which has had the effect of cutting down "domestic mechanisms of democratic accountability" and so "perverting" the constitutional balance between executive and legislative organs at national level.[25] Similarly, relocation of power to the European judiciary, anti-democratic in the sense that it substitutes one form of elite government in the Community for another, can "subvert" national democracy by indirectly shifting the balance of power at national level. That a substantial horizontal relocation of power from parliamentary institutions towards a non-elected judiciary is already occurring, and that this transfer of power to the judiciary is visible at both national and Community levels, is widely

---

[22] J Scott, "Law, Legitimacy and EC Governance: Prospects for 'Partnership'" (1998) 36 *Journal of Common Market Studies* 175, 177.

[23] K-H Ladeur, "Towards a Legal Theory of Supranationality—The Validity of the Network Concept" (1997) 3 *European Law Journal* 33.

[24] See M Delmas-Marty (ed.), *Corpus Juris: introducing penal provisions for the purpose of the European Union*, (Paris: Economica, 1997); W van Gerven, "Constitutional Conditions for a Public Prosecutor's Office at the European Level", in G De Kerchove and A Wyenbergh (eds.), *Vers un espace judiciaire européen*, (Brussels: Editions ULB, 2000).

[25] D Wincott, "Does the European Union Pervert Democracy? Questions of Democracy in New Constitutionalist Thought on the Future of Europe" (1999) 4 *European Law Journal* 411. See also D Chryssochoou, "Democracy and Symbiosis in the European Union: Towards a Confederal Consociation?" (1994) 17 *West European Politics* 1.

accepted; indeed, it is a matter of self-congratulation for many lawyers. These developments are dangerous in that they inhibit and supersede democratic discussion and debate.

Law as Culture

Formalist or positivist traditions of legal scholarship present law as a special system of reasoning, characterised by a quality of coherence or as a set of principles arranged as a system of artificial logic. As the distinguished comparativist F H Lawson once observed:[26]

> "All law tends to become a collection of lines of systematic thought made to follow logically from a limited number of premisses; or rather, from a number of decisions of one kind or another, legislative or judicial, systematic bodies of principle are established by a process of induction, and those principles acquire a sanctity of their own which turns them into axiomatic premisses from which other rules and principles can be deduced. This is a process which cannot be avoided".

The view of law as a set of coherent and systematic body of legal norms cemented by a specialised method of reasoning is a central feature of the civilian legal tradition[27] and is widely accepted by lawyers as applying to the Community legal system.[28] To complete the positivist picture of orderliness and coherence, the concepts which form the building blocks of the system are seen as autonomous and neutral. Legal concepts become empty vessels, superficially similar and transferable, at least within a given legal family or closely related families.[29] At this level of abstraction, for example, it is possible to say that fault is the basis of delictual liability in European legal systems. Similarities between legal systems may also be enhanced by drawing a distinction between the *structure* of legal reasoning, presented as similar inside European legal families, and *presentation* of legal argument, seen as a surface variant.[30] The view of legal concepts as readily comparable and interchangeable is naturally attractive to EC lawyers because it facilitates and downplays problems of harmonisation and integration of Community legal systems.

---

[26] "Comparative Law as an Instrument of Legal Culture", in F H Lawson, *Selected Essays*, (Oxford: Oxford University Press, 1977), Vol II, p. 73.

[27] J H Merryman, *The Civil Law Tradition: An Introduction to the Legal Systems of Western Europe and Latin America* (Stanford: Stanford University Press, 1969).

[28] F Snyder, in "General Course on Constitutional Law of the European Union", in *Collected Courses of the Academy of European Law* (Oxford: Oxford University Press, 1997), p. 50, cites to this effect classic texts by J-V Louis, *The Community Legal Order* (2nd edn., Brussels: European Community, 1990), p. 13 and G Isaac, *Droit communautaire général* (Paris: A Colin, 1983), p. 111.

[29] For the concept of legal families (discussed further below), see R David and J Brierly, *The Major Legal Systems in the World Today* (3rd edn., London: Butterworths, 1985), pp. 17–20.

[30] J Bell, "English and French Law—Not so Different?" (1995) 48 *Current Legal Problems* 63. The argument is justifiably critiqued by B Markesinis, "The Comparatist (or a Plea for a Broader Legal Education)" (1995) 15 *Yearbook of European Law* 262, 269.

Even at the simple level of legal concept, however, harmonisation and convergence may often be illusory. Familiar words like "fault", with apparently similar or even identical meanings when translated, may be differently understood and applied in different legal cultures. This is the underlying message of Pierre Legrand:[31]

> "[R]ules and concepts alone actually tell one very little about a given legal system . . . They may provide one with much information about what is apparently happening, but they indicate nothing about the deep structures of legal systems. Specifically, rules and concepts do little to disclose that legal systems are but the surface manifestation of legal cultures and, indeed, of culture *tout court*. In other words, they limit the observer to a 'thin description' and foreclose the possibility of the 'thick description' that the analyst ought to regard as desirable".

Legal systems are here seen as built up through habits, customs and practices which infuse law and dictate the way in which it will be interpreted. To this cultural package, Legrand attaches the term *"mentalité"*.

Legrand's thesis can be misrepresented as an extremist argument against any form of convergence, harmonisation or incorporation, a claim which would not only render legal systems wholly immune from outside influence but which argues against the course of European history.[32] An alternative way to read his core argument concerning *mentalité* is, however, rather persuasive. Legrand points to several features of the common law, such as the way it moves from fact to principle and remedy to rights, which form its "deep structure". When apparently simple concepts such as good faith or fault are transferred from one legal system to another, the methodology of the system will operate to limit the effect of the transplantation. If fault, for example, is installed as the basis of delictual and tortious liability in every European legal system, what is construed as fault may vary as considerably over spatial boundaries as it has been seen to do over time periods. Fault is a flexible concept, variable along a spectrum, and a system can easily instal or reinstate strict liability through the doctrine of "presumptive fault"; systems protective of defendants may in practice require proof of "grave fault". Something very like this has happened with the interpretation of the uniform EC Products Liability Directive, where harmonisation has in practice come to mean approximation. Legrand's *mentalité* concept explains why the reality of incorporation is so often "translation". It can indeed be compared with the original notion of the directive in EC law, which required member states to work towards a given goal, with the flexibility to work with the *mentalité* of their own legal system and not against the grain. This conception has, however, been rendered partially nugatory by the ECJ's promotion of the doctrine of "direct effect".

---

[31] P Legrand, "European Legal Systems Are Not Converging" (1996) 45 *Internatonal and Comparative Law Quarterly* 52, 56.

[32] R van Caenegem, *An Historical Introduction to Private Law*, (Cambridge: Cambridge University Press, 1992).

Somewhat similar is Gunther Teubner's conception of "legal transplants" as,[33]

> "a fundamental irritation which triggers a whole series of new and unexpected events . . . [they irritate] law's 'binding arrangements' . . . they unleash an evolutionary dynamic in which the external rule's meaning will be reconstructed and the internal context will undergo fundamental change".

Like Legrand, Teubner rejects the idea that that foreign transplants are easily absorbed by the host system and draws on sociological research to argue that proponents of harmonisation are moving in precisely the wrong direction. Globalisation will not necessarily result in a "convergence of social orders and in a uniformisation of law" because "different sectors of the globalised society do not face the same problems for their laws to deal with".[34] Basil Markesinis provides a telling example drawn from the area of tort law harmonisation.[35] Tort law and welfare law, he argues cogently, are two closely related areas of law which have been allowed to proliferate in uncoordinated fashion inside national legal systems, largely because the first is categorised as civil law and the second primarily as administrative. In the light of different national attitudes to welfare, vertical convergence of tort laws is likely to increase horizontal disjunction of tort and welfare law; yet to attempt at one and the same time vertical and horizontal convergence would be an impossible exercise—complicated in the Community by the absence of clear competence in either area.

This is why Christian Joerges, reflecting on efforts by the European Commission to harmonise consumer protection law, deduces that reform is always best undertaken at national level:[36]

> "The compulsory incorporation of 'foreign' concepts . . . affects deeper structures of private law systems. Every legal concept, every dogmatic construction, every line of legal argument operates in pre-determined traditional contexts. Legislative acts of national parliaments remain rooted in these contexts, even when they are perceived as destructive interventions. Moreover, they are still subject to control by case law, which is formulated with the objective of maintaining coherence within private law".

To summarise, conceptual differences between legal systems go much deeper than procedure, presentation of argument or methods of construction. They spring from different cultural traditions, reflecting "different justifications for the imposition of legal obligations and the creation of rights", which derive

[33] G Teubner, "Legal Irritants: Good Faith in British Law Or How Unifying Law Ends Up in New Divergencies" (1998) 61 *Modern Law Review* 11, 12.

[34] *Ibid.* 13.

[35] B Markesinis, "Why a Code is Not the Best Way to Advance the Cause of European Legal Unity" (1998) 5 *European Review of Private Law* 519, 521.

[36] C Joerges, "The Europeanization of Private Law as a Rationalization Process and as a Contest of Disciplines—an Analysis of the Directive on Unfair Terms in Consumer Contracts" (1995) 3 *European Review of Private Law* 175, 183. On the difficulties, see N Questiaux, "Implementing EC Law in France: The Role of the French Conseil d'État", in P Craig and C Harlow (eds.), *Lawmaking in the European Union* (Dordrecht: Kluwer, 1998).

from "the moral and political foundations" of different societies. Law—and here the earlier example of welfare law is highly pertinent—reflects "accepted principles of distributive justice in a community".[37]

If concepts represent only the tip of the iceberg of law then, in thinking about law as a cultural artifact, we may need to enlarge our definition. David Nelken[38] depicts legal culture as a "multi-layered" concept which includes as well as legal norms, "salient features of legal insititutions and their infrastructure, social behaviour in creating, using and not using law, as well as legal consciousness in the legal professions and amongst the public". Lawrence Friedman's conception of law is still wider. He includes,[39]

> "the values and attitudes which bind the system together, and which determine the place of the legal system in the culture of the society as a whole. What kind of training do the lawyers and judges have? What do people think of law? Do groups or individuals willingly go to court? For what purposes do people turn to lawyers; for what purposes do they make use of other officials and intermediaries? Is there respect for law, government, tradition? What is the relationship between class structure and the use or nonuse of legal institutions? What informal social controls exist in addition to or in place of formal ones? Who prefers what kind of controls, and why? . . . It is the legal culture, that is, the network of values and attitudes relating to law, which determines when and why and where people turn to law or government, or turn away".

Here law and legal culture are presented as an onion, whose skins can be stripped away to reveal deeper layers. But whether these background values are described as making up the *mentalité* of the judge and lawyer or are incorporated into a "thick" definition of law is really immaterial. The point is that they need to be taken into consideration whenever harmonisation and convergence are in question. Harmonisation and convergence are complex issues, not to be undertaken lightly. They may even be impossible goals. Attempts at harmonisation and convergence may, as argued in the next section, even if ultimately rejected by the host system, cause it substantial harm.

Law and Political Culture

Public law has particularly deep roots inside a cultural and political framework. It is difficult to see it at all in terms of a set of neutral, apolitical concepts and it has been defined as "a sophisticated form of political discourse".[40] Stripping away its skins reveals administrative law encased in constitutional law by which it is nourished and to which it owes its being. Constitutional law is in turn

---

[37] H Collins, "European Private Law and the Cultural Identity of States" (1995) 3 *European Review of Private Law* 353, 356 and 360.

[38] D Nelken, "Disclosing/Invoking Legal Culture: An Introduction" (1995) 4 *Social and Legal Studies* 435, 438.

[39] L Friedman, "Legal Culture and Social Development" (1969) 4 *Law and Society Review* 29, 34.

[40] M Loughlin, *Public Law and Political Theory* (Oxford: Clarendon Press, 1992), p. 4.

wrapped in, and permeated by, the prevailing political and governmental culture. It is these deeper values which help to determine, amongst other things, "when and why and where people turn to law or government". The mirror-image of Legrand's notion of *mentalité* is the terminology of "background theory" or "mindset",[41] in use amongst English public lawyers to describe the deep values which infuse constitutions and legal systems. Behind rules and concepts, the argument runs, lie habits, customs and ways of thought derived from historical experience. These inarticulate premisses infuse both constitutional law and judicial decision-making.

Even if globalisation is bringing European societies closer together, there remains a considerable cultural divergence. National and subnational culture is still strongly reflected in modes of government and in public administration. It is the state or region which still possesses the crucial role in ensuring continuity of effective government. It is national institutions which at present provide the central unit of governance within the Community. As Alan Dashwood puts it:[42]

> "The individual citizen . . . continues to experience government as, essentially, a Member State phenomenon . . . Rules touching the lives of individuals in all kinds of ways may no longer be home-produced; but the sometimes unwelcome consequences of the rules are exacted by officials with familiar accents and uniforms and owing their allegiance to political masters who are answerable through the national democratic process".

Nor are we yet ready to conform to some "European model or ideal type of public administration which the countries of the European Union are reaching towards, leave alone a model of modernisation".[43] At one end of a theoretical spectrum we find the strong public service ethos central both to French public administration and administrative law;[44] at the other, the public management theories of Thatcherite Britain.[45] There is admittedly much exchange of ideas; privatisation and agencies have proliferated, regulation is recognised across Europe as a useful technique for control of the private sector[46] and managerialism exerts a growing influence in national civil services.[47] But recruitment, personnel, techniques of administration, continue to vary[48] and the reality is still a

---

[41] C Harlow, "Changing the Mindset: The Place of Theory in English Administrative Law" (1994) 14 *Oxford Journal of Legal Studies* 419; P Craig, *Public Law and Democracy in the United Kingdom and the United States of America* (Oxford: Clarendon Press, 1990), p. 3.

[42] A Dashwood, "States in the European Union" (1998) 23 *European Law Review* 201, 213.

[43] A Claisse and M-C Meininger, "Les fonctions publiques à l'épreuve de la modernisation", in L Rouban and J Ziller (eds.), Special Issue: "Les Adminstrations en Europe: d'une Modernisation à l'Autre" (1995) 75 *Revue française de droit administratif* 345 (author's translation).

[44] E Malaret Garcia, "Public Service, Public Services, Public Functions, and Guarantees of the Rights of Citizens: Unchanging Needs in a Changed Context", in M Freedland and S Sciarra (eds.), *Public Services and Citizenship in European Law, Public and Labour Law Perspectives* (Oxford: Oxford University Press, 1998).

[45] C Hood, "A Public Management for All Seasons" (1991) 69 *Public Administration* 3.

[46] G Majone, "The rise of the regulatory state in Europe" (1994) 17 *West European Politics* 77.

[47] D Farnham et al., *New Public Managers in Europe* (Basingstoke: Macmillan, 1996).

[48] J Burnham and M Maor, "Converging Administrative Systems: Recruitment and Training in European Union Member States" (1995) 2 *Journal of European Public Policy* 185.

plural Europe of many administrative cultures, valid in their own national cultural context. The situation is further complicated where states possess strong local or regional traditions (as in Belgium) or in federal states (notably Germany), where implementation by regions cannot be dictated by a strong central government. At the level of service delivery variance remains very great; the reality here is a "Europe of many speeds" in which "levelling up" can be undertaken only slowly.[49] Systems and processes which work in one member state may be largely ineffectual in others—and effectiveness in the real, grass roots, sense provides the strongest of arguments for pluralism.

Empirical research shows that national administrative attitudes and culture profoundly affect implementation of Community directives and policies; where these do not harmonise well with national administrative structures, they may be transposed and lip-service may be paid to them, but they will remain largely a dead letter. An empirical study made of the implementation of visa and asylum procedures, for example, revealed enormous divergence in implementation at national borders, where the inbred culture of immigration officers allowed traditional practices to continue unchecked.[50] Enlargement is particularly relevant to this picture. In states emerging from the shadow of totalitarianism, the struggle against Stalinist bureaucracy has been acute and recruitment of sufficient capable personnel dedicated to the methods of western democratic capitalism is a special problem. Especially in environmental matters, there is talk of a prolonged period for conformity. The argument is not one for stasis. Convergence and harmonisation may still remain ultimate goals. Yet implementation will not be achieved through working against the grain of national cultural traditions; backlash and anti-European sentiment are the more likely outcome.

Legal as well as political and administrative systems have internal dynamics which give them their special character. John Bell identifies four very different European administrative law traditions.[51] The French-influenced systems of France, Belgium, Luxembourg, Italy, Portugal and Spain all acknowledge a classical demarcation line between civil and administrative jurisdictions. In the Germanic tradition the distinction is blurred with greater overlap and (though Bell does not say this) there is a marked emphasis on justiciable constitutional rights.[52] Bell remarks of the common law countries of Britain and Ireland that they, in common with the Netherlands could be seen as possessing "a strong tradition of administrative *non-law*". The same is true of the Scandinavian family where, at least in Sweden and Denmark, judicial review takes second place to

---

[49] W Kickert, *Public Management and Administrative Reform in Western Europe* (London: Edward Elgar, 1997).

[50] S Peers, *Mind the Gap! Ineffective Member State Implementation of European Union Asylum Measures* (London: Immigration Law Practitioners' Association and Refugee Council, 1998).

[51] J Bell, "Mechanisms for Cross-fertilisation of Administrative Law in Europe", in J Beatson and T Tridimas (eds.), *New Directions in European Public Law* (Oxford: Hart, 1998), pp. 149–51.

[52] J Schwarze, "The Convergence of the Administrative Laws of the European Union Member States" (1998) 4 *European Public Law* 191, 192.

the ombudsman. Bell's criteria, as he would be the first to admit, merely scrape the surface; deeper examination would reveal further fissures between members of the same family. Moreover, the families under consideration are fairly closely related; this will not necessarily continue to be the case when the Community begins to accept further members from the ex-Eastern bloc or—in the South— Turkey.

Six of the present member states place great emphasis on Parliaments in securing accountability; in the case of the United Kingdom, the telling phrase "political constitution"[53] is apposite. In English constitutional law, the central doctrine of parliamentary sovereignty can be seen to serve a dual purpose: on the one hand, it simply establishes the hierarchy of legal norms; on the other, it constitutes the fundamental principle of democratic legitimacy. Statute law is paramount because it is established, legitimated and underpinned by the system of parliamentary democracy by which we have come to be governed. The cultural resonance of the second idea in English law canot be underrated, any more than we can ignore the very different constitutional settlements of other European nations in which a separate administrative jurisdictional distinction has become entrenched and where in consequence the public/private divide has developed deep conceptual accretions which constitute the prevailing mindset.[54] Again, take the rule of law principle, entrenched in the Treaties as a key principle of European constitutional settlements. The divergent terminology— rule of law, *règne de la loi, rechtstaat, état de droit*—all captures something of the spirit of the doctrine but is by no means synonomous. It is important too to note that formal or thin, and substantive or thick, interpretations of the concept exist side by side, often within the same legal culture.[55] There is not one rule of law but many.

Bell's reference to a tradition of administrative non-law is also highly significant. Law—as Friedman signals [56]—is one of a number of pathways which link, and provide access to, a society's social and political systems. One of the key functions of administrative law is to provide the citizen with these pathways. In no society does law have a monopoly, but in some societies it is less highly prized than others. It has, for example, been said that "the idea that there could be any state activity which may not be challenged in court is alien to German law".[57] Other European societies, as Bell indicates, evince a distinct preference for alternative dispute-resolution, as in the robust Scandinavian ombudsman tradition.

---

[53] J A G Griffith, "The Political Constitution" (1979) 42 *Modern Law Review* 1.

[54] J Allison, "Cultural Divergence, the Separation of Powers and the Public/Private Divide" (1997) 9 *European Review of Public Law* 305 and *A Continental Distinction in the Common Law, A Historical and Comparative Perspective on English Public Law* (2nd edn., Oxford: Clarendon Press, 2000), advances a very similar argument to that of Legrand.

[55] P Craig, "Formal and Substantive Conceptions of the Rule of Law: An Analytical Framework" (1997) *Public Law* 467.

[56] n. 39 above.

[57] W Rufner, "Basic Elements of German Law on State Liability", in J Bell and A W Bradley (eds.), *Governmental Liability, A Comparative Study* (London: British Institute for Comparative Law, 1991), p. 252.

One cannot be sure what will result from blocking one of the pathways or widening another. Complaints may be diverted into a system where they cannot be appropriately handled or they may dry up altogether. Damage may then be caused to the political culture, ultimately impinging on a society's concept of citizenship.

It is important to stress once more that this paper is not arguing for stasis, cultural purity or isolationism. European societies have been influenced over the course of centuries by each others' cultures and, to quote Marc Galanter,[58] "legal cultures, like languages, can absorb huge amounts of foreign material while preserving a distinctive structure and flavour". But when we talk of legal transplants as an irritant, we must realise that they may operate to destabilise legal and political institutions or change the balance of institutional power in a way which a given society finds unacceptable. When legal transplants impinge in this way on the wider political practices of a society, the democratic system is indeed perverted. The "open flank" argument is here applied through law.

EC LEGAL CULTURE

Creating a Constitution

At national level, public law operates in the framework of a working democracy. This is not the case in the EU where the institutional environment of the legal order is not securely embedded. The Community has never become a state, though it does possess some statal characteristics, nor have the member states been able to decide whether they are moving towards or away from federation or whether the ultimate destination of Europe is "union" or, as this author prefers, "community".[59] The institutional structure is in a state of flux, revolving around inter-governmental conferences at which the Treaties undergo an irregular process of incremental change. More important, the structure of the Community fails properly to mirror the democratic beliefs and cultures which characterise the institutions of the member states. It could be said to profess democracy without being democratic.

Although the fragility of the democratic structure and political institutions can today be seen as reflecting on the legitimacy of the EC legal order,[60] at first the actual consequence for the Court of Justice was an unusual degree of autonomy. In contrast to national judicial organs, the ECJ became accustomed to operating in a political vacuum, secure from institutional competition and

---

[58] M Galanter, "Predators and Parasites: Lawyer-Bashing and Civil Justice" (1994) 28 *Georgia Law Review* 633, 674.

[59] J Weiler, "The Community System: The Dual Character of Supranationalism" (1981) 1 *Yearbook of European Law* 267.

[60] D Wincott, "The Role of Law or the Rule of the Court of Justice?" (1995) 2 *Journal of European Public Policy* 583.

largely insulated from public opinion. A tight epistemic community of court, legal services and commentators[61] helped to foster easy acceptance of the ECJ as constitution-maker—hardly a late twentieth-century conception—with little reflection as to whether any mandate for such a role existed.[62]

Even if it was not born into an established constitutional culture, the infant legal order was quick to develop one. At one and the same time the Court was engaged in manufacturing for itself a constitutional jurisdiction, transforming the Treaties into a Community constitution, concretising the rules of the new legal order and legitimating each in terms of the other.[63] Integrationism—"a genetic code transmitted to the Court of Justice by the founding fathers"[64]— emerged as a central feature of its mindset, while concern for "top down" reception of the infant Community legal order promoted the doctrine of supremacy.

A significant step in the evolution of a constitutional culture was the conceptualisation of the Treaties as the "basic constitutional charter"[65] of a "Community based on the rule of law"—at best a contestable claim. The plural construction of the Community was less often noted, nor did the Court's confident judgments tend to reflect uncertainty surrounding the ultimate constitutional destination. For member states and national jurisdictions, the effect was restrictive and exclusive:[66]

> "[B]y declaring the supremacy of Community law on the basis of a teleological reading of the Treaties and without reference to the constitutions of the Member States, the European Court saw the question of the scope of the competence of this new legal order as one which could be answered exclusively by reference to the Treaties, of which it was the sole, authoritative interpreter . . ."

Assuming that the Treaties are accepted to be constitutional in character,[67] then its origins have led to an unusually one-sided constitution. At its heart we

---

[61] The phrase is borrowed from M Shapiro, "Comparative Law and Comparative Politics" (1980) 53 *Southern California Law Review* 537, 538. For the make-up of the relevant epistemic community in the EC context, see H Schepel and R Wesseling, "The Legal Community: Judges, Lawyers, Officials and Clerks in the Writing of Europe" (1997) 3 *European Law Journal* 165.

[62] F Mancini, "The Making of a Constitution for Europe" (1989) 26 *Common Market Law Review* 595.

[63] R Dehousse, *The European Court of Justice* (Basingstoke: Macmillan, 1998).

[64] F Mancini and D Keeling, "Democracy and the European Court of Justice" (1994) 57 *Modern Law Review* 175, 186. On the role of the Court in integration, see J Weiler, "A Quiet Revolution— The European Court of Justice and its Interlocutors" (1994) *Comparative Political Studies* 510.

[65] R Cooter and D Schmidtchen, "Introduction", in "Special Issue: Conference on the Constitutional Law and Economics of the European Union" (1996) 16 *International Review of Law and Economics* 277.

[66] I Maher, "Community Law in the National Legal Order: A Systems Analysis" (1998) 36 *Journal of Common Market Studies* 217, 244. See also B de Witte, "The Nature of the Legal Order", in P Craig and G de Búrca (eds.), *The Evolution of EU Law* (Oxford: Oxford University Press, 1999), pp. 196–8.

[67] Further discussed by T Schilling, "The Autonomy of the Community Legal Order: An Analysis of Possible Foundations" (1996) 37 *Harvard International Law Journal* 389; P Eleftheriadis, "Aspects of European Constitutionalism" (1996) 21 *European Law Review* 32; K Armstrong, "Theorizing the Legal Dimension of European Integration" (1998) 36 *Journal of Common Market Studies* 155, 161; B de Witte, "International Agreement or European Constitution?", in J Winter et al. (eds.), *Reforming the Treaty on European Union—The Legal Debate* (Dordrecht: Kluwer, 1996), p. 3.

find the ideology of market crucial to the conception, first of the common market, and later of the European Economic Community which supplanted it. As Seidel puts it, it is "*The Treaty* [which] obligates Member States to ensure their economies are organised and run in accordance with the principles of the market and competition".[68] The move to constitutionalise the Treaties has thus been driven equally by the desire to promote deeper integration; to entrench economic values at constitutional level, thus rendering them incontrovertible; and by a wish to legitimate free market economic doctrine as a value of "constitutional" rank. In this the influence of German ordo-liberal doctrine has been very marked.[69] As John Gray remarks, "[t]he late-twentieth-century free market experiment is an attempt to legitimate through democratic institutions severe limits on the scope and content of democratic control over economic life".[70] What opponents fear is the entrenchment of a political credo at a level beyond political reach. Hostility thus extends beyond the substance to procedure, here the claims of constitutionality and of legal supremacy.

Buttressing the economic constitution stand the "four freedoms", which possess for some the mantra and status of the civic and political rights often found in constitutional bills of rights. The early priority given to economic, commercial and property rights was hardly surprising, but their dominance helped to point up the absence of formal protection for civil and political rights in the EC "constitution". Failure to recognise human rights more widely emerged as a significant ground of conflict with the German Constitutional Court.[71] It also created the potential for significant argument over values, when economic rights were seen as taking precedence over other rights valued at least as highly by national communities. Value pluralism and national identity were moving on to the legal agenda.

Supremacy, Equality and Effectiveness

The foundations of the EC legal order rest in the Treaty, more especially the rule of law ideal embedded in the Preamble. This Treaty status of "high constitutional principle" provides a theoretical legitimation for the whole judge-made construction of EC law; in addition, Article 220 (ex 164) establishes the Court as guardian of the Treaty, its duty being to see the law observed. In line with the

---

[68] M Seidel, "Constitutional Aspects of the Economic and Monetary Union", in F Snyder (ed.), *Constitutional Dimensions of European Economic Integration* (Dordrecht: Kluwer, 1996), p. 476 (emphasis mine). See also M Streit and W Mussler, "The Economic Constitution of the European Community: 'From Rome to Maastricht' ", in F Snyder (ed.), *ibid.*

[69] D Chalmers, "The Single Market: From Prima Donna to Journeyman", in J Shaw and G More (eds.), *New Legal Dynamics of European Union,*(Oxford: Oxford University Press, 1995), pp. 56–66. And see E-J von Mestmacker, "On the Legitimacy of European Law" (1994) 58 *RabelsZ* 617.

[70] J Gray, *False Dawn, The Delusions of Global Capitalism* (London: Granta Books, 1998), p. 9.

[71] J Kokott, "Report on Germany", in A-M Slaughter, A Stone Sweet, J Weiler (eds.), *The European Courts and National Courts—Doctrine and Jurisprudence* (Oxford: Hart, 1998), pp. 81–102.

requirements and liberal ideology of the EC constitutional culture, the rule of law principle early acquired an unashamedly formalist and procedural interpretation—the classic liberal model. Cotterell reminds us of the cultural link between this "thin" interpretation of the rule of law principle and capitalist societies,[72] in which category the Community stands. The "thin" version of the rule of law requires a legal order with fixed and stable general principles; formal rights of access to courts for the resolution of disputes are also necessary. Both have been provided and flourished.

A further tenet of the formal rule of law principle is the doctrine of equality before the law. Here we have the kernel of the "level playing field" of EC legal rights. Equality as a facet of the rule of law legitimates the EC legal order. The Court itself has argued that:[73]

> "The success of Community law in embedding itself so thoroughly in the legal life of the Member States is due to its having been perceived, interpreted and applied by the nationals, the administrations and the courts and tribunals of all the Member States as a uniform body of rules upon which individuals may rely in their national courts".

Formal equality pays no heed to outcomes. No attempt need be made to clothe the bare bones of the concept in reality. Friedman's wider, socio-legal definition of law[74] and his admonition to consider the use made of the legal system and the purposes for which people turn to lawyers can be ignored. Not only does the formal version of the rule of law flourish in capitalist societies but it is particularly attractive to economic actors. Because of "the stability and predictability that legal-political, as opposed to purely political, institutions have to offer . . . [l]egalization, and thus judicialization, fits an 'economic community' particularly well".[75] Galanter makes the same point when he observes how the dominance of American multi-national commercial concerns has created a pressure to judicialisation in Europe.[76]

Ami Barav lists as fundamental doctrines of the EC legal order: supremacy, irreversibility, direct applicability and the binding force of EC law, the last three of which are indeed further aspects of legal supremacy.[77] Supremacy is the fundamental doctrine of EC law, essential to integration. Supremacy is buttressed

---

[72] R Cotterell, *Law's Community: Legal Theory in Sociological Perspective* (Oxford: Oxford University Press, 1995), pp. 164–77, discussing F Neumann, *The Rule of Law: Political Theory and the Legal System in Modern Society* (Oxford: Berg, 1986). This is not a novel argument of course.

[73] Report of the Court of Justice (and Court of First Instance) on Certain Aspects of the Application of the Treaty on European Union, Luxembourg, May 1995, para. 4.

[74] n. 39 above.

[75] M Shapiro, "The European Court of Justice", in P Craig and G de Búrca, *The Evolution of EU Law*, (Oxford: Oxford University Press, 1999), pp. 328, 330. See also H Schermers, "The Role of the European Court of Justice in the Free Movement of Goods", in T Sandalow and E Stein (eds.), *Courts and Free Markets* (Oxford: Oxford University Press, 1982).

[76] M Galanter, "Predators and Parasites", n. 58 above.

[77] A Barav, "Ominpotent Courts", in D Curtin and T Heukels (eds.), *Institutional Dynamics of European Integration* (Rotterdam: Martinus Nijhoff, 1994), vol II, p. 268. See similarly, P Pescatore, "Aspects judiciaires de l'acquis communautaire" (1981) 17 *Revue trimestrielle de droit européen* 617, 649.

by the ingenious use made by the ECJ of the simple obligation imposed on member states by Art 10 EC (ex 5) "to take all appropriate measures" to fulfil their Treaty obligations. This has been transmuted into a novel legal principle of fidelity.[78] A "command and control" idea of law is being set in place and with it a connection between the rule of law and the power of command (sovereignty).

Command is carried into the doctrine of "effectiveness", another notion to feature centrally in the case law of the ECJ. The link between the principles is spelt out in an extraordinary extra-judicial statement by the ECJ:[79]

> "Any weakening, even if only potential, of the uniform application and interpretation of Community law throughout the Union would be liable to give rise to distortions of competition and discrimination between economic operators, thus jeopardising equality of opportunity between economic operators and consequently the proper functioning of the internal market".

An "effective" judicial system starts with the articulation of legal principle. Principles must next be transposed by national courts. In building the new legal order, the ECJ borrowed heavily from the conceptual vocabulary of national legal systems: e.g., from France, the concept of *principes généraux* with constitutional weight; from Germany, the proportionality principle; from England the *audi alteram partem* principle; and so on.[80] In borrowing, the ECJ looked naturally for solutions "most compatible with the legal order of Community law and that most closely correspond to the functional capacity and the goals of the Community".[81]

Awkward problems of "horizontal divergence" were then created when a principle borrowed from a national system or compounded of elements from several was re-introduced in a reformulation devised by the ECJ. The impact of the "superior" legal order on national legal systems might then be detrimental and contested. The contribution of national legal systems to EC law has been by no means equal. Some national systems may thus find greater difficulty in adaptation than others. Though France had a head-start, the Six came from the same or similar legal families. Diversity increased sharply in 1972, when the accession of the UK and Ireland for the first time introduced the common law family and the entry of Denmark brought in the Scandinavian family. If Pierre Legrand is right,[82] the mindset of common law judges would introduce a particular problem. That new member states are deemed to accept on accession an *acquis*

---

[78] See M Blanquet, "Acceptation et Consecration d'un Concept Communautaire: La Fidelité Communautaire", in S Poillot-Peruzzetto (ed.), *Vers une culture juridique européenne?* (Paris: Montchrestien, 1998).

[79] *The Future of the Judicial System of the European Union (Proposals and Reflections)* 1999.

[80] T Koopmans, "The Birth of European Law at the Cross-Roads of Legal Traditions" (1991) *American Journal of Comparative Law* 493. Emergent general principles of EC law are explored more fully by J Schwarze, *European Administrative Law* (London: Sweet & Maxwell, 1992 (English edition)) and J Schwarze (ed.), *Administrative Law under European Influence* (London: Sweet & Maxwell/Nomos, 1996).

[81] J Schwarze, *European Administrative Law*, n. 80 above, p. 17.

[82] n. 31 above.

created *before their arrival* leads to further difficulties. Heavy use of preliminary reference procedure means that differential patterns of reference may influence a national contribution.[83] To attempt "convergence" by judicial process is, in short, always a complex and essentially haphazard process of "approximation". It satisfies the formal equality requirement of the rule of law principle but cannot guarantee real equality or effectiveness.

Effectiveness does not stop with transposition. Implementation is also necessary, creating a need for enforceable remedies. The case begins to be made for a Community-wide system of judicial remedies, obtainable from all national courts. In the well-known case of *Factortame*, where the applicants applied for interim relief to English courts, the ECJ argued that:[84]

"[T]he full effectiveness of Community law would be . . . impaired if a rule of national law could prevent a court seised of a dispute governed by Community law from granting interim relief in order to ensure the full effectiveness of the judgment to be given on the existence of the rights claimed under Community law. It follows that a court which in those circumstances would grant interim relief, if it were not for a rule of national law, is obliged to set aside that rule".

In the controversial *Francovich* case, the Court justified the creation of a new remedy in damages, unauthorised by the Treaties, in identical language:[85]

"The full effectiveness of Community rules would be impaired and the protection of the rights which they grant would be weakened if individuals were unable to obtain redress when their rights are infringed by a breach of Community law for which a Member State can be held responsible".

But no system of judicial remedies is complete in itself. Neither Court nor Commission is "sufficient alone to ensure the effectiveness of Community law in the broader social sense, in particular in so far as it entails the commitment of citizens, popular participation and political legitimacy. For this purpose, it may be suggested, other institutions, processes, tools and techniques are also required".[86] In other words, implementation depends on national administrative authorities, a dependence likely, as argued in an earlier section, to produce very variable outcomes.

---

[83] For statistics, see A Stone Sweet and T Brunell, "The European Courts and National Courts: A Statistical Analysis of Preliminary References, 1961–95" (1998) 5 *Journal of European Public Policy* 66.

[84] Case C–213/89 R v. *Secretary of State for Transport ex p Factortame (No 3)* [1990] ECR I–2433.

[85] Joined Cases 6, 9/90 *Francovich and Bonafaci* v. *Italy* [1991] ECR I–5357.

[86] F Snyder, "The Effectiveness of European Community Law: Institutions, Processes, Tools and Techniques" (1993) 56 *Modern Law Review* 19, 52.

The early case law of the ECJ recognised national procedural autonomy. The *Saarland* ruling stated that "in the absence of Community rules on this subject, it is for the domestic legal system of each member state to designate the courts having jurisdiction and to determine the protection of the rights which citizens have from the direct effect of Community law".[87] This principle was subject only to the proviso that procedural rules must not (i) be less favourable than those governing similar domestic actions nor (ii) render virtually impossible or excessively difficult the exercise of rights conferred by Community law.

Gradually, this autonomy was eroded. A key ruling was *Johnston*,[88] where the ECJ held that a statutory "ouster clause", which required an employment tribunal to treat a ministerial certificate of "public interest immunity" as conclusive, must cede to the "general principle of effective judicial protection". *Factortame* and *Francovich* mark further key stages in the process of "constitutionalisation", whereby EC law can penetrate with impunity the area of legal procedure previously supposed to be reserved for the national legal systems. By the 1990s, the procedural rights of defendants were being described as "principles of higher rank which prevail over all other rules" and commentators were speaking of the virtual erosion of the rule of national procedural autonomy.[89]

Procedures can also permeate national systems in the guise of human rights law. ECHR Articles 5, 6 and 13 all guarantee access to justice[90] and *Johnston* merely mirrors in EC law the right of access to court recognised and protected by ECHR Article 6(1). It is fair to say that ECHR Article 6(1) has been generously interpreted; indeed, a case law has developed around it which would certainly not have been foreseen by the original signatories.[91] The degree of judicially ordained procedural convergence has been so great as to induce the complaint that Article 6(1) risks bringing within the ambit of the ECHR nearly the whole of administrative justice.[92] In the name of "levelling up", the extension of ECHR

---

[87] Case 33/76 *Rewe* v. *Landwirtschaftskammer Saarland* [1976] ECR 1989, 1997. See also Case 158/80 *Rewe-Handellgesellschaft Nord mbll and another* v. *Hauptzollamt Kiel* [1981] ECR 1805.

[88] Case 222/84 *Johnston* v. *Royal Ulster Constabulary* [1986] ECR 1651. See also Case C–208/90 *Emmott* v. *Minister for Social Welfare* [1991] ECR I–2925.

[89] K Lenaerts and J Vanhamme, "Procedural Rights of Private Parties in the Community Administrative Process" (1997) 34 *Common Market Law Review* 531; R Craufurd Smith, "Remedies for Breaches of EU Law in National Courts: Legal Variation and Selection", in P Craig and G de Búrca (eds.), *The Evolution of EU Law* (Oxford: Oxford University Press, 1999), p. 287.

[90] ECHR Art. 5 deals with pre-trial process; Art. 13 demands an "effective remedy" for infringements of ECHR rights; Art. 6 requires a fair and public hearing by an independent and impartial tribunal in the determination of a person's civil rights and obligations.

[91] D Harris, M O'Boyle and C Warbrick, *Law of the European Convention on Human Rights* (London: Butterworths, 1995), ch. 6.

[92] R Abraham, "Les principes généraux de la protection juridictionnelle administrative en Europe: L'influence des jurisprudences européennes" (1997) 9 *European Public Law Review* 577, 582. A classic example is Case C–222/86 *UNECTEF* v. *Heylens* [1987] ECR 4097.

Article 6(1) to the standard fare of administrative justice is imperilling established and respected administrative adjudicatory systems.[93]

The Maastricht Treaty introduced a provision on human rights in the TEU
that was made justiciable by the Treaty of Amsterdam requiring the EU to
"respect fundamental rights, as guaranteed by the European Convention for the
Protection of Human Rights and Fundamental Freedoms signed in Rome on
4 November 1950 and as they result from the constitutional traditions common
to the Member States, as general principles of constitutional law".[94] An EU
Charter of Rights can only accelerate the process of convergence. Article 47 of
the Charter[95] parallels ECHR Article 6(1), while Article 41 creates a "Right to
Good Administration", which includes in paragraph 2 the right to a hearing
and reasoned decisions. The ECJ technique of constitutionalising human
rights principles, directly or indirectly borrowed from the ECHR, is thus
legitimated.

At first sight, the extension of human rights into relations between citizens
and the administration seems a wholly benign development. If the universality
of human rights is accepted as axiomatic, then their extension and co-ordination
must surely be a "levelling up". This is, however, a dangerous simplification. An
impugned procedure may not be inferior; it may simply be different. There is,
for example, no absolute advantage of adversarial over inquisitorial procedure;
one is not inevitably more independent or inherently less arbitrary than the
other; each can operate fairly.[96] Yet by stressing the independence criterion, the
Court of Human Rights may prioritise the paradigm of adversarial justice, in
which an impartial judge mediates between opposing parties. Again, some societies have strong cultures of "non-law", a preference which may be reflected in
their procedures. To rule out ombudsmen as a remedy because their recommendations are not technically binding alters the very concept of justice in a society.
As Ronny Abraham argues, cultural uniformity precludes experiment and
creates a real danger of stultification. He sees too a threat to minority cultures
in the[97]

> "condemnation of minority institutions and procedures, first considered curious, then
> abnormal, finally suspect in terms of the principles of due process. It is not because an

[93] E.g., the Dutch procedure of Crown appeal in *Benthem* v. *Netherlands* (1985) 8 EHHR 1;
noted by Verheij, "Dutch administrative law after Benthem's case" (1990) *Public Law* 23. The practice of allowing members of administrative formations of a Conseil d'Etat to participate in adjudication, *Procola* v. *Luxembourg* (1996) 22 EHRR 193; noted by R Drago, "Un nouveau juge
administratif", in *Ecrits en hommage à Jean Foyer* (Paris: Presses Universitaires de France, 1997) pp.
454–5; English habeas corpus procedure in *Vilrajah* v. *UK* (1992) 14 EHRR 248 and judicial review
procedure in *Lustig-Prean and others* v. *UK* (judgment of 27 Sept. 1999) 29 EHRR 548 (not on Art.
6(1) case).
[94] TEU, Art. 6. See Part Four of this book.
[95] n. 7 above.
[96] M Damaska, *The Faces of Justice and State Authority* (New Haven: Yale University Press,
1986). And see H Lindblom, "Harmony of the Legal Spheres" (1997) 5 *European Review of Private
Law* 11, 20.
[97] Abraham, "Les principes généraux", n. 92 above, p. 582.

institution or rule is to be found only in one, or in a small number of countries, that it is to be adjudged bad; the majority is not always right".

Note how Abraham, like Friedman, links procedures with culture.

When EC law is in tension with national constitutional law, culture clashes may be particularly acute because of the sanctity which nations (rightly) attach to their constitutions, often categorised as "higher" law. In the celebrated case of *SPUC* v. *Grogan*,[98] a "right to life", rated as "fundamental" and protected by a prohibition on abortion in the Irish Constitution, came into conflict with the economic freedom of access to services in the EC Treaty. Even though the ECJ managed to avoid an outright clash, the case came under fire because of the clash of competing norms.[99]

Cases which seemingly raise quite simple questions of procedure may in practice involve significant clashes of value. *Factortame* overturned the doctrine of parliamentary sovereignty, keystone of the British constitution.[100] In *Peterbroeck* and *van Schijndel*,[101] the question was whether a national judge, faced with a situation in which EC law may be applicable but has not been pleaded, must raise the point of his own motion. Behind this technical question lay a deep constitutional question concerning the nature of adjudication in French-style legal systems.[102] In thoughtful and considered opinions in these cases, A-G Jacobs set out the case for self-restraint:[103]

> "[I]f the view were taken that national procedural rules must always yield to Community law, that would . . . unduly subvert established principles underlying the legal systems of the Member States. It would go further than is necessary for effective judicial protection. It could be regarded as infringing the principle of proportionality and, in a broad sense, the principle of subsidiarity, which reflects precisely the balance which the Court has sought to attain in this area for many years. It would also give rise to widespread anomalies, since the effect would be to afford greater protection to rights which are not, by virtue of being Community rights, inherently of greater importance than rights recognized by national law".

---

[98] Case C–159/90 *SPUC* v. *Grogan* [1991] ECR I–4685. The Court ruled that an information service on abortion facilities was a "service" but that the students' union involved did not provide a service either directly or indirectly through funding.

[99] From the torrent of comment, see J Coppel and A O'Neill, "The European Court of Justice: Taking Rights Seriously" (1992) 12 *Legal Studies* 227.

[100] P Craig, "Report on the United Kingdom" in A-M Slaughter, A Stone Sweet, J Weiler (eds.), *The European Courts and National Courts—Doctrine and Jurisprudence*, (Oxford: Hart, 1998), p. 196.

[101] Case C 312/93 *Peterbroeck, Van Campenhout et Cie* v. *Belgium* [1995] ECR I–4599. Here the Court rejected the advice of the Advocate-General, rulng that the Cour d'Appel must raise a point of EC law of its own motion where appeal is the first opportunity on which the point can be raised. In joined Cases C–430, 431/93 *van Schijndel & van Veren* v. *Stichting Pensioenfonds voor Fysiotherapeuten* [1995] ECR I–4705, a similar action failed on the narrow ground that a point of EC law based on *new facts* cannot be raised on appeal.

[102] On the consequences for the French legal system, see J Delicostopoulos "L'Influence du droit européen quant aux pouvoirs du juge judiciare national sur le fait et le droit" (1997) 6 *Justices* 117.

[103] *van Schijndel*, paras. 24, 25, 27.

To resolve such clashes merely by reference to the operation of the supremacy doctrine, a short cut to a pre-ordained result, is deeply problematic; it resolves the problem superficially but not at a deep level. According to John Gray, rights are[104]

"never the bottom line in moral or political theory or practice. They are conclusions, end-results of long chains of reasoning from commonly accepted premises. Rights have little authority or content in the absence of a common ethical life. They are conventions that are durable only when they express a moral consensus. When ethical disagreement is deep and wide an appeal to rights cannot resolve it. Indeed, it may make such conflict dangerously unmanageable . . . Looking to rights to arbitrate deep conflicts—rather than seeking to moderate them through the compromises of politics—is a recipe for a low-intensity civil war".

This is difficult stuff for lawyers, trained to view the legal system as a rational ordering or ranking of legal principle, and naturally inclined towards the conception of judicial decision as the "single right answer", unchallengeable save by appeal.[105] But to pretend—as lawyers so often do—that rights are uncontestable is to divest them of their deep content and meaning; to substitute a thin for a thick, a legal for a political, definition of rights. The purpose and effect of articulating judgements about values in the language of rights is, by endowing them with the sanctity of law, to transfer the power of decision from legislatures to courts. When this process takes place in the EC legal system, the doctrine of legal supremacy operates so as to remove the power of decision from national to European level, entrenching the rights in question at a level beyond political reach. This is Wincottt's "perversion of democracy" duplicated.

CONCLUSIONS

The case for pluralism advanced in this chapter forms part of a broad political debate about governance in the Community: integrationism versus subsidiarity. Integrationism was once seen as something of a loyalty test; today pluralism is squarely on the political agenda. We are becoming accustomed to the concept of subsidiarity introduced by the Maastricht Treaty and (more gingerly) to the "multi-speed Europe" and "variable geometry" of the Treaty of Amsterdam. Treaty status is making the ideas respectable. If the Community is to embrace within its boundaries a new swathe of entrants with different cultural traditions, political expectations and capabilities, acceptance of diversity will become a necessity. It will be essential to treat the Community as a confederal association,

---

[104] J Gray, *False Dawn, The Delusions of Global Capitalism* (London: Granta Books, 1998), p. 109. See also A Bayefsky, "Cultural Sovereignty, Relativism and International Human Rights: New Excuses for Old Strategies" (1996) 9 *Ratio Juris* 42.

[105] R Dworkin, *Taking Rights Seriously* (London: Duckworth, 1977) and *Law's Empire*, (London: Fontana, 1986).

weighted to the bottom level.[106] Co-operative political activity will be based on strong existing national and sub-national structures which legitimate it.

The purpose of this chapter is to link this wide, general debate about constitutions and governance to a narrower debate, conducted mainly between lawyers, about harmonisation and convergence of legal systems. In so doing, it has questioned the use of law as an instrument of political integration, arguing that legal integration in a political vacuum tilts the balance of power from government and legislature unacceptably far towards the judiciary, modifying in the process relationships between the EU and member states (the double perversion of democracy.) Implicitly, the chapter also questions law's integrative force. Paradoxically, legal integration may be disintegrative. Essentially parasitic in nature, the EC legal order balances precariously on the props of national legal orders. Clashes between the orders which cause repercussions on national constitutions will in time rebound directly on the Community.

Again, the chapter has attacked both the vision of a "level playing field" of procedural rights and the concept of "levelling up" as essentially simplistic and misleading ideas. The realities which underlie the legal doctrines of equality and efficiency demand a more complex and sophisticated argument about the commensurability of rights and values. Arguing that legal systems are culturally linked, the chapter notices differing attitudes to legal remedy and judicialisation. The first division of competences between national legal orders and the EC was sensitive to these differences but a blurring of the boundary has been noted. Border raids in the name of integrationism have led to expanded competence for EC law and its progenitor, the ECJ.

The ECJ was designed as an international tribunal with a strictly limited remit but it made short work of this restricted mandate. It soon moved to establish the supremacy of the law which it administered and had ruled itself alone competent to administer, while alongside it fitted itself out with a toolkit of powerful remedies, used to bind the legal orders of the member states. A model of law emerged more formalist and more coercive than the national legal orders of any member state would offer and arguably ill-adapted to the non-statal constitutional context in which it has to operate. The supremacy principle represents the installation at the heart of a postmodern "Community of Nations" of a Kelsenist conception of legal sovereignty. Pooled sovereignty ought to imply the acknowledgement of "co-ordinately valid legal systems"[107]—the EC legal system as one among equals.

But if it is proving difficult to move far from the concept of sovereignty in the political arena, then it is harder still to eliminate it inside the legal order. The theory of law as an instrument of command and coercion has qualities of

---

[106] P Eleftheriadis, "Begging the Constitutional Question" (1998) 36 *Journal of Common Market Studies* 255.

[107] N MacCormick, "Liberalism, Nationalism and the Post-sovereign State", in R Bellamy and D Castiglione (eds.), *Constitutionalism in Transformation: European and Theoretical Perspectives* (Oxford: Blackwells, 1996).

endurance; the tiger is not dead but sleeps. The rush to "constitutionalise" human rights and to extrapolate general constitutional principles has permitted the ECJ to buy into the classic hierarchy of legal norms. Rights, in Dworkin's inimitable phrase, are "trumps" through which courts gain power and legitimate their own claim to sovereignty. And sovereignty is very much the business of courts.

A plural legal framework not only implies respect for national legal orders but also a non-hierarchical method of mediating conflict. Writing in a federal context, Fritz Scharpf spells out the consequences of a plural adjudicative regime:[108]

> "[T]he recognition of a bipolar constitutional order prevents the one-sided orientation of judicial review towards the enumerated powers of the central government, which is otherwise characteristic of federal states. It requires the court to balance competing jurisdictional claims with a view not only to their substantive justification, but also to the manner in which the powers are exercised. The criterion is *mutual compatibility*, and the characteristic outcome is not the displacement of one jurisdiction by the other, but the obligation of both to choose mutually acceptable means when performing the proper functions of government at each level".

The initial intention for the EC was of non-confrontational, non-hierarchical, co-operative judicial machinery; under EC Article 234 (ex 177), the ECJ enjoyed a *consultative* function, advising in case of doubt on the meaning of EC law. Later, as the Court's integrationist culture and mindset hardened, a distorted vision surfaced of a "quasi-federal instrument for reviewing the compatibility of national laws with Community law".[109] The erstwhile adviser had stepped into the untenable position of partisan umpire—Scharpf's asymmetrical monster—and had into the bargain acquired enforcement powers. There was over-use of a reference procedure which had shown itself insensitive to the balancing exercises for which it came to be used.[110] There is need for a true "judicial dialogue", with an opening for national courts to indicate the potential impact of decisions on the national legal system. This would force them to articulate their reasoning in the language of that system, reinforcing domestic accountability by submitting judgments to scrutiny in the national arena where their impact needs to be weighed and tested. The ground rule of national procedural autonomy needs to be reinstated, with departures from that rule justified by reference to the twin principles of proportionality and subsidiarity.

The argument of this chapter has been presented somewhat starkly. There is room for a median position between the extreme poles of integrationism and unregenerate pluralism. There are today signs that the ECJ is beginning to understand this. Recent case law is more tentative, more thoughtful and more

---

[108] F Scharpf, "Community and autonomy: multi-level policy-making in the European Union" (1994) 1 *Journal of European Public Policy* 219, 225.

[109] F Mancini and D Keeling, "Democracy and the European Court of Justice", n. 64 above, at 184.

[110] A point developed by T de la Mare, "Article 177 and Legal Integration", in P Craig and G de Búrca (eds.), *The Evolution of EU Law* (Oxford: Oxford University Press, 1999), at 227.

sensitive to national sensibilities. The Court has recently suggested too that national courts should "apply Community law themselves, and not . . . resort too hastily to the solution afforded by a reference to the Court of Justice".[111] These could be signs of a new judicial mindset which would welcome legal diversity manifested in "co-ordinately valid legal systems". Yet this welcome development in no way undercuts the argumentation of this chapter. Case law can change. It is a pluralist mindset which needs to be permanently installed at Luxembourg.

Essentially the case for harmonised judicial protection rests on theories of the market:[112]

> "If a market is to flourish, disputes arising out of business conducted in the market must be resolved consistently with one another, and that requires more than a uniform substantive law. Distortion is bound to occur if the mode of litigation, with all that that implies both by way of procedural techniques and by way of their implications for costs, delays, appeals, enforcement of judgments and so on, varies substantially from one place to another. The idea of a single 'internal market' requires for its complete realisation a single system for the judicial resolution of disputes."

Surely this is a thin argument to set against the deep values of heritage, legal culture and constitutional legitimacy?

---

[111] Court of Justice, "The Future of the Judicial System", n. 79 above, p. 24. Contrast C Barnard and E Sharpston, "The Changing Face of Article 177 References" (1997) 34 *Common Market Law Review* 1113; D O'Keeffe, "Is the Spirit of Article 177 under Attack? Preliminary References and Admissibility" (1998) 23 *European Law Review* 509.

[112] T Jolowicz, "Introduction", in H Storme (ed.), *Approximation of Judiciary Law in the European Union* (Dordrecht: Kluwer and Martinus Nijhoff, 1994), p. xiii.

12

Public Law, Europeanisation, and Convergence: Can Comparatists Contribute?

PIERRE LEGRAND

INTRODUCTION

M^Y PROPOSED ANSWER to the question that forms the title of this essay is organised into four parts which can be summarised thus.

1. "[T]he comparati[st] presumes similarities between different jurisdictions in the very act of searching for them".[1] As long as it remains driven by the reductionist urge to confine its analytical framework to the identification of sameness in the formulation of statutes or the outcome of judicial decisions across jurisdictions, comparative legal studies has little to offer the debate on Europeanisation (other than the pseudoscientific respectability connected with institutional fetishism). In fact, this brand of comparative research is positively misleading in the way it propounds the presence of commonalities across legal "systems" which can exist solely at the most superficial level and are, therefore, devoid of epistemological value.

2. Only if it is prepared to move beyond the juxtaposition of substantive and adjectival posited law and if it is willing to overcome its seemingly obsessional urge to suppress difference across laws can comparative research about law meaningfully influence the ongoing conversation concerning legal convergence in Europe.

3. As the discipline fundamentally reconstructs itself and as comparatists undertake to show greater sensitivity to the characteristic features of laws and experiences of law that are not theirs, comparative legal studies can be expected to address the limits within which any "convergence" agenda must operate and the constraints which, ultimately, must defeat it.

4. The realisation that legal convergence can never fully transcend the manifestations of localism, including the historicity of law, is not to be regretted. No

---

[1] J Vining, *The Authoritative and the Authoritarian* (Chicago: University of Chicago Press, 1986), p. 65.

matter how insistently the bureaucratic ethos of technical/universal homogeneity promotes its centralising and uniformising ambitions, the reformulation of legal Europe cannot condone a disempowering of local histories in a context where the specificity of European legal discourse arguably lies precisely in its historicity.

Ex abundante cautela, I want to make three brief observations regarding terminology. First, I regard the categorical division between "public law" and "private law" as a social construction of limited analytical value because of the way in which this scheme distorts legal thought and practices by conveying a false sense of the orderliness of both.[2] Moreover, I bear in mind that while these labels are "terms of art" in the civil-law world they are but "plain English words" in the common-law tradition.[3] Second, I use "Europeanisation" to refer to legal integration within the European Community only. Third, I understand "convergence" in its ordinary meaning. This word is derived from the Latin "*convergere*", that is, "to tend toward the same meeting point together". "Convergence", therefore, suggests "merger" or "fusion"; it connotes "unity" or "uniformity". That which "converges" is that which purports to reach the same point. In physics, for instance, converging rays are rays that merge at a given point. And, one will say that various roads converge on the village from different directions. The notion of a common meeting point, therefore, underlies the idea of convergence. Without it, the rays or the roads would be parallel or perpendicular or whatever.

COMPARATIVE LEGAL STUDIES AND REDUCTIONISM

Not everyone would concur with Nietzsche who claimed that, along with love, avarice, envy, conscience, "pious respect for tradition", and cruelty, comparative legal studies "give[s] color to existence".[4] To illustrate: comparative work about law has been described as "voluminous, obsessively repetitious, and sterile—a literature that feeds and grows, like a psychic cancer, upon logical classification and reclassification and technical refinement and sub-refinement, without limit and with a minimum of external reference and relevance".[5] It is

---

[2] For critical observations on "public law", see G Frankenberg, "Remarks on the Philosophy and Politics of Public Law", (1998) 18 *Legal Studies* 177. For an argument advocating the artificial character of the distinction between "public law" and "private law", see D Oliver, *Common Values and the Public–Private Divide* (London: Butterworths, 1999).

[3] G Samuel, "The Impact of European Integration on Private Law: A Comment" (1998) 18 *Legal Studies* 167, pp. 167–8 and 171.

[4] F Nietzsche, *The Gay Science*, trans. by Walter Kaufmann (New York: Vintage, 1974), p. 81 [originally published in German in 1882].

[5] M S McDougal, "The Comparative Study of Law for Policy Purposes: Value Clarification as an Instrument of Democratic World Order" (1952) 1 *American Journal of Comparative Law* 24, p. 29.

also said to "[t]urn a blind eye to everything but surfaces",[6] castigated as "super-ficial",[7] pronounced as marking "a somewhat disappointing field",[8] or rejected as "a grossly impoverished genre".[9] Other references to the "extremely prob-lematical, if not precarious, condition" of comparative legal studies,[10] "the mediocre quality of analyses allegedly comparative",[11] the "theoretical poverty" of comparative work,[12] or to comparative analysis of law as an "exhausted scholarly tradition" remain current.[13] Indeed, it is argued that comparative legal studies "finds itself in the condition of botany and zoology before Linnaeus and of anatomy before Cuvier":[14] it is plagued by composite empiricism; it is aggregative rather than interpretive.

Stigmatised as "bankrupt", comparative legal studies features "scholarship that scorns ideas and fixes its gaze lovingly on the black-letter rules of the pri-vate law".[15] In effect, the "Muse Trivia"—"the same Goddess who inspires stamp collectors, accountants, and the hoarders of baseball statistics"—has been the "animating spirit" within the field.[16] Thus, "[o]ne of the enduring problems of comparative law has been its inability to demonstrate convincingly the theoretical value of doctrinal comparisons separated from comparative analysis of the entire political, economic and social . . . matrix in which legal doctrine and procedures exist".[17] Richard Tur's indictment summarises the position well: "[t]he not yet discredited conception of comparative law as the comparison of the law—that is, of the detailed content of the positive law—of two or more countries, a process which ends when one runs out of countries, as

---

[6] L M Friedman, "Some Thoughts on Comparative Legal Culture", in D S Clark (ed.), *Comparative and Private International Law: Essays in Honor of John Henry Merryman on His Seventieth Birthday* (Berlin: Duncker & Humblot, 1990), p. 52.

[7] A Watson, *Legal Transplants* (2nd edn., Athens, Georgia: University of Georgia Press, 1993), p. 10.

[8] M Shapiro, *Courts* (Chicago: University of Chicago Press, 1981), p. vii.

[9] S Roberts, "Comment [on Lawrence Rosen: 'Islamic Law as Common Law']", in J Feest and E Blankenburg (eds.), *Changing Legal Cultures* (Oñati: International Institute for the Sociology of Law, 1997), p. 44.

[10] J Hall, *Comparative Law and Social Theory* (Baton Rouge: Louisiana State University Press, 1963), p. 6.

[11] F Rigaux, "Le droit comparé comme science appliquée" (1978) *Revue de droit international et de droit comparé* 65, p. 73 ["*la médiocre qualité des analyses prétendues comparatives*"].

[12] L-J Constantinesco, *Traité de droit comparé*, vol. 3: *La science des droits comparés* (Paris: Economica, 1983), p. 21 ["*misère théorique*"].

[13] J H Merryman, "Comparative Law and Social Change: On the Origins, Style, Decline and Revival of the Law and Development Movement" (1977) 25 *American Journal of Comparative Law* 457, p. 482.

[14] Constantinesco, n. 12 above, p. 21, n. 5 ["*(le droit comparé) se trouve dans la situation de la botanique et de la zoologie avant Linné et de l'anatomie avant Cuvier*"].

[15] W Ewald, "Comparative Jurisprudence (II): The Logic of Legal Transplants" (1995) 43 *American Journal of Comparative Law* 489, p. 492.

[16] W Ewald, "Comparative Jurisprudence (I): What Was it Like to Try a Rat?" (1995) 143 *University of Pennsylvania Law Review* 1889, p. 1892.

[17] R Cotterell, "The Concept of Legal Culture", in D Nelken (ed.), *Comparing Legal Cultures* (Aldershot: Dartmouth, 1997), p. 13.

it were, ought by now to have been rejected as incompetence masquerading as jurisprudential expertise".[18] Such banishment, however, has yet to happen.

The proliferation of books claiming to bear on comparative legal studies in recent years, especially in Europe, has become farcical. The more there are, the more they prove comparative analysis of law to be disoriented and insubstantial. These snippety compilations—the legal equivalent of guides to car mechanics—are a symptom of disease, not a proof of health. If comparatists knew what they were doing, they would not tolerate them, let alone adulate them. Typically, the texts on offer propound normalised schemes based on rational and (so-called) scientific principles showing small regard for context and none for contingency. They relegate the cognitive asymmetries between the civil-law and common-law worlds, for example, to ignorable differences, to the realm of epiphenomena, and show confusion between the legitimate desire to overcome barriers of communication across legal traditions and the alleged need to elucidate presumed similarities. To focus on selected titbits of black-letter law without any consideration of the historical, social, economic, or cultural environment is to deceive the reader on a massive scale by intimating to him that the brittle similarities as regards fact-patterns and judicial outcomes matter more than the traditionary differences that dictate the epistemological framework within which a case is addressed (an approach evidently unconvincing to anyone who has studied and taught both in the civil-law and common-law worlds). Insensitivity to questions of cultural heterogeneity fails to do justice to the situated, local properties of knowledge which are no less powerful because they may remain inchoate and uninstitutionalised. In the way it refuses to address plurijurality at the deep, cultural level, the rhetoric of comparative legal studies simply deprives itself of intercultural and epistemological validity. It deserts serious thought for earnest prostration before the instrumentalist sabotage of cognition.

As long as the apparent intellectual demands associated with entry into the field remain so low, the situation is unlikely to improve: comparative work about law will continue to elide and occlude the difficulty of the comparative enterprise. No one will impersonate a physicist, because the extensive formation in mathematics is a well-known pre-requisite. Curiously, it is thought that comparative work about law can be achieved without particular skill or preparation. A smattering of a foreign language is sufficient for many of my colleagues and students boldly to engage in so-called "comparative" legal studies and, seemingly without any compunction, openly to style themselves as "comparatists". While the consequences of poor propaedeutics may be less spectacular for an apprentice-sorcerer playing comparatist rather than physicist, they remain no less present. The formalised and totalised description of those foreign rules or precepts of law regarded as relevant that will be offered as comparative

---

[18] R H S Tur, "The Dialectic of General Jurisprudence and Comparative Law" (1977) *Juridical Review* 238, p. 238.

analysis will suffer from distortions (such as the presentation of materials through a maladapted intellectual framework or the introduction of arguments from the "system" under observation through a misconceived prioritisation), but mostly from omissions; it will sin less through what it asserts than on account of what it will have failed to ask. For the comparatist, to formulate the apposite questions is at least as important as to devise a response. Any comparative analysis of law is a corollary of what counts as an interesting question for a comparatist operating in a certain place at a certain time. All the data is in existence, if virtually so, before the comparatist comes to it. But it will be his to label and organise—to "reify"—only if he thinks of asking the questions that will allow it to be seized.[19]

LEARNING TO COMPARE WITH CULTURE

I argue that comparatists should move away from hubristic programmes engendering a frenetic and hasty search for commonalities-which-clearly-must-be-there-since-we-want-them-there. My goal is to redeem local knowledge, best described in terms of its plasticity, pliability, diversity, and adaptability. I advocate a general theoretical framework for an innovative and militant approach to comparative legal studies which argues for greater sensitivity to the characteristic features of laws and experiences of law that are not ours. I claim that meaningful comparative work demands the public intervention of critical individuals who accept that, within the structural constraints set by the human interpretive apparatus, understanding of a law or of an experience of law other than one's own can only arise from thorough cultural contextualisation. Comparative legal studies, so I claim, is best envisaged as a perspective fostering a resistance to the trends toward the ever-increasing technological standardisation of law and the ready political subordination of the lawyer (within or without the academy) to the comforting values of orthodoxy and reiteration. In my view, the vocation of comparative work about law is intrinsically scholastic and its agenda is, therefore, incongruent with that of practitioners or lawmakers seeking to elicit epigrammatic answers from foreign laws.[20] What is required in an age of globalisation is not so much yet more technical knowledge about what a foreign law says on any given point at any given time, for one can relatively easily consult an encyclopaedia or enlist the help of a foreign lawyer to ascertain such rudimentary data. Rather, there is an urgent need to understand how foreign legal communities think about the law, why they think about the law as they do, why they would find it difficult to think about the law in any other way, and *how their thought differs from ours.* If Joseph Weiler is correct,

---

[19] I paraphrase P Veyne, *Comment on écrit l'histoire* (Paris: Seuil, 1971), p. 152.
[20] E.g., P W Kahn, *The Cultural Study of Law* (Chicago: University of Chicago Press, 1999), p. 5: "the intellectual project of understanding a culture of law should not be held hostage to the question of its practical consequences".

"[t]he treatment of the celebrated 'other', the other in our selves, in our midst, and the other clamoring at our doors or shores is an issue extremely high on the public agenda in most European societies".[21] It is this kind of fundamental information about alterity-in-the-law that comparatists are uniquely suited to provide and that they should be seeking to disseminate, leaving the technical updates to practitioners specialising in a given foreign law. I suggest that this approach to comparative legal studies can best be effectuated by securing pertinent anthropological, sociological, philosophical, historical, and psychological insights. Indeed, I claim that the comparatist can only account in a meaningful way for how the law is constructed in a foreign jurisdiction through an interdisciplinary investigation.

For instance, in enacting a *loi* for the reasons they do and in the way they do, as a product of the way they think, with the desires and ambitions they have, in enacting a particular *loi* (and not others), the French are not just doing *that*: they are also doing something typically French and are thus alluding to a modality of legal experience that is intrinsically theirs. In this sense, because it communicates the French sensibility to law, the *loi* can serve as a focus of enquiry into legal Frenchness and into Frenchness *tout court*. It need not be regarded only as a *loi* in terms of its effectivity as rule. There is more to *loi*ness than *loi*-as-rule. Indeed, *loi*-as-rule is a "cognitive intoxicant" bound to entail persistent miscognition of the French experience of the legal.[22] A *loi* is necessarily an incorporative cultural form. As a compactly allusive accretion of cultural elements, of traditionary features that constitute individual autonomy and identity within a community, it is supported by impressive historical and ideological formations. A rule does not have any empirical existence that can be significantly detached from the world of meanings that characterises a legal culture; on the contrary, it is "encrusted, beyond lexical-grammatical definition, with phonetic, historical, social, idiomatic overtones and undertones. It carries with it connotations, associations, previous usages, and even graphic, pictorial values and suggestions (the look, the 'shape' of words)".[23] The part never states its own meaning, for it is an expression and a synthesis of the whole assumptive background: it conveys morally and politically resonant ascriptions.[24] And it is precisely this ability to

---

[21] J H H Weiler, *The Constitution of Europe* (Cambridge: Cambridge University Press, 1999), p. 326.

[22] M A Schneider, *Culture and Enchantment* (Chicago: University of Chicago Press, 1993), p. 40.

[23] G Steiner, *Errata* (London: Weidenfeld and Nicolson, 1997), pp. 18–19.

[24] See J Bell, "English Law and French Law—Not so Different?", in *Current Legal Problems 1995*, vol. 48, pt 2 (Oxford: Oxford University Press, 1995), p. 82: "[i]f an English lawyer says that his legal system does not accommodate 'gratuitous contracts', because a 'contract' is conceptually a promise for reward, what he is really saying is that English law is not convinced, as a matter of values, that gratuitous promises, as such, should be enforced (though they may be enforced sometimes as trusts, bailments, etc.)". A related point was made by Mill in more general terms as he observed that "[d]ifferences of legislation are not inherent and ultimate diversities are not properties of Kinds". Rather, he wrote, "[i]f . . . two nations differ in this portion of their institutions, it is from some difference in their position, and thence in their apparent interests, or in some portion or other of their opinions, habits, and tendencies; which opens a view of further differences without any assignable limit, capable of operating on their industrial prosperity, as well as on every other feature

see the whole in the part, to move away from the underbrush of detail and lead to a clearing of responsive perception, that defines the interpretive competence of the comparatist.[25] The task of comparative legal studies is the understanding of the semantic field to which the rule belongs, the appreciation of the latent patterns of interest and struggle that shape the existence of postulated realities, the production of associations to which the rule is a clue. These connections can be "horizontal" or "vertical", that is, they can take place across fields as the rule is linked to what can be found elsewhere at the same time (including other rules) or within the same field as prior expressions of the rule are highlighted in order to allow for a diachronic panorama.[26] A comparison is an archipelago.

Because a manifestation of posited law exists in a larger cognitive framework, the comparatist must apprehend it as being more than a short-lived event with a clearly ascertainable beginning and an identifiable end and relate it to other, whether prior or concurrent, legal-cultural phenomena in a way that will make the particular proposition look less like an arbitrary incident and more like the manifestation of a coherent and intelligible pattern. Thus, the rule becomes the unknowing articulator or vector of a cultural sensibility which, while it is actually inscribed in the textual fragments themselves, requires the observer's ampliative acts of interpretation to come to light. A rule can be regarded as compressed knowledge. As the comparatist invests meaning into the language of the text through a process of abstraction from the particular, he discloses the effect of compression by showing the rule to be expandable.

AN EXCURSUS ON CULTURE

It is probably fair to say that one of the most pervasive beliefs encountered in the humanities is the conviction that in some meaningful way the individual owes his existence to society; in other words, that personalities, needs, and wants are nurtured and sustained by the community in which human beings live. But the idea of the social nature of the individual is as elusive as it is ubiquitous, because it seems at once to be saying something so incontrovertible as to be devoid of methodological significance *and* to be advancing a thesis so radical as to threaten the very possibility of human individuality and self-determination. *How does culture work?*

of their condition, in more ways than can be enumerated or imagined": J S Mill, *A System of Logic Ratiocinative and Inductive*, in *Collected Works of John Stuart Mill*, ed. by J M Robson, vol. 8 (Toronto: University of Toronto Press, 1974), bk 6, ch. 7, p. 882 [originally published in 1843].

[25] H-G Gadamer, *Truth and Method*, 2nd rev. edn. trans. by J Weinsheimer and D G Marshall (London: Sheed and Ward, 1989), p. 190: "the meaning of the part can be discovered only from the context—i.e., ultimately from the whole" [originally published in German in 1960]; C Taylor, "Interpretation and the Sciences of Man", in P Rabinow and W M Sullivan (eds.), *Interpretive Social Science: A Second Look* (Berkeley: University of California Press, 1987), p. 36.

[26] See C E Schorske, *Fin-de-siècle Vienna* (Cambridge: Cambridge University Press, 1979), pp. xxi–xxii.

As he engages in social forms of activity, the individual ascribes significance and value to his environment. Objects, for instance, are endowed with social meaning beyond their materiality or strictly physical nature. This ascription of significance is a function of the purposes for which the object was created and of the uses to which it is put. When "that thing" is called a "pen", it acquires an additional form of existence at the level of meaning which was never part of its physical nature as such. It is through this ascriptive process that the world becomes an object of significance beyond its raw materiality and that it can, therefore, become an object of thought. This is to say that thought can only emerge in an environment of socially constituted meanings or that thought is only possible for an individual once he has been socialised into the practices of a community (for example, within the family or at school). It is the appropriation or internalisation of these practices which, literally, "creates" the individual mind. Since the practices themselves inscribe various collective allegiances, such as national, geographical, ethnic, religious, and linguistic affiliation, the individual mind can reasonably be said to be formed as it is inaugurated into the thought processes or beliefs of collectivities.[27] Rather than stand in opposition to society, the individual is thus "one of its forms of existence".[28] It is in this way that Karl Mannheim observes how the thinking which arises within a community is not the product of individuals, but rather that of a group having developed a particular "style of thought" by way of continual responses to a range of situations which members of the group confront on account of the specific position in which the group finds itself.[29] Thought is, therefore, culturally constituted in a very significant way. Otherwise, responses to events would be *ad hoc*, springing not from a sense of meaning, but only from ideas called into being by the immediate circumstances or the current mental state of the individual.

For comparative legal studies to apprehend law as culture thus attests to a commitment to a unit of analysis that includes individuals and their social milieu and that no longer regards the technical dimension of the posited law as a controlling centre of the action. Culture is made to function as an omnibus category which allows the comparatist to point to the posited law not only in terms of its materiality (the rules and so forth) but, more importantly, at the level of its meaning which alone can reveal why the posited law was created in the way it was (and not otherwise) and disclose the goals sought by the community as it invests itself into its posited law. No formulation of the posited law

---

[27] I follow D Bakhurst, "Activity, Consciousness, and Communication", in M Cole, Y Engeström, and O Vasquez (eds.), *Mind, Culture, and Activity* (Cambridge: Cambridge University Press, 1997), pp. 147–63. Bakhurst himself draws on the work of psychologists belonging to the so-called "Vygotsky school" named after the Russian psychologist Lev S Vygotsky (1896–1934). See also C Strauss and N Quinn, *A Cognitive Theory of Cultural Meaning* (Cambridge: Cambridge University Press, 1997).

[28] P Bourdieu, *Questions de sociologie* (Paris: Minuit, 1984), p. 29 ["*Le corps socialisé (ce que l'on appelle l'individu ou la personne) ne s'oppose pas à la société: il est une de ses formes d'existence*"].

[29] K Mannheim, *Ideology and Utopia* (New York: Harcourt Brace Jovanovich, 1936), p. 3 [originally published in German in 1929].

can safely escape a cultural interpretation and all formulations of the posited law can, therefore, be helpfully envisaged as expressions, if at times discontinuous, of "legal tradition" understood here to mean something like "a set of deeply rooted, historically conditioned attitudes about the nature of law, about the role of law in the society and the polity, about the proper organisation and operation of a legal system, and about the way law is or should be made, applied, studied, perfected, and taught".[30] Put differently, all law may be seen "not as a response to the immediate circumstances or current mental state of an interlocutor or of oneself, but as part of an unfolding story".[31] The comparatist's task thus becomes "a venture into cultural hermeneutics".[32]

As suggested by John Merryman,[33] culture is concerned with regularities or recurrences over the *longue durée*. It entails sustained, intensive, and imaginative reflection on persistence. For Fernand Braudel, the analyst must be preoccupied primarily with the realm of the permanent or semi-permanent.[34] While not denying that culture is also the product of the activities of subjects who constantly reformulate experience within a symbolic order, the comparatist's assumption must be that "there are historical structures operating over the long term which are the foundation of the collective identity of men and women who have lived together for a long time across generations".[35] Braudel observes that

[30] J H Merryman, *The Civil Law Tradition*, (2nd edn., Stanford: Stanford University Press, 1985), p. 2.

[31] M Carrithers, *Why Humans Have Cultures* (Oxford: Oxford University Press, 1992), p. 82.

[32] M A Glendon, *Abortion and Divorce in Western Law* (Cambridge: Harvard University Press, 1987), p. 8. Observe that the presence of legal phenomena operating on the global level in relative insulation from the State does not mean a fundamental de-traditionalisation of law. Although global legal processes may indicate a weakening of the State as a source of identity, that is, a measure of de-territorialisation, it is hard to see how a transnational corporation, for instance, can offer a competing source of "cultural resonance" to the national bond and its history and mythology. While the specialised and technical global legal discourse cannot usually be regarded as the expression of one society or one culture in particular, it remains that manifestations of the global can be traced to local, "cultural" ties. The idea of an *acultural* law, whether global or not, cannot be envisaged. Even global phenomena are not above culture, for they arise from a cultural diversity which is already there; they are the outcome of cultural flow. In this sense, a meta-culture must never be taken to suggest a *tabula rasa*. Any *consensus gentium*—say, the distinctive cluster of meanings, symbols, and practices associated with the *lex mercatoria* or international arbitration—finds its anchorage in the variations in meaning systems that individuals from different communities gather to assemble such that the finished product continues to reveal a dependence upon a certain kind of learning which sets limits to cultural variability. In other words, I argue that even the globalisers—the frequent flyers and the frequent faxers—are, to an extent at least, constructed out of their own culture's materials of meaning and expression and remain possessed by their culture. Unsurprisingly, therefore, Teubner shows that even as the legal notion of "good faith" is being "globalised", cultural embeddedness continues to be strong such that the German model cannot be transferred to Great Britain, because it is linked to a specific production regime—what the author calls "Rhineland capitalism"; see G Teubner, "Legal Irritants: Good Faith in British Law or How Unifying Law Ends Up in New Divergences" (1998) 61 *Modern Law Review* 11.

[33] Above, at text accompanying n. 30.

[34] F Braudel, *Grammaire des civilisations* (Paris: Flammarion, 1993), p. 60 [originally published in 1963].

[35] J Le Goff, *La vieille Europe et la nôtre* (Paris: Seuil, 1994), p. 67 ["*il y a dans l'histoire des structures de longue durée qui sont le fondement de l'identité collective des hommes et des femmes qui ont vécu longtemps ensemble à travers les générations*"].

a *mentalité,* "which dictates attitudes, orients choices, roots prejudices", is "the fruit of distant legacies, of beliefs, of fears, of ancient anxieties".[36] Culture, of course, goes beyond the formalised practices operating in a given group. Although it *will* embrace conscious and formal beliefs, the constitution of legal identity is also accomplished through "less conscious, less formulated attitudes, habits and feelings, or even unconscious assumptions, bearings and commitments".[37] Equivocal perceptions, inchoate awareness, or unconscious assumptions are, in fact, particularly significant elements of the relevant legal-cultural data as has been underlined by anthropologists who note that "what informants find difficult to verbalize is more important, more fundamental, in the cultural organisation of ideas than what they can verbalize".[38] In sum, allowing for the complexity and ambiguity of individual perceptions of external realities, a *mentalité*—which suggests a cluster of predispositions, propensities, or inclinations—is the outcome of a process of transformation of often unconscious aspirations or expectations according to the concrete indices of what is probable, possible, or impossible for a given group into relatively durable tendencies that are internalised intergenerationally through socialisation and that crystallise into courses of action.

Building on this reflection, I want to suggest some further thoughts pertaining to the study of law as a culturally-embedded discourse. "Culture" is said to be "one of the two or three most complicated words in the English language".[39] A key feature accounting for culture's elusive contours—its implicit or tacit character—can, it seems to me, usefully be seized by way of a metaphor and an anecdote. The figure of speech is Edward Hall's who, acknowledging the difficulty of offering a rigorous definition and insisting upon the fact that "no constant elemental units of culture have as yet been satisfactorily established", refers to culture as "the silent language".[40] The following story captures the point. It is taken from an essay published in Russian in 1926 whose title was translated into English as "Discourse in Life and Discourse in Poetry":

> "Two people are sitting in a room. They are both silent. Then one of them says, 'Well!'. The other does not respond.
>
> For us, as outsiders, this entire 'conversation' is utterly incomprehensible. Taken in isolation, the utterance 'Well!' is empty and unintelligible. Nevertheless, this peculiar colloquy of two persons, consisting of only one—although, to be sure, one expressively

---

[36] Braudel, n. 34 above, p. 53 [*"dicte les attitudes, oriente les choix, enracine les préjugés"*;*"le fruit d'héritages lointains, de croyances, de peurs, d'inquiétudes anciennes"*].

[37] R Williams, *Culture* (London: Fontana, 1981), p. 26.

[38] R A LeVine, "Properties of Culture: An Ethnographic View", in R A Shweder and R A LeVine (ed.), *Culture Theory* (Cambridge: Cambridge University Press, 1984), p. 76.

[39] R. Williams, *Keywords,* 2nd edn. (London: Fontana, 1983), p. 87. See also J G Herder, *Ideen zur Philosophie der Geschichte der Menschheit* (Wiesbaden: Fourier, 1985), p. 39: "[n]othing is more indefinite than this word" [*"Nichts ist unbestimmter als dieses Wort (Kultur)"*] (originally published in 1784). For a critical exploration of the meaning of "culture" (including a useful array of references), see G H Hartman, *The Fateful Question of Culture* (New York: Columbia University Press, 1997), pp. 21–59 and 205–24.

[40] E T Hall, *The Silent Language* (New York: Doubleday, 1959), pp. 20 and 25, respectively.

intoned—word [the word in Russian is *tak*], does make perfect sense, is fully meaningful and complete.

In order to disclose the sense and meaning of this colloquy, we must analyze it. But what is it exactly that we can subject to analysis? Whatever pains we take with the purely verbal part of the utterance, however subtly we define the phonetic, morphological, and semantic factors of the word *well*, we shall still not come a single step closer to an understanding of the whole sense of the colloquy.

Let us suppose that the intonation with which this word was pronounced is known to us: indignation and reproach moderated by a certain amount of humor. This intonation somewhat fills in the semantic void of the adverb *well*, but still does not reveal the meaning of the whole.

What is it we lack, then? We lack the 'extraverbal context' that made the word *well* a meaningful locution for the listener. This *extraverbal context* of the utterance is comprised of three factors: (1) *the common spatial purview* of the interlocutors (the unity of the visible—in this case, the room, a window, and so on), (2) the *interlocutors' common knowledge and understanding of the situation*, and (3) their *common evaluation* of that situation.

At the time the colloquy took place, both interlocutors *looked up* at the window and *saw* that it had begun to snow; *both knew* that it was already May and that it was high time for spring to come; finally, *both* were *sick and tired* of the protracted winter— they were both *looking forward* to spring and *both were bitterly disappointed* by the late snowfall. On this 'jointly seen' (snowflakes outside the window), 'jointly known' (the time of the year—May), and 'unanimously evaluated' (winter wearied of, spring looked forward to)—on all this the utterance *directly depends*, all this is seized in its actual, living import—is its very sustenance. And yet all this remains without verbal specification or articulation. The snowflakes remain outside the window; the date, on the page of a calendar; the evaluation, in the psyche of the speaker; and nevertheless, all this is assumed in the word *well*."[41]

The reference to an elaborate "extra-verbal context" ascribing meaning to one word contributes to the intelligibilisation of culture as occupying a middleground between what is common to all human beings—such universals might include an appreciation of the difference between "to hit" and "to be hit"[42]—and what is unique to each individual. As a term attempting to delineate identity, "culture" refers to features that are not universal, but that transcend the individual; it marks what Marc Augé calls a "collective singularity".[43] Culture helps us to realise that the individuals we encounter are part of a community and forces us to escape the dichotomy whereby we see ways either as universal—especially when we focus on our own—or as idiosyncratic—when we meet someone with a different world-view from our own. The notion of "culture", indeed, captures the idea of shared mental programmes that have

[41] M Holquist, *Dialogism* (London: Routledge, 1990), pp. 62–63 [emphasis original]. Although the paper is signed by Valentin Voloshinov, its authorship became contentious once Mikhail Bakhtin claimed that he had published some of his work under the names of friends, including Voloshinov; see *ibid.*, pp. 8 and 193–4.

[42] J Bruner, *The Culture of Education* (Cambridge: Harvard University Press, 1996), p. 36.

[43] M Augé, *Le sens des autres* (Paris: Fayard, 1994), p. 90 ["*singularité collective*"].

formed not on account of the fact that we live on this planet nor because of our uniqueness, but as a function of the community to which we belong. Thus, "[w]hat one means by legal culture . . . is best illustrated by reference to [such commonalities as] legal language, legal reasoning, legal argument and legal justification".[44] Culture takes us beyond mere words and leads us into an unstated and assumed realm which itself operates in juxtaposition to words, qualifies them, and makes them meaningful.[45] Often, that entire realm finds itself located not only beyond words, but beyond awareness, that is, beyond the awareness of the observed and possibly beyond that of the observer (who still tends to act as if the word or, in law, the rule or precept was the whole).

Culture is, therefore, a different type of eloquence; it consists of an alternative, wider-ranging message system. It is concerned with "collective consciousness" or what is imprecisely termed the "history of collective ideas". It purports to ascertain, for instance, the factors underlying the constitution of specific legal climates and the shaping of collective re-presentations within a given community. To argue that discrete patterns of reasoning or of discourse or of implicit beliefs can be inferred from the respective modes of behaviour followed by various legal communities is to accept that these characteristics, in order to qualify, need not only be distinctive, but also recurrent and pervasive; they must, in other words, inform a substantial part of the ideas, beliefs, and assumptions of the legal group concerned. These remarks raise the difficult questions of uniformity and constraint.[46]

First, culture is not uniform. Obviously, collectivities do not think, and the anthropomorphisation of a legal culture runs the risk of having individuals pictured as being somehow disembodied and entirely subjected to a community. It also raises the equally serious trap of minimising intra-cultural dissonances, inconsistencies, and contradictions.[47] The point is not to claim that a *mentalité* is monolithic so that every individual within a community would act within precisely the same cognitive framework in response to typical objects and events (nor is it, incidentally, to propound that individual world-views are internally consistent). There is no question of "disciplining" adherents to a legal tradition, say, into a single and authentic identity. Such stereotypical inflexion suggesting the dominion of some principle of noncontradiction should be avoided, for the shared meanings, attitudes, and values that form a *mentalité* are simply not experienced by everyone; no two individuals cook pasta or play the violin in the

[44] G Wilson, "English Legal Scholarship" (1987) 50 *Modern Law Review* 818, p. 845.

[45] Hall, n. 40 above, p. xi.

[46] As I elaborate upon these questions, I am mindful of some of the observations directed at my work in J Bell, "Mechanisms for Cross-Fertilisation of Administrative Law in Europe", in J Beatson and T Tridimas (eds.), *New Directions in European Public Law* (Oxford: Hart, 1998), pp. 154–7; J W F Allison, "Transplantation and Cross-Fertilisation", in Beatson and Tridimas, pp. 172–6; B Schäfer and Z Bankowski, "Mistaken Identities: The Integrative Force of Private Law", in M Van Hoecke and F Ost (eds.), *The Harmonisation of European Private Law* (Oxford: Hart, 2000), pp. 21–45.

[47] See G E R Lloyd, *Demystifying Mentalities* (Cambridge: Cambridge University Press, 1990), p. 5.

same way. To suggest otherwise would be a dangerous idea. It is essential to account for a measure of heterology within a culture at any particular time, since every culture is tested and contested by individuals who inhabit it and whom it inhabits. Thus, a culture has to accommodate internal tensions and instabilities (which it will ignore, suppress as deviance, or strive to re-locate within mainstream orthodoxy).[48] The comparatist must ensure that reference to the notions of "tradition" or "culture" does not, despite "its cosy invocation of consensus", "serve to distract attention from social and cultural contradictions, from the fractures and oppositions within the whole".[49] Meanings are not reducible to common meanings. For instance, one can easily imagine divisions as to the merits of judicial activism taking place within a society. Arguably, then, there would be a lack of "common meaning" as regards the limits of judicial activism. Yet, this failure of consensus occurs within the ambit of the practice of adjudication as it is experienced in that society. This "common reference world" constitutes the web of intersubjective meaning "which [is] constitutive of the social matrix in which individuals find themselves and act" or "the background to social action". As comparative legal studies seeks to accommodate intersubjectivity, it continues to allow, therefore, for dissensus within a community.[50]

Culture, being an integral part of the game of social control, social conflict, and social change, hides relations of power which manifest themselves, for instance, through the distribution of knowledge amongst members of the group. Not all actors are equally situated to understand and act upon the world in similar terms. In fact, actors classify and construct their understanding of the social world from particular positions in a hierarchically structured social space. An understanding of legal culture must, therefore, involve an appreciation of the distribution of knowledge across the interpretive (or sub-interpretive) communities within the culture. The distribution of knowledge and the perception of that distribution from within the legal culture affect the way the legal culture produces and reproduces meanings. Discursive formations (such as a civil code or a constitution) function rhetorically through their narratological and tropological structures to prejudice judgement, elevating or protecting some elements in society by repressing others. They reveal certain hierarchies of power, of repressor and repressed, within the social fabric of the moment, whereby individuals feel the force of symbols and are led to behave according to them. Any comparative analysis of law, therefore, is also a cratology, that is, a study of power. But even the heterodox, antinomian, and rebellious orientations seeking to reconstitute from within the boundaries of collective identity do not detract

---

[48] For a detailed statement arguing against the notion that culture is always and everywhere a fully integrated phenomenon, see M S Archer, *Culture and Agency*, 2nd edn. (Cambridge: Cambridge University Press, 1996).

[49] E P Thompson, *Customs in Common* (London: Penguin, 1991), p. 6. See also J Clifford, *The Predicament of Culture* (Cambridge, Mass.: Harvard University Press, 1988), p. 232.

[50] For the distinction between "common" and "intersubjective" meaning, see Taylor, n. 25 above, pp. 57–62. The quotations are from *ibid.*, pp. 60, 57, and 57, respectively.

from the existence of "a system of cultural principles, a method of organising and attributing meanings, a practice of cognitive mapping that is held, with little variability, by large numbers of people" within a given legal community.[51] Consider this well-known contribution to socio-psychological studies:

> "The political revolutionary does not refuse to cast his revolutionary songs in the modal structure and scale progressions of the culture he is in process of changing; his formations, if his organized forces are strong enough, will operate in terms of accepted patterns of military procedure. The one who rebels against the religious and moral system of his time will couch his appeals in the linguistic patterns of his people, use established affect symbols, and employ accepted aesthetic standards in heightening the responses of his followers".[52]

Second, culture defines a realm of possibility. Relative to a given socio-historical situatedness, certain values and visions cannot but constitute the ultimate horizons for what can plausibly be considered rhetorically convincing and morally acceptable: "*all* aspects of social life are pervaded by decidedly non-neutral assumptions whose acceptance by a member of the culture define what is 'possible' for that person".[53] This observation recalls the significance of

---

[51] J Arditi, "Geertz, Kuhn and the Idea of a Cultural Paradigm" (1994) 45 *British Journal of Sociology* 597, p. 614. The fact is that differentiated thought within a legal tradition or culture must assume a measure of epistemological commonality if it is to lay any claim to cognitive (or political) effectivity: how could opposite positions speak to one another—or against one another—unless they were situated within a homogeneous epistemological field? For this argument, see M Foucault, "*Il faut défendre la société*", ed. by M Bertani and A Fontana (Paris: Gallimard, 1997), p. 185 [being the transcript of a lecture delivered in March 1976].

[52] M J Herskovits, "On Cultural and Psychological Reality", in J H Rohrer and M Sherif (eds.), *Social Psychology at the Crossroads* (New York: Harper, 1951), p. 153. For an argument to the effect that even famous and influential sixteenth-century figures like Copernicus and Vesalius used classical models throughout their work and remained committed as fervently to traditional concepts as to empirical data, see A Grafton, *New Worlds, Ancient Texts* (Cambridge, Mass.: Harvard University Press, 1992), p. 115, where the author observes that "[b]oth Copernicus and Vesalius expected that their innovations could coexist with—and even rest on—the very structures we now see them as attacking".

[53] S Levinson, *Constitutional Faith* (Princeton: Princeton University Press, 1988), p. 156 [emphasis original]. See also I M Young, *Justice and the Politics of Difference* (Princeton: Princeton University Press, 1990), pp. 45–6. For arguments in favour of strong cultural determinism, see B M Berger, *An Essay on Culture* (Berkeley: University of California Press, 1995), *passim*; S Fish, *Doing What Comes Naturally* (Durham: Duke University Press, 1989), pp. 430, 459, and 246; R Rosaldo, *Culture and Truth* (Boston: Beacon Press, 1993), p. 25. For an influential reflection on how the self is constituted in important ways by group affinities, see generally P Bourdieu, *La distinction* (Paris: Minuit, 1979), *passim*; *ibid.*, *Le sens pratique* (Paris: Minuit, 1980), *passim*; *ibid.*, n. 28 above, *passim*, where the author develops the notion of "*habitus*" which he seems to have derived from E Panofsky's work and which he presents as an array of permanent, transferable, limiting, and explanatory dispositions underwriting practices and images as they arise within a lived environment. Indeed, Bourdieu translated into French Panofsky's celebrated challenge to positivism which draws arresting parallels in terms of "habit-forming forces" between the building of cathedrals and Aquinas's *Summa Theologiae*; see *ibid.*, *Architecture gothique et pensée scolastique*, transl. by P Bourdieu (Paris: Minuit, 1967). For an acknowledgement of Bourdieu's indebtedness to Panofsky, see *ibid.*, p. 142. For a helpful discussion of Bourdieu's idea of "habitus", see D Swartz, *Culture and Power* (Chicago: University of Chicago Press, 1997), pp. 95–116. Interestingly, Bourdieu has observed that "culture" would be "a better term than *habitus*". However, he thought the notion was "overdetermined"; see P Bourdieu, "Structuralism and Theory of Sociological Knowledge", (1968) 35 *Social Research* 681, p. 706, n. 23.

historical analysis for comparative legal studies; "it is only through history that one can discover the conditions of possibility of psychological structures".[54] Pierre Legendre remarks, for instance, that "French law cannot produce or take into account just anything since it is linked to the mythical structure of nationalist truth".[55] I also claim that, even though cultural meanings are neither fixed nor static (*"tradere"*, the etymological source of "tradition", connotes that which is in movement), the adaptive dimension of culture must, despite its undoubted significance, be apprehended as subservient to the theme of cultural reproduction. Because a legal culture functions as an ongoing integrative process, what one encounters by way of an alternative experience is incorporated into an existing whole within which it is readily intelligibilised against the background of the whole, if at the cost of a measure of dissonance reduction. Indeed, the power of a culture inheres in its capacity to assimilate data through a didactic of conflict resolution operating in its favour so that a new experience appears to conform to existing structures of thought and belief. Resorting to powerful imagery, Algirdas Greimas thus highlights the matter of "cultural persistence", or perhaps inertia, by equating "legal culture" with "'good legal manners' (in the way there are table or conversation 'manners', *etc.*)".[56]

This is not to say that the comparatist should suppress all traces of an intentional structure of practice and reduce practice exclusively to temporally non-emergent constraints, that is, to constraints that are stable over time (Andrew Pickering rightly mocks the notion of tacit knowledge "as hovering nonemergently in some special epistemic heaven and controlling practice from without").[57] Of course, the idea of a community being incarcerated in a place or in a mode of thought is a fiction of the anthropological imagination. Communities should not be unduly typified through a static and univocal notion of culture. Even Edward Sapir's "classic" perspective warned against this danger.

> "The so-called culture of a group of human beings . . . is essentially a systematic list of all the socially inherited patterns of behaviour which may be illustrated in the actual behavior of all or most of the individuals of the group. The true locus, however, of these processes which, when abstracted into a totality, constitute culture is not in a theoretical community of human beings known as society, for the term 'society' is itself a cultural construct which is employed by individuals who stand in significant relations to each other in order to help them in the interpretation of certain aspects of their behaviour. The true locus of culture is in the interactions of specific individuals and, on the subjective side, in the world of meanings which each one of these individuals may

---

[54] M Foucault, *Maladie mentale et psychologie* (Paris: Presses Universitaires de France, 1954), p. 90 [*"C'est dans l'histoire seulement que l'on peut découvrir les conditions de possibilité des structures psychologiques"*].

[55] P Legendre, *Jouir du pouvoir [:] traité de la bureaucratie patriote* (Paris: Minuit, 1976), p. 72 [*"Le droit français ne saurait produire ni prendre en compte n'importe quoi, car il est lié à la structure mythique de la vérité nationaliste"*].

[56] A J Greimas, *Sémiotique et sciences sociales* (Paris: Seuil, 1976), p. 111 [*"de 'bonnes manières juridiques' (comme il existe des 'manières' de table, de conversation, etc.)"*].

[57] A Pickering, *The Mangle of Practice* (Chicago: University of Chicago Press, 1995), p. 200.

unconsciously abstract for himself from his participation in these interactions . . . It is impossible to think of any cultural pattern or set of cultural patterns which can, in the literal sense of the word, be referred to society as such. There are no facts of political organization or family life or religious belief or magical procedure or technology or aesthetic endeavor which are coterminous with society or with any mechanically or sociologically defined segment of society".[58]

In other words, the presence of socially differentiated knowledges, discourses, and meaning systems within a culture should be recognised and the contestatory nature of discourses within communities acknowledged. And it is the case that, even as it reproduces itself, culture changes on account of the fact that the frameworks which it delineates and within which it operates are inevitably modified as they address new empirical data. However, since present situations are addressed in terms of past experiences, only exceptionally will the new information effectively *challenge* the whole. As a leading naturalist reminds us, "[c]ulture conforms to an important principle of evolutionary biology: most change occurs to maintain the organism in its steady state".[59] And if psychoanalysis is to be credited with any discoveries, one is surely that our psychological state, our past experience, and our memories curtail our field of action such that we only enjoy interstitial freedom.

In the end, therefore, while I am certainly not defending the view that the old dichotomy of structure and agency should be resolved in favour of a complete incapacitation of the power of choice, I do maintain that there is an important sense in which individual identity is supervenient upon unchosen participation in common forms of life, that the life of a culture determines the resources of perception, that there exists something like "cultural suggestibility". Furthermore, such overdetermination increases over time as the sphere of elective choice progressively contracts itself.[60] In any event, there is simply no such thing as the unencumbered self creating itself by acts of will unmediated by any constitutive cultural inheritance.[61] Because individuality is produced through culture, personal style is never more than a deviation in relation to the style of a group so that it always relates back to the common style either through its conformity with it or on account of its difference from it.

---

[58] E Sapir, "Cultural Anthropology and Psychiatry", in *Selected Writings in Language, Culture, and Personality*, ed. by D G Mandelbaum (Berkeley: University of California Press, 1949), p. 515 [originally published in 1932].

[59] E O Wilson, *In Search of Nature* (London: Allen Lane, 1997), p. 107.

[60] See P Bohannan, "Ethnography and Comparison in Legal Anthropology", in Laura Nader (ed.), *Law in Culture and Society*, 2nd edn. (Berkeley: University of California Press, 1997), p. 405: "a cultural tradition has a character that becomes 'more so' as it develops". Ultimately, it can not be denied, of course, that "past endurance tells us nothing about what will happen tomorrow": Pickering, n. 57 above, p. 207.

[61] In Marx's blazing version of this assertion, the philosopher claimed that "[t]he tradition of all the dead generations weighs like a nightmare on the brain of the living": K Marx, *The Eighteenth Brumaire of Louis Bonaparte*, in D McLellan (ed.), *Karl Marx [:] Selected Writings* (Oxford: Oxford University Press, 1977), p. 300 [originally published in German in 1852].

*

In the realisation that conceptions of law-as-rules-or-precepts are impoverished, the comparatist is attracted to the explicatory power which an appreciation of the legal as culturally constituted may yield. The indeterminacy of "culture" or, if you will, the impossibility of distinguishing between "culture" and "non-culture" in a way that would allow the identification of empirically verifiable causal relationships through which control over social life could be effectively attained ought to be a handicap only for the positivist seeking the kind of clear and determinate guidance usually associated with computer programmes.[62] But comparative legal studies wishes to subscribe to a very different cognitive project. The comparative enterprise does not purport to be serviceable in the sense of providing an instrumental programme oriented toward technical ends. For comparatists, plausible explanations can be more profitable and, hence, preferable to causal demonstrations. In fact, comparative analysis of law is best apprehended as a hermeneutic investigation aiming to achieve understanding about the life of the law and life in the law through the invention of meaning. To be sure, such understanding may then be used to encourage new forms of problem-solving. Yet, it remains that the primary role of comparative legal studies is to awaken assumptions, that is, to answer what Jürgen Habermas calls an "emancipatory" interest.[63] Comparative analysis of law wishes to liberate individuals from repressive and confining forces regarded by them as natural rather than as socially constructed. It can do so by heightening awareness of the constraints imposed by a symbolic "system" and by helping to overcome the closing of the mind otherwise generated by habit, socialisation, or tradition. It is, ultimately, engaged in a phenomenological inquiry of what is *possible* for a legal community and the semiotic sub-groups it harbours, such as practitioners, judges, and academics. Indeed, one cannot afford to study legal experience without examining what kind of legal experience is possible, for culture limits possibilities of experience: it constrains. In this sense, culture is both a liminal and a finite space. At a more general level, comparative-legal-studies-as-hermeneutics

---

[62] E.g., Taylor, n. 25 above; P Winch, *The Idea of a Social Science* (London: Routledge and Kegan Paul, 1958), p. 115. For a considered critique insisting upon the fact that the notion of "legal culture" is imprecise, arbitrary, and devoid of causal significance so that it lacks "sufficient analytical precision . . . to allow it to indicate a significant explanatory variable in empirical research", see Cotterrell, n. 17 above, p. 14 and *passim*. It is interesting to note, however, that the pertinence of culture is not limited to "soft" subjects, but is also regarded (by some analysts at least) as crucial for economic theory concerned as it is with predictability and quantifiable accuracy. See, e.g., D C North, *Institutions, Institutional Change and Economic Performance* (Cambridge: Cambridge University Press, 1990); J Knight and D North, "Explaining Economic Change: The Interplay Between Cognition and Institutions" (1997) 3 *Legal Theory* 211; P A David, "Clio and the Economics of QWERTY" (1985) 75 *American Economic Review* 332, who argues that there are path-dependent sequences of economic changes, that is, "non-ergodic" processes, which are inherently historical in character and where stochastic elements rather than systematic forces play a dominant role. For an argument to the effect that the amorphous character of cultures makes them neither indecipherable nor insubstantial, see L Rosen, "The Integrity of Cultures" (1991) 34 *American Behavioural Scientist* 594.

[63] J Habermas, *Knowledge and Human Interests* (Boston: Beacon Press, 1987), pp. 302–17 [originally published in German in 1968].

intends to counteract (latent) ethnocentrism. A re-presentational strategy seeking critical enlightenment in this way hardly suffers from the notion of "culture" not being ascribed a restricted and precise meaning *qua* mechanistic explication of experience. The malleability surrounding the notion of "culture" does not prevent the ascription of determinative efficacy and the articulation of various characteristics which can prove of direct relevance to the pursuit of deep or thick comparative legal studies.

The comparatist must, therefore, re-present a legal culture in ways which have greater interpretive power than is offered by the traditional rule-based model. The idea for the comparatist is to refuse to take experience as a given and to try to see how it is conditioned and shaped, how patterns of consciousness evolve. Legal experience is immersed in a cultural context: it is modulated. It is, indeed, the legal culture—a notion which makes specific reference to the subculture that is constituted amongst law specialists, especially as regards the repository of those elements that partake in the stable, general, and unconscious—that provides the "internal logic" of the law.[64] Although groups and identities are necessarily fluid, the legal culture remains the cement that binds normality and normativity, that accounts, through the posited law, for a "govern*mentalité*" (a useful notion which connotes at once the ideas of government, governance, and *mentalité*).[65] The comparatist's range of options in the pursuit of his task is vast, since there is nothing for the observer of a legal culture that is quintessentially "legal"; rather, the quality of "legality" (if this be the apposite word) is conferred onto the object of observation on the basis of what the comparatist understands that the observed culture understands as legal and, also, in the light of what he himself understands as legal.

*

I must now enter a melancholy note. A measure of how much work, how so much work, remains to be done before comparative legal studies moves to the kind of analysis I advocate can be illustrated anecdotally. On the occasion of a debate at the European Academy of Legal Theory in Brussels, on 3 November 1997, a distinguished Belgian colleague who regards himself (and, I understand, is regarded by others) as a comparatist, suggested that my doubts concerning the desirability of a convergence of legal "systems" within the European Community and my sentiment that "convergence" was not the inherent and unalloyed good that it was frequently stated to be were irrelevant to the discussion, *because it said in the Treaty of Rome that convergence must happen.*[66] In

---

[64] J H Merryman, "On the Convergence (and Divergence) of the Civil Law and the Common Law", in M Cappelletti (ed.), *New Perspectives for a Common Law of Europe* (Leyden: Sijthoff, 1978), p. 224. See also E Örücü, "An Exercise on the Internal Logic of Legal Systems" (1987) 7 *Legal Studies* 310.

[65] See M Foucault, "La 'gouvernementalité'", in D Defert and F Ewald (eds.), *Michel Foucault [:] Dits et écrits [,] 1954–1988*, vol. 3: *1976–1979* (Paris: Gallimard, 1994), p. 655 [originally published in 1978].

[66] From a strictly formalistic perspective, this claim is mistaken for the Treaty of Rome nowhere mentions the word "convergence". See text below at p. 253.

the same vein, as I was questioning the warrant of the oft-repeated (but, to my mind, unsubstantiated) argument that there are to be found common principles underwriting the range of posited laws across the Community, the reply came that Article 288 (formerly 215) of the EC Treaty expressly stated that such principles existed. "Surely", my colleague claimed, "those who wrote that Article knew what they were doing". Such display of presumption shows that for this Belgian jurist, the Treaty of Rome has become so realistic that it can properly speak on behalf of reality. The legislative text has indeed displaced reality; *it* is right. I claim that my colleague pays undue attention to the texts of written language to the detriment of the frameworks of intangibles within which interpretive communities operate and which have normative force for these communities, even though not coherently and completely instantiated. Moreover, his attitude betrays a *political* decision to marginalise difference. My colleague discards the existence of qualitatively differentiated phenomena and the concrete contents of experiences and values in order to achieve "certainty, predictability and control".[67] His hegemonic strategy creates a false consensus which can only be established through exclusive reference to the formalised elements of law and through the delegitimation of a notion such as "tradition" or "culture" which, in its intricacy, would intervene as an irrational interloper interfering with the production and the perception of formalistic autarky.

Of course, the refusal or inability to see that law acts as a site of ideological refraction of deeply embedded cultural dispositions does not make reality go away: bananas *do* exist even if I do not like them and the continental drift *is* happening even if I do not perceive it. But can my colleague and others who think like him ever free themselves from this commitment to a seemingly endless and all-encompassing textuality? Can they ever transcend "the system of selfmade concepts that serve . . . to cover up the living process of society"?[68] Michael Oakeshott answers that rationalists are "essentially ineducable", because they are wedded to formal models of truth and cognition and could only be trained out of them by "an inspiration which [they] regar[d] as the great enemy of mankind".[69] If Oakeshott is even partially correct, the claims that European legal "systems" can converge and that they are indeed converging are not about

---

[67] B de Sousa Santos, *Toward a New Common Sense* (London: Routledge, 1995), p. 73.

[68] T W Adorno, *Negative Dialectics* (London: Routledge, 1973), p. 311 [originally published in German in 1966].

[69] M Oakeshott, *Rationalism in Politics* (London: Methuen, 1962), p. 32. For a recent observation to the same effect, see B H Smith, *Belief and Resistance* (Cambridge: Harvard University Press, 1997), p. 119: "For those who conduct their intellectual lives primarily or exclusively through transcendental rationalism, that set of densely interconnected, mutually reinforcing ideas (claims, concepts, definitions, and so forth) operates as a virtually unbreachable cognitive and rhetorical system, or, one might say, as a continuously self-spinning, self-repairing, self-enclosing web. . . . Everything in the system fits together tightly and securely. Whatever does not fit *into* the system is identified by the system as irrelevant or unauthentic. . . . The rigorous, unremitting work of Reason creates a tight, taut web, intertextual and interconceptual" [emphasis original]. See also P Schlag, *The Enchantment of Reason* (Durham: Duke University Press, 1998).

to fall silent, no matter how epistemically ignorant of the reality these assertions are, no matter how much they illustrate an instance of cognitive impairment.

COMPARATIVE LEGAL STUDIES AND TRANSMIGRATION

Assuming that comparative legal studies were finally to advance beyond its entrenched ahistoricism and reveal a cultural consciousness, it could not but attest to the inevitability of acculturation. Even the same inscribed words will not generate the same understanding in two different legal cultures. Consider this statement drawn from ongoing anthropological research on cognition: "The fact that exactly the same word gets printed or uttered again and again does not mean that exactly the same meaning (which is half the word) spreads from minds to minds".[70] As words cross boundaries, there intervenes a different morality to underwrite and effectuate them: every culture continues to articulate *its* moral inquiry according to traditional standards of justification. The disjunction between the bare propositional statement and its meaning thus prevents the displacement across cultures of the words *themselves*. This point is only made more obvious if the inscribed words are different because they have been written in different languages; a passage from Benjamin indeed reminds us that "the word *Brot* . . . mean[s] something other to a German than what the word *pain* means to a Frenchman".[71] As the understanding of a word changes, the meaning of the word changes. And as the meaning of the word changes, the word itself changes. In sum, meaning simply does not lend itself to transplantation, because "[i]n order to transport a single word without distortion, one would have to transport the entire language around it"—and, one would have to add, for present purposes, the entire legal culture and the entire culture *tout court*.[72]

On account of every legal culture's inherent assimilative capacity, any imported form of words is inevitably ascribed a different, local, meaning which makes it original. Because every import finds itself within a world that is already there, it is indeed a *sine qua non* condition of any import making sense within the recipient culture that the borrowing should rapidly find itself indigenised—in other words, that each de-traditionalisation should find itself re-traditionalised. Pure hospitality is, therefore, impossible.[73] I argue that the presence of an irreducible

---

[70] D Sperber, "Learning to Pay Attention", *The Times Literary Supplement*, 27 Dec. 1996, p. 14, col. 3.

[71] W Benjamin, "The Task of the Translator", in *Selected Writings*, ed. by M Bullock and M W Jennings and trans. by H Zohn, vol. 1: *1913–1926* (Cambridge, Mass.: Harvard University Press, 1973), p. 257 [originally published in German in 1923].

[72] E Hoffman, *Lost in Translation* (London: Minerva, 1991), p. 272.

[73] E.g.: F S C Northrop, "The Comparative Philosophy of Comparative Law", (1960) 45 *Cornell Law Quarterly* 617, p. 657: "in introducing foreign legal and political norms into any society, those norms will become effective and take root only if they incorporate also a part at least of the norms and philosophy of the native society".

element of autochthony constraining the epistemological receptivity to the incorporation of an exogenous text limits the *possibility* of effective convergence and, in the case of law, of effective legal convergence.

Critics of "culture" in effect claim that the idea suggests homogeneity, stability, coherence, and boundedness in a context where social interaction is characterised by conflict, change, discontinuity, and open-endedness. Not unlike the notion of "race", "culture" would tend to "freeze" difference.[74] There is no doubt that "culture" is a construct or an abstraction in the sense that the word does not refer to any concrete "reality": one cannot see a culture. This means, of course, that the identification of certain features of the lifeworld as "cultural" can only be more or less persuasive and can never be "true". It is precisely this artificial and, therefore, contestable aspect of "culture" that its detractors use as a target. To reject "culture", however, is to accept that identifiable ways of feeling, thinking, and acting are randomly distributed across individuals—something disproved by anthropological research. Despite the dangers associated with simplification and reification, I argue that, just as one can usefully speak of "the Gothic style", "[t]here are many situations in which 'Japanese culture' is a convenient shorthand for designating something like 'that which many or most Japanese irrespective of gender, class, and other differences regularly think, feel, and do by virtue of having been in continuous social contact with other Japanese'".[75] Speaking of "culture" in this way does not automatically privilege coherence, does not entail essentialism, does not necessarily preclude temporal variation, and does not efface individual variations or contestations that can take the form of participation in a range of subcultures. Nor does "culture" need to be understood as positing a number of discrete heritages organically tied to specific homelands and considered best kept separate (like the laboratory specimens in petri dishes we also call "cultures"). Nor does "culture" need to deny their cosmopolitanism to the people being studied. In other words, "culture" allows for a transnational public sphere and certainly need not connote nationalism or isolationism, that is, something like "cultural fundamentalism". Nor does "culture" need to be linked with ethnicity. Again, the point is simply to acknowledge that "[e]verywhere we find sets of certain learned features that are shared more extensively by people who interact with each other than between these people and others with whom they do not interact or among those others".[76] The fact that the notion can be

---

[74] L Abu-Lughod, "Writing Against Culture", in R G Fox (ed.), *Recapturing Anthropology* (Santa Fe: School of American Research Press, 1991), p. 144. See also A Kuper, *Culture* (Cambridge, Mass.: Harvard University Press, 1999), pp. 245–47; A Appadurai, *Modernity at Large* (Minneapolis: University of Minnesota Press, 1996), p. 12.

[75] C Brumann, "Writing for Culture" (1999) 40 *Current Anthropology* S1, p. S7. My summary owes much to this paper.

[76] *Ibid.*, p. S9.

abused by those who exaggerate the patterning and uniformity of human action, the fact even that such an extreme event as the Holocaust can be regarded as a form of culture-consciousness is no reason to jettison "culture". Who would consider no longer resorting to the word "democracy" because the Soviet regime abused it for much of the twentieth century?

*

A number of instances can be adduced to demonstrate the inevitability of the domestication of legal meaning and the correlative impossibility of convergence across legal "systems". In each case, the national character of constitutional and administrative law (possibly owing as much to the different conceptions of the State developed in the nineteenth century as to the differentiated reception of the Roman notion of *imperium*) shows remarkable persistence in the face of extraneous influences. In fact, there is a sense in which constitutional and administrative law is even more national-specific than private law to the extent that it is more closely imbricated in the distinctive polity prevailing at local level.[77]

One spectacular illustration of naturalisation, of course, is the way in which Montesquieu's appreciation of the separation of powers in England has led to a complete subordination of the judiciary in France where, under the 1958 constitution, it is not even a "*pouvoir*" but a mere "*autorité*".[78] Another instance concerns the Roman distinction between "public law" and "private law" which, once it had travelled to England from civil-law jurisdictions, was reformulated in remedial terms thus confirming the view that "the public/private distinction depends quite squarely on an underpinning of political theory".[79] Given the contrast between the Continental "State-led societies" and the British "society-led State",[80] where "[t]he emphasis on flexible regulation and administrative discretion finds its expression in the legal system with its preponderance of procedural regulation and the missing comprehensive system of public law principles to guide and control administrative action",[81] it is unsurprising that

---

[77] "[P]ublic law is simply a sophisticated form of political discourse [and] controversies within the subject are simply extended political disputes": M Loughlin, *Public Law and Political Theory* (Oxford: Oxford University Press, 1992), p. 4.

[78] Amongst his many pronouncements to the same effect, Montesquieu famously stated that "the judges of the nation are but the mouthpiece that utters the words of the statute; they are inanimate beings which can neither moderate its strength nor its rigour": *De l'esprit des lois*, in *Oeuvres complètes*, ed. by R Caillois, vol. 2 (Paris: Gallimard, 1951), bk XI, ch. 6, p. 404 ["*les juges de la nation ne sont (. . .) que la bouche qui prononce les paroles de la loi; des êtres inanimés qui n'en peuvent modérer ni la force ni la rigueur*"] (originally published in 1748).

[79] *O'Reilly v. Mackman* [1982] 3 All ER 1124 (HL). For a thorough study of the difficulties attendant upon this reception, see J W F Allison, *A Continental Distinction in the Common Law* (Oxford: Oxford University Press, 1996). The quotation in the text is from N E Simmonds, *The Decline of Juridical Reason* (Manchester: Manchester University Press, 1984), p. 131.

[80] See generally B Badie and P Birnbaum, *Sociologie de l'Etat* (Paris: Grasset, 1982), especially pp. 171–217.

[81] C Knill, "European Policies: The Impact of National Administrative Traditions", (1998) 18 *Journal of Public Policy* 1, p. 16. See also K H F Dyson, *The State Tradition in Western Europe* (Oxford : Martin Robertson, 1980), especially pp. 186–202 ; M R Damaška, *The Faces of Justice and State Authority* (New Haven: Yale University Press, 1986).

various manifestations of "localism" are already apparent as regards the incorporation of the European Convention on Human Rights into British law via the Human Rights Act 1998. First, the new statute is unlikely to change the fact that British judges have traditionally been concerned with the protection of residual liberties rather than with the advancement of abstract rights. Second, the British statute enacts less than a full patriation of Convention rights. Third, while the higher courts will enjoy the power of declaring an Act of Parliament to be incompatible with Convention rights, such declaration must coexist with the doctrine of parliamentary sovereignty which means, in effect, that the courts must continue to enforce and apply the problematic legislative text until it has been amended.[82]

A further example of local "resistance" occurred when English courts were invited to adopt the principle of proportionality on the Continental model and rejected the idea because they thought it would favour undue interference with the merits of administrative decisions rather than the more limited supervisory jurisdiction traditionally exercised by the judiciary.[83] Even if the principle of proportionality had been received, however, it is clear that it would promptly have adopted a local sociological colour.[84] The concept ("proportionality") might have been the same as that prevailing in Berlin or Luxembourg, but the *conception* of it governing locally would have differed. An interpretation is always a subjective product and that subjective product is necessarily, in part at least, a cultural product; the interpretation is, in other words, the result of a particular understanding that is conditioned by a series of factors (many of them intangible) which would be different if the interpretation occurred in another place or in another era (for, then, different cultural claims would be made on interpreters). As Malcolm Ross aptly notes, "deciding whether something is reasonable, proportionate or fair will only yield consistent or recognisable results in different systems or jurisdictions if the underlying yardstick demanded by those terms reflects shared values as to what is necessary or proper behaviour, or the priorities to be attached to particular choices and resources".[85] I claim that it would be "*un très grand hasard*" if such concurrence of values were to materialise.[86] In other words, external influences, rather than generate a kind of immanent rationalisation across legal cultures, lead to a local *métissage* which, because the elements in the

---

[82] See generally K D Ewing, "The Human Rights Act and Parliamentary Democracy" (1999) 62 *Modern Law Review* 79.

[83] *Brind* v. *Secretary of State for the Home Department* [1991] 1 All ER 720 (HL).

[84] Indeed, Lord Hoffmann argued extra-judicially that the acceptance of proportionality in English law would change little. According to him, "[p]roportionality is not a new principle but another and sometimes better way of explaining how we apply our existing principles": "A Sense of Proportion", in M Andenas and F Jacobs (eds.), *European Community Law in the English Courts* (Oxford: Oxford University Press, 1998), p. 161. This is "domestication by anticipation", so to speak.

[85] M Ross, "Behind Proportionality: The Cultural and Constitutional Context", in M Andenas (ed.), *English Public Law and the Common Law of Europe* (London: Key Haven, 1998), p. 88.

[86] The words are Montesquieu's as he addresses the improbability that a law designed for one jurisdiction would fit another: n. 78 above, bk 1, ch. 3, p. 237 ["a very great coincidence"].

mix are specific to a given historicity, is itself idiosyncratic and, in the end, ethnocentric on account of the inevitable domestication process that I have outlined.[87] The following statement is apposite: "At least until the one great, comprehensive, universal, political truth is revealed and accepted, every legal system is an expression of the culture that called it into being. Each is a system among a network of interdependent systems functioning together to form that culture. The interdependence of systems creates resistance to change and increases the risks that planned change will bring unplanned consequences".[88] There is always at work, if you like, an active agent of articulation, and that agent lives locally.[89]

The point is not, therefore, that legal change can not happen (since constellations of significations are clearly not immobile) or that it can not emerge from external influences (since cultures are obviously not window-less monads), but that whatever legal change materialises will take the form, as a result of a constructive cognitive process, of a specifically local mutation usually denying convergence across jurisdictions other than at the brittle and superficial level (while, incidentally, highlighting the crucial role assumed by the individual within a culture through whom the process of cultural dissemination operates). Thus, although a decision like *M. v. Home Office*,[90] concerning the matter of interim relief against the Crown, represents an important step as regards the development of domestic remedies, the judgment of the English court shows that any talk of European convergence, any idealisation away of difference, is either wishful thinking or bad faith.[91]

In *M.*, Lord Woolf aimed to remedy a local anomaly to the effect that the Crown and government bodies do not enjoy legal personality at common law so that they cannot be subject to injunctive relief. No European dimension was involved in the case and Lord Woolf's remark concerning the merit of avoiding "inconsistency" with European Community law was evidently made *obiter*. In any event, Lord Woolf stressed that "[the] jurisdiction to grant interim and final injunctions against officers of the Crown does not mean that that jurisdiction

---

[87] This observation suggests a more general remark: cultural diversity does not rest on cultural autonomy but rather on an original configuration of "interconnections": U Hannerz, *Cultural Complexity* (New York: Columbia University Press, 1992), p. 266.

[88] P D Carrington, "Aftermath", in P Cane and J Stapleton (eds.), *Essays for Patrick Atiyah* (Oxford : Oxford University Press, 1991), pp. 114–15.

[89] For what I would regard as variations on this argument with reference to the integration of "private law" within the European Community, see H Collins, "European Private Law and the Cultural Identity of States" (1995) 3 *European Review of Private Law* 353; and "Formalism and Efficiency: Designing European Commercial Contract Law" (2000) 8 *European Review of Private Law* 211; Teubner, n. 32 above; Christian Joerges, "The Europeanisation of Private Law as a Rationalisation Process and as a Contest of Disciplines—An Analysis of the Directive on Unfair Terms in Consumer Contracts" (1995) 3 *European Review of Private Law* 175 and "European Challenges to Private Law: On False Dichotomies, True Conflicts and the Need for a Constitutional Perspective" (1998) 18 *Legal Studies* 146.

[90] [1993] 3 All ER 537 (HL).

[91] I borrow the formulae from D Kennedy, *A Critique of Adjudication* (Cambridge, Mass.: Harvard University Press, 1997), pp. 191–4.

should be exercised except in the most limited circumstances",[92] thereby point-ing to the persistent specificity of English law.

At this stage, a number of questions can usefully be raised against the back-ground of *M*. Has the English conception of "Crown" now moved closer to the French conception of "*Etat*"? Is the English understanding of "public law" now more akin to the French notion of "*droit public*"? Does the English equitable remedy of "injunction" now bear more resemblance to the French "*référé*" or "*injonction*"? Have "the most limited circumstances" within which the injunc-tion can be granted in English law anything in common with the situations where a "*référé*" or "*injonction*" can be secured under French law? Has the English tradition of "administrative non-law" now moved significantly toward the French approach?[93] Does the erosion of parliamentary sovereignty through judicial assumption of power bring English law closer to the French model of separation of powers? Will an English judge now be less concerned with facts than has traditionally been the case and favour a rights-based approach? Will an English judge now discard factual analogies with precedents and substitute a more conceptual or systemic perspective? Will an English judge now begin to lay down "rules"? Further questions arise. Are the socio-legal role and responsibil-ities of public officials now constructed in the same way by the lay population in both jurisdictions? Are the social and legal dynamics of the relationship between individuals and public officials now constructed in the same way by the lay population in both jurisdictions? Is the fear that a public official will suffer a social stigma or will find himself the object of legal proceedings by a dissatis-fied litigant now experienced in the same way by public officials in both juris-dictions? Is the fear (and realistic likelihood) that a complaint will be made by a litigant against a public official now experienced in the same way by public offi-cials in both jurisdictions? Is the information regarding available legal remedies or rights in the possession of litigants now the same in both jurisdictions? Are the eventual costs associated with a complaint from the point of view of the lit-igant now internalised in the same way by litigants in both jurisdictions? Is access to justice now the same for litigants in both jurisdictions? Is the likelihood of an order being made against a public official in the courts now the same in both jurisdictions? Is this information now available to litigants in the same way in both jurisdictions? In other words, *what* is converging?[94]

It is crucial to reiterate the distinction between two phenomena: that of national developments deriving inspiration from extraneous ideas, on the one hand, and that of convergence of laws, on the other.[95] In fact, the story told by

---

[92] n. 90 above, p. 564.

[93] Bell, n. 46 above, p. 150.

[94] Related questions could be asked with respect to cases such as *Woolwich Building Society* v. *Inland Revenue Commissioners* [1992] 3 All ER 737 (HL), as regards the restitution of *ultra vires* receipts by public authorities, or *Osman* v. *United Kingdom* (1998) 5 BHRC 293 (ECHR), dealing with the immunity of police officers from liability in negligence.

[95] See Ross, n. 85 above, p. 87. See also Bell, n. 46 above, *passim*.

M. is largely unexceptional, for all that *M*. shows us, ultimately, is that ideas travel, even in law. What one can see in *M*. is that a reform-minded judge on occasion finds it convenient, presumably in the interest of economy and efficiency, to adopt and adapt a pre-existing idea which was formulated outside of the jurisdiction within which he operates—not unlike the way writers on occasion quote or derive inspiration from other authors some of whom are foreigners. What is at issue here is a rhetorical strategy involving the ordinary act of appropriation as an enabling discursive method made more compelling, perhaps significantly so, by the existence within the European Community of regulatory structures and the imposition of a judicially-driven discipline nurturing local dispositions to extraneity (legal, economic, social, or otherwise) through the dissemination across the laws of the member states of ideas endorsed by Community institutions.[96] This distribution process may possibly be best understood using something akin to Dan Sperber's epidemiological model.[97] But to assert that change within the local law can be driven by a kind of transcultural negotiation is not to say any more—or any less—than that individuals can engage with alterity as they proceed with the historical construction of a specific position of historical enunciation. This is as plain in law as it is in literature or mathematics. But does the fact that Baudelaire was inspired by Edgar Allan Poe mean that French and American poetry have been converging? And does the fact that Niels Bohr's scientific findings drew on Rutherford's work on particle physics mean that the scientific cultures of Denmark and New Zealand (or Britain) have been converging? On each occasion, one rather witnesses a local transformation which *de-specifies* local specificity in a most limited manner and in fact may well serve to highlight particularism. Consider *M*. which tells us that, exceptionally, English litigants will now enjoy the opportunity to get an interim injunction against the Crown. Given that civil-law jurisdictions do not have anything like the English notion of "the Crown", or the English notion of "injunction", or the English notion of "equitable remedy", by linking the English and civilian law-worlds via European Community law, Lord Woolf has arguably dramatised their cognitive disconnections and made possible a new awareness of difference. This is especially the case if one envisages a situation where, say, an English and a French court would each render a decision in a dispute involving relief against a public official.

---

[96] For a study showing how the distinctive characteristics of different national administrative traditions influence the implementation of European Community legislation (with specific reference to the institutional embeddedness of respective administrative practices, the structural capacity for administrative reform, and the preferences, capabilities, and resources of subordinate administrative actors), see Knill, n. 81 above. Predictably, the author concludes that implementation is easier in jurisdictions with a high potential for administrative reform especially if embedded institutional equilibria regarding regulatory styles and structures (including the number and tightness of institutional linkages) are not unduly challenged.

[97] D Sperber, *Explaining Culture* (Oxford: Blackwell, 1996). There is, of course, a crucial qualification underlined by Sperber himself: the transmission of infectious diseases is characterised by the replication of pathogenic agents while legal representations are transformed each time they are transmitted.

To simplify the matter, let us imagine that the facts are precisely the same in both countries and let us further accept that the law is exactly the same in both countries. Clearly, one must still bear in mind that the French judge is French and that the English judge is English.[98] Now, the way in which the French and English judges are to approach the merits of the case will vary. Inevitably, the judge comes to the issue as a socialised human being, that is, as a product of his cultural and legal environment. But there is more. Different evidentiary rules (themselves reflecting different social and political values developed over the long term) will make for a different construction of the facts in the eyes of the law. In other words, even if the facts are the same (as I assume they are for present purposes), it remains that the facts will not be the same in the eyes of each law. Likewise, different judicial drafting techniques will thematise certain dimensions of the problem and ignore others. When French decisions, for instance, appeal to the comforting idea of interpretive stability that a grammatical discourse connotes so as to suggest that, although they are clearly not "the law", they are no more than a vehicle allowing for the stable production of the legislative texts' necessary legal solutions, they are doing much more than simply gesturing toward formalism. They thereby advocate a particular vision of adjudication and of the values served by adjudication. The felt need to obfuscate, or at least to de-prioritise, the role of hermeneutical readings of the law in order not to invest the generative matrix of the decision with the insecurity associated with purposive hermeneutics is in itself of considerable significance to an understanding of judicial governance and, more broadly, of a legal *mentalité*.[99]

In sum, I suggest that any attempt at globalisation ultimately resolves itself as an original experience of "glocalisation".[100] The similarities that require to be postulated if the "convergence" thesis is to prove creditable are simply unrealistic. In fact, the "convergence" thesis can only hold if its proponents are prepared to pretend that the problems which the law addresses and the solutions which the law provides to these problems are somehow unconnected to the cultural environment from which the problems and solutions arise. In other words, the "convergence" thesis compels one to regard social problems and their legal treatment as occurring in a cultural vacuum. Only if one is willing to ignore the cultural dimension of the law can one say that the problem of "relief against public officials" and its treatment by the law can be considered irrespective of geography. What is unclear is whether the defenders of "convergence" take the view that unlike art or literature, law is somehow completely disconnected from the society by which it is produced or whether they accept that law necessarily

---

[98] "[I]t must be clear that one of the difficulties for English lawyers trying to understand French law is the fact that it is French and not simply that it contains technicalities unfamiliar to them": G Wilson, "English Legal Scholarship" (1987) 50 *Modern Law Review* 818, p. 831.

[99] See M Lasser, " 'Lit. Theory' Put to the Test: A Comparative Literary Analysis of American Judicial Tests and French Judicial Discourse" (1998) 111 *Harvard Law Review* 689.

[100] R Robertson, "Glocalization: Time-Space and Homogeneity-Heterogeneity", in M Featherstone, S Lash, and R Robertson (eds.), *Global Modernities* (London: Sage, 1995), pp. 25–44.

partakes in the culture from which it emanates but prefer to close their eyes to this fact leaving the matter to sociologists or other such "marginal" figures to consider. In either case, the "convergence" approach perpetuates a brand of "rightwing Hegelianism [which] conceals a stark downgrading of historical contingency and human freedom".[101] In an insightful observation, Martin Loughlin highlights how the historical rootedness of law means that "law is thoroughly a cultural construct",[102] although the fact may be inconvenient for lawyers to acknowledge given the limits of their expertise:

> "The journey of finding effective, enlightened and liberating conditions of government is a journey through history and on tracks formed within specific cultural traditions. The maps drawn by societies other than our own are undoubtedly of innate interest; indeed, their strangeness and their difference make us welcome. But as guides to the journey they must be treated with great circumspection. It is precisely those aspects that welcome us which pose major barriers to understanding them as practical guides. Their accessibility is deceptive since we read them as outsiders and this leads too easily to distortion. If we are serious about confronting the complex issues raised by an inquiry into democracy and public law, I believe that we must start by recognising that there can be no elsewhere which underwrites our existence".[103]

Ultimately, the reality of European legal convergence becomes as problematic as the idea of convergence of European societies, at least from the moment one takes the issue beyond the superficial level of rules and precepts. This is because convergence of a group of legal cultures does not appear any more feasible than would convergence of the different world-views privileged by a wide range of societies. Since the legal is also cultural, "convergence", a "common meeting point" across laws, is a promise that law is simply ontologically incapable of fulfilling.[104] To the extent that one is prepared to value cultural and moral commitment over abstract and instrumental frameworks, this situation is certainly not to be deplored especially if the following facts concerning European Community law are borne in mind.

(*i*). The fundamental points underlying the Treaty of Rome are that there should be an opening of economic borders within the European Community; that the member states should recognise each other's law; and that "market citizens" should have the opportunity to select the legal regulation that best suits them. This structure, therefore, assumes difference across the legal "systems" of the various member states.

---

[101] R M Unger, *What Should Legal Analysis Become?* (London: Verso, 1996), p. 9. See also *ibid.*, pp. 72–73 and 76–77.

[102] B Z Tamanaha, *Realistic Socio-Legal Theory* (Oxford: Oxford University Press, 1997), p. 128.

[103] M Loughlin, "The Importance of Elsewhere" (1993) 4 *Public Law Review*, p. 57. As the author himself notes, his text is indebted to P Larkin, "The Importance of Elsewhere", in *Collected Poems* (London: Marvell Press and Faber, 1988), p. 104 [originally published in 1955].

[104] For a thoughtful slant on this argument, see P B Stephan, "The Futility of Unification and Harmonization in International Commercial Law" (1999) 39 *Va J Int'l L* 743. I owe this reference to Professor Hiroo Sono.

(*ii*). The Treaty of Rome itself accepts the presence of differences across legal "systems" within member states, for the Treaty's concern with the harmonisation of laws expressed in Article 94 (formerly 100) acknowledges either that these differences are insurmountable or that they ought not to be fully transcended. (In this respect, the doctrine of "direct effect" developed by the European Court of Justice arguably suffers from a legitimacy problem.) Indeed, "harmonisation" does not connote the idea of a "common meeting point" and certainly means neither "uniformity" nor "equivalence". It does not, therefore, require any "convergence" of national laws in order to materialise. The preamble of the 1992 Treaty of European Union and Article 7 of the protocol on subsidiarity and proportionality appended to the 1998 Treaty of Amsterdam both recognise the inevitability or value of legal pluralism as do, in effect, all European directives by conceding a national margin of appreciation to the member states.[105]

(*iii*). The European Court of Justice, which is entrusted with the interpretation of the Treaty of Rome (as subsequently amended), has no adjudicative power to eliminate differences across the laws of the various member states not even as regards those member states' readings of European Community law itself. According to Article 234 (formerly 177) of the Treaty, its role is strictly consultative. Once the European Court of Justice has pronounced on what it regards as the correct interpretation of European Community law, it falls to the national courts, embedded as they are in diverse legal cultures, to apply the law, including European Community law. Again, the structure of this interpretive framework shows how differences across legal "systems" are not meant to be erased. (The European Court of Justice's proactive stance in favour of the assimilation of laws across member states, therefore, also raises a serious issue of legitimacy.)

LEARNING TO LIVE WITH DIFFERENCE

In the face of a Europeanisation that operates in a deracinating world of markets, it falls to identity politics to fulfil a humanising role. To allow difference to act as the pertinent dialogical vehicle between European legal traditions is, of course, vastly more complicated than designing a homogeneous legal culture oriented only toward one center. Yet, the *understanding of diversity* must be seen as the privileged way to attenuate the heterogeneity of meaning that acts as an impediment to communication and to foster the respect due the variety of

---

[105] In fact, the piecemeal, at times spasmodic, character of European Community interventions regularly causes the disintegration of "systemic" interdependencies within the various member states both in law and between law and other discourses. Given that the nature or extent of these discontinuities depends upon the particular discursive configuration governing locally, every Community measure generates new, if unintended, differences *across* the discursive configurations (including law) prevailing in the various member states. The production of "difference" across member states is, therefore, inherent to European law-making. See generally Teubner, n. 32. above.

lived experiences that sustain intersubjective world-views and practices across European interpretive communities. The specificity of Europe lies not in the abolition of difference but in the deft management of the cultural heteronomies within the whole, in the assumption of pluralism, in the acceptance of a coexistence of non-harmonised rationalities on its territory, in the willingness to enlarge the possibility of intelligible discourse between legal traditions, and in the steady practice of a politics of inclusion ensuring an equally significant role for each of the two legal traditions historically represented in its midst. In short, difference must be understood and the temptation to reduce it resisted. Europe's distinctive circumstances throughout its history have repeatedly involved the recognition of insurmountable alterities arising from within. Today, "the *duty* to answer the call of European memory dictates respect for difference, the idiomatic, the minority, the singular and commands to tolerate and respect everything that does not place itself under the authority of reason"; in fact, "this responsibility toward memory is a responsibility toward the concept of responsibility itself which regulates the justice and the justness of our behaviour, of our theoretical, practical, and ethico-political decisions".[106]

In French, one can refer to a "*parti pris*" and talk about "*prendre son parti*". Either formulation connotes three meanings that jointly capture three important facets of my argument. First, one can have a "*parti pris*" in the sense of showing purposefulness. For example, a French sentence could run thus: "*Chez lui, le parti pris de faire du bien se remarquait vite*" ("In him, the determination to do good could easily be noticed"). A variation on this sentence would read: "*Il avait pris le parti de faire du bien*" ("He had determined to do good"). Second, a "*parti pris*" refers to a prejudice as in the sentence, "*il y a trop de parti pris dans ses jugements*" ("there is too much prejudice in his opinions"). Third, "*prendre son parti*" can mean "to resign oneself". After one has lost an important vote, it can be said that "*il en a pris son parti*", that "he has resigned himself to it". Purposefulness, prejudice, and resignation are three cardinal features of the brand of comparative legal studies I advocate. I claim that comparatists must resign themselves to the fact that law is a cultural phenomenon and that, therefore, differences across jurisdictions can only ever be overcome imperfectly. Disclaiming any objectivity (and, therefore, bringing to bear their own prejudices as situated observers), they must purposefully privilege the identification of differences across the laws they compare lest they fail to address singularity with authenticity.

---

[106] J Derrida, *L'autre cap* (Paris: Minuit, 1991), pp. 75–7 "[*le devoir de répondre à l'appel de la mémoire européenne (. . .) dicte de respecter la différence, l'idiome, la minorité, la singularité (. . . et) commande de tolérer et de respecter tout ce qui ne se place pas sous l'autorité de la raison*" (emphasis original)]; *ibid.*, *Force de loi* (Paris: Galilée, 1994), p. 45 ["*Cette responsabilité devant la mémoire est une responsabilité devant le concept même de responsabilité qui règle la justice et la justesse de nos comportements, de nos décisions théoriques, pratiques, éthico-politiques*"].

CONCLUSION

Coming to the matter of "convergence" as a comparatist—and, therefore, as someone who values diversity as a good and who is prepared to affirm it as a good—I urge common-law lawyers to resist the drive toward cultural uniformity by emphasising, explaining, and justifying their particularity, thus claiming for themselves the power to transform the negative meanings associated with difference into positive ones. Above all, common-law lawyers must overcome the inclination to fall for a devaluation of their own experience of life in the law in the face of ever more ponderous intimations emanating from various Continental universities and capitals that "good Europeans" cannot oppose legal convergence across the European Community, because to contest "convergence" is supposedly to deny the merits of the European construction. In fact, it must be appreciated that to master, absorb, and finally reduce difference to sameness just cannot make for a "good Europe". James Tully correctly observes that "[t]he suppression of cultural difference in the name of uniformity and unity is one of the leading causes of civil strife, disunity and dissolution today".[107] The law of the European Community can only possibly prove itself to be a workable amelioration over the extant variety of national and infranational laws if it is prepared to draw upon both the civil-law and common-law traditions, that is, upon two discrepant historical reservoirs of ideas which between them allow all communities and individuals across Europe to recognise the comforting legal-cultural forms established over the long term that resonate with their sense of identity (including spheres of "non-law" that have deliberately fashioned themselves as legitimate modes of conflict resolution).

To stress difference as a value, to militate in favour of the recognition, respect, and implementation of difference in all its complex ramifications, is not to subvert the Enlightenment commitments to human emancipation and liberty and is not *a fortiori* to insist upon a return to a pre-Enlightenment cast of mind which denied parity for all before the law and favoured exclusion based on

---

[107] J Tully, *Strange Multiplicity [:] Constitutionalism in an Age of Diversity* (Cambridge: Cambridge University Press, 1995), p. 197. But see for an argument *in terrorem* suggesting that to defend legal pluralism is to oppose peace, J Schwarze, "Introduction", in *ibid.* (ed.), *Administrative Law Under European Influence* (London: Sweet & Maxwell, 1996), p. 21: "For a continuation of the endeavours towards European unity that have, up to now, brought peace and wealth for the Member States and for which there is hardly any political alternative, an even closer intertwining of the administrative law systems of the Member States is becoming necessary in order to further intensify and deepen European integration. In this context, the Member States are required to make concessions in a field that has always been a classical domain of the national State". As a German academic asserts such antiparticularism, he is seemingly giving effect to the nineteenth-century view that "[o]nly by transcending what distinguished Swabia from Prussia, or Bavaria from Schleswig-Holstein, could Germany become, in law as in ideology, one". This quotation is from W T Murphy, *The Oldest Social Science?* (Oxford: Oxford University Press, 1997), p. 44, n. 22. For general evidence supporting the view that German academics tend to address European matters as if *German* history was repeating itself, see J Laughland, *The Tainted Source* (London: Little Brown, 1997), pp. 22–3, 26, 31–3, 110–11, 116–17, 120, and 137.

status. Nor is it to promote indifferentist relativism or to stand against Europeanisation or to display pessimism. My argument lies elsewhere. Given that the diversity of legal traditions and the diversity of forms of life in the law they embody remain the expression of the human capacity for choice and self-creation, I seek affirmatively to encourage oppositional discourse in the face of a totalitarian rationality which, while claiming to pursue the ideal of impartiality by reducing differences in the lifeworld to calculative and instrumental unity, effectively privileges a situated standpoint—that favouring capital and productivity, regulation and juridification—which it allows to project as universal. I contend that this exercise must be apprehended for the fiction that it is and that one must accept, therefore, that a universalisation can only prove persuasive if it will work *through* difference rather than against it by acknowledging as equally meaningful each legal tradition's characteristic discursive formation. Only in deferring to the non-identical can the claim to *justice* be redeemed.

Today's comparatists in law faculties throughout Europe are expected to subscribe to a script of underlying European unity and ultimate European transcendence where particularism is assumed to be epiphenomenal and fated to play but a peripheral role in the future of human affairs. It is easy to sympathise with the desire for a more orderly, circumscribed world. The obsession to find and impose order possibly answers a most basic human drive (in fact, the common law is an order too—as is the alphabet). But it is quite another thing to underwrite the search for a monistic unifying pattern not unlike the Platonic belief in a final rational harmony, that is, to endorse reason acting as the corrosive solvent of custom and allegiance. And this is why the programmatic engagement that I advocate for comparative legal studies must aim for a relentless disruption of the immoderate confidence in regulatory formalisation somnolently reiterated by those who seek to rob the law of its historical integrity.

13

Culture, Democracy and the Convergence of Public Law: Some Scepticisms about Scepticism[1]

NEIL WALKER

INTRODUCTION

IN THEIR CONTRIBUTIONS to the present volume, Pierre Legrand and Carol Harlow present formidable cases for treating the distinctiveness of domestic systems of public law more seriously than is often the case in discussions of the integrative potential of public law across states in general, and in the context of EU law in particular. The point of departure for Legrand's argument is the theme of culture, while for Harlow it is democracy that provides the analytical baseline and normative lodestar. It would be fair to say, however, that the two arguments complement—indeed presuppose—one another, and in fact this is made explicit in Harlow's paper.[2]

In the present contribution, I seek to endorse much of the general messages of Legrand and Harlow while qualifying them in important particulars. I argue, first, that Legrand and Harlow's arguments threaten to throw out the baby along with the bathwater. They correctly criticise what we might call "convergence fundamentalism"—that is, the belief amongst many academics, politicians and bureaucrats, as often implicit as explicit, that the convergence of systems of public law is *essentially* and so *generally* a good thing; yet in so doing it is arguable that neither Legrand nor Harlow sufficiently specifies on what terms, to what extent and through what transmission mechanisms *particular* convergent movements of law between or above legal systems might *contingently* be a good thing—or for that matter even a feasible project. Secondly, and closely related, the ideas of "culture" and "democracy" that they elaborate in order to defend their theses are, on careful analysis, revealed to have conflicting ramifications. On the one hand, they do indeed provide the foundations of

---

[1] The title is borrowed from William Twining, who was engaged in a quite different project concerned with the law of evidence: W Twining, "Some Scepticisms about Scepticism" (1984) 11 *Journal of Law and Society*, pp. 137–72 and 285–316.

[2] Above, pp. 205–08.

strong presumptive arguments against convergence. On the other hand, a deeper exploration of the very same concepts also challenges the normative claims of the "units"—that is, the domestic polities and legal systems—against whose convergence they argue, and does so in a manner which seems to suggest the desirability of *some measure* of "contingent" convergence. Yet, as we have noted, it is this intermediate possibility—or, to be more accurate, the vast range of intermediate possibilities of selective convergence—which tends to be marginalised by the single-mindedness of the authors' attack on convergence fundamentalism.

AGAINST CONVERGENCE FUNDAMENTALISM

No-one with remotely sensitive sociological antennae—whether professionally tuned or not—could fail to be impressed by Legrand's well-known and compelling analysis of the limitations of the traditional comparative method before the cultural embeddedness of law.[3] Law is not simply a set of rules, but a way of thinking—a *mentalité*—which is grounded in the social practice of legal communities and of the broader communities of which they are part and which underpins and breathes life into the legal rules. For Legrand, much traditional comparative law has either simply ignored or underplayed the significance of legal culture. For him, by contrast, "a rule does not have any empirical existence that can be significantly detached from the world of meanings that characterises a legal culture".[4] Legal culture, which is complexly interwoven with wider forms of culture within a society, thus adds its own distinctive texture to the rules of a system. In turn, this distinctiveness creates an "irreducible epistemological chasm"[5] between legal cultures, leading to an incapacity on the part of those immersed in one legal system to appreciate the deep context and meaning of other systems. It is imperviousness to or arrogant dismissal of this epistemological chasm which encourages comparativists in their labours of mistranslation, transferring rules between systems without serious reflection upon the different meaning and import of the transferred rule when transplanted to and re-rooted in a different cultural sub-soil.

  Legrand addresses two possible objections to his thesis in some detail. In the first place, he defends his notion of distinctive legal cultures against the well-known and frequently rehearsed argument that the essentialisation of difference implicit in this notion is both flawed in explanatory terms and dangerous in normative

[3] Many of Legrand's best known studies are collected in *Fragments on Law-As-Culture* (Deventer: W E J Tjeenk Willink, 1999). For a comprehensive and well-balanced overview of comparative law's recent contribution to debates over unification and harmonisation, see L Nottage, "Convergence, Divergence and the Middle Way in Unifying or Harmonising Private Law", EUI Working Papers, LAW No.2001/1 (Florence: European University Institute).
  [4] Above, p. 230.
  [5] J W F Allison, "Transplantation and Cross-fertilisation" in J Beatson and T Tridimas (eds.), *New Directions in European Public Law* (Oxford: Hart, 1998) p. 173.

terms.[6] For him, cultures need not be uniform or monolithic. Individuals are not mere sociological dupes, fated to follow behavioural tramlines dictated by common material and ideational conditions. Neither, he claims, can he be accused of falsely romanticising culture as necessarily or even tendentially egalitarian. Membership of a common culture does not preclude asymmetries of power and knowledge, nor eliminate conflicts of interest between the members of that common culture. Equally, the idea of culture, as it is elaborated by Legrand, does not and should not freeze or fetishise difference. Cultural forms and units are not immutable, and the differences that manifest themselves between cultures do not justify political projects of "cultural fundamentalism"[7]—the dismissal of the cultural "other" as alien or inferior.

Nevertheless, for all their internal heterogeneity and openness to external influence, cultures, according to Legrand, necessarily denote boundedness and some sense of collective identity. They define "a realm of possibility",[8] a set of limiting assumptions within which social actors operate. In other words, the relatively open-texture of cultural units does not in the final analysis deny their unity or integrity—their very identity as cultural units. And, Legrand asserts, convergence fundamentalists cannot ignore these loose but resilient cultural units and the normative and epistemological frontiers that they establish as easily and as readily as they might mock, and so dismiss the popular caricature of culture as an undifferentiated monad.

In the second place, Legrand defends his thesis against the more specific, limited and less well-trodden objection that it is only applicable to private law, where the major part of his work has been concentrated, and has no relevance to the domain of public law. As he points out, the very boundary between public law and private law is a culturally specific and so culturally variable one, as demonstrated by the way in which the traditional Roman law distinction was reformulated in remedial terms through the prism of English law.[9] Yet, as the logic of Legrand's position dictates, this does not make the public/private divide meaningless, merely *differently* meaningful in different legal systems. This can be illustrated by reference to the recent work of Dawn Oliver.[10] She devotes a book-length argument to the thesis that in the United Kingdom public law and private law are ultimately concerned with the protection of a common core of values—namely individual dignity, autonomy, respect, status and security. She does not deny, however, even from a position which makes an ambitious claim about the existence of a common, boundary-transcending, normative core, that

---

[6] See e.g. Allison, n. 5 above; J Bell, "Mechanisms for Cross-Fertilisation of Administrative Law in Europe," in Beatson and Tridimas, n. 5 above; B Schafer and Z Bankowski, "Mistaken Identities: The Integrative Force of Private Law," in M Van Ost and F Ost (eds.), *The Harmonisation of European Private Law* (Oxford: Hart, 2000) pp.21–45.
[7] Above p. 245.
[8] Above p. 238.
[9] Above p. 246. Here Legrand draws on the work of J W F Allison, *A Continental Distinction in the Common Law* (Oxford: Oxford University Press, 1996).
[10] See D Oliver, *Common Values and the Public-Private Divide* (London: Butterworths, 1999).

the binary divide between public law and private law remains a resilient part of the self-understanding and self-representation of the system; a kind of cultural "shorthand for a whole collection of ideas"[11] about the distinctions, however hazy and imperfect and however deficient in terms of their mutual coherence, between different types of institutions, functions, interests and procedures. Essentially, this cultural shorthand, while its perception of the limits and edges of public law may be distinctly fuzzy, serves to locate "the distribution and control of state power"[12] as the traditional and continuing centre of gravity of the discipline.

Legrand duly accepts the significance of the public/private divide as part of the self-understanding and self-presentation of the system, and in a move which is paralleled in Harlow's paper,[13] quotes Loughlin in support of the thesis that public law is but "a sophisticated form of political discourse"[14] about the nature, limits and purposes of state power. And as a sophisticated political discourse, far from being less resonant of domestic cultural norms than private law, public law becomes even more "national-specific".[15] On this view, the values, customs and ways of thought inscribed in constitutional and other public law rules are at the very heart of what distinguishes and characterises the polity,[16] which in turn, typically[17] provides the individuating point of reference and authoritative container for the legal system as a whole. Rather than being above or beyond the distinctive culture of the system, therefore, public law actually *frames* that distinctive culture—is deeply constitutive of it.

In what way is the cultural thesis about the distinctiveness of public law and the fallacies of convergence fundamentalism complemented by Harlow's democratic thesis? For Harlow, the case for diversity and against convergence fundamentalism rests upon the idea of "pluralist democracy", with democracy for these purposes defined as "popular political self-government [in which] 'the people of a country decide for themselves the contents of the laws that organise and regulate their political association'[18]".[19] The pluralist element appears to be twofold. In the first place, if the "community" of the EU is taken as the relevant level of analysis, then a plurality of different democratic voices emanating from

---

[11] See D Oliver, *Common Values and the Public-Private Divide*, (London: Butterworths, 1999). p. 14.

[12] *Ibid.*, p. 31

[13] Legrand, above p. 246; Harlow, p. 208.

[14] M Loughlin, *Public Law and Political Theory*, (Oxford: Oxford University Press, 1992) p. 4.

[15] See above, p. 246.

[16] This leaves open the question of which, if any, is normatively prior—(public) law or polity. For interesting recent analyses, drawing upon but modifying the Kelsenian perspective, see, e.g. N MacCormick, *Questioning Sovereignty* (Oxford: Oxford University Press, 1999) ch. 2; H Lindahl and B van Roermund, "Law Without a State? On Representing the Common Market" in Z Bankowski and A Scott (eds.), *The European Union and Its Order: The Legal Theory of European Integration* (Oxford: Blackwell, 2000) pp. 1–17.

[17] Though not, of course necessarily as, for example, in the case of the *Scottish* legal system and the *United Kingdom* polity.

[18] The quote is from F Michelman, "Brennan and Democracy: the 1996–97 Brennan Centre Symposium Lecture" (1998) 86 *California Law Review* 399.

[19] Harlow, above p. 201.

the different member states—constituent "countries"—require to be heard. However, this emphasis upon statist democracy does not imply that Harlow subscribes to a strong version of the thesis that there exists "no demos" at the wider European level, a thesis famously associated with the 1993 Maastricht decision of the German Constitutional Court.[20] This is indicated by the second limb of Harlow's democratic pluralism, namely her acceptance of the need for—and thus the value and legitimacy of—strong representative institutions invested with supreme law-making powers at the European level. This presupposes the existence of a coherent political community at the European level alongside the political communities at the state level.

Nevertheless, a fair and rounded reading of Harlow's paper would undoubtedly have the state democratic level as the more powerful, the more conducive to popular political identification and involvement. In turn, this connects to the thesis of cultural diversity. If the level of state politics is accorded an elevated status within the plural democratic framework on account of its being the level with which "the people" most closely identify, then that identification is in turn connected with a sense of common culture. On this view cultural community and political community are mutually supportive, certainly within normative political theory if not always within actually existing political orders. The democratic empowerment of the local polity can be *democratically* more effective because the local community has a prior sense of identity with that polity, while it is *culturally* protective in that it guarantees respect for local culture against the universalising imperatives and the monolithic tendencies of the supranational order.

Furthermore, Harlow argues, to the extent that political authority flows up to the European level, a double democratic danger arises. Not only is the sense of political community—of the *demos*, rather thinly stretched over this wider constituency, but also the institutional balance of the Union tends to favour the judicial organs over the more democratically sensitive political organs. The mechanisms of legal integration, including the early-asserted doctrines of supremacy and direct effect, and the later and continuing development of jurisprudences of uniform procedural enforcement and protection of human rights involve "a substantial horizontal relocation of power from parliamentary institutions towards an unelected judiciary".[21] Through these doctrines, which are not based upon any simple reading of the Treaties but involve much creative judicial work, the judges arrogate to themselves the power to make significant value judgements and to precipitate significant changes in national legal orders. They thus squeeze the authoritative space of representative institutions—a

---

[20] *Brunner* v. *European Union Treaty* [1994] 1 CMLR 57. This has spawned an enormous literature. See, e.g. M Everson, "Beyond the *Bundesverfassungsgericht:* On the Necessary Cunning of Constitutional Reasoning", in Bankowski and Scott (eds.), n. 16 above, pp. 91–112; J H H Weiler "Does Europe Need a Constitution? Demos, Telos and the German Maastricht Decision", (1995) 1 *European Law Journal* 217.

[21] Harlow above, p. 204. See also D Chalmers, "Judicial Preferences and the Community Legal Order", (1997) 60 *Modern Law Review* 164.

process exacerbated by the fact that the main national interlocutors of ECJ judges are often other judges—and threaten the integrity of the expressions of local political will and local cultural sensibility which domestic legal systems represent.

CULTURE AND DEMOCRACY REASSESSED

So the convergence fundamentalists appear to have been well and truly routed, but how do we construct a more balanced sense of the appropriate mechanisms of transmission between systems of public law from the wreckage of the battle-field? Both Legrand and Harlow are conscious of the need to address this question. They are thus clearly not divergence fundamentalists. They do not make the equal and opposite error of the convergence fundamentalists of assuming that difference should be supported for its own sake, or that a simple trajectory of diversification should be encouraged or expected. Rather, each favours dialogue between legal systems—between the different domestic systems and between domestic systems and supranational systems. Legrand talks of the "legitimate desire to overcome barriers of communication across legal traditions" and of how a deeper understanding across legal cultures "may then be used to encourage new forms of problem-solving".[22] For her part, Harlow talks of "co-ordinately valid legal systems",[23] of "a plural legal framework" to match a pluralist conception of democracy, and of the need for mutual respect and "a non-hierarchical method of mediating conflict".[24]

These are suggestive formulations, but both their underlying motivation and their implications remain rather vague. Many contemporary theorists of the European Union would have sympathy with the basic idea of a plurality of inter-acting normative orders for both epistemological and normative reasons. Epistemologically, the notion of legal pluralism flows from the idea that the different legal orders—national and supranational—of the developing European—indeed global—political mosaic of the post-Westphalian age make competing and incommensurable claims to ultimate legal authority; that there is no Archimedean point from which we can judge the relative weight of these claims; and that what we have in consequence is a heterarchically organised rather than a hierarchically organised configuration of legal authority.[25] Normatively, this pluralism is attractive for many commentators—indeed many

[22] pp. 228 and 241 above.
[23] The quotation is from N MacCormick, "Liberalism, Nationalism and the Post-Sovereign State", in R Bellamy and D Castiglione (eds.), *Constitutionalism in Transformation: European and Theoretical Perspectives*, (Oxford: Blackwell, 1996). See also MacCormick, n. 16 above.
[24] Harlow, pp. 222–3 above.
[25] See e.g. MacCormick n. 16 above; C Richmond, "Preserving the Identity Crisis: Autonomy, System and Sovereignty in European Law" (1997) 16 *Law and Philosophy* 377–420; J Shaw, Postnational Constitutionalism in the European Union" (1999) 6 *Journal of European Public Policy* 579–97; N Walker, "Flexibility within a Metaconstitutional Frame: Reflections on the Future of Legal Authority in Europe" in G de Búrca and J Scott (eds.), *Constitutional Change in the EU: From Uniformity to Flexibility?* (Oxford: Hart, 2000) pp. 9–30.

of the same commentators[26]—because, in the absence of categorical inter-systemic rules for making decisions or resolving disputes in areas of overlapping competence, it encourages more flexible modes of bargaining and more deliberative modes of dialogue[27] between actors occupying authoritative sites in different systems, whether this be between the ECJ and national courts, between the Council (in its legislative mode) and national legislatures, or between the Commission and national executives.

Yet it is not clear whether and to what extent Legrand or Harlow would share the epistemological starting-point or approve the normative implications. The explicitness of Harlow's endorsement of the pluralist literature suggests that she does share the epistemological premise of the pluralist school, although, as we shall see, this may be in some tension with her democratic analysis. Legrand's work is of course more tangential to the debates around constitutional pluralism, and so his position on this question is less clearly focused, and in some degree has to be extrapolated from his more general approach. As we have observed, the incommensurability of legal cultures and systems is absolutely central to that general approach. Yet it does not follow that, on the basis of such incommensurability, he would doubt the ultimate authority of national constitutional orders over the putative constitutional order of the European Union, since even for the question of incommensurability to be sensibly posed in this particular context requires the prior concession that the putative constitutional order of the EU deserved to be taken seriously as a competing site of authority. And insofar as he addresses this prior question in his remarks on the EU Treaty framework's endorsement of the continuing diversity of national legal systems, on its restricted constitutional mandate, and on the doubtful legitimacy of the ECJ's efforts to deepen the original mandate through the direct effect and supremacy doctrines, Legrand appears unprepared to make this concession.[28]

---

[26] One prominent exception who subscribes to normative but not epistemological pluralism is J Weiler; see his *The Constitution of Europe* (Cambridge: Cambridge University Press, 1999) esp. ch. 8; for an exploration of this distinction in the context of an overview of Weiler's work, see N Walker "All Dressed Up," (2001) 2 *Oxford Journal of Legal Studies* 563 82.

[27] On which see e.g. J Cohen and C Sabel, "Directly-Deliberative Polyarchy" (1997) 3 *European Law Journal* 313–42; O Gerstenberg, "Law's Polyarchy: A Comment on Cohen and Sabel" (1997) 3 *European Law Journal* pp. 343–58.

[28] See Legrand, above pp 252–3 Each of these lines of argument might reasonably be questioned. To the point that the Treaties allow continuing diversity of national legal orders through doctrines such as subsidiarity and proportionality and through the endorsement of harmonisation rather than unification of domestic laws, one might respond that while the constitutional autonomy of the EU requires a plausible claim to authority within certain fields of competence, it does not require a "statist" (or superstatist) strategy of comprehensive subordination of the national legal orders; indeed, it is a central feature of constitutional pluralism that no such comprehensive subordination is feasible or appropriate. To the point that the constitutional mandate of the EU is restricted, *inter alia*, by the merely "consultative" character of the ECJ's preliminary reference jurisdiction, one might respond that while national constitutional courts may retain a degree of bounded (by their interpretation of the requirements of EU law) discretion both in the decision whether to refer a question to the ECJ and also in their reception and assimilation of the answer, this is quite different from the power of outright rejection of the ECJ's conclusions implied by the "consultative" label. To the point that the authority of the ECJ to deepen the constitutional mandate in the way that it has its

As to normative implications, again it is not clear to what extent either author would endorse the compromises, accommodations and other forms of co-ordinate authority which have already grown up within the framework of EU law as manifestations of the attitudes of mutual respect and dialogue which they claim to endorse; or, indeed, which alternative or additional transmission mechanisms they might endorse. Legrand in particular is critical of the ECJ's aggressive interpretation of the Article 234 reference procedure,[29] and Harlow of its *dirigiste* approach to procedural harmonisation, or to the development of a cross-sectoral European human rights jurisprudence.[30] But it is less apparent what, particularly for Legrand, *would* pass muster as an acceptable form of communication or co-ordination. For example, would it include existing legislative techniques of minimum harmonisation, where states are allowed to set higher standards of regulation than those set out in a directive? [31] More broadly, which, if any, of the complex range of general or sectoral flexibility provisions contained in the Treaty of Amsterdam, and strengthened by the Treaty of Nice, show sufficient respect for the aspirations of those member states who wish to opt-out of or opt-in to initiatives which do not involve the Union as a whole?[32] Or to pitch the debate at an even higher level and pose the question of respect from the opposite standpoint: should the European Parliament, in the spirit of good communication between systems, be granted the formal voice, perhaps even a voting voice in the Treaty amendment process, which it does not presently possess?[33]

These details of co-ordination and of the balance between convergence and divergence matter, I would argue, because the ideas of culture and democracy on which Legrand and Harlow rest their arguments imply, on deeper inquiry, the normative permissibility, perhaps even desirability, of some level of communication and convergence between systems. Take, first, the idea of culture. In his conclusion Legrand quotes approvingly from the work of James Tully,[34]

doubtful, one might respond that it is a normal, indeed inevitable, part of the role of a constitutional court to interpret, and in some respects deepen the mandate handed down by the constitutional text, and, indeed, that all but the original six member states made the national constitutional decision to join the EU *after* the major constitutional landmark decisions of the ECJ in the 1960s, so conferring additional political legitimacy upon its expansionist jurisprudence. See e.g. Weiler n. 26 above, at ch. 8; Walker "Late Sovereignty in the European Union" European Forum Paper (Florence, European University Institute, February 2001.) For a position within European public law which offers robust and detailed support to the line sketched by Legrand, see Schilling, "The Autonomy of the Community Order—An Analysis of Possible Foundations" (1996) 37 *Harvard Journal of International Law* 390–409; and "Rejoinder: The Autonomy of the Community Legal Order," Harvard Jean Monnet Working Paper 10/96.

[29]   Above p. 253.

[30]   Above, pp. 218–21.

[31]   See S Weatherill, *Law and Integration in the European Union* (Oxford: Oxford University Press, 1995) pp. 151–7

[32]   See N Walker, "Sovereignty and Differentiated Integration in the European Union" (1998) 4 *European Law Journal* 355–88, at 362–9.

[33]   Art. 48, TEU. For recent developments, including the initiation of a new round of constitutional debate under the Treaty of Nice, see B De Witte's contribution to the present volume.

[34]   Above, p. 255.

citing his warning that the suppression of cultural difference is a leading cause of social conflict and disintegration in the contemporary world order.[35] Legrand, of course, is invoking this sentiment in defence of national culture against the monolithic pretensions of the EU. But, as we have already argued, Legrand is also sensitive to the fact that his *own* thesis is open to precisely the same objection at a lower level of analysis. His concession of internal cultural heterogeneity and of asymmetries of power and knowledge, and his critique of cultural insularity, suspicion and imperialism all testify to this. Yet it is arguable whether his critique and reconstruction of cultural formation goes far enough, or that he is sufficiently diligent of the political implications of such a critique.

Tully's own work is instructive in this regard. For Tully, "([T]he modern age is intercultural rather than multicultural".[36] Interculturality implies that cultures overlap geographically; that they are complexly interdependent in their formation and identity; and that, in consequence, their internal heterogeneity is highly developed; "[T]hey are continuously contested, imagined and reimagined, transformed and negotiated, both by their members and through their interaction with others". What this implies for Tully, unlike Legrand, is that there is no privileged site of cultural formation—no fixed cultural unit which is presumptively central to individual experience and collective identity. In other words, the demands for cultural recognition from the nation state, and from its defining cultural products, such as its legal system, must be balanced against the alternative demands for cultural recognition from ethnic and linguistic minorities; from national minorities within multi-national states; from "intercultural" epistemic and functional communities such as refugees, religious movements, business and trading communities and feminist movements; and, indeed, from crossnational or supranational movements trying to sustain, develop or defend regional or continental identities.[37]

---

[35] J Tully, *Strange Multiplicity: Constitutionalism in an Age of Diversity* (Cambridge: Cambridge University Press, 1995). For discussion in the context of the EU, see Shaw n. 25 above.

[36] *Ibid.*, p. 11.

[37] Of course, one response which might be made to this line of argument, and which was in fact suggested by Legrand himself in the course of the Aberdeen seminar, is that while culture *tout court* might admit of such an open-textured definition, legal culture is a more limited and specific idea, one in which the identifying criteria and boundaries of specific units remain relatively distinctive. This suggestion opens up a deep well of theoretical and empirical inquiry into the relationship between culture in general and legal culture (see e.g. D Nelken (ed.), *Comparing Legal Cultures* (Aldershot: Dartmouth, 1997)). A short essay with a more general object of inquiry is not the place to explore this in any depth. Neither is it fair to use an impromptu remark by Legrand as a peg on which to hang a reasoned critique, particularly as he has not had the opportunity in the present volume to elaborate and refine his thoughts further on this matter. I will restrict myself, therefore, to a few modest observations. First, as Legrand's own work amply demonstrates, any sensitive approach to the relationship between theoretical objects as open-ended, multi-dimensional and mutually implicated as culture in general and legal culture on the other is bound to encounter great difficulty in defining the boundaries and charting the complex web of connections between the two. The burden of proof, therefore, lies on those who would assert that the more specific (but still very broad) concept is more easily individuated in national (or indeed any other) terms than the more general concept to demonstrate how and why that is the case. Secondly, in seeking to discharge such a burden, one might begin by isolating those parts of legal cultures which are most institutionally facilitated and intensely concentrated. This would involve drawing some variation on Friedman's

What political and legal architecture is needed to balance and accommodate these alternative claims to cultural recognition? To begin to answer this question, we should return to Harlow's more political frame of reference, and to her conception of democracy. As noted, while Harlow concedes the need for a pluralist multi-level democracy, there remains a strong emphasis upon the state level, as the most powerful source of cultural and political identity. On one view, therefore, even if we accept Tully's radical account of "interculturality", in the type of democratic vision endorsed by Harlow the nation state and its legal system, perhaps in structured co-ordination with sub-national federal or devolved units, continues to trump other levels of cultural formation. It is difficult to avoid this inference from Harlow's democratic theory, even if it is at odds with her explicit acceptance of pluralism and co-ordinate authority between legal systems. To put matters bluntly, even if there is a significant tension between nation-state cultural identity and the interests, aspirations and

distinction between the relatively closely-knit "internal" legal culture of legal professionals (the specialist doctrinal knowledge and related normative values and strategic capacities of judges, lawyers, "repeat player" litigants, public or private institutional actors systematically operating in the shadow of the law etc.) on the one hand and a much more diffuse "external", "popular" or "lay" legal culture on the other (see e.g. L M Friedman, *The Legal System: A Social Science Perspective* (New York: Russell Sage Foundation, 1975)). But thirdly, such a move, by tending to identify the relatively fixed components of legal culture with the knowledge and practice of powerful sections of the community, throws up two separate challenges to Legrand's thesis. In the first place, it might suggest that, at least as regards these aspects which are reasonably identifiable, the *mentalités* associated with national legal systems and cultures, and which are deemed worthy of protection, are rather more elite-driven and elite-orientated than Legrand would be comfortable with. It is one thing, as he does and must, to concede in principle the possibility of asymmetries of power and knowledge and latent or active conflicts of interest within a common culture, but the more marked these asymmetries and conflicts appear the less easily normatively defensible the idea of a common culture becomes. In the second place, an emphasis on internal culture also points us towards a possibility not considered by Legrand, namely the development of a specific and separate EU legal culture. Although this has been a "relatively neglected" (F Snyder, "The Unfinished Constitution of the European Union: Principles, Processes and Culture" in J H H Weiler and M Wind (eds.), *Rethinking European Constitutionalism* (Cambridge: Cambridge University Press, 2001) field to date, recent studies have begun to examine the ways in which European judges, lawyers, clerks and officials and transnational law firms operating within the institutional and juridical environment of the EU are forging a distinctive set of attitudes and practices (see e.g. Snyder above, A Von Bogdandy, "A Bird's Eye View on the Science of European Law: Structures, Debates and Development. Prospects of Basic Research on the Law of the European Union in a German Perspective" (2000) 6 *European Law Journal* 208–38; H Schepel and R Wesseling, "The Legal Community: Judges. Lawyers, Officials and Clerks in the Writing of Europe" (1997) 3 *European Law Journal* 165–88.). Indeed, since the history of national polities and nationalism is one of complex *mutual* causation and reinforcement of shared loyalties and world-views on the one hand and common institutional forms on the other, we should not be surprised that the common institutional forms of the nascent post-state polity of the European Union also provide a sympathetic environment for the development of distinctive cultural traits. Of course, the dangers of elitism associated with national legal culture are arguably even greater in a relatively youthful post-national polity whose initial common cultural heritage was rather limited and fragmented, which has as yet had little time to develop thick and widely shared forms of common identity, and where instead technocratic expertise centred on the European Commission has played a major part in polity development. But this has less to do with the integrity, viability and durability of the distinctive legal-cultural unit, which is Legrand's primary concern, and more to do with its democratic credentials and general political legitimacy, which is Harlow's.

sensibilities associated with it on the one hand, and other sites of cultural formation on the other, it would seem to follow from her analysis that there should be only one ultimate winner. If the business of politics, and of law-making requires one central point of reference, the stronger cultural, and so democratic credentials of the state means that it should continue to provide that point of reference. It must be the axis around which other levels of interest and cultural formation are finally accommodated—or, as the case may sometimes be, not accommodated.

Arguably, however, this focus on statist democracy both sells our constitutional heritage rather short and fails to have adequate regard to the multi-level institutional design and legitimacy requirements of the new Europe. As Harlow understands and acknowledges, our understandings of constitutional virtue have never rested on the single pole of democracy. Nevertheless, Harlow talks in her chapter of the need to redress the balance of contemporary constitutional discourse on Europe towards democracy and liberty and away from respect for fundamental rights and the rule of law.[38] Yet while one might have sympathy for her concern about some aspects of the prevailing European constitutional mind-set, particularly where it is insufficiently alert to the democratic concerns of allowing a strong role in government to judges and functional experts, her approach courts the danger of overcompensating. To stress "the political components of democracy"[39] over other values, as she sets out to do, implies that democracy, especially in the state environment where it is most fully developed, if not the only constitutional virtue is nevertheless the most important one. But can such an assertion of democratic primacy provide an adequately balanced and nuanced starting-point for a normative investigation of such a complex and novel configuration as the emerging European polity?

In suggesting that it cannot, I would make four points. In the first place, even where democracy is treated as the primary value in state-based political and constitutional theory, its meaning is by no means settled. It is, to use a well-worn phrase, "an essentially contested concept",[40] not least because for some its value is largely counted in instrumental terms, as an unrivalled means towards other virtues such as fair or effective government, whereas for others its value is largely intrinsic, to do, for example, with the dignity or solidarity implicit in deliberative or otherwise participative decision-making.[41] Accordingly, the weight of opinion, such as it is, behind democracy as a primary value, is in fact a diversity of opinion. This is not in any sense to belittle the moral and political force of the considerable overlapping consensus of sentiment and argument which is marshalled behind the concept of democracy, but merely to suggest that it may be more difficult than is sometimes imagined by those who march

---

[38] Above, p. 201.
[39] *Ibid.*
[40] W B Gallie, "Essentially Contested Concepts" (1956) 56 *Proceedings of the Aristotelian Society.*
[41] See e.g. MacCormick, n. 16 above, ch. 9.

under that banner to isolate a compelling and internally coherent argument in political theory for democratic primacy.

Secondly, the implications in institutional and doctrinal terms of an argument in political theory for the primacy of democracy are by no means clear or uncontroversial, and may indeed lead to the privileging of other mechanisms and standards alongside democratic process. This is partly because of the essential contestability of the concept of democracy, but also partly because, regardless of their agreement or otherwise on questions of general normative political theory, different theoretical schools and political traditions differ as to the legal-institutional implications of their normative starting positions. That is to say, not only does the umbrella of democracy cover deep controversy within normative political theory, but it also, and in a manner by no means entirely derivative of this deeper controversy, embraces an equal diversity of theories of institutional *praxis*, some of which do not transcribe the deep primacy of democracy at the level of design proposals.[42] To take a single example, there is one well-known and influential variant of national procedural constitutionalism which views democracy as the primary virtue but which nevertheless argues for the countermajoritarian entrenchment of rights-based constraints which are deemed to be directly or indirectly constitutive or supportive of democracy.[43] Here, democratic primacy at the fundamental level translates into a finely calibrated balance of democratic process and rights protection at the institutional level.

Thirdly, putting to one side the internal diversity and complexity of the argument from democratic primacy, we must in any case acknowledge that within national constitutional discourse the perspective or range of perspectives associated with the premise of democratic primacy by no means holds general sway. Indeed, in many theoretical perspectives and, moreover, in the broader sphere of political symbolism and ideology, constitutionalism, and public law generally, tend to be invoked as a counterpoint to democracy. Constitutionalism is typically seen not only in terms of the establishment of public authority but also in terms of its legitimation, whether against autocratic or oligarchic abuse or— of more immediate pertinence—against the tyranny or myopia of the transient democratic majority. So modern constitutionalism, from Montesquieu and Tocqueville to Dworkin and Habermas, from the *Federalist Papers* to the contemporary global "rights revolution",[44] incorporates a strong, even predominant, tendency, which concedes the inevitability and fundamental legitimacy of democratic processes and values, but which, both in its underlying political

[42] For a similar, but much more developed argument with regard to the notion of rights—rather than democracy—in political theory and in constitutional design, see J Waldron, *Law and Disagreement* (Oxford: Clarendon Press, 1999) ch. 10.

[43] See in particular, J H Ely *Democracy and Distrust: A Theory of Judicial Review* (Cambridge, Mass.: Harvard University Press, 1980).

[44] For an insightful recent overview of the development of modern constitutionalism in its broad historical and constitutional context, see M Loughlin, *Sword and Scales: An Examination of the Relationship Between Law and Politics* (Oxford: Hart, 2000) esp. chs. 11–13.

theory and in its institutional design, seeks to avert the dangers of complacency and avoid the oversimplifying reductionism implicit in the premise of democratic primacy.[45]

Fourthly, if we accept the robust institutional fact of transnational and supranational governance in the modern age as a means of addressing collective action problems in the economic and social domain which are no longer within the effective control of individual states,[46] this additional layer of complexity poses further questions of democratic primacy as an adequate point of departure. Thus, an influential range of European constitutional theory would argue that either (and in some cases both) in terms of underlying normative theory or in terms of institutional design, democracy must and should occupy a less prominent position in the supranational theatre than it does in its traditional statist context. Common to this broad approach is a rejection of the idea that the current absence of strong preconditions of democratic will formation in the European context requires us to rewind to some "golden age" of nation state democracy or even, as appears to be the tendency in Harlow's approach, to concentrate our design efforts on consolidating what remains of that legacy. For those who would continue to emphasise the underlying primacy of democracy even in the European arena, a more urgent institutional priority is instead accorded to finding new and imaginative forms of democratic voice which concentrate less on the search for holistic solutions in the name of the collective "demos" and more upon participative and deliberative structures within particular transnational communities of interest or attachment.[47] In turn, this shades into another approach, exemplified in different ways by prominent commentators such as Weiler, MacCormick and Scharpf, who, while confirming the continuing importance of democracy as a value and as a guiding principle of institutional design at the European level, suggest that in the absence of a thick nation state-style *demos* at the European level, we should place more emphasis upon other fundamental virtues of governance. These may be defined in terms of expertise,[48] negotiated consensus and other "output-oriented"[49] and effectiveness-centred values, or even, to turn the absence of a strong *demos* into an

---

[45] That is not to assert that this wide range of thinking is in any overall sense theoretically more sophisticated or normatively more attractive than that which starts from a position of democratic primacy, still less that some aspects of it are not seriously neglectful of the value of democracy, but simply to suggest that it is a mistake to assume that on the whole it tends not to take democracy seriously enough and on that basis stands in need of *general* correction.

[46] See e.g. F Scharpf, *Governing in Europe: Effective and Democratic?* (Oxford: Oxford University Press, 1999) ch. 1.

[47] See e.g., Cohen and Sabel, n. 27 above; Gerstenberg, n. 27 above; E O Eriksen and J E Fossum (eds.), *Democracy in the European Union- Integration Through Deliberation?* (London: Routledge, 2000); P C Schmitter, *How to Democratize the European Union . . . And Why Bother?* (Maryland: Rowman and Littlefield, 2000); R Bellamy and D Castiglione, "The Normative Turn in European Union Studies: Sovereignty, Identity and the Legitimacy of the Euro-Polity and its Regime" (unpublished paper, 2001); see also, and relatedly, the new "comitology" literature, in particular C Joerges and E Vos (eds.), *EU Committees: Social Regulation, Law and Politics* (Oxford: Hart, 1999).

[48] See e.g. MacCormick, n. 16 above, ch. 9.

[49] Scharpf, n. 46 above.

explicit virtue, in terms of supranationalism's structural opportunity to curb the nationalist or majoritarian excesses of state democracy through the cultivation of transnational toleration and mutual recognition.[50]

Some of the general themes explored above may be brought out more clearly by taking, as an illustrative example, an insightful recent work by Miguel Poiares Maduro.[51] For him, there are two basic fears underlying constitutional discourse and organisation, whether at national or supranational level, namely "the fear of the few and the fear of the many". Democratic representation, rights protection, separation of powers and other institutional values are all ways of addressing these fears. Different institutional values may be balanced against each other in order to reconcile these fears, as in judicial review of majoritarian-validated legislation. But even within particular institutional forms, one may find the fear of the few and the fear of the many to be in tension. Thus the ever-shifting balance of majoritarian versus unanimous decision making within the nationally-mediated democratic organ of the Council reflects a concern to reconcile the tension between majoritarian and minoritarian bias. The relationship between the two fears becomes even more complex if one moves between political levels, in that responding to one type of bias at one level can give rise to the same type of bias at the other level. Thus, the call for strong national democracy and cultural self-determination, which lies at the heart of Harlow and Legrand's arguments, is one way of countering the fear of the many at the European level, but it can also stimulate fear of the many at national level on the part of national or cross-national minorities.

The key point is that within constitutional discourse democracy is just one, albeit one vitally important normative value which tracks deeper problems of governance (for Maduro, the fear of the few), and only one, albeit diversely articulated institutional form through which increasingly complex and multi-level constitutional solutions are sought for these problems. Sometimes this diverse institutionalisation may involve balancing democratic process against other institutional values, such as rights protection or the ring-fencing of expert decision-making from direct political interference. Sometimes it may involve an internal balance between different levels and forms of democracy. In turn, echoing the concerns of some of the writers mentioned above,[52] the need for a versatile institutional response to constitutional puzzles may involve severing the umbilical chord between cultural community and democratic community more cleanly than Harlow seems prepared to do, and encouraging the proliferation of democratic forms—based upon civic rather than ethnic forms of citizenship and identity—at non-state levels.[53]

[50] See, in particular Weiler, n. 26 above, esp. chs. 7 and 10.

[51] "Europe and the Constitution: What if this is as Good as it Gets?" in Weiler and Wind (eds.), n. 37 above.

[52] See nn. 46–50.

[53] Indeed, within the present volume both Keating and Scott's papers are additional powerful testimony to the argument that the articulation of the institutional value of democracy at the supra-national level may, within a complex multi-level institutional balance, be one of the ways of

CONCLUSION

It is, of course, an endlessly complex task in applied political theory to develop a balance of institutional values which optimises the possibility of meeting the aspirations and minimising the abuse of minorities and majorities at every level and in every sector of our political community. But it is in the final analysis a task for public law. The institutions, mechanisms and techniques of public law, like the political theory which underpins it, may, as Loughlin insists, be rooted in cultural particulars; but just as political theorists do not for that reason give up the struggle to make their message pertinent at different times and places, so public lawyers should not give up the struggle to make their designs relevant to different times and places. This may involve difficult problems of translation, and here the warnings of Legrand and Harlow are well-expressed and well-taken. In the final analysis, however, in a world of densely competing claims for cultural recognition, in which the circuits of economic power and their social ramifications extend well beyond the state, and in which, in consequence, multi-level governance is already deeply embedded, there is simply no other option.

allowing minority regional or functional voices to be heard—and the fears of the many to be assuaged—within majoritarian national polities.

Index